A HISTORY OF
RUSSIAN
PHILOSOPHY

A HISTORY OF

RUSSIAN PHILOSOPHY

From the Tenth Through the Twentieth Centuries

VOLUME I

edited by Valery A. Kuvakin, Ph.D.,
Moscow State University

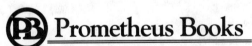 **Prometheus Books**

59 John Glenn Drive
Buffalo, New York 14228-2197

Published 1994 by Prometheus Books

98 97 96 95 94   5 4 3 2 1

Library of Congress Cataloging-in-Publication Data

A history of Russian philosophy : From the tenth through the twentieth centuries / edited by Valery A. Kuvakin.
        p.   cm.
    Translated from the Russian.
    Includes bibliographical references.
    ISBN 0-87975-780-9
        1. Philosophy, Russian. I. Kuvakin, Valerii Aleksandrovich.
B4201.H57   1993
197—dc20   93-26895
                                                                    CIP

Printed in the United States of America on acid-free paper.

Contents

VOLUME ONE

5

PART TWO: THE AGE OF ENLIGHTENMENT AND PHILOSOPHY

PART THREE: THE IDEALISM OF THE FIRST HALF OF THE NINETEENTH CENTURY

PART FOUR: PHILOSOPHY AND RADICAL PUBLICISTIC WRITING

PART FIVE: PHILOSOPHY AND THE REVOLUTIONARY MOVEMENT

From the Contributors

This is the first work by Russian historians on their national philosophy to be published in English. Through it we hope to acquaint English-speaking students with the wide diversity of thought that spans the thousand years of Russian history from the tenth to the twentieth centuries. We have endeavored to discuss in readable form the most interesting pages from the intellectual life of Russia: its leading thinkers' understanding of the universe, history, and the sense of human existence and conceptions of the individual and society, including Russian ideas of true knowledge and the ideals of a worthy life.

Russian philosophy is at once national and international. It is such because it has never developed in isolation from the national soil or from the most influential and profound ideas of East and West. Despite their national coloring the problems with which Russian philosophers have contended are basically close to the perennial problems of world philosophy.

On the whole, Russian philosophy has reflected the content of, and qualitative shifts in, Russia's development. In that sense it has been a form of national self-awareness, Russia's understanding of its fundamental values and perspectives of development, and its place in world civilization.

Russia's fate and destiny have been determined by a set of powerful if qualitatively different factors: (1) her geographical position between East and West; (2) the adoption of Christianity in its Orthodox form in A.D. 988; (3) the Tatar-Mongol invasion, which began in the thirteenth century, and thrust the Russians into nearly a quarter of a millennium of fighting for their freedom.

Understandably, the period of the Grand Duchy of Muscovy, which succeeded the periods of Kievan Rus and the Tatar-Mongol subjugation, was characterized by a determination to achieve maximum state security. The consolidation and realization of that goal not only ensured national independence, but also generated a psychology and policy of rigid centralism,

13

though the central control confronted constant disruption arising from Russian peasants' natural colonization of the free expanses, particularly to the east of Moscow.

The disparity between the striving to strengthen the power of the state on the one hand, and personal freedom and material and moral well-being of its subjects on the other, became particularly sharp on the eve of the reign of Peter the Great (1672–1725). His vigorous reforms and military activity led to his "opening a window" onto Europe, with the building of St. Petersburg and the establishment of close state and cultural ties with the West. But the modernization he carried out did not become a stable social process after his death: his changes were too sharp and involved great human sacrifices, as well as an artificial break with many national traditions. The weakest aspect of Peter's reforms was that they did not include effective machinery for self-regulation. There was no basic framework by which they could be adapted to the changing conditions of Russia's historical development. As a result, the desire to become equal to the West in the standards and quality of economic and cultural life began to take the form of abrupt, painful leaps and outbursts of change whose results were both positive and negative. One of the negative results was disruption of the more or less organic social structures of pre-Petrine Rus and the rise, on the one hand, of artificial formations (for example, the imperial officialdom, forerunner of bureaucracy and a new conservatism) and, on the other, of the rudiments of an intellectual elite, the intelligentsia, that was alien both to the people and to the state structures. Peter the Great's "unhappy child" was doomed to oppositionism and to isolation from both the people's way of life and the official state and cultural system.

All of this largely determined the psychology both of the intelligentsia and of the state's attitude to it. The split between the people, the authorities (state), and the intelligentsia colored Russian thought with clearly expressed tones of anthropocentrism and the philosophy of history. Up to the end of the nineteenth century the character of Russian philosophy, in the main uninstitutionalized and unacademic, reflected the internal divorce in the life of Russian culture. And although, as Nikolai Berdyaev said, "we lived on different floors of culture," the main drawback was the very narrow communication lines between these "floors."

These features in turn created a specific psychological atmosphere for Russian thought: the intelligentsia's oppositionist spirit and negative attitude to the authorities were synthesized with the sense of being persecuted and not wanted, which was often transformed into its opposite, viz., into a feeling of the intelligentsia's mission of suffering, belief in its special calling, and messiahism. That, too, colored Russian philosophy with clear tones of moralism and prophetism, evolving its social radicalism or, at the opposite pole, its mysticism and apocalypticism. These found their most striking embodiment in the intellectual situation at the turn of the century, when there was a simultaneous flourishing in Russia of materialism, Marxism, cosmism, and a religious philosophy saturated with eschatology.

* * *

A few words on the structure of this study are in order. The opening chapter surveys the molding of Russian philosophical thought, the course of its proto-national birth in Kievan Rus, and its development to the end of the seventeenth century. The first and second sections trace the leading trends in philosophy from the period of the Petrine reforms to the Decembrists' uprising (1825). In the third section attention is focused on the idealist views of the first half of the nineteenth century, which was a key time for philosophy. The Slavo-phile, Westernist, and radical democratic trends, which determined the whole further development of both idealism and materialism in Russia right to the end of the century, took shape in Russian social consciousness in the 1830s and 1840s.

The fourth to eighth sections reflect the not unimportant circumstance that Russian philosophy, which was never noted for academism or a passion for developing self-sufficient theoretical systems, demonstrated particularly clearly in the nineteenth century its propensity for some field of culture and social activity or other. Its aspiration to a synthesis with various forms of social consciousness and practical realization is evident there. For the radical democrats of the 1840s to 1860s—Vissarion Belinsky, Alexander Herzen, Nikolai Ogarev, Nikolai Chernyshevsky, Nikolai Dobrolyubov, and Dmitri Pisarev—philosophy was inseparable from literary and social criticism. The revolutionary Populists—Mikhail Bakunin, Pyotr Lavrov, Pyotr Tkachev, and Nikolai Mikhailovsky—sought to unite philosophy with political practice. The flowering of philosophical thought in literature is associated with the names of Dostoyevsky and Tolstoy. A tendency to regard reality philosophically through the prism of religious consciousness was inherent in Nikolai Danilevsky and Konstantin Leontiev, Pamfil Yurkevich, and Vladimir Solovyov. An inter-penetration of philosophical and scientific comprehension of objective reality, and of man's place in it, became a distinct phenomenon of Russia's intellectual life after the abolition of serfdom during the period from 1861 to 1863. Philosophically minded scientists like Ivan Sechenov, Dmitri Mendeleyev, Konstantin Tsiolkovsky, and Vladimir Vernadsky not only gave a powerful stimulus to psychology, chemistry, astronomy, cosmology, and biology, but also formulated a number of original philosophical ideas that allow us to speak of Russian cosmism and the theory of the noosphere.

The turn of the century became a significant stage in the development of Russian philosophy, when social thought attained special depth and dif-ferentiation. New systems of idealism, from pan-eroticism to existentialism, from sophiology to mystical realism (to which Part 9 is devoted), took shape against a background of the acute sharpening of autocratic-imperialist Russia's social contradictions in conditions of intensive intellectual and spiritual searchings dramatized by fierce revolutionary clashes and the catastrophe of a fratricidal civil war.

From the standpoint of the history of philosophy, the former USSR's dramatic experience in the twentieth century had a dual result. On the one hand, a Russian philosophical diaspora was formed, whose members gave the shape of mature systems to the initial intuitions of the Russian cultural renaissance of the early twentieth century; on the other hand a phenomenon appeared that was abstractly defined by the term "Soviet philosophical science."

The authors of these essays in the history of Russian philosophy have not set themselves the task of analyzing this very contradictory phenomenon. The history of "Soviet philosophical science" is now studied in the former USSR in the context of other fields of research, particularly in the context of the history of Marxism and Leninism.

This book focuses on an analysis of the thought of the most influential Russian philosophers. For a better understanding of these ideas within their original social and cultural milieu, we recommend that the readers first acquaint themselves with the political and civil history of Russia. Suggested reading would include: J. Billington, *The Icon and the Axe. An Interpretive History of Russian Culture,* New York: (n.p.), 1967; F. Copleston, *Philosophy in Russia. From Herzen to Lenin and Berdyaev,* Notre Dame: University of Notre Dame Press, 1986; P. N. Milyukov, *Outlines of Russian Culture,* New York, 1962; *A Documentary History of Russian Thought from the Enlightenment to Marxism* translated and edited by W. J. Leatherbarrow and D. C. Offord, Ann Arbor: Ardis, 1987; and various works of the historians G. Vernadsky, M. Raeff, and R. Pipes.

*   *   *

At the present time there is broad discussion of Russian philosophy in Russia, and programs are being undertaken for the "revival of forgotten names." The works of Chaadayev, Berdyaev, Solovyov, Fedotov, Rozanov, and many others are being printed in press runs of 50,000 to 200,000 copies. At the same time the distinguishing national features of Russian thought and the meaning of the concept "Russian philosophy" are being discussed.* This has proved to be a complicated matter, not so much theoretically as psychologically and culturally, since answers depend directly on the level of awareness and social and cultural maturity of the people involved. Before perestroika the picture of Russian philosophy had been evaluated by two criteria, namely, according to how close, similar, or dissimilar it was to Marxism, and according to the

---

*For the latest in English about that, see *Studies in Soviet Philosophy.*

philosophical ideas of the West that had penetrated Russia and been assimilated by Russian thought. In that connection we spoke of Russian Wolffianism, Russian Schellingianism, Russian Kantianism, and the like. An opposite tendency, observable today, is to counterpose Russian philosophy to, say, German or some other, and to overrate or exaggerate its specific national features. Fortunately, democratization in the field of culture in science is helping to avoid these two evils, the Scylla of national nihilism and the Charybdis of nationalism.

On an abstract level the answer to the question of the national features of Russian philosophy is simple and obvious: It is unique from the standpoint of its *existence*—in its thinkers, doctrines, works, the stages of development in its chronology, and its interactions with all forms of national and world culture—and from the standpoint of its *essence,* i.e., in its embodiment of specifically interpreted traditional problems of philosophy.

It is pointless to argue which national philosophical culture is better or worse, higher or lower. Yet the existence of philosophy in a society is inseparable from the sphere of national values. For Russians, therefore (as for Americans or Indians, Germans or Englishmen), Russian philosophy is closer and dearer than any other in direct proportion to the individual's level of national consciousness and self-awareness and to his or her involvement in national life and culture. National philosophical traditions are closer—or should be—to persons who find themselves in the area of the nation's historical development and ecology. One does not have to be a Russian for that. For Russian philosophy is itself multinational not only as a phenomenon of culture, but also as a chain of successive and simultaneously existing ideas, systems, and doctrines, inasmuch as its creators have been people of various nationalities—Russians, Ukrainians, Greeks, Jews, Moldavians, Germans, Kalmucks, and so on.

However, the essence of philosophizing and of philosophical problems is universal, a factor that enables a person of any nationality and national culture to understand and sympathize with the world of ideas of any other national philosophy. The national cultures of the world are thus open to one another, and that openness can lead to mutual understanding and friendship between nations and provide the basis for creating a universal culture of mankind free from hostility and estrangement, ready to tackle the global problems of the third millennium of our era.

We thus introduce you to the diversity of Russian thought and hope that acquaintance with it will not leave you indifferent but will, on the contrary, stimulate an interest in other aspects of Russian culture.

Editor's Note

In preparing this volume for Western readers I am very aware that familiarity with the original source material, enhanced by competent exposition, must take precedence over the more sophisticated tasks of interpretation and analysis. To encourage an objective assessment of Russian philosophy by interested nonprofessionals as well as scholars of philosophy, history, political science, and related fields, this volume contains selections from the most important and pertinent writings of such exemplary Russian philosophers as Alexander Radishchev, Pytor Chaadayev, Alexis Khomyakov, Vissarion Belinsky, Mikhail Bakunin, Nikolai Chernyshevsky, Nikolai Mikhailovsky, Konstantin Leontyev, Vladimir Solovyov, Nikolai Berdyaev, Nikolai Lossky. Like most editors of collected works, I faced many problems: (1) limited space, (2) selecting the most representative names in the history of Russian philosophy, and (3) determining if the contents of selected source material coincided exactly with the topics that contributors to this book discussed in their chapters. I had some latitude to include ideas related to the basic focus of the exposition. Not surprisingly, I have had to reconcile these three goals and some inevitable compromises had to be made. Each selection is prefaced by a short editorial remark that will, I hope, assist the reader in appreciating the relevance of the excerpt.

Valery A. Kuvakin
Moscow University

Introduction

The Beginnings of Russian Philosophy

Mikhail Gromov and Nikita Kozlov

Russian philosophy as a phenomenon of culture and intellectual history took shape in the period from the ninth to the seventeenth century. Having initially taken up some elements from the Slavonic pagan outlook, from the tenth century on, after the introduction of Christianity, it intensively absorbed (via Byzantium and the South Slavs) theoretical theses of sophisticated Eastern Christian philosophical and theological thought that were important for its intellectual evolution. Old Rus received from Byzantium, the main guardian of the classical heritage, names, images, and concepts of Hellenistic civilization basic for European culture, not however in pure form, but in a Christianized guise.

In contrast to sophisticated, refined Western European scholasticism, whose language was Latin, philosophy in Rus right from the start followed the tradition of the Slavonic missionaries such as Cyril (c. 827–869) and Methodius (c. 815–885), who created an alphabet and laid the foundations for translating the Bible, the main source of medieval notions about the world and man, into Old Slavonic. Typical features of Russian medieval philosophizing were its spread throughout the whole context of culture; a leaning toward the living, colorful word; a fervent public spirit; special interest in historical, moral, and esthetic problems; and a close alliance with literature and art. As a result many philosophical ideas were embodied in artistic, malleable images rather than in the form of conceptual-logical and systems-forming constructions. These features can be considered achievements that affected Russian mentality, but they also had a retarding effect on the molding of philosophy as a special form of professional activity, which it had been in the West from the time of the medieval universities.

The terms "philosopher," "philosophy," and "philosophize" are often found in old Russian writings, but their meaning was much broader and more poly-semantic than in modern Russian. By "philosophers" could be meant the clas-sical Greek and Roman thinkers whose ideas and names were known from many sources, including the anthology of aphorisms *The Bee* (*Pchela*); the Church Fathers (it was said of Maxim the Confessor, for example, that he was a philosopher renowned for his life and word to the end of his days); Christian preachers versed in dogmatism, as *The Tale of Bygone Years* (*Po-vest vremennykh let*) called the Byzantine theologian who had come to Rus on the eve of its baptism and addressed the "Speech of the Philosopher" to Prince Vladimir (?–1015); masters of exegesis, like Clement Smolyatich, who profoundly interpreted the hidden meaning of the venerable books; edu-cators of a high cultural level like Maxim the Greek (1475–1556), "the very wise in philosophy"; art-workers, like the icon-painter Theophanes the Greek, who knew how to embody philosophical images in perfect artistic forms, who was called the "master philosopher" by his contemporary Epiphanius the Sage; and, finally, people capable of extraordinary thought. Wise rulers were also ranked among the philosophers. In the Hypatian chronicle it was said of Prince Vladimir of Volhynia: "Vladimir understood the parables and obscure words and talked much with the bishop about books, because he was a great book-lover and philosopher the like of which there has not been on earth, nor will be after him." Statements like this reflect the respectful attitude to, and high social status of, philosophy in medieval Rus and show indirectly how our ancestors understood philosophy and the meaning of philosophizing.

A direct idea of philosophy is clearly expressed in its definitions. The views of John of Damascus, the eighth-century Byzantine thinker, theologian, and poet, sometimes called the Eastern Thomas Aquinas, enjoyed the greatest respect in Rus. In his fundamental *Fount of Knowledge*, which anticipated the *Summae* of Western scholastics, and in the *Philosophical Chapters*, often called *The Dialectic,* John of Damascus gave six definitions of philosophy: "Philosophy is knowledge of the existent . . . knowledge of things divine and human . . . thinking about death, both caused and natural . . . likening to God . . . the art of arts and science of sciences . . . and love of wisdom."[1] Further he formulated the all-embracing system of knowledge in which the whole aggregate of knowledge was understood as philosophy. In the spirit of the Peripatetic tradition he divided philosophy into the *theoretical* and *practical*, breaking down the former into *theology*, *physiology* (the theory of nature), and *mathematics*, and the latter into *ethics* (the theory of the individual's behavior), *economics* (management of the household), and *poli-tics* (government of the state).

John of Damascus's definitions were essentially revised in the sixteenth century by metropolitan Daniel of Moscow, who has long been known in the history of Russian literature as a passionate polemical writer, but was quite unknown as a philosopher. Yet he was the author of an interesting philosophical work *Read Philosophy Carefully So as to Avoid Erring* (*O filosofii vnimai razumno, da ne pogreshishi*).

He added three more definitions to John's six in this work and augmented the text roughly threefold by supplementing it with pious maxims of a moral and ascetic nature. Daniel distinguished between "carnal philosophizing" and "spiritual wisdom," deeming only the latter to be true. His emotional, excited effusions differed strikingly from John's clear, analytical style, but his work became very popular and was often to be found in various anthologies of the sixteenth and seventeenth centuries.

Saint Cyril, called the Philosopher for his high cultural achievements, gave a brief but expressive definition of philosophy (the first one in Slavonic). In a *Life* of him it is said that he understood by philosophy "knowledge of things divine and human—as far as man could come near to God—which taught man to be by his deeds in the image and likeness of his Creator."[2] The *Life* described philosophy as a sublime striving after *Hagia Sophia* (Divine Wisdom), who had appeared to the intellectually curious lad in a prophetic dream as a beautiful maiden surpassing all in her dazzling beauty. In old Russian thought wisdom was initially interpreted in the spirit of the Platonic eros, which comprised both passional and intellectual aspects, a moral attitude to philosophy as the supreme value and an esthetic contemplation of its bewitching unearthly image.

The image of Hagia Sophia, which represented a Christianized synthesis of the Greek Pallas Athena and the biblical Wisdom, was a key one in Russian medieval philosophy. It was expressed not only in written texts but also in majestic cathedrals and churches dedicated to Saint Sophia, in magnificent frescoes and icons, in sculptures, and in solemn, uplifting anthems in her honor. This image played a major role in shaping a tradition in Russia that united philosophy with artistic and symbolic comprehension of being.

The fundamental division of philosophy into "internal" and "external"— a method originating with the Church Fathers—was important for the old Russian understanding of it. By "internal" was meant Christian, God-inspired philosophy, the supreme philosophy whose aim was salvation of the human soul; by "external" was meant pagan, worldly, less important philosophy, because it was aimed at knowledge of material things. Sometimes it was condemned but more often considered expedient, as Maxim the Greek wrote, "for amending the mind," and in this sense it was regarded as logic. The understanding of philosophy as practical, life-building spiritual tutorship, teaching by deed rather than word, and, as healing of the human soul, was a peculiarly Christian interpretation of its Socratic understanding as practical morality.

One of the colorful forms of expression of folk wisdom were the brief sayings, aphorisms, and proverbs long common in the culture of the East

Slavonic peoples. Having arisen in the pre-state, pre-literate period, they had become recorded in books from the days of Kievan Rus, fixed in works of art and articles of folk life, and recorded in many other ways. After the translation of works of antiquity and Eastern and Near Eastern books into Slavonic, local traditions soaked up a wealth of aphoristic literature of world significance.

There are sayings of sages in the earliest important pieces of Russian writing, both original works and translations: in *The Tale of Bygone Years*; *The Discourse on Law and Grace* (*Slovo o zakone i blagodati*); the *Anthologies* (*Izborniks*) of 1073 and 1076; and in many collections of hagiographic, narrative, epistolary, and apocryphal genres. Of special interest are the anthologies of aphorisms like the *Hundred Words* (*Stoslovets*) by Gennadius, which was employed by Grand Prince of Kiev Vladimir Monomakh (1053–1125). *The Wisdom of Menander* (*Mudrost Menandra*), *The Sayings of Hesychius and Barnabas* (*Izrecheniya Isikhiya i Varnavy*), and also the *Physiologue* (*Fiziolog*), *Alexandria*, and *Conversation of the Three Holy Hierarchs* (*Beseda tryokh svyatitelei*), close to them in their moralizing, parabolizing character, were known in Rus. Some anthologies, homilies, and sermons with aphoristically expressed ideas possessed colorful grandiloquent titles: *The Golden Stream* (*Zlatostrui*), *Emerald* (*Izmaragd*), *Pearl* (*Margarit*), *Golden Chain* (*Zlataya zep*). By their titles, content, and appearance, these books, often illustrated and decorated with painted ornamentation and miniatures and with rich bindings, were meant to express visually the great value of wisdom and knowledge.

The most popular book of the aphoristic genre was *The Bee,* translated from a Greek anthology by the same title (*Melissa*). The Byzantine original had been compiled by the monk Anthony in the eleventh century from Joannes Stobaeus's fifth-century collection of the sayings of classical authors, and Maxim the Confessor's seventh-century collection of statements by Christian authorities. It has been suggested that *Melissa* was translated at the end of the twelfth century; it was supplemented with the sayings of old Russian authors and creatively adapted, and has come down to us in many versions. The longest Russian edition contains seventy-one chapters and more than 2,500 quotations from biblical, classical, and medieval authors.

Its title was connected with the image of the "busy bee" already common in antiquity—flying from flower to flower and diligently gathering the nectar of many plants. So a person who wanted to acquire the honey of wisdom should zealously gather the nectar of thoughts. That symbolic image is ascribed to Isocrates, the famous Athenian orator and publicist of the fourth century B.C. The sayings in *The Bee* were arranged thematically: "On Wisdom," "On Truth," "On Courage and Fortitude," "On Wealth and Poverty," "On Industry and Diligence," "On Truth and Lies," and so on. They might give an indication of the author (Socrates, Plato, Epicurus, Solomon, Philo, Nil Sinaites, Saint

John Chrysostom) of the source (the Psalms, the Gospels, the Apostles), of some unidentified sage ("Philosopher Nemo," "a wise man"), or give no indication of the original source. Some thoughts, it should be noted, were only ascribed to respected authorities (pseudo-epigraphs); many were distorted or adapted.

Nature and society, the world and man, object and subject were not differentiated in medieval consciousness but were thought of as one on the basis of a supreme principle personified in the image of God. The God of the Russian Middle Ages was not only a religious notion about the Maker of the world and Providence, but also a philosophical concept of a single spiritual substance (because he was eternal, infinite, and possessed absolute being). To experience God meant to unite with him as with the ideal, i.e., the maximum of human capabilities (because he was all-wise, all-merciful, and all-good). It is not surprising that this superconcept, central to medieval consciousness, enjoyed such esteem that all modes of natural, social, and personal being were reduced to it as the primary substance.

In ancient Rus the conception of the universe was not only expressed in abstract terms, but also took artistic, malleable forms. *Trinity*, the famous icon by Andrei Rublev (c. 1360/70–c. 1430), was as philosophical as Hegel's triad or Kant's trichotomy.

In it the Trinitarian conception of the universe is expressed in the images of three pensive angels bending toward each other in mute conversation. The left-hand angel depicts Jehovah, the Creator of the world and Earth; the middle one, the divine Logos of Jesus Christ; and the right-hand one, the spirit of truth of the Paraclete, the Holy Ghost. Each detail has profound symbolic meaning. The image of the city above the left-hand angel embodies the notion of the socium as harmonized, well-ordered being. A mountain above the right-hand angel is the symbol of the ascension of the spirit. The tree of Mamre above the middle angel is the tree of life, the oldest archetype of human consciousness, reconceived as the cross. In the center of the whole composition is a chalice as the symbol of sacrificial redemption, the supreme humanistic ideal—"greater love hath no man than this, that a man lay down his life for his friends"—and at the same time the symbol of the innermost penetration of the essence of being through the image of the Lord's Supper, calling man to be satisfied with spiritual goods and not to guzzle the fruits of the earth. If one remembers that the icon was painted "in memory and praise" of Saint Sergius of Radonezh in order to overcome "the hateful discord of this world," it takes on a social, and even concrete historical significance. It is precisely that "speculation in paints" (*umozrenie v kraskah*), a special form of wisdom developed in Rus to a level of perfection, when philosophical, esthetic, moral, social, and historical content was concentrated in one integral image within a polysemantic symbol, admitting of endless multi-level development of its semantics.

There were also philosophical conceptions of nature in Rus, more un-

derstandable to present-day consciousness, about the hierarchical structure of
the universe in the spirit of Dionysius the Areopagite, about the three parts
of the soul (rational, volitional, and sensual), of man as the crowning point
of creation (or, in modern terms, the pinnacle of the evolution of matter),
who was a "microcosm" reflecting the whole infinite world or "macrocosm."
The doctrine of elements, already classically formulated by Empedocles, was
widely accepted. In the *Anthology* of 1073 it was said that man's body, like
the whole world, was "constituted of fire, air, water, and earth." Various natural phenomena and human nature were linked with the struggle, combination, and interpenetration of the four primary elements. There were many
such ideas in the apocryphal literature, repudiated and not encouraged by
the Church, but nevertheless very popular.

In the early sixteenth century the *Lucidarius* (*Enlightener*), widely known
in Europe, was translated from the German. The authorship of the original
Latin version has been attributed to Saint Anselm of Canterbury, who enjoyed great authority in the Catholic world, and to Honorius of Autun. This
book, which was categorized as apocryphal in Rus, was a kind of "popular
scientific" work constructed in the form of a dialogue of teacher and pupil
and intended "to teach the marvelous wisdom." What was secret in other
wise books "was set out outspokenly in this book."

The pupil asked the teacher various questions (how the world was
constructed, what the planets were, where hell was and where heaven, and
so on) and received answers to them in which the same classical conception
of the four primary elements of being was expounded. Thus the Greeks'
cosmogonic theories of the creation of the world from chaos, in which the
primary elements were still in undifferentiated form, continued to exist in
the late Middle Ages, sanctified by the names of Justin the Philosopher, John
of Damascus, Thomas Aquinas, Saint Anselm of Canterbury, and other
authorities.

There is an interesting idea in certain editions of the *Lucidarius* about
the nonannihilability of matter (together with the idea of the nonannihilability of the soul). It occurs in descriptions of how the elements constituting
a person were returned to their initial positions after his death. The idea of
a dialectical interconnection of the microcosm and the macrocosm was perceived by medieval man as human nature's dependence on the nature of the
heavenly bodies under which a person was born and which affected his character and his fate (the notion has survived, incidentally, to our times). Here
the elements appeared in the form of their inherent properties—dryness or
moisture, heat or cold—and man received these same qualities from the stars.

To understand the medieval mode of philosophizing it is important to
consider the special role of *symbolizing* as a kind of prototype of a theoretical, scientific method of cognition. Symbols made it possible to discern beyond the external, empirical manifestations of being its inner sense, visible

only with the "eyes of the soul." The whole Universe was likened to an open book full of shimmering symbols that philosophers were called on to interpret. The symbolism of colors, jewels, plants, animals, numbers, and natural phenomena, apprehended as meaningful "signs," permeated and organized medieval consciousness and all its creations.

A characteristic feature of old Russian consciousness was its historical depth. A striving to trace sources from the Creation, to fit the history of its people into the history of mankind, to determine the role of the individual in history, and to explain the essence of the past, present, and future by the philosophy of history, shines through in the annals and chronicles and in many narrative and publicistic works.[3] The sense of history was revealed through the dramatic struggle of the two world principles, God and the Devil. The former personified the powers of good, the latter of evil. The medieval conception of the turbulent dynamics of society and the nature inseparable from it can be conditionally called one of *panethicism,* in which all phenomena were interpreted from an emphatically ethical point of view.

Reflection on the historical fate of Rus, on the equality of the Slavs among the earlier civilized peoples, affirmation of the superiority of the new faith (Christianity) understood as grace and truth, the panegyric to Prince Vladimir Svyatoslavich, who baptized the Russian people and brought it into the world arena, and praise of Yaroslav the Wise (c. 978–1054), who built the first "House of Wisdom" in the Russian lands, the cathedral of St. Sophia in Kiev—such was the content of one of the best publicistic and philosophical works not only of the Russian Middle Ages but also of the European: *The Discourse on Law and Grace* by the metropolitan Ilarion (eleventh century).[4]

Several masterpieces of literature were devoted to substantiating Russian statehood in the period of the rise of Moscow, among them *The Legend of the Princes of Vladimir (Skazaniye o knyazyakh vladimirskikh)* that contained two legends that became fundamental tenets of the official ideology of the Russian state in the sixteenth and subsequent centuries. The first tried to prove the Rurik dynasty's descent from the Roman Emperor Augustus, the second described how the Byzantine Emperor Constantine Monomachus handed over the ensigns of supreme power (the Cap of Monomachus, a royal necklace, and a gold chain) to his grandson, Grand Prince Vladimir II Monomakh, the ruler of Rus. This set of regalia was to symbolize the inheritance of supreme power materially and visibly, and was intended for the ceremonial consecration of the Russian autocrats.

This *Legend* had significant political repercussions: its ideas were widely reflected in the chronicles, in official documents and anthologies, in diplomatic practice, in the messages of Ivan IV (the Terrible), and other works. It was translated into Latin and became known in Europe. It was employed in the procedure for the crowning of the czar (*Chin venchaniya na tsarstvo*) compiled by the metropolitan Makarius in 1547 for the coronation of Ivan the Terrible. The latter rejected the title of king offered him by the pope and the German emperor, and for the first time in Russian history, proclaimed himself "czar" (Caesar) i.e., equal to the Roman and Byzantine emperors. Makarius also compiled *The Book of Degrees of the Imperial Genealogy* (*Stepennaya kniga tsarskogo rodosloviya*) from Vladimir Svyatoslavich, who Christianized Rus, to Ivan IV, who became the first Russian autocrat.

Interest in the classical heritage increased in this same period. In many churches in Moscow and other cities frescoes, icons, and works of applied art appeared that figured Plato, Aristotle, Anaxagoras, Homer, Virgil, and many other personages of the Greco-Roman world. The ideas of the continuity of the world monarchies, and of the transfer to and establishment in Rus of a new universal political and sacerdotal center were reflected in the murals of the Kremlin cathedrals, in the wall paintings of the Golden Chamber, and in numerous icons of the time.

The ideal social arrangement was conceived in Rus as a harmonious combination of the secular and ecclesiastical powers. The former ruled the state, the latter educated the people morally. Rulers should heed the advice of wise mentors, as Alexander the Great had heeded the words of Aristotle; they should be conscious of their responsibility to the people, as was attributed in *The Bee* to Plato: "He who accepts great power must have a great mind."

The *Instructive Chapters for the Orthodox Rulers* (*Glavy pouchitelny nachalstvuyushchim pravoverno*), compiled by Maxim the Greek for the still-young Ivan the Terrible,[5] are illustrative of the intellectual influence exerted by the thinker on the monarch. The "glorious philosopher" counseled the czar to curb the three sinful passions ("voluptuousness," "pride," and "avariciousness") and to turn to the three saving virtues—"justice," "chastity," and "meekness"—understood as right judgment, high morality, and a solicitous attitude to his subjects. But the tyrant who usurped power did not heed the advice of Maxim the Philosopher, himself fell low, and involved Russia in a very serious crisis that nearly ended in the loss of her independence in the Time of Troubles at the beginning of the seventeenth century.

Problems of the structure of society, of the relation of authority to morality, of the relations of the estates, of the interaction of traditions and innovations, of the influence of foreign ideas and the preservation of distinctive Russian features were broadly discussed in the correspondence of Ivan the Terrible and Andrei Kurbsky (1528–1583); in the disputes between the followers of Iosif Volotsky (1439/40–1515) and the so-called nonpossessors; in the struggle between the followers of the reformist patriarch Nikon (1605–1681) and the Old Believers; in the works of Fyodor Karpov, Zinovi Otensky, Silvestr Medvedev, and many other thinkers, publicists, and statesmen of the fifteenth to seventeenth centuries.

Knowledge of the world was possible, in the opinion of old Russian thinkers, by both "internal" and "external" means. In the first case man became directly aware of the universal action of a single spiritual substance intuitively, through illumination, bypassing exhausting examination of the empirical diversity of being; in the second, he attained divine wisdom gradually, through long reflection, through harmony of nature and society, the created world, and the sphere of activity accessible to him.

Knowledge was considered inseparable from the moral principle. In his *Discourse on Wisdom* (*Slovo o premudrosti*), Bishop Cyril of Turov (c. 1130–c. 1182) quoted a parable whose sense was that meekness was the mother of wisdom and reason and good thoughts and all wise deeds. Sublime wisdom was only possible through awareness of one's own insignificance in the face of the infinity of the universe. The wisdom of humility was counterposed to philosophical pluming of oneself or boasting and foolish pride in one's limited reason.

The views of Artemius of St. Sergius Trinity Monastery, a contemporary of Ivan the Terrible, are close to Hesychastic conceptions and an example of Russian medieval epistemology. He considered the comprehending of being an endless process; "there was no end to the journey of wisdom," he said, and differentiated false philosophizing of the mind that strove for self-assertion from an altruistic soul's striving for truth. The soul rose to the heavenly Wisdom through "humble wisdom," for which a concentration of spiritual forces, improvement of body and mind, and moral self-perfection were necessary. Instead of idle, pompous talk one should love "blessed silence" and retire to a small, secluded monastery. Artemius saw three elements in man: the carnal, the emotional, and the spiritual.

Alongside the ethicizing of cognition, there was also a process of its estheticizing. The frequent lauding of book learning; the form of the medieval book itself, which aspired to absorb the quintessence of wisdom, bound in jeweled covers and decorated with miniatures; astonishment at the capacity of human consciousness to illuminate the whole Universe like lightning; the depiction in paintings of ascetics and sages with lofty brows and a penetrating glance—all this reflected the purposive conferring of esthetic significance (which was highly valued in the Middle Ages) to men's intellectual activity. It was not the aggressive pagan Prince Svyatoslav of Kiev (?–972), but Yaroslav the Wise, who cared for the enlightenment of his subjects, and the hermit Theodosius of the Kiev Caves (?–1074), who instructed them, who were the models to be imitated.

The passional element played a major role in the process of cognition. Rejecting the rational way of reason that gazed dispassionately at the world, the old Russian strove to comprehend being by "laying up thoughts in his heart," with impassioned soul and belief in justice, good, and beauty. The "heavy-hearted" and "high-minded in the heart" were not capable of knowing the essence of things. Love was inseparable from the heart. Their epistemological link was that love purified the heart while the heart brightened the intellect. As Saint Augustine, who was honored in Old Rus, said: "We know insofar as we love."

The distinguishing features of the thinking established in Russia by the seventeenth century were reflected in compilations of an encyclopedic and lexicographic kind arranged in alphabetical order—*azbukovniks*—which were a special type of manuscript book. They combined the various traditions of interpreting the obscure passages of esteemed literature; were rich in phrases of living, everyday language; and reflected information accumulated over the centuries and the level of knowledge of their time. While not wholly superseding the dictionaries and explanatory books of various kinds that had preceded them, *azbukovniks* became the dominant type of universal dictionary and short encyclopedia. The explanation of terms in these compilations had a general theoretical, philosophical sense and not just a grammatical one. Mastery of them promoted development of thinking, stimulated knowledge of the world, and broadened the general outlook of the Russian people of pre-Petrine times.

The semantics of medieval concepts often did not correspond to the modern, so that careful linguistic analysis of old Russian terminology is called for. Dialectics, for example, was understood as an ability to use words, as a means of correct thinking, as the art of carrying on a dialogue, dispute, or talk. A more adequate term here would have been "logic."

Logic also existed in the structure of philosophical knowledge in Russia and was represented by translations and original works (certain articles of the *Anthology* of 1073, Moses Maimonides' *Logic, The Book Called Logic* [*Kniga, glagolemaya logika*], Andrei Kurbsky's *Talk about Logic* [*Skaz o logike*], and others). One can say, on the whole, that in spite of the predominance of religious, artistic, and symbolic methods of comprehending existence a scientific method of its cognition was also developed. But they were not differentiated, so that Old Russian texts usually represent a combination of all four methods. As semiotic analysis shows, one and the same linguistic expression may function as a word-image, as a word-symbol, as a concept-word, and as a word-revelation, Logos.

Russian medieval thought, while the same unique cultural phenomenon as old Russian painting, blended typologically into the general structure of Russian, European, and world philosophy. It expressed the initial, fundamental, and longest period of national spiritual self-existence; it established traditions, created a terminology of abstract thinking, and determined the high social status of philosophy—as all-encompassing wisdom, a lofty synthesis of the ideal and the empirical experience, and the most important life-building doctrine. The exalted odes of Lomonosov and Derzhavin, Herzen's passionate publicistic writings, Tolstoy's philosophy of history, Dostoyevsky's moral quests, Solovyov's "sophiology," the philosophy of Pavel Florensky, and much else in Russian culture of the eighteenth to twentieth centuries find their sources in the period of Old Rus.

Russian medieval philosophy was not self-contained and exclusive or limited but strove to absorb the achievements of European peoples. That process evolved particularly rapidly in the seventeenth century when, after the founding of the Kievo-Mogilyanskaya Academy, the Slavonic-Greek-Latin Academy was opened in Moscow. Many figures of Slavonic culture were then attracted to Russia; there was an intensive effort in translating books from Latin, Polish, German, and other languages; and teaching of philosophical disciplines began. Pyotr Postnikov, a graduate of the Slavonic-Greek-Latin Academy, became the first diplomated Russian philosopher, having received the degree of Doctor of Philosophy from Padua University in 1694. He became very actively involved in the Petrine reforms of the late seventeenth and early eighteenth centuries, when the gradual change began from the medieval to the modern European type of thinking.[6]

NOTES

1. *Antologiya mirovoi filosofii* (*Anthology of World Philosophy*) 4 vols. (Moscow, 1969), vol. 1, pt. 2, p. 622.

2. *Skazaniya o nachale slavyanskoi pismennosti* (*Legends about the Beginning of the Slavonic Written Language*) (Moscow, 1981), p. 73.

3. *Chelovek i istoriya v srednevekovoi filosofskoi mysli russkogo, ukrainskogo i belorusskogo narodov* (*Man and History in the Medieval Philosophical Thought of the Russian, Ukrainian, and Byelorussian Peoples*) (Kiev, 1987).

4. *Ideino-filosofskoye naslediye Ilariona Kievskogo* (*The Philosophical Heritage of Ilarion of Kiev*) (Moscow, 1986), pts. 1 and 2.

5. Maxim Grek, *Sochineniya* (Works) (Kazan, 1860), pt. 2, pp. 157–84.

6. For more detail on Old Russian philosophy and culture see A. F. Zamaleyev, *Filosofskaya mysl v srednevekovoi Rusi* (*Philosophical Thought in Medieval Rus*) (Leningrad, 1987); M. N. Gromov and N. S. Kozlov, *Russkaya filosofskaya mysl X–XVII vekov* (*Russian Philosophical Thought in the 10th–17th Centuries*) (Moscow, 1990); G. P. Fedotov, *Svyatye drevnei Rusi* (The saints of old Rus) (Paris: YMCA Press, 1989); *Medieval Russian Epics, Chronicles, and Tales,* 2d ed., edited, translated, and with an Introduction by Serge A. Zenkovsky (New York: E. P. Dutton, 1974).

Part One

The Era of Modernization and the Rise of New Philosophy

1

Peter the Great's "Brain Trust"
Yulia Senchikhina

THE SOCIAL AND CULTURAL CONTEXT

The historical features of Russia's development in the late seventeenth and early eighteenth centuries, viz., the process by which she had begun to overcome her backwardness, and the confrontation between the various social strata and political groups in the country, were mirrored almost exactly in the Russian thought of that time and in the social and philosophical ideas of its most outstanding representatives. The Petrine reforms found support among Western-oriented nobility, whose spokesmen were the "brain trust": the eminent thinkers Feofan Prokopovich, Vassily Tatishchev, and later Antioch Kantemir. The Russian state's increase in might and power and international prestige was seen as theoretical substantiation of radical reforms. At the same time the social thinking of the nascent capitalist structure against the background of the old, feudal system reflected all the difficulties and contradictions of this era. Thus, the legacy of the members of the "brain trust" can be considered the key that opens the door not only to the eighteenth century but also to deeper layers of the history of Russian philosophy.

It should be taken into consideration that religion dominated social consciousness in Russia and permeated all spheres of intellectual life. It was natural that the predominance of theology in the social and intellectual life could not help but foster the dogmatic, obsolete style of thinking and also the authoritarian method of providing scientific evidence, which employed biblical texts and the works of the Church Fathers, etc., as criteria of truth.

The general culture and science of this period in Russia, however, had already matured to the extent that nature and people's relation to it could be explained without the interference of supernatural forces. But since this relation was mediated by social connections that were burdened by their feudal content, the thinkers of the seventeenth century and those of the eighteenth who remained influenced by religion in their understanding of history faced difficulties developing more rational and realistic world outlooks. Nevertheless, they brought the philosophical and social thought of their period to more mature, modernized forms.

The profound socio-economic processes that were shaking patriarchal Russia were bound to create a need for educated people, for secular science and European culture. The increase in lay elements in the sphere that was under the authority of philosophy proceeded in two opposite directions. On the one hand, a freeing of ideas about God from their anthropomorphic expression in the Christian religion to a conversion of God into an abstract suprasensuous absolute led from theology to philosophical idealism and deism. On the other hand, a tendency developed toward a materialist explanation of reality that became more and more incompatible with the religious outlook.

Prokopovich, Tatishchev, and Kantemir played a major role both in the spread of philosophical knowledge and in the working out of ideas that constituted the direct basis of the philosophy of the Russian Enlightenment.

FEOFAN PROKOPOVICH

Feofan Prokopovich (1677–1736), the leader of the "brain trust," was a professor and rector of the Kiev-Mogilyansk Academy and the author of a number of textbooks and historical works. He was well acquainted with West European philosophical traditions and was also known as the statesman who Peter the Great commissioned to compile the *Spiritual Regulations* (*Dukhovnyi reglament*) (1720), a political, historical pamphlet aimed against the claims of the Church Fathers and the abuses of the clergy. He had not only assimilated the best of Russian culture, but had also become the leader of the Russian thinkers who defended and substantiated the Petrine reforms. In his philosophical legal treatise *The Right of the Monarch's Will* (*Pravda voli monarshey* [1722]) and in his speeches and sermons, Prokopovich put forward ideas of enlightened absolutism. His substantiation of the idea of Russia's need for accelerated development of the productive forces, science, education, and culture, as well as centralization of the state, was fresh and challenging for his day and corresponded to the interests of the nascent entrepreneurs and the nobility in the czar's service, which undoubtedly testified to the educational thrust of his legacy.

In philosophy Prokopovich tried to reconcile faith and knowledge and find a relationship between religion and science that would allow the latter to develop successfully under the domination of a religious worldview. He criticized the materialist tendency in the philosophy of Aristotle and opposed the atheism of Epicurus and Spinoza. Nevertheless, while rejecting the scholastic reasoning of Thomas Aquinas's successors, he strove to disseminate the discoveries of natural science, especially knowledge of mathematics and astronomy. While sometimes departing from a traditionally religious explanation of history, he expressed ideas that were in harmony with the conceptions of natural law and the social contract.

VASSILY TATISHCHEV

The Russian statesman and scholar Vassily Tatishchev (1686–1750) is noted in the history of Russian thought primarily as the author of the works *Russian History (Istoriya Rossiyskaya)* and *A Conversation of Two Friends about the Benefit of the Sciences and Schools (Razgovor dvukh priyateley o polze nauk i uchilishch)*. The main content of his philosophical and sociopolitical views was elaborated in these works. His outlook had a deistic character. He understood God as the creator of the world, but he made people's worldly well-being depend on science and, in striving to limit belief, called for a separation between philosophy and theology. As a dualist Tatishchev recognized two substances—the corporeal and spiritual worlds—treating man as a unity of "the two very different properties of soul and body." He attached paramount importance to philosophy, considering it "the chief science by which man could know himself." The sphere of divinity, according to him, extended to purely theological, scholastic problems. While not denying religious perspective, Tatishchev criticized theologians and clericalism. On matters concerning the Universe he was a supporter of the heliocentric theory and was well acquainted with the works of Copernicus, Galileo, and many other European scientists, both mathematicians and naturalists. His well-stocked library (which has not yet been fully studied) is evidence of this.

Tatishchev was one of the first Russian thinkers specifically to examine questions of knowledge; he had a particularly high evaluation of its sensory level. Intellect, he considered, was formed only through the sense organs. A materialist tendency can be detected in his assertion that knowledge about objects was accumulated through the effect of things on the sense organs. He assigned a major place in cognition to memory, ideas, and abstractions. In his classification of the sciences, he distinguished between "corporeal" and "spiritual" sciences, and, in addition, between the "useful" (natural and humanitarian), the "needed" (theology), and the "false" (astrology, alchemy, etc.).

Tatishchev opposed religious, fatalistic, and providentialist conceptions of history. Sociopolitical events, he suggested, did not depend on Providence, but rather on objective factors, population, the developmental needs of industry, commerce, and education. Universal intellectual enlightenment was the motive force of historical progress. He advocated universal education and intellectual enlightenment as the best way to modernize Russia.

ANTIOCH KANTEMIR

The name of Antioch Kantemir (1709–1744), son of the Moldavian ruler Dmitry Kantemir, became well known in both Western Europe and Russia during his lifetime. Poet, diplomat, and passionate admirer of the science and philosophy of modern times, he caught the attention of Voltaire and Montesquieu and was acquainted with such major scientists of his day as Maupertuis and Fontenelle.

Kantemir's legacy—satires in various different editions, translations (in particular of Fontenelle's *Conversations on the Plurality of Worlds* [*Entrétiens sur la Pluralité des Mondes,* 1730]), and his philosophical treatise *Letters on Nature and Man* (*Pisma o prirode i cheloveke*)—is evidence of his broad range of interests and contains significant material for study of the history of the philosophical thought of the European Enlightenment.

Kantemir's world outlook was contradictory. Characteristic of him was a peculiar combination of theological, secular, and rationalist ideas, as well as notions of a rigid separation of soul and body in man, attacks on classical atomism and materialism, a cosmological proof of the existence of God, and so on. At the same time there was in his views of this period a noticeable humanist orientation combined with certain ideas of rationalism, which inevitably predetermined a glorification of human reason that "wisely arranges all matters of behavior." Reason was also the main driving force of social affairs.

In his early works Kantemir had already drawn a general picture of the world from the latest data of the science of his time. He made heliocentrism the basis of his conception of the structure of the Universe: "It is now the common opinion of learned astronomers that our Earth revolves around the Sun, and not the other way round."

His work on the translation of Fontenelle's *Conversations on the Plurality of Worlds* was associated with a new, more mature period in his philosophical development, since this book contained an exposition of Copernicus's theory, a critique of the Ptolemaic and religious views about the Universe, and the fundamentals of physics and Descartes's "theory of vortices." The translation of the philosophical terms and his explanation of the meaning of the philosophical categories help us to evaluate the views of Kantemir himself. At the same time, he laid the foundations of Russian philosophical terminology.

When defining the subject matter of philosophy, Kantemir gave preference to "natural matters," so that physics, which taught how "to know the cause and circumstances of all natural effects and things," preceded metaphysics, which discussed the existent in general and the properties of the soul and spirit. His interest in the natural sciences led him to separate philosophy from theology in the spirit of the principle of the "duality of truth."

The philosophical basis of Kantemir's understanding of the world was a deism. He adopted an idea that only the act of creating the world was the First Creator's. Unlike theists, the Russian deists of that time recognized not only the objective existence of the external world, but its self-sufficiency and independence from supernatural forces as well.

In the theory of knowledge Kantemir sided with sensualism, regarding sensation as the basis of an idea. An idea was secondary to the external thing and was its representation in man's mind. A representation arose from sensations, which reflected the various qualities of a thing. Kantemir treated sensation, perception, and memory as necessary prerequisites for generalizations, logical comprehension of reality, and deductions. These statements brought him close to the tradition of sensualist rationalism.

In his philosophical treatise *Letters on Nature and Man* (1742), Kantemir treated the world as the creation of the divinity. According to him, science, which studied nature and man, confirmed the wisdom of the Creator. While close to Cartesian rationalism, he did not explain the origin of abstract concepts, especially those without a direct sensual basis, and referred to a supernatural force.

As a social thinker, Kantemir exposed conservative views. While seeing in serfdom a "natural" distribution of social forces, he did, however, condemn its extremes. His political and sociophilosophical views linked up in an original way with the theory of natural law and the principle of the "common good."

The thinkers who emerged from the Western-oriented strata of the Russian nobility of the early eighteenth century made considerable progress in developing the philosophical idea compared with their predecessors and contemporaries who represented a pre–Petrine, traditional religious outlook. The range of philosophical reflections of the "brain trust" included problems of the essence of philosophy, matter and the development of the theory of knowledge, the individual, society, and history.

THE PROBLEM OF PHILOSOPHY

Prokopovich, following Aristotle, considered philosophy to be concerned only with investigation of the general: "It considers things taken in general, and not singly, because science does not arise from particulars (as dialecticians put it)."[1]

Tatishchev demarcated philosophy and theology more rigorously than Prokopovich, considering that philosophy should have knowledge of nature and man as its subject matter rather than questions of theosophy and soul-saving. Tatishchev treated it as a science that brought people practical results.

In this respect his eleventh question and answer in *Conversation of Two Friends* is characteristic:

> I find all that you say very strange: that the supreme good is knowledge of oneself and the acquisition or maintenance of perfection, being, and satisfaction, which, it seems, does not agree with the teaching of the Church, because it teaches that eternal bliss is in salvation of the soul and not in satisfaction; and salvation is acquired by faith, hope, and love. . . .
>
> *Answer.* I did not think that you wanted to draw me so far into a discussion about theology which does not pertain to this, but I intended including the same in some short speeches, and therefore I told you that the teaching consisted in knowing oneself, in which all else is included.[2]

This was a new answer to the question of the role of science, and thus of philosophy, in society. Tatishchev stressed further that "philosophers originally divided the sciences exclusively by their declared properties: spiritual—theology, and corporeal—philosophy."[3] It follows from this that he was trying to separate divinity and philosophy and liberate the latter from the influence of the former. In defending the independence of philosophy and revealing the reasons for the clergy's fight against it, he sometimes expressed more radical ideas than the French enlighteners, or even the materialists of the eighteenth century.

Young Kantemir fully sympathized with Tatishchev in his understanding of the essence of philosophy. For him it was the sum of the sciences that cognized the "natural," i.e., what Tatishchev defined as "corporeal." "Philosophy," Kantemir wrote, "is the general name for fundamental, clear knowledge of natural and pre-natural matters that results from diligent discussion and investigation of these matters. Philosophy is divided into Logic, Ethics, Physics and Metaphysics."[4]

In contrast to Tatishchev, Kantemir saw philosophy as including not only "corporeal" sciences, but also "spiritual" ones, viz., logic, ethics, and—what is more—metaphysics.

It should be stressed that Tatishchev expressed a number of interesting ideas about the development of science since antiquity, and about the separation of the sciences from philosophy into independent branches of knowledge. He correctly noted the difference in content of philosophy between antiquity and his own time, which is undoubtedly of interest in the study of the development of sciences, especially philosophy.

Prokopovich's book *Argument about Godlessness* (*Rassuzhdeniye o bez-bozhii*) remains one of the first memorials to the bitter struggle between materialism and idealism in Russian philosophy. In comparison with Prokopovich, Tatishchev took a more advanced philosophical stand, spoke directly about his sympathy with doctrines that recognized both principles (the materialist and the idealist), and in his *Conversation* opposed both materialism and idealism, thus adopting a contradictory position. He did not agree with the antique materialists or with Hobbes and his successors that, "the essence of man is just body, and the soul is only an inclusion, and only an empty word that signifies nothing."[5]

But Tatishchev could not maintain this dualist point of view, because the realistic course of his meditations ultimately demanded an unambiguous answer to the problem of spirit and matter. Like Descartes, he claimed that the soul was eternal and perfect and the body suffering, transient, and imperfect. Following Descartes, he recognized that body and soul were created by God. He thus inclined, in the end, to objective idealism.

Kantemir also held an idealist position when dealing with the question of the priority of the material or the ideal. When speaking of nature and God, he asserted that nature was secondary and created by the law of divine purpose, so that everything in the world was permeated by a spiritual element. "I do not know a dual being in my nature: one that knows, and another that has no comprehension; . . . the soul knows itself, and understands and reflects on everything we see."[6]

He regarded man's unity as a unity of spirit and body, giving priority to the spirit, or reason. "Thus it is clear that the one depends equally on the other; the power of the mind over the body is altogether the greater; the mind conceived: at once all limbs and joints are set in motion, drawn powerfully as if by a machine. On the other hand, the power of the body over the mind is no less obvious. The body moves, the mind is immediately compelled to think with joy and grief, according to what happens."[7]

While recognizing "the sharpness and perspicacity of mind" of materialists, of whom there were "a great number," he dissociated himself all the same from materialism and criticized it.

As a result of their study of the natural sciences, however, these Russian thinkers came to a certain limitation in their initial idealist premises, which they did either by introducing elements of pantheism in a spirit close to that of the Renaissance, or by turning to separate deistic ideas. The ideas of pantheism and deism were combined, moreover, with a critique of the anthropomorphic understanding of God. In many of Prokopovich's works, for instance, God was depicted as an omnipotent, invisible force, as the guarantee of the immutability of the laws of nature, as the first impulse and the first cause— as the "cause without beginning." He also often brought God and nature closer together and identified them.

MATTER, NATURE, AND THE IDEA OF DEVELOPMENT

In Prokopovich's natural philosophy there was clearly visible a striving to get to know nature from itself and reveal the laws governing it by experiment, the senses, and reason. References to the Bible were not authoritative enough for him when studying nature.

Tatishchev also expressed the same idea, believing that no proof from Scripture was required in matters of philosophy and the natural sciences; proof had to be confirmed by natural circumstances.

The deistic and pantheistic ideas that these thinkers adopted as a result of cognizing nature objectively helped Russian philosophical thought break away from Church orthodoxy and consolidate rationalist and materialist tendencies. What had been embryonic and an element in Prokopovich was taken further by Tatishchev, partly by Kantemir, and especially by Lomonosov.

When the relation between matter and form is examined in their works, much can be found that they took not only from Aristotle but also from the Scholastics. That was due to some extent to the underdevelopment in the philosophy of their time of the theory of the self-motion and inner activity of matter, the elaboration of which could not be adequately stimulated by a science based on mechanics. Activity was transferred to form, in agreement with Aristotelianism. In correlating matter and form, Prokopovich, Tatishchev, and Kantemir frequently concluded that matter was passive and a potential or possibility, while form was the vector of activity, reality, and the act. Such statements, however, did not take the form of a system, but were combined with other, often contradictory views, characteristic of a higher degree of philosophical assimilation of reality than Aristotelianism and scholasticism. An idea was discussed, for example, that the passivity of matter did not rule out its activity as a component of substance, physical body, and nature.

Assertion of the precedence of matter in relation to form brought these Russian thinkers' views closer to the ideas of the Renaissance and counterposed them to Thomism. While recognizing that God created the world, they did not deny (in contrast to the successors of Thomas Aquinas) its continuous creation. Prokopovich, for instance, considered that the forms, essence, and being of things were not sent down from on high but were inherent in the things themselves, which originated from one another in nature. "What can be clearer in the whole world than that the multitude of things have their own essence, being, difference, and division one from the other?"[8]

These philosophers' theory of motion, space, and time lacked many of the extremes of philosophical mechanism, in part because they assimilated a number of spontaneous dialectical ideas of antiquity. This is particularly noticeable in Prokopovich, who pointed out the link between movement and the contradictoriness of things. Motion, Prokopovich said, arose from opposition. The struggle of opposites, in his opinion, was a necessary condition of the continuation of motion. But he laid more stress on the disruptive aspect of contradiction than on the constructive.

When speaking about the causes of motion and trying to explain them from nature itself, these Russian thinkers touched on problems of the relation between motion and rest, showing both their link and their opposition. Prokopovich wrote that it was more necessary to cognize motion because explanation by means of it included almost all knowledge of nature.

Acknowledgment of the fact that any motion tended to rest, corresponding to Aristotle's physics, was characteristic of the level of development of the Russian seventeenth-century science. Understanding of inertia was essentially deepened in Russian natural science, and the priority of the state of rest began to be eliminated. In that connection the concepts of finite and infinite, continuous and discontinuous were analyzed in detail. During discussion of the divisibility of particles of matter there was a rapprochement of the atomistic and corpuscular conceptions with all the contradictions inherent in that. In his notes on Fontenelle's *Entrétiens,* for instance, Kantemir recognized the existence of atoms of different shape and size, moving in a void. But, as is obvious from his *Letters on Nature and Man,* he denied the indivisibility and eternity of atoms and the infinitude of motion. Like Prokopovich he rejected the doctrine of Epicurus on the grounds that it did not presuppose God's creation of the world and admitted its primordial character. In spite of statements like that, however, a first step was taken toward accepting atomism; its further affirmation and development called for surmounting the initial deistic assumptions and limiting the physical sense of the idea of God's creation of the world. Tatishchev was already defending Epicurus' theory as a whole in his *Conversation.*

Russian scholars' ideas about the universality of motion and the unlimited divisibility and inexhaustibility of matter, in short, merged into the common stream of the advanced ideas of the philosophy of modern times, and led to an understanding of motion as change in general, as well as other conflicting ideas.

THE THEORY OF KNOWLEDGE

The same contradictoriness, still unrecognized by the science of the time, was also inherent in the interpretation of the problem of truth. In the epistemology of that period the content of a judgment or statement that corresponded to the object was understood as true, and one that did not as false. This Aristotelian definition contained the dual possibility—materialist and idealist—of resolving the problem of truth, depending on how the object and reality, to which the statement should correspond, were understood. The early Russian enlighteners' understanding of truth was primarily expressed in its division into the logical and the metaphysical.

By logical truth was understood the correspondence of logical operations to objects and the world of material things, and nature. In this way, God was regarded either as nature or as an object of reflection beyond the bounds of philosophy. Logical operations themselves, according to Prokopovich, not only corresponded to objective operations and relations but also coincided with them. This idea was very important as a first approximation and approach to understanding the correspondence of the laws of logic to those of the objective world. The notion of logical truth mainly reflected materialist tendencies in its interpretation. Their existence was confirmed by the critique of Thomism and of the thinkers of the Second Scholasticism (Arriaga). A similar understanding of truth is also contained in the works of Tatishchev, Kantemir, and Lomonosov.

PHILOSOPHY OF SOCIETY AND HISTORY

At the turn of the eighteenth century the idea that Russia's strength, power, and historical future depended on the spread of education and development of science, the arts, and crafts became an inseparable part of the national consciousness of society. The philosophers of Peter the Great's time, who held idealist views on social phenomena, linked the changes meant for the "people's good" with the activity of the enlightened ruler, who had been called to serve his Fatherland by divine Providence. However, reference to that was more a tribute to the times, a verbal cover behind which was hidden recognition of historical necessity and law. The fact that the activity of the "philosopher on the throne" was being realized in the creation of a regular army and navy and the building of mills and factories, i.e., in multiplication of social wealth, was much more important in their eyes. Also it was being done "everywhere with inquisitive searching and with the aid of mathematical tools, physical experiments and the discussions of philosophers."[9]

The idea of enlightenment as the foundation of historical development and social well-being permeates all the works of Prokopovich and his sympathizers. While expressing the interests of Russia's reformers, this idea corresponded primarily to the vital needs of the early enterprise.

In trying to fuse together profound patriotism, old Russian traditions, and enlightenment ideas, these thinkers relied on the anti-scholastic principles and experience of eminent humanist enlighteners and reformers, and started from the point that education should be universal and everyone, including the peasants, should be made literate. It does not need saying that this idea was revolutionary in an age of serfdom because it opposed the clergy's monopoly of knowledge and science and the religious character of education as a whole inherent in feudalism.

The description of the views of supporters of enlightened absolutism in

Russia would be incomplete if it did not deal with their ideas about the relation between enlightenment and science and ignorance, superstition, and obscurantism.

BELIEF AND KNOWLEDGE

First, it should be stressed that Russian thinkers of the first half of the eighteenth century in practice affirmed the priority of knowledge in matters of the relation between knowledge and belief, although they did not exclude belief. None of them was an atheist, though contemporaries considered them such. They were not opponents of faith in general and did not strive to liberate social consciousness from it. While rejecting belief based on superstition and ignorance, they defended "true faith." Their attitude to this belief was dualistic. Prokopovich, for example, strove to remove it from the realm of positive knowledge (philosophy, physics, history, etc.), making it the subject of theology. But he so rationalized belief, requiring it to meet the same criteria as knowledge, that he introduced the concept of reason into the definition of faith itself and proposed it as the main thing. Thus, by rationalizing belief, he took its interpretation to the ultimate boundary at which the sovereign dominance of reason began, excluding faith as a dogma. But he himself was not yet aware that by introducing reason and its criteria of truth into the sphere of belief, he was thereby undermining the foundations of any faith.

The secular element increased considerably in the works of Tatishchev and Kantemir. The choice of science over the medieval theological outlook and the authority of the Church was made more definitely. But Prokopovich essentially proposed a reformist version of Russian Orthodoxy. This fully corresponded, objectively, to the needs of the rising free trade and enterprise, because the offensive against feudalism was always linked with a critique of Church restrictions. Like all reformers, he considered the Bible the sole faultless, impeccable source of belief. Unlike his brother-in-arms Tatishchev, he did not rise to denying the divine inspiration of this source. It is not denied, however, that some of his statements did not express his true views but were made for tactical considerations during his exhausting combat against the opponents of the Petrine reforms in the boyar-clerical camp.

Prokopovich, Tatishchev, and Kantemir belonged to the scientific, enlightenment trend and made themselves known as outstanding theorists in the solving of ontological and epistemological problems. But their talent was still better expressed in the social sphere, where they came forward not only as scholars justifying the enlightened-absolutist version of the theory of natural law in Russia, but also as statesmen and politicians whose views on society and the state were closely linked with their understanding of the individual and his essence and purpose.

MAN IN THE LIGHT OF PHILOSOPHICAL REFLECTIONS

The idea of man as a microcosm, inherited from classical antiquity, took on new life during the Renaissance. Being directed against denigration of the human and elevation of the divine, it drew attention to worldly matters and emotions, forming a real world of the spiritual in which man became the creator of his own happiness.

Denial of divine creation was not inherent in Prokopovich's theory. Yet he constantly strove to stress the independence, strength, and activity of man, who was made great by his intellect, deeds, and virtues, irrespective of any divinity. "All the virtues divided into parts in nature are concentrated in him as one, and he emerges as something else, not in size, but in the fullness of perfections equal to the whole of nature."[10]

Prokopovich's man was still abstract; his essence did not come from social relations but was natural. But this "man in general" was not simply equal to the rest of nature but also surpassed it, subordinating natural forces to himself by means of labor (understood as an innate natural quality in people). In his view man and his intellect and body were governed by natural law, whose core was conscience. Prokopovich believed that nature laid the foundation of good deeds, or the capacity to do good in man. This natural gift acquired moral elements, however, only when man did good consciously, basing himself on freedom of choice. From that it followed that reliance on natural law was not an adequate condition for morality, because man's actions should also be based on consciousness and a free choice of good. Involuntary or forced actions could not be regarded as moral.

Elucidation of the meaning of life had a major place in the works of these thinkers. Prokopovich, in particular, associated it with the works and deeds that filled people's lives. Death he regarded as "the worst of all evils." Similar views that ran counter to the orientation toward salvation and bliss in the next world, traditional for Christian morality, were also expressed by his associates. These ideas were close to the theses that later thinkers, like Chernyshevsky, for example, developed in the theory of "rational egoism."

When discussing the relation between man and work in terms of ethics, Prokopovich, Tatishchev, and Kantemir pushed eudemonism into the background and laid stress on the ethics of duty or deontology. In their view, labor was easy and pleasant only in the natural state as a "joyful dance of health," but later became forced and hard and was converted from pleasure into a duty in regard to the family, society, and the state.

Neither Prokopovich nor his sympathizers were opponents of feudalism as a social system, but, in morally condemning luxury, they were thereby in favor of a humane, liberal attitude to the poor. They thought that burdening the peasant with work beyond his strength was equivalent to murdering him. Prokopovich called on the lords not to employ cruel punishments against serfs, but "to punish paternally with the intention of correcting them, and not to foment the heart of the savage; not to impose an inordinate burden of due services or work, not to levy exorbitant taxes on peasants, and not to withhold deserved reward."[11]

On the other hand, he called on peasants to work diligently for their lords. Although he believed it was "best to be legally free from slavery," neither he nor his fellows rose to protest serfdom. Their liberalism was nevertheless not just a means of social reconciliation and justification of the existing system. It already contained a kernel, albeit weak and small, of social freethinking, as was especially noticeable in Kantemir's satire. The seed sprouted and developed "to the envy and pride of the immoral gentry" in the works of spokesmen of future generations who rose to expose serfdom in the latter half of the eighteenth century, and then to demand its abolition.

The work of Prokopovich et al. reflected the change taking place in Russian philosophy in the significance and subordination of its components. Development of technology was bringing the sciences of nature to the fore, while the study of the latter ceased to be an introduction to theosophy. That led to an essential reorganization of the theory of knowledge, to changes in the style of thinking, methods of proof, and criteria of truth. In the works of the "brain trust" there was already quite a marked tendency toward recognizing the irrefutability of the laws of nature. The enlighteners of this period lauded the strength and power of human reason, opposed authoritarianism and dogmatism, and insisted on the benefit and practical applicability of knowledge. Their works promoted the formation of a Russian enlightenment and were the soil on which Lomonosov, Radishchev, and other Russian thinkers of the eighteenth century developed.

NOTES

1. Cited from N. S. Tikhonravov, *Sochineniya* (Works) (Moscow, 1898), vol. 2, p. 134.

2. V. N. Tatishchev, *Izbrannye proizvedeniya* (Selected works) (Leningrad, 1979), pp. 52–53.

3. Ibid., p. 89.

4. A. Kantemir, Foreword to *Razgovory o mnozhestvennosti mirov* (St. Petersburg, 1740), footnote 2.

5. Tatishchev, *Izbrannye proizvedeniya*, p. 53.

6. *Sochineniya, pisma i izbrannye perevody knyazya A. Kantemira* (Prince A. Kantemir's works, letters, and selected translations), (St. Petersburg, 1868), vol. 2, p. 51.

7. Ibid., p. 59.

8. F. Prokopovich, *Rassuzhdeniye o bezbozhii* (*Argument about Godlessness*) (Moscow, 1774), p. 12.

9. F. Prokopovich, *Sochineniya* (Works) (Moscow-Leningrad, 1961), p. 66.

10. F. Prokopovich, "A Word About Love of God," in *Khristianskoye chteniye,* 2d ed. (n.p., 1838), pt. 23, p. 183.

11. F. Prokopovich, *Pervoye ucheniye otrokam* (*A First Lesson for Sprigs*) (St. Petersburg, 1723), p. 14.

2

Mikhail Lomonosov

Vitaly Bogatov

"THE FIRST RUSSIAN UNIVERSITY"

The greatest national poet of the nineteenth century, Alexander Pushkin, called Mikhail Lomonosov (1711–1765) "the first Russian university." There is much truth and justice in that evocative metaphor. The appearance of so outstanding a personality in the early eighteenth century was extraordinarily fortunate, yet at the same time to be expected. The efforts of Peter the Great and his kindred spirits had accelerated the rates of development of the economy, culture, and science in Russia. Russia had consolidated her international position. Conditions had been created for further socioeconomic progress. But this progress was contradictory, since it occurred simultaneously with an increase in economic pressure on the peasantry. There had been a further consolidation of the monarchy and the gentry's empire. Export of farm produce had increased. Discontent of the working people had grown and unrest had increased.

Lomonosov was the spokesman of Russia's historical needs. He was a true encyclopedist, a man who was at the source of many branches of knowledge and industry. He expressed the interests of those strata of Russian society that wished to modernize the country's economic and military might as the foundations of state independence, and of those who advocated development of the national culture and the thriving and enlightenment of their people. Mathematician, physicist, chemist, astronomer, geologist, geographer, poet, linguist, historian, and philosopher—this is an incomplete list of the spheres of his theoretical and practical activity.

Lomonosov came from a family of Russians (Pomors) of the White Sea littoral in the Archangel Province. He showed an early interest in studies, and in 1730 left for Moscow. Although he experienced great material difficulties, he successfully mastered the fundamentals of the sciences and, after studying at the Slavonic-Greek-Latin Academy, was sent to St. Petersburg. From there, as one of the three best pupils, he went to Germany to continue his education. In Germany he successfully applied himself to problems of metallurgy and mining, and studied philosophy and other humanitarian and natural sciences.

In 1741 he began his twenty-five-year period of fruitful work as enlightener, scientist, and philosopher, a period full of intensive activity—sometimes dramatic in its tension—to train national scientific and other personnel. He was the first Russian professor and member of the academy and initiated the founding of Moscow University, where he helped to introduce lecturing in Russian. He struggled constantly against conservatism in science and against bureaucracy in the field of education. Lomonosov thought a great deal about Russia's scientific and spiritual development, linking advance in this field with young people and their enthusiasm and curiosity.

HIS SOCIAL AND POLITICAL PHILOSOPHY

In his social and political sympathies Lomonosov was a supporter and defender of the cause of Peter the Great, who became an ideal for him. He approved of Peter's reforming activity and held in high esteem his efforts in the field of economic development. Lomonosov wanted to see his native land an enlightened monarchy.

Life itself was demanding drastic reforms and social changes. In that context Lomonosov's activity was very fruitful and timely because his efforts were anti-feudal and in the final analysis had a democratic character. In a letter to Ivan Shuvalov (of November 1, 1761) Lomonosov proposed the following plan for resolving social problems that he considered paramount: (1) reproduction and maintenance of the Russian people; (2) elimination of idleness; (3) correction of morals and greater enlightenment of the people; (4) improvement of agriculture; (5) improvement and spread of arts and crafts; (6) better benefits for the merchantry; (7) a better state economy; (8) maintenance of the military arts during a long-term peace. He then commented: "These very important headings call for deep and long-term discussion, skill in public affairs to make them understood, and cautiousness in carrying them out."[1]

This program was included in Lomonosov's work that was given a title coinciding with the first of the listed problems. It gave priority to his concern for easing the living conditions of the peasantry as a way to maintain the Russian people, in whom lay "the wealth of our state."

When defining the role of the people in public affairs he put their well-being first, writing: "The prosperity, glory, and flourishing condition of the state come from three sources: (1) internal quiet, and the security and satisfaction of subjects; (2) victorious actions against the enemy and from the conclusion of a favorable and glorious peace; and (3) mutual exchange of internal surpluses with distant peoples through the merchantry."[2]

But in the final analysis he regarded the Russian population as a passive estate, assigning the active role in history to the enlightened monarch. He saw the sense of his own life and activity in promoting enlightenment and the economic and cultural prosperity of the people of Russia.

PHILOSOPHICAL MATERIALISM

Lomonosov was the first Russian materialist philosopher, the founder of the Russian materialist tradition. He was a thinker and naturalist who was able to combine concrete scientific interpretation of nature with philosophical comprehension of it. His materialism was based on the natural sciences and study of inanimate nature. On the whole it was mechanistic and, what is more, inconsistent, since it relied on intuitions of deism and recognition of the existence of God-Creator. On the other hand, as far as nature, science, and the process of cognition were concerned, Lomonosov's materialism was free of mystical, religious ideas. He was a critic of the institutions of the Church.

He came to materialism and freethinking in science through the impact of the ideas of Russian and West European scholars. He highly appreciated Christian Wolff as his teacher, but Wolff himself admitted that he had not succeeded in converting Lomonosov to the idealist outlook that he himself advocated.

Lomonosov answered the question of the relation between matter and spirit in a materialistic way: the external world was primary and existed outside and independent of man. He divided the objects of nature into three constituent parts: inanimate nature, plants, and animals. Matter underlay everything that existed; it was "that from which the body was constituted and on which its existence depended."[3] Matter was manifested in two states: (1) as solid, liquid, and gaseous; and (2) as ether, which filled all the interstices between the particles of bodies. "A body is an extension possessing the force of inertia," and the "essence of bodies is extension and inertia"; "Everything that is and happens in bodies is governed by their essence and nature," and "nature consists of action and reaction." Thus, Lomonosov in fact rejected the existence of any phenomena and substances outside nature (phlogiston, fluids, etc.). He considered the main attributes of matter to be extension, inertia, imperviousness, and motion. He interpreted space as the place occupied by a body, as its extension, therefore "a body consists of physical, insensitive particles that have extension."[4]

Lomonosov paid special attention to so-called primary and secondary qualities. That was not a new problem for European philosophers and naturalists. Galileo and Locke in particular had racked their brains to solve it. It boiled down to the following: were such qualities of matter as extension, weight, shape, motion, etc., on the one hand, and taste, color, sound, smell, etc., on the other, objective? The latter were often declared to be derived from our feelings and mind, i.e., not to exist objectively.

Lomonosov opposed a sharp division between primary and secondary qualities. In his opinion, both had an objective basis. Furthermore, he was deeply convinced of their organic unity. He saw the difference between them in the fact that primary qualities are universal, i.e., inherent in all nature, and secondary ones lack that universality, i.e., are specific. He gave his answer from a mechanistic standpoint. While recognizing that there was an infinite variety of both qualities in nature, he represented the specificity of secondary qualities itself in an oversimplified way, although the science of the time could not provide any other solution.

MATTER AND MOTION

The concept of motion had a central place in Lomonosov's theory of matter. In the seventeenth and eighteenth centuries mechanics, astronomy, and mathematics were the most developed of the natural sciences. On their bases a mechanistic view of nature had become predominant in the natural sciences and philosophy. But the naturalists were accumulating more and more facts and conclusions that provided evidence that science was beginning to feel the limitations of the mechanistic and mathematical methods of understanding the universe. An idea of the need for a historical view of the past of the Universe was gradually gaining ground, and evolutionary views were acquiring considerable influence. Lomonosov made a marked contribution to developing of the theory of evolution.

In his celebrated work *First Principles of Metallurgy or Mining* (*Pervye osnovaniya metallurgii, ili rudnykh del* [1763]) he gave an original definition of the global change in the Earth. Having examined the processes taking place on its surface and in its interior, he drew a significant conclusion:

Thus many think, without reason, that everything, as we see, was initially made by a Creator; not only mountains, valleys, and waters, but allegedly also various kinds of minerals emerged together with the whole world; so that there is no need to investigate the reasons why they differ in inner properties and position of place. Such arguments are very harmful to the growth of all the sciences and consequently to natural knowledge of the globe, and especially to the art of mining, although it is easy for some

smart fellows to be philosophers by learning three words by rote—God
so created—and giving this as an answer instead of all the reasons.[5]

These considerations struck a blow at metaphysical notions in the natural sciences. But on the whole Lomonosov remained within the boundaries
of the mechanistic method of thinking. It is important at the same time to
stress that he did not conceive motion without matter and explained all changes
in it by various forms of mechanical movement (translational, oscillatory,
rotary). According to him motion was a process of continuous creation and
destruction.

Lomonosov's theory was confirmed in part by his scientific achievements,
in particular by his discoveries in the theory of heat. He formulated an important proposition that motion in the material world could be external (visible) and internal (accessible only to speculation). The phenomenon of heat
was the internal motion of material particles. Of course, he also explained
internal motion mechanistically.

Lomonosov had already written in his *Reflections on the Cause of Heat
and Cold* (*Razmyshleniya o prichine teploty i kholoda*), in 1748, that "heat
is excited by motion," and that this motion was rotary. The conclusion read:
"*There are sufficient grounds of heat in motion.* And since motion cannot
happen without matter, it is necessary that *sufficient grounds for heat consist
of the motion of some matter.*"[6]

The problem of motion could not be answered scientifically without
elucidation of its source. Like the other best minds of the eighteenth century,
Lomonosov sought an answer to this matter. Formally, he assumed a first
impulse, but the main direction of his scientific search was analysis of the
dynamics of nature. Moreover, he did not mystify the first impulse (it is also
a problem for modern science) but interpreted it mechanistically, i.e., again
as natural necessity and the inevitability not so much of a first impulse as
of primary movement. This is confirmed by his philosophical, methodological
arguments in his short work "On the Weight of Bodies and the Eternity of
the Primary Motion" (*O tyazhesti tel i ob izvechnosti pervichnogo dvizheniya*),
in which he stressed that "primary motion is that which originates in itself,
i.e., does not depend on other dynamics." He then advanced the following
proposition: "Primary motion cannot have a beginning but must exist eternally," and suggested the following proof:

> Assume that primary motion does not exist eternally; then it follows that
> there was a time when there was no motion and that which moved was
> at rest but was finally forced into motion. Hence one can conclude that
> there was something external that moved it and, consequently, primary mo-
> tion was not primary, which however contains a contradiction. It is there-
> fore necessary to accept the opposite assertion and to admit that primary

motion could never have a beginning but must have existed since time immemorial.[7]

ATOMISM

Lomonosov's philosophical ideas were scientifically supported by his atomism, on the problems of which he worked throughout his scientific career. Before the principle of the "corpuscular philosophy" was formulated, he had to make a critical appraisal of the atomistic conceptions of Gassendi, Boyle, Newton, and others. He rejected the notions of the Newtonians who declared that particles of matter were separated by an absolute void, and he did not agree with Boyle who had in fact come to deny the real existence of chemical elements as qualitatively different kinds of atoms. The Cartesian identification of matter and space did not satisfy him either. But the main thrust of his criticism was directed against Leibniz's monadology. The German philosopher and scientist treated the primary corpuscle-monad as a "fulguration of the Divinity," declaring it a spiritual substance.[8] He also rejected the views of Leibniz's follower, Christian Wolff.

Lomonosov's greatest accomplishment was that he was one of the first to suggest a concrete scientific conception of the atomic-molecular structure of matter. This theory was based on the latest achievements of physics, chemistry, and mathematics of that time. In 1741, in his *Elements of Mathematical Chemistry* (*Elementy fizicheskoy khimii*), and rather earlier, in 1739, in his *Physical Dissertation* (*Fizicheskaya dissertatsiya*), he substantiated this principle and defined the atom (element) and molecule (corpuscle). The atom, he said, was "the part of a body that did not consist of any other smaller bodies different from it."[9] The molecule (corpuscle) consisted of several atoms.

Corpuscles were complex, invisible entities, but the properties of the bodies of nature had to be sought in their qualities. Corpuscles had extension, and their essence had to be cognized through experiment and reflection.

Lomonosov's contribution to the development of atomism was (1) that he was one of the first who managed to unite theoretical notions about atoms with experimental data; (2) that he substantiated the existence of two qualitatively different levels of the organization of matter (atoms and molecules), recognizing the fact that discrete forms of matter (particles) tended to become more complex; (3) that he opened the way in science to discovery of the basic law of the chemical composition of matter (the law of permanent and divisible relations); and (4) that he linked chemistry (the atomic level) and physics (the molecular level).

DISCOVERY OF THE LAW OF THE
CONSERVATION OF MATTER AND MOTION

Lomonosov's name has gone down in world science and philosophy as a pioneer of the universal law of the conservation of matter (substance) and motion. That became possible only through his development of scientific atomism, which enabled him to make a major advance in the study of nature.

Scientists knew that matter and motion were eternal, but the question of the dynamics of the quantity of substance and the forms of its existence remained open. In concrete scientific investigations it often happened that the quantity of the substance used for an experiment proved different, more or less, at the end of it. Such unscientific concepts as "fire principle," phlogiston, etc., were employed to explain this phenomenon.

Lomonosov first formulated the law of the conservation of matter and motion in a letter to Leonhard Euler in 1748, but that was in a private communication, and the idea of the law remained closed to the broad scientific public. That is why he returned to it twelve years later in his *Disquisition on the Solidity and Fluidity of Bodies* (*Rassuzhdeniye o tvyordosti i zhidkosti tyel* [1760]). It contains an almost word-for-word formulation of the law as it appears in the letter to Euler. Here is this celebrated excerpt: "But all the changes which happen in nature amount in essence to the fact that the amount taken from one body is added to another, so if some substance is diminished in one place, it is added in another; the hours a person is awake are diminished by those he spends asleep. This universal natural law also extends to the laws of motion themselves."[10]

Lomonosov justly considered this a *universal* law of nature that applied equally to matter and motion as an integral quality of it. Furthermore, he provided *experimental* confirmation of the law of the indestructibility of matter, and carried out his celebrated experiment on combustion in a sealed vessel.

METHODOLOGY AND THE THEORY OF KNOWLEDGE

Lomonosov's methodological principles relating to epistemology were an interesting aspect of his work. While approaching the achievements of human knowledge in a respectful, critical way, he stressed: "I shall not attack people who have made a contribution to the republic of science for their mistakes, but shall try to put their good ideas to use. . . . Noticing the mistakes is not worth much; to do things better—that is what befits a worthy man."[11]

But he was categorically against canonizing authorities, and favored a historical evaluation of the contribution of every eminent scholar to science, calling for an independent and critical comprehension of the history of thought, because knowledge became out of date and obsolete, and science and philosophy searched for and found new truths. He defined the moral and patriotic sense of his life in science as follows: "As for me, I will devote myself to the struggle against the enemies of the Russian sciences until I die, as I have been doing for twenty years; I stood for them in my youth and shall not betray them in old age."[12]

Lomonosov's scientific and philosophical works were extraordinarily vital and practical. In that sense he can be called a realist. He conducted his search for truth in several directions.

He attempted to create an integrated materialist theory of knowledge. He was aware that the search for truth was being carried out in a one-sided way in science. Naturalists relied on experiment in their struggle against medieval scholasticism. In his opinion the naturalist was obliged to be analytical and study a phenomenon profoundly and in a thorough way; and he had to have a clear idea of the object being investigated. A scientist's experimental activity was aimed at studying "the historical knowledge of changes" in matter, and examining how new bodies developed from a combination of known ones. All of this constituted the initial stage of science's movement toward truth. Philosophy's task was to generalize and synthesize the experimental data and seek out the laws and causes of the phenomena taking place. It is the scholar's theoretical, generalizing thought that leads to scientific truth. Lomonosov's final conclusion reads as follows: "To establish a theory from observations, and to correct observations through theory, is the best means of seeking the truth."[13]

Lomonosov was a passionate champion of the truth not only because it was necessary as such, but also for the practical benefit of people. Science and philosophy should promote the prosperity of Russia, improve the quality of life, be fundamentally associated with the "arts," i.e., with industry, and serve the people.

Problems of epistemology were not a subject of special philosophical examination for him, but in his quest for a correct, objective method of finding scientific truth he expressed many interesting ideas that provide grounds for evaluating his theoretical, cognitive principles as materialist. We have already mentioned his historicism in studying nature and the relationship between theory and practice. His interpretation of the concept "truth" itself, and his appraisal of the vital importance of natural science, impelled him to study the mechanism for obtaining reliable knowledge.

As a philosopher and scientist Lomonosov recognized the essential role of reason in cognitive activity, which required unity of the sensual and the rational. Being deeply convinced of the omnipotence of human reason, he began with the fact that the process of cognition starts with the effect of the external world on man's senses. Particles of matter that had definite properties excited appropriate nerve endings of the organs of the sense of touch; this combination of actually existing properties with sense organs was passed to the brain where it was registered. Such stimuli of the external world, repeatedly confirmed through the sense organs, created notions that were later processed by the brain into general concepts and categories called ideas.

According to Lomonosov, scientific knowledge and truth were the end result of man's sensory-rational activity and constituted a movement from ignorance to ever greater comprehension of nature's secrets and employment of them for the good of society. He opposed the idealist conception of "innate ideas" from that standpoint, and the interference of the Church in the affairs of science.

Lomonosov called reason the "ruler of our actions." But man lived among other beings like himself. The scholar therefore could not and should not remain the sole possessor of truth. Everyone needed knowledge. Considering that the result of a scientist's thought activity became the property of everyone through the word as a means of transmitting thought to others, Lomonosov himself did much to propagate knowledge, was a reformer of language, and a fighter for enlightenment of the people. He laid down the traditions of a realistic, or rather materialistic, attitude to traditional philosophical problems and the social and spiritual development of Russia.

NOTES

1. M. V. Lomonosov, *Izbrannye filosofskiye proizvedeniya* (*Selected Philosophical Works*) (Moscow, 1950), pp. 598–99.

2. Ibid., p. 624.

3. Ibid., p. 93.

4. Ibid., pp. 97, 99, 109.

5. Ibid., p. 397.

6. Ibid., p. 137.

7. M .V. Lomonosov, *Polnoye sobraniye sochinenii* (Complete works), (Moscow, 1951), vol. 2, p. 201.

8. See: *The Philosophical Writings of Leibniz*, selected and translated by Mary Morris (London: J. M. Dent & Sons, 1934), p. 11.

9. M. V. Lomonosov, *Izbrannye filosofskiye proizvedeniya*, p. 89.

10. Ibid., p. 341.

11. Ibid., pp. 92–93.

12. Ibid., p. 697.

13. Ibid., p. 330.

Part Two

The Age of Enlightenment and Philosophy

3

The Russian Enlightenment of the Late Eighteenth Century

Vitaly Bogatov and Alexi Boldyrev

The ideas of the Enlightenment, whose first heralds in Russia were Lomonosov and Radishchev, became particularly widespread in the second half of the eighteenth century. The Enlightenment reflected the struggle of the early bourgeois forces of Russia against feudalism. The development of capitalism in Russia took place against a background of consolidation of absolutism and intensification of serfdom. But Russia's involvement in European civilization made her transition to new social relations irreversible.

The enlighteners threw doubt on the legitimacy of traditional social relations, opposed estate regulation, advocated secular humanistic moral standards, raising the social welfare of the population, and democratization of public affairs. Unlike Radishchev they were protagonists of gradual improvements and legal and political reforms. There was an absence of complete unanimity among them on matters of state organization. Although reformism did not include ideas about people's power and republicanism, there was much humanism, common sense, and humane moral values in it. The Russian Enlightenment was the cause of the highly educated people of the time, who were aware of the need to improve the situation of the people and create an atmosphere of respect for the individual. A broad range of scholars, writers, and statesmen was drawn into the enlightenment movement. They included such striking personalities as Anichkov, Desnitsky, Fonvizin, Kozelsky, and Novikov. We shall examine the views of some leading figures who had a marked influence on the development of Russian philosophical ideas of the period.

SEMYON DESNITSKY

Semyon Desnitsky (1740–1789) was born to a middle-class family, graduated from Moscow University in 1759, and then studied at Glasgow University, where he received first a master's degree (1765) and then an LL.D. (1767). After eight years in Scotland he became professor of law at Moscow University, where he worked until 1787.

Desnitsky was a specialist in legal studies and a sociologist. He expounded his views in a number of books on jurisprudence and allied subjects. Among them were *The Shortest Way to Jurisprudence* (*Slovo o pryamom i blizhaishem sposobe k naucheniyu yurisprudentsii*, [1768]); *Death Penalty in Criminal Cases* (*Slovo o prichinakh smertnykh kaznei po delam kriminalnym*, [1770]); *A Legal Discourse on the Beginning and Origin of Matrimony in Primary Peoples* (*Yuridicheskoye rassuzhdeniye o nachale i proiskhozhdenii supruzhestva u pervonachalnykh narodov*, [1775]); and *A Legal Discourse about the Different Ideas Which People Have Concerning the Ownership of Property and Different Conditions of Society* (*Yuridicheskoye rassuzhdeniye o raznykh ponyatiyakh, kakiye imeyut narody o sobstvennosti imeniya i razlichnykh sostoyaniyakh obshchezhitelstva*, [1781]).

In 1768 he drafted a *Proposal Concerning the Establishment of Legislative, Judicial and Punishment Authorities in the Russian Empire* (*Predstavleniye o uchrezhdenii zakonodatelnoi, suditelnoi i nakazatelnoi vlasti v Rossiiskoi imperii*). In it he opposed absolutism and demonstrated the need for a constitutional monarchy. He translated a number of legal and political treatises from English, supplying them with his own forewords, in which he condemned serfdom. In 1783 he became a member of the Russian Academy of Sciences.

Desnitsky's social ideas were an important part of the intellectual arsenal of the Russian enlightenment of the latter half of the eighteenth century. He worked on the most important problems of the essence of social relations and the state system and legal institutions, and explored the problem of property.

Desnitsky's works on political economy, jurisprudence, and social philosophy, their conclusions and general trends, clearly showed his critical attitude to the official ideology, clericalism, absolute monarchy, and serfdom. He considered the driving force of progress to be human reason expressed in ideas, science, and enlightenment. Basing himself on the theory of "natural law" and "social contract," he substantiated the need for a significant limitation of the monarch's power, and for elected representative authorities. He considered a constitutional monarchy of the British type to be the model of a social system. In his *Proposal Concerning the Establishment of Legislative, Judicial and Punishment Authorities in the Russian Empire* submitted to Catherine the Great, he set out an integral program for restructuring the state that posed the problem of transferring state power from the monarch to a "governing" Senate guided by the monarch. The Senate would define the taxes, declare war, determine foreign policy, control the budget, and so on. Although he did not envisage depriving the empress of any power, the conservatives looked on his plans as an attempt to create an "organ of people's representation" in Russia. Their fear was not ill-founded, because it was proposed to elect the Senate by provinces, and to recognize the right of the nobility, merchants, clergy, representatives of higher educational institutions, and scholars to be elected to it.

Desnitsky proposed judicial reform and a limitation of the arbitrary power of the czar's courts, and advised introduction of an institution of lawyers. He recommended granting power in the provinces to elected bodies in which merchants would predominate. His proposals for dealing with the peasant problem were interesting and amounted to a marked limitation of the power of landowners and a ban on a further enserfing of peasants. He criticized the clergy, in the spirit of Lomonosov, for their opposition to science, and advocated secular education for the people.

Desnitsky expressed his social ideas in *A Legal Discourse about the Different Ideas Which People Have Concerning the Ownership of Property in Different Conditions of Society.* In it he seriously posed the problem of social evolution of humankind for the first time in Russian socioeconomic and legal literature and attempted to answer it through analyzing the evolution of the forms of property.

He believed that mankind had passed through four stages in its development: (1) hunting, (2) husbandry, (3) land-tilling, and (4) commerce.

The first stage in this development was marked by hunting. Under those conditions people did not have a fixed abode and led a nomadic life. "Among peoples who live by trapping animals the majority of material goods are not divided but are common to all. . . . They have joint, undivided possession and use, and since they eat together their edible stores are common to all."[1] On that basis he concluded that, "When, among peoples who live by trapping animals and eating wild-growing fruits, there is no divided, separate possession of goods, the difference between *thine* and *mine* among them is hardly intelligible."[2]

At this stage of mankind's evolution private property did not yet exist, which made the idea of its eternal existence unsound.

Husbandry was a higher level of life, and private property came into being at this stage. But it was not yet private ownership of land. Land was at the disposal of large families and tribes. Private property appeared in the form of domesticated animals and everything associated with their care. Mankind was raised to a new level of material well-being and culture. "In short, in this pastoral and cattle-raising state, peoples had an increasing concept of property because they began to own a greater number of very durable and long-lasting goods."[3]

Property was not only a guarantee of survival but also a sign of social status; at the same time it did not yet disrupt the traditional forms of people's intercourse. The collectivist principle predominated.

The "land-tilling state" changed the picture in a very radical way. The nomadic period came to an end. People went over to a settled way of life. They settled in "a land chosen by them," built permanent dwellings, worked the land, and began to secure it to those who tilled it. Private property developed in land, and the right of ownership and of bequeathing land was legalized at that stage.

This state finally secured movable and immovable private property (chattels and real estate), and agriculture became highly developed. A manufacturing industry, crafts, and trade arose. All of this was consolidated in laws that protected private property, which gave it "the general usefulness of sanctioned property," "a person was permitted to use his things at will" by law. The law also protected the owner, encouraged exchange of commodities, the development of communications, and so on.[4]

The "commercial state" of society, in which capitalist society was readily recognized, was the supreme achievement of mankind in Desnitsky's opinion. He should be given some credit for striving to question the eternity of monarchy and serfdom in Russia.

Like a true enlightener he exaggerated the role of "reason," and of "benefit" ("profit"), which he understood in an abstract way. He claimed that private property was its highest form. Basing himself on Scottish sociologists and lawyers he introduced several ideas into Russian social thought (for example, the difference between private property and common ownership, and so on). He brought out the close link between legal institutions and the distribution of property in society, and showed that the law served whoever had economic power. His studies were objectively aimed at the development of "commercial," i.e., free-enterprise relations in Russia.

Desnitsky's *A Legal Discourse on the Beginning and Origin of Matrimony in Primary Peoples* (*Yuridicheskoye rassuzhdeniye o nachale i proiskhozhdenii supruzhestva u pervonachalnykh narodov* [1775]) was organically united with the work mentioned above. And it was presumably the impulse for the writing of his main work, which analyzed problems of property. Study of the forming of the family inevitably posed the question of the living, social, economic, and moral conditions in which it could arise and function in the various stages of human development.

Desnitsky regarded the family as well as property historically. In opposition to the biblical myth of the first family, Adam and Eve, he treated the family not as created by a divine act but as arising during the evolution of society, as a result of people's changing relations in the labor process and the forms of their intercourse. He called only the monogamous family a family, and for this reason he put its origin in the third period of social evolution—in the "land-tilling stage" when private property arose. During the inception of "commercial society" not only were the socioeconomic foundations of the existence of the family laid, but the legal foundations as well.

Desnitsky understood, however, that this did not mean the advent of ideal family relations. In that connection he drew attention to the hard position of the woman and insisted that a marriage should be entered into for the mutual benefit of the man and the woman.

In eighteenth-century conditions, when absolute monarchy and patriarchal family relations prevailed in Russia, Desnitsky's ideas of a secular, social, and legally defended family were quite realistic.

His contributions to Russian sociophilosophical thought were considerable. He was in the front rank of the outstanding thinkers of his time for the depth and clarity of his theoretical solutions and his scholarly activity for Russia's advance and the well-being of all those who created her wealth and prosperity.

DMITRY ANICHKOV

Dmitry Anichkov (1733–1788) came of a *raznochintsy* family* and received a good education. He studied in the seminary of the St. Sergius Trinity Monastery, and in 1755 became one of the first students of the university just founded in Moscow.

His dissertation titled *An Argument from Natural Theology about the Principle and Origin of Natural Divine Worship* (*Rassuzhdeniye iz naturalnoy bogoslovii o nachale i proisshestvii naturalnogo bogopochitaniya* [1769]) was considered a major event in the intellectual life of Russia. In it he posed the question of the natural origin of religion. Because of his critical attitude to mysticism and clericalism, he was not confirmed as a professor for eight years.

Anichkov taught mathematics, philosophy, and logic in Moscow University. In addition to the above-mentioned work, he wrote several books on philosophical and theological subjects and textbooks on arithmetic, algebra, geometry, and trigonometry.

As a philosopher he adhered to the main principles of materialism, expressed in deistic form. He believed that philosophy should play a major social role, and that the "duty of a philosopher was to seek out the causes of many things," and to answer the problem of "the union of soul and body."[5] Philosophy's task was to study and explain the surrounding world in keeping with common sense and logic. His thought was directed on the whole against theology and medieval scholasticism. Like the other enlighteners, he fought to teach philosophy in Russian, was a supporter of heliocentrism, and a popularizer of the latest advances in science.

---

* *Raznochinets*—intellectuals not belonging to the gentry in nineteenth-century Russia.—*Ed.*

Anichkov considered the world to be filled by material substance. In spite of the synod censorship, he managed to introduce the idea of the dependence of the soul on the body into his works. In a polemic with Leibniz and Wolff he demonstrated the thesis that the ideal (soul) was engendered by the material (body).

Anichkov did much in the field of the theory of knowledge. He rejected the concept of "innate ideas," and substantiated a thesis of materialist sensualism. The basis of knowledge was sense perceptions, which were the result of the effect of external objects on man's sense organs. In *A Word on the Properties of Human Knowledge* (*Slovo o svoystvakh poznaniya chelovecheskogo* [1770]), the critical aspect of the argument against Masons, Scholastics, and religious conceptions of knowledge was clearly expressed. Anichkov attached great importance to experimental science and human experience.

Anichkov took a mechanistic stand on matters of the theory of knowledge. He called the sensual stage the lowest (it was inherent, he suggested, in some animals). The highest degree of knowledge was the capacity of understanding, reasoning, reflecting, paying attention, and abstracting—unique to man because he was gifted with intellect. He divided human knowledge into three stages: sense perception, the soul's development of a concept of the perceived object, and reasoning.[6]

In his opinion, cognition was a complicated, contradictory process. In that connection he recalled Francis Bacon's "idols" and Descartes's doubt. Anichkov divided all cognitive fallacies into the "theoretical" and the "practical." The latter were the most dangerous. He counted approximately ten reasons for misconceptions, but at the same time did not doubt that man was capable of attaining truths, and did so. On the whole his cognitive principle was based on a profound belief in human reason, and the inexhaustible possibilities of empirical, rational knowledge. His materialism was inconsistent, of course. In addition, given censorship, he could not frankly express his thoughts. Nevertheless, his contribution to development of the theory of knowledge was very fruitful and substantially enriched Russian philosophy.

A distinctive feature of Anichkov's outlook was his opposition to the clergy. He based his views on the origin of religious notions and on the social role of the Church, on a broad range of literature and the authority of eminent scientists.

He denied the idea of the innateness of religious emotions in the individual; they had a quite explicable origin, he suggested, and an earthly basis. In his search for answers to the genesis of divine worship and religious beliefs he turned to the early periods of mankind. People (he wrote) initially came up against nature and its terrible elements and inexplicable phenomena. Nature overwhelmed them, generated in them a feeling of their own helplessness and instilled terror in them. Inability to explain what was happening in nature and people's ignorance led them to worship. Strong and wise people, who astounded their fellow tribesmen by their actions, became objects of worship. "And so, from wonder a new earthborn divinity arose, to whom altars and temples were erected in deep antiquity. . . . The descendants, gazing with admiration on this man-created creature, in the end counted them as heavenly and called these ages heroic."[7]

The next stage in the development of religious notions and ideas was associated with the fact that power and wisdom began to be attributed no longer to separate, concrete personalities but to some third, abstract being who stood above the strong and wise. So belief in the transcendental, supernatural, i.e., in God, came into being.

Anichkov did not limit himself to analyzing the origin of pagan gods. He extended his analysis to the causes of the genesis of Christianity, criticizing the authenticity of Bible stories about heaven and hell. His anticlericalism led him to oppose religious education for children and to call, in essence, for separation of the school from the Church.

PAFNUTY BATURIN

Little is known of the life of Pafnuty Baturin (1740–1803). He came from the gentry and was in military service from the age of fourteen. In 1782 he retired with the rank of colonel. He lived in St. Petersburg, Kaluga, Tula, and Kiev. He wrote several satirical plays of an educational character, and a critical article against Gavrila Derzhavin's "Ode to the Wise Kirghizkaisak Queen Felicia" (*Oda k premudroy kirkizkaysatskoy tsarevne Felitse*). The grounds for including him among thinkers of Russia's enlightenment are his two works titled *A Short Narrative about Arabians* (*Kratkoye povestvovaniye o aravlyanakh* [1787]) and *Examination of the Book of Errors and Truth* (*Issledovaniye knigi o zabluzhdeniyakh i istine* [1790]).

These works attest that Baturin was a polemicist, a talented enlightener, philosopher, and social thinker, educated on the best models of Russian and European culture. In the first of these two books he greatly appreciated the value of historical knowledge and called for drawing moral lessons from the past and the use of historical knowledge to mitigate cruelty and injustice in human relations. In his opinion, ruling classes should be concerned with the common good, cultivate a sense of benevolence and justice in their milieu, and bring it to the people. Spread of "salutary" enlightenment was called upon to play an immense role in improving society.

Baturin's attitude to serfdom was close to that of Desnitsky and most of the other Russian enlighteners, and he can be described as a moderate reformist. At the same time he proclaimed in the censored press (and therefore in cautious form) the exceptional importance of liberty in human life. For him, freedom was a synonym of absolute value; he expressed his opposition to slavery and subordination, although he did so in a very vague way. He admitted a "right to slavery" for rulers, not without bitter sarcasm, and as an exception to the general rule.

Baturin condemned religious mysticism, and prejudices of any kind, irrespective of their confessional character. He cast doubt on the commonly accepted view of the beneficence of the Church's social and moral effect as a social institution.

He expounded with sympathy in his own works the ideas of Epicurus and "the glorious atheist Spinoza."[8] His own philosophical opinions can be defined as materialist, but expressed in a deistic form. Nevertheless, he criticized even divine actions. Man's supreme aim was to know the laws of the external world in all their diversity in order to put them to use. Citing the authority of Bayle and Locke, Galileo and Newton, he suggested that sense experience was the main source of this knowledge; the soberly practical view of the "investigator of nature" should discard ideas of emanation and hidden mysterious forces as the fruit of ignorance and superstition, a chimera of the Middle Ages.

Baturin is known in the history of Russian philosophy primarily as an irreconcilable opponent of the Masonic doctrine. His *Examination of the Book of Errors and Truth* was written as a philosophical, publicistic pamphlet against the book of the French mystic Saint-Martin *Des erreurs et de la verité,* popular among the Russian "brothers." This work of Baturin's was clear evidence of the profound ideological differences between the enlighteners and orthodox Freemasons in Russia.

His analysis of Masonic ideas was distinguished by its thoroughness and elaborateness. While treating Masonry as a "moral and political phenomenon," he tried to explain why it had become so widespread in Russia. He not only pointed out the host of Saint-Martin's formal and logical contradictions and "incomprehensible metaphysics," but also demonstrated its lack of originality and the similarity of the various propositions of Masonry to the ideas of ancient Indian philosophy and Zoroastrianism. He also expressed his own judgments on important philosophical problems, affirming that the criterion of the truth of knowledge could not be prophetic self-assurance founded on belief in a mysterious divine presence, but only the facts of science and everyday experience. "A reasonable observer (naturalist) who esteems justice will never," he wrote, "propose his own convictions that have not, so to say, the stamp of truth in place of facts of nature confirmed by repeated experiments."[9]

He understood "nature" or "matter" as a moving and complexly structured substance in its actual and potential being. "Nature . . . signifies substance in general and the being of all possible corporeal creatures, and their motion, relations, and action on one another."[10] Knowledge of matter in all the diversity of its manifestations was an endless, complicated business "because there is still much in the nature of acts and creatures that is unknown, the same as there are many still unknown relations in the host of known things."[11]

When speaking of sense experience as the main source of the diversity of information about the external world, Baturin refuted Saint-Martin's thesis of some pre-established harmony between the sensual and rational levels of knowledge. This relationship was established spontaneously during the study of nature and was wholly the result of human activity. Man's knowledge was not absolute and could therefore lead, Baturin considered, both to error and to truth. The intervention of a "ruling cause" in cognition should exclude mistakes, but that contradicted experience.

The tendency of Baturin's views to materialist sensualism was an example of how deism became a specific form of materialism capable of freeing the theoretical-cognitive and methodological problematic in philosophy from an exclusively religious interpretation of it.

YAKOV KOZELSKY

Yakov Kozelsky (1728–1794) was born into a military family in the Ukraine. He was educated at the Kiev Theological Seminary and in the grammar school (gymnasium) of the St. Petersburg Academy of Sciences. He taught mathematics and mechanics in the Artillery Cadet Corps. In 1752 he began military service, and in 1788 he entered the civil service. His last years were spent on his estate near Poltava.

Kozelsky's philosophical views were influenced by Lomonosov's ideas, as well as the traditions of the German and French enlightenment. In style of thinking, he was close to members of the school of Leibniz and Christian Wolff, although his philosophy was largely original. He published several original works and translations on mathematics, physics, and history. His main works were *Philosophical Propositions* (*Filosofskiye predlozheniya* [1768]) and *Discourse of Two Indians, Kalan and Ibrahim, on Human Knowledge* (*Rassuzhdeniye dvukh indiytsev Kalana i Ibragima o chelovecheskom poznanii* [1788]).

He defined philosophy as the science of the sciences, which did not, however, absorb their whole content but only "general knowledge of things and human affairs."[12] He divided it into the theoretical (logic and metaphysics), intended to demonstrate the correct road to knowledge of the truth, and the practical, which contained the rules of human behavior and of establishing harmonious relations between people. Kozelsky set out his own sociopolitical views within the context of practical or moral philosophy. On the whole they were close to the ideas of Desnitsky, Fonvizin, Novikov, Tretyakov, and other Russian enlighteners. Basing himself on the theory of "natural right" and "social contract," he demonstrated the need to limit serfdom, emancipate the individual, and introduce representative institutions and universal subordination to the supreme "sovereign"—one law for all—that limited the will of czars and rulers.

His warning to authorities rang unambiguously: "Owners' respect for the law is their security."

The supreme aim of politics was to establish social harmony, and the most important consequence was a wide dissemination of good morals in society. While pointing out the important role of enlightenment and education of the people, he noted their inadequacy when discord of interest prevailed in society. "No people," he wrote, "can be made virtuous otherwise than through a union of the special good of each with the common good of all."[13]

When polemicizing against Rousseau, Kozelsky stressed the utopian character of the idea of a return to man's "natural state," but, in his view, Rousseau was right in pointing out the lack of coincidence of society's socioeconomic and moral progress. From Kozelsky's standpoint, however, purification of morals in contemporaneous conditions should be expected from a proper development of precisely what had once been distorted and had become a negative social factor. The historical development of society was irreversible, as "the sciences, arts, and crafts" were irreversible in their development. "In such a state of the learned world and the impossibility of man's being naturally happy, it is necessary to take refuge in art and science."[14] It was the development of science and education, and strict observance of the social contract that would ultimately demonstrate the progressive character of mankind's transition from the "natural" to the "civil" state. He noted that, "Man also gets moral freedom in the civil state, which makes him lord of himself, because the incitement of wishing is slavery while submission to prescribed laws is freedom."[15]

Kozelsky suggested that, with the development of scientific knowledge, its link with people's practical needs would become more complicated and significant. At the same time he remarked that a tendency had arisen in science to separate itself from the real world, which was why he sharply condemned the rationality and formalism that were affecting both the particular and the philosophical sciences, and turning science in on itself.

Though he had put forward a program for the reform of philosophy, Kozelsky could not, however, overcome schematicism in both his mode of exposition and the content of his ideas.

While rejecting the doctrines of Leibniz and Wolff about "pre-established harmony" and about "Providence" and freedom of will, and counterposing the "natural order of science" to "natural theology," Kozelsky boldly declared that he defined the main categories of his philosophy—"matter," "space," and "infinity"—according to the teaching of the French materialist Helvetius.

Like many of the materialists of the eighteenth century Kozelsky identified matter ("nature") with a substance that possessed material force and generated all the diversity of the world around man from itself. In his striving to explain nature and reality, starting from it itself, he drew a sharp line between the natural and the supernatural and suggested that the latter would not be the subject matter of philosophical analysis.

Nature existed eternally, preceding man and his consciousness (science), so that strictly scientific knowledge of them must be based on study of nature and its laws. Sciences like physics, mathematics, chemistry, physiology, and medicine should encourage this.

Like Anichkov, Kozelsky shared the corpuscular philosophy of Lomonosov when speaking of the structure of matter, and pointed out the material nature of light and the ether. His theory of knowledge can be defined as materialist sensualism. At the same time he did not gloss over the significance of rational methods of cognition and the role of concepts, and considered that "philosophizing" was often the sole means of finding the reasons for one phenomenon or another. In developing his theoretical, cognitive ideas, he resolutely opposed the thesis of an irreconcilable difference between the psyche of animals and the consciousness of man, and showed that the lowest stages of knowledge, i.e., "sensation, imagination, and memory" were not only inherent in man but were also largely so in certain animals.

As we can see, the Russian enlighteners of the latter half of the eighteenth century considered many philosophical problems, were materialists in their general trend, and were oriented to science. And although the materialist orientation of Anichkov, Desnitsky, Baturin, Kozelsky, and others had deistic garb, the propositions about the immortal soul, the existence of God, and His creation of man, were introduced rather formally, by tradition.

In conditions where serfdom predominated they defended an ideal of a free, integral, and independent creative personality capable of understanding the laws of nature and its own being so as to employ them for the good of man and human society.

NOTES

1. *Izbrannye proizvedeniya russkikh myslitelei vtoroi poloviny XVIII veka* (*Selected Works of Russian Thinkers of the Latter Half of the Eighteenth Century*), 2 vols. (Moscow, 1952), vol. 1, p. 274.

2. Ibid., p. 275.

3. Ibid., p. 280.

4. Ibid., p. 284.

5. Ibid., p. 171.

6. Ibid., pp. 139, 140.

7. Ibid., p. 127.

8. Ibid., vol. 2, p. 422.

9. Ibid., p. 396.

10. Ibid., p. 526.

11. Ibid., p. 484.

12. Ibid., vol. 1, p. 428.

13. Ibid., p. 530.

14. Ibid., p. 415.
15. Ibid., p. 525.

4

The Challenge of Conservatism: The Masons and M. M. Shcherbatov

Alexi Boldyrev

THE HISTORICAL SITUATION

One paradoxical peculiarity of the situation that had taken shape in Russia in the eighteenth century was the absence of an "official ideology." The Russian Orthodox Church could no longer serve, as before, as a reliable and effective support of the autocracy and serfdom. Its influence in Russia's intellectual life, substantially limited by Peter the Great's reforms, continued to diminish in the second half of the century. The absence of developed intellectual traditions in Orthodox theology, its marked conservatism, and its retrospection played no small part in its decline. The efforts of such Church hierarchs as the Archpriest Alexius, the Metropolitan Platon, the Archimandrite Feofilakt, and Bishops Baibakov and Gedon Krinovsky to hold back the development of science, art, and philosophy, and to curb "freethinkers" in lay culture, were unsuccessful. The Age of Enlightenment was knocking at all doors, not just at those of the nobility but also on the walls of the monasteries. The new, more dynamic sociocultural conditions evoked by the forming of a free enterprise system within the economy of Russia, the broadening of contacts with West European countries, the growth of the influence of natural science, and development of a press forced those in power to modernize the traditional outlook. In view of the pressing economic and sociopolitical crisis of Russian feudalism, the authoritarian state was looking assiduously for new forms of social policy, different from both the dogmatism and the formalism of Church orthodoxy—and even more from "atheism," materialism, and "Voltaireanism"—and from the historically new, liberal, and democratic-in-spirit ideology of the Enlightenment. That is why such a symbiotic ideological formation as enlightened absolutism or "palace enlightenment" became possible, and such a specific variety of it as *Masonry*.

FREEMASONS IN RUSSIA

The theoretical constructs of Russian "Freemasons" absorbed fragments of the social, political, and philosophical ideas of the European Enlightenment in an original way, so as to deformalize religious truths, make religion attractive, or (as they said then) render it "a moral force."

In Russia Freemasonry was called upon to become an effective counterweight to the scientific, philosophical, and sociopolitical views of the Enlightenment. Subjectively, for the majority of educated people, it was a long-awaited moral and philosophical doctrine that not only fixed the universal, spiritual foundations of human existence in theoretical form, but also introduced them, through joint "fraternal works" in the lodges, into the practice of everyday life. Freemasonry cultivated spiritual "wholeness," and was attractive by its attempt to reconcile faith and knowledge, religion and science, and thought, feeling, and will to act. For the Russian gentry, among whom, at the end of the century, even the most radical ideas of the Enlightenment were no longer regarded as something daring and exotic, the "royal craft of Freemasons" had become something in the nature of a "religion of today." It overcame the temptation of enlightened freethinking and claimed to no less than a theoretical, moral, and practical synthesis of all world culture as a whole— Western and Oriental, lay and religious.

The earliest reliable information on the existence of Masonic organizations in Russia dates from 1731, when the first lodge of the English system was formed, headed by a Capt. D. Philipps. Freemasonry, introduced from the West,[1] spread at first among foreigners living in Russia; later it gradually recruited "neophytes" from the Russian nobility.

Two main periods are distinguished in the history of Russian Freemasonry. The first, roughly the 1750s to 1770s, can be called the stage of Russian society's initial acquaintance with this singular religious-moral movement. In those three decades there was a numerical increase in lodges and members. But Russian Masonry lacked its own ideological and national face then and experienced, as N. I. Novikov remarked, an age of "crisis and humiliation." This aristocratic pastime from overseas, surrounded by an aura of mystery, had become fashionable. By the close of the 1770s almost all the great noble families were represented in Masonry. Only the fanciful Masonic rituals distinguished the activity of the lodges from the ordinary lay routes and salon small talk. It was then that Russian Masons were attracted simultaneously by Rousseau, the philosophy of deism, and by the "clairvoyant sages" Swedenborg, Weigel, and Arndt. Masons translated Voltaire and articles from the celebrated French *Encyclopedia*. It was not by chance that the terms "Mason," "Martinist," "Voltairean," and "freethinker" were almost synonymous in both the conversation and the belles lettres and poetry of those years. Freemasonry was still inseparable then from the broad wave of enlightenment that enveloped the gentry right up to the highest levels of authority, with Catherine the Great at the head.

In the second stage, in the 1780s and 1790s, a turn toward authentic Masonry was noted in Masonic circles, i.e., to Christian and often extraconfessional mysticism and irrationalism. Moderate trends like Rosicrucianism and Templarism became predominant, members of which called Voltaire, without mincing words, "the plenipotentiary minister of Hell," and the brilliant leaders of the French Enlightenment his "sinister" servants.[2] The abrupt changes in Catherine the Great's policy after the revolutionary explosion in France in 1789 led to a decided curtailing of "palace enlightenment"; the masks were thrown off, and any hypocrisy abandoned. The monarch's enlightenment proved superficial, covering up a spirit not proper to it; it was a kind of ideological "Potemkin village," i.e., scenery.

Russian Masonry appeared equally in its true colors precisely in the last quarter of the eighteenth century, becoming a notable phenomenon of Russian culture, and an effective factor in public consciousness. The creative, propagandist, publishing activity of Freemasons reached its peak. The best-known propagandists of Masonry were I. P. Elagin, I. V. Lopukhin, and N. N. Trubetskoy, among others. Several Masonic journals were published: *Magazin svobodnokamenshchitskiy* (*The Freemason Magazine* [1784]); *Pokoyashchisya trudolyubets* (*The Laborer at Rest* [1784]); *Vechernyaya zarya* (*Afterglow* [1782]), and others. In spite of the whole anti-enlightenment tenor of the Masons' speeches and articles, they were inevitably more "left" than the position of official government circles. Masons continued to be suspect as godless, political conspirators; in the years of reaction, which intensified after the exile of Radishchev and the arrest of N. I. Novikov, Masons began to be persecuted by the government. Yet, neither that, nor the fact that Masonry had experienced a semi-official existence in Russia when in better times its adherents and patrons had been recruited in court circles, gives direct grounds for concluding how far Masons were opportunist or, on the contrary, in opposition.

THE UNIVERSAL AND THE PARTICULAR IN THE IDEOLOGY OF MASONS

Masonry, as an international—or at least European—phenomenon, contained national cultural features of various countries. That was reflected in the names of the Masonic systems: English, Swedish, French. In addition, some devotees of Masonry created their own lodges and trends, calling them by their own names (the systems of Zinnendorf, Fessler, and Saint-Martin). The many Masonic systems differed considerably from one another. The Illuminati, for instance, tended to sociopolitical ideas of an enlightened tinge, and their activity had a conspiratorial character. At the same time the popular Rosicrucians (Masons of the rose and cross) put forward an ideal of the sage ascetically isolated from the world, who avoided any kind of social activity.

A number of Masonic lodges, for example, the "New Israel," were based on the religion of Judaism; others preferred Christianity, but the majority tried to formulate their credo without any confessional partiality. Nevertheless there were a number of common features, including ideological-philosophical ones, that allow us to speak of Masonry as a special phenomenon of culture.

One feature is the comprehensive organizational and theoretical hierarchical character of Masonry. The system of views and ideas of Freemasons was presented as strictly divided and multilevel. The "brother" "seeking wisdom" passed from the lowest stage or "degree" to the highest, not so much going more deeply into knowledge of a certain doctrine as simply discarding that previously mastered. Thus the initial grades of initiation—entered apprentice, fellow craft, master—presupposed observance of certain principles of Christian morality: love of near ones; resignation of pride; cultivating of "good works"; philanthropy; sincere talks; special "prayers," and so on. The higher degrees called for blind devotion to the Masonic banner. As in the Jesuit Order, in Masonry it was held that everything was moral, noble, and true that favored consolidation and spread of Masonry. The highest titles disclosed the "secrets" of communion with spirits and taught black and white magic. Elements of unorthodox mysticism in the interpretation of biblical canons were brought to the fore. At that stage of the Masonic pyramid—at the level of the highest knowledge—the philosophical foundations of the genuine, and not feigned, world-outlook program that the secret "brotherhood" offered were revealed to its initiates.

The doctrine of Masonry was anthropocentric. It hardly presents significant interest for the history of philosophy in its natural philosophical divisions because it was fragmentary and schematic; it is important to stress, however, that it reproduced almost with no change the cosmology of the Pythagoreans, and ideas popular in medieval alchemist treatises. Masonic ideologists constantly stressed that knowledge of the world is only the threshold to self-knowledge. Man is the closest of the points of the cosmos accessible to his senses and reason, in which there is an intensive contact of the two worlds, the physical and the moral, the spirit and nature. All questions of being and knowledge of the secret of the "corporeal" and "angelic" world and the laws of the social world are reduced to man and derived from various interpretations of his essence.

In a programmatic article in a Russian Masonic journal of the eighteenth century it was said: "Our spirit, not disturbed by any external clamor, surrenders itself to longing for nature herself . . . and by turns flies to its Creator, goes deeper into the mystery of nature, endeavoring to lift the veil of this Goddess, or coming into itself, finds all things in itself and explains everything by man."[3]

In their answers to the main question of the essence of man, the leading theorists of Russian Masonry took a religious, idealist stand, so that the general character of the Masonic doctrine is more exactly defined as religious, anthropocentric. One must also stress that Masonic religiosity was a very peculiar phenomenon and diverged quite far from Russian Orthodoxy. It was a simple matter for the Masonic author, when proclaiming his credo, to put the celebrated Socratic formula into the mouth of the Christian God, speaking moreover in his name: "O my son! Learn to know yourself" ("God's Word to Man" [*Glas boga k cheloveky*]).[4]

The sources of the specific religiosity of Russian Masonry, as of this doctrine as a whole, were very diverse. It was widely held in Masonic circles, for instance, that "the light of wisdom" came to humanity from the East. That predetermined the special interest of several trends of so-called Egyptian Masonry in traditions about the cult mysteries of the ancient Egyptian priesthood, the religion of countries of the Near East, the antique mysteries, and in the symbolic interpretation of Old Testament texts. The patriarch of Russian Masonry, I. P. Elagin, known mainly as the author of a historical work *Attempt at Narration about Russia* (*Opyt povestvovaniya o Rossii*), who was the first Russian recognized in Western Europe as a provincial Grand Master, wrote in his notes that "the science of Freemasons was preserved as a mystery in the temples of the Chaldeans, Egyptians, Persians, Phoenicians, Jews, Greeks, and Romans . . . in the lodges of the Persians and the Pythagorean and Platonic schools, and among the Indian, Chinese, Arab, and Druid philosophers."[5]

The works of the Church Fathers were equally copiously cited in Russian Masons' works, as well as the works of theosophists, and theologians who were outside the direct line of the Christian Church tradition, like Jacob Bohme, Paracelsus, and Swedenborg. Russian Masons' doctrine absorbed the irrationalist trends in eighteenth-century European philosophy associated with the names of J. G. Hamann, F. H. Jacobi, and Moses Mendelssohn (although not all Masons were irrationalists). Masonic nonconfessional religiosity was also formulated under the strong influence of new trends within Christianity itself, attracted to unorthodox mysticism (pietism, quietism, Quakerism, and Methodism). The works of Blaise Pascal and Saint-Martin, and of preachers of various kinds of a religious, mystic turn of mind, were translated, published, and highly appreciated in Masonic circles.

THEIR DOCTRINE OF MAN

Elagin, I. D. Shaden, and others tried to overcome the clear eclecticism of their religious-idealist anthropology, claiming that man's divine essence was one and immutable. One esoteric doctrine, not subject to dogmatization, had therefore existed in incomplete form at all times and among all peoples, and in various religions and philosophical systems. The aim of Masonry was to find it, to gather it together into a "living" symbolic religion, to free it from historically transient forms and, having given it a modern cast, to disseminate it. It was not by chance that various expressions were common in the theoretical lexicon of Freemasons, like "outspoken religion," "true Christianity," "inner Christ," which were used to discuss and argue outside confessions, schools, trends, and cultures, as if on behalf of an intuitively attained and omnipresent "Divine Wisdom."

As for the science of modern times and the materialist deistic trend in philosophy, the theorists of Masonry often perceived them as an honest delusion of spiritually helpless sufferers, "lost in darkness." Yet Masonic thinkers readily borrowed both separate facts or ideas and the system of argument of these "lost sheep." The Russian Freemasons Lopukhin and Elagin, like their West European "spiritual brethren," waged a struggle for natural science in its idealist interpretation. It was claimed in authoritative Masonic publications that "a real knower of nature cannot help being a freethinker" and, at the same time, "true theology" could not exist "without knowledge of God in nature and society." Masons, moreover, did not limit themselves to conceptions of the dual nature of truth. They understood that at a time of rapid growth of the sciences of nature, and of their high authority in the culture of the Age of Enlightenment, general arguments about the created world that reflected the wisdom of the Creator were clearly inadequate. They did not affirm a parallelism of philosophy, science, and theology, but endeavored to join them together in a single doctrine of the divine essence of man.

The image of man was divided in Masonic works: spirit and soul were the divine spark that illumined the gloom of the "burdensome edifice" of the human body, possessed by "carnal lusts" and enfeebled by various passions. It is important to stress that recognition of this division was, from the standpoint of Masonic theorists, a kind of convention and a necessary admission, because when one spoke of the "bodily" or "carnal" one had to remember that it did not exist in man apart from his spiritual nature. On the contrary, the spiritual principle was inconceivable in him apart from the bodily. The different forms of this combination gave rise to a hierarchy of human types, at the summit of which was the man-god, and at the bottom the Old Adam. "Man [Masons said] in the whole of his essence is not single but dual. Truly dual. There is the outer man and the inner man, there is the bodily and carnal man, and the spiritual man."[6]

Man was not only a microcosm containing an interiorized analogue of the earthly dust and of the world spirit invigorating it, he was also a microgod, because man was like unto God in his spirit, or—as Masons liked to express it in their "building" terminology—"the Great Architect of the Universe." Man as given, i.e., worldly, sinful, fallen man, was—Masons repeated after Bohme—the "Old Adam," symbolically portrayed in the form of a rough, undressed ("wild") stone. Many of the theses of philosophical materialism were justified, in principle, with regard to such a man. His soul and spirit displayed a high degree of unfreedom, and often a truly slavish dependence on the body and the functions of the bodily organs. The theory of sensualism, Masons considered, splendidly described the imperfect process of knowing by the Old Adam, "enveloped" by the body and of necessity comprehending the world through "bodily sensation." But the man turned toward God, or all the more the neophyte, entering the Masonic "Academy of Divine Enlightenment," discovered in himself a certain *intention* or principle of spiritual dynamism that, when developed, could lead to a different qualitative state: the Old Adam could be converted into a New Adam. Masons considered that the trouble with and main mistake of naturalists (as they called materialists, deists, and the natural scientists close to them) was that they wholly denied such a possibility. Yet, on the road of spiritual self-building to the New Adam (who was symbolized as a "cube" or "perfect polyhedron"), i.e., in movement from the "Land of Trial" to the "Land of Bliss," the most radical changes of both an ontological and an epistemological quality happened to man.

First of all the character of the relationship of the physical and spiritual was itself altered: the substantial dualism of soul and body developed into a spiritual-divine monism. Just as in Christian anthropology, the liberating of the inner, spiritual man from the shackles of the bodily was understood as total spiritualization of the flesh and as the birth of a new "spiritual" body. At the pinnacle of enlightenment the secret was disclosed to the Freemason that during the birth of the New Adam the soul appeared as a modification of the spirit, and the body as a modification of the soul. Their deep-hidden identity was thus presupposed despite their external differences.

The most prolific Russian Mason, I. V. Lopukhin, whose *The Spiritual Knight* (*Dukhovnyi rytsar* [1791]) and *Some Features of the Inner Church* (*Nekotorye cherty o vnutrenney tserkvi* [1798]) were popular in Western Europe in translations during his lifetime, devoted no few pages to the problem of the mystic merger of the spirit and matter, which he treated according to the well-known Neoplatonic formula of "unity without merger." During the transformation of "wild stone" into a "perfect polyhedron," he wrote, the human body "has to be the cradle of the rebirth and the earthly abode of the true inner and spiritual man, created in the image and likeness of the Merciful."[7] To return to man the pure image of the First Adam who inhabited Eden meant, in his opinion, to create a perfect body as the temple of the

renewed spirit, through ascetic denial of the flesh and all-round spiritualization of human existence.

THE PROBLEM OF KNOWLEDGE

On the theoretical, cognitive plane the forming of the "inner man" meant
an awakening of supersensory faculties in perception of the world and God,
and also in the act of self-knowing. From the Masons' standpoint, both the
French sensualists and the rationalists, for example, of the school of Leibniz
and Wolff, substantially impoverished human spirituality and did not allow
for its qualitative diversity. But spiritual experience witnessed to the existence
of a "secret, innermost capacity to extend the gaze beyond oneself to other
remote objects and to acquire such concepts and knowledge of things there
as could not be acquired through the spiritual forces known to us."[8] As to
what these faculties and this knowledge represented, Masons spoke with a
large dollop of poetic indeterminacy. They singled out insight into the future,
supersensory intercontact of "kindred souls," mystical intuition that yielded
absolutely reliable knowledge, and so on. It was emphasized, in the Masonic
literature, that the whole strength and power of human reason that had so
clearly declared itself in the Age of Enlightenment had divine revelation as
its source. To elevate reason meant to subordinate it to faith, Masons argued.
The Bible as the "external word" had to be given a profound reading and
a symbolic interpretation. Truths were revealed to people and thus the alternative—faith or knowledge—became senseless.

    The death of the Old Adam and the birth in man of the New Adam,
who was identified with Christ, was the moment, according to Russian Masonic
doctrine, when the process of self-knowing merged with knowledge of God
and with the ontological forming of man in God. On this, from the standpoint of Christian dogmas, the Masonic theorists very freely operated with
a dialectic of the divine and the human. Specific religious perfectionalism led
Russian Masons to take the idea of imitation of Christ common in Christianity
to recognition of the possibility of identity with Christ, which objectively threw
doubt on his uniqueness. For many of them, Christ and, for example, Bohme
were different faces of one divinity that any Mason skilled in the wisdom
of Solomon could approach; and not only approach but even "merge centrally
with the Highest Sun of pure light."

    The humanist pathos of the Age of Enlightenment that entailed faith
in the unlimited possibilities of human reason figured in this case in false
form as conviction in the transcendental potentialities of the human spirit.
Masons did not pretend to theoretical originality and repeated (with insignificant
variations) courses of religious thought already known in history. The central
point for them was the moral and practical conditions of the spiritual rebirth

of man on the road to God. Numerous rules, prayers, admonitions, songs, confidential talks, confessions, and meditations were employed precisely for these ends, constituting the "work" of Masonic lodges. In addition, a new ritual instead of the traditional one used by the "external Church," new symbols, and hieratic inscriptions were offered to the Mason brothers.

The deciphering of Masonic symbols as a special epistemological procedure oriented to an integral, spiritual type of perception by "reason," the "heart," and the "will" was obligatory for brothers of all degrees and titles, all of which provided, in their views, a chance of purifying a human's nature of sinful defects and opening up a prospect of building the "inner Church" in his soul, serving of which made religious truths alive, revealed their secret meaning, and made the transcendental man's intimately personal and spiritual achievement.

SOCIAL MAXIMS

In contrast to the radical trends of Freemasonry in the West, Russian Masons of the highest degrees called for minimizing social contacts with the world of the "profane" in their search for "inner light," on the principle of rendering to God what was God's and to Caesar what was Caesar's. Russian Masons of the eighteenth century preached an esoteric doctrine of spiritual self-perfection, preferred to remain "outside politics," and usually refrained from any judgments in this field. Pushkin, who personally knew certain members of this generation of Russian Masons, described his impressions as follows: "One cannot deny that many of them belonged to the discontented but their hostility was limited to grumpy censure of the present, naive hopes for the future, and equivocal toasts at Freemason suppers."[9]

At the same time we cannot consider the long-known letters and published speeches of Lopukhin, Kutuzov, and Turgenev deliberately insincere; they expressed the feelings of faithful subjects and loyalty to the powers that be, and even an approval of the arrest of Radishchev and Novikov. All that relates to the period when Catherine the Great had begun a campaign of persecution against Masons, branding them as godless, political conspirators. These testimonies cannot therefore be regarded as objective or characteristic of their real social and political views.

MIKHAIL SHCHERBATOV

One of the most notable and colorful figures espousing the Russian conservative outlook in the latter half of the eighteenth century was Mikhail Shcherbatov (1733–1790). A defender of big landed property, and an advocate for serfdom, he even considered "free thought" the ideal of an enlightened monarchy and wanted to limit the autocracy by the power of the old hereditary aristocratic families. It was not by chance that he made an impact on Russian culture as a historian: all his thoughts and hopes were turned to the past, to pre-Petrine Russia when, in his opinion, estate barriers clearly demarcated the serf-peasant and the lord, the base-born and the boyar.

In 1857 Herzen, in the foreword to the London edition of Shcherbatov's pamphlet *On the Damage to Morals in Russia* (*O povrezhdenii nravov v Rossii*) and Radishchev's *Journey from Petersburg to Moscow* (*Puteshestviye iz Peter-burga v Moskvu*), treated them as exponents of two diametrically opposed points of view on the development of Russia. "Sorrowful sentries at two different doors, they, like Janus, look in opposite directions. Shcherbatov, turning away from the dissolute court of his day, gazes at the door to which Peter I ascended, and behind it sees ceremonious, pretentious Moscovite Russia."[10]

Nostalgia for the past not only impelled Shcherbatov to archive studies, but largely determined the badly concealed irritation with which he gazed at the destruction of medieval values, regulations, and all the style of Old Russian life, which was inexorably passing away in the reign of Catherine the Great. But Shcherbatov was not a limited contrarian in his world outlook. The fruits of enlightenment and science had put their stamp on the character of his views, on everything he wrote as a historian, publicist, economist, and philosopher, and on much of what he stood for as a public servant.

Shcherbatov was the son of a rich aristocratic family belonging to a very old princely clan that had Rurik as one of its ancestors. After private tutoring at home, he was enlisted at seventeen in the Semyonovsky Life Guards, in which he rose to the rank of captain during the period preceding Catherine the Great's accession to the Russian throne. In 1767, while already in public service as a deputy of the Yaroslav gentry, he took part in the work of the Codifying Commission. His speeches against liberal-minded deputies became widely known in court circles. In the same year, after the official presentation to Catherine II, he was given access to the Patriarchal and Typographical Libraries, in which the manuscripts of the chronicles had been gathered together by an edict of Peter the Great, with the aim of writing a history of Russia. He worked tirelessly on his multivolume project titled *Russian History from Ancient Times* (*Istoriya Rossiyskaya, ot drevneyshikh vremen*).* Shcherbatov went beyond his predecessor V. N. Tatishchev: he broadened the range of chronicle sources and archive materials, and was more cautious and circumspect in his work on them.

In addition, Shcherbatov was interested in political, philosophical, and economic matters. In 1776–1777 he wrote his *Statistics About Russia* (*Statistika*

---

*It was published in the main during his lifetime; only the last two volumes, brought up to the beginning of the seventeenth century, were published after his death, i.e., in 1791.

v rassuzhdenii Rossii), an encyclopedic work containing comprehensive geo-graphical, ethnographic, socioeconomic, and political descriptions of the Russian Empire in the 1770s. Though a secret critic of Catherine the Great's policy and of the morals of the court, Shcherbatov was able to conceal his opposition and his morality (much too rigorous for the time) and enjoyed the empress's regard and financial support, while occupying high posts of state. From 1778 he was president of the Kammer-Collegium and a privy counsellor, and from 1779 a senator.

Like his political allies, influential aristocratic statesmen A. R. Vorontsov, N. I. Panin, and A. B. Kurakin, Prince Shcherbatov was a member of various Masonic lodges throughout his lifetime. But Masonic ideas affected only his views on religion and the Church. His sober, practical turn of mind and great interest in experimental science were revealed, for example, in his essay "On the Benefit of Sciences," in which he stressed the importance of the discoveries of Newton, Galileo, Boyle, Kepler, and others. His endeavor to construct his arguments on the model of the "mathematical method," as in Spinoza's *Ethics,* and his predominant orientation on the whole to the traditions of secular philosophical culture enable one to conclude that the prince was a certain exception among Russian Masons.

Shcherbatov strove to base his philosophical speculations on reliable facts and "to take as his guide science and exact experiments."[11] The possibilities of scientific knowledge were vast; there were no secrets in nature that would not be discovered sooner or later. But, according to him, the "philosopher of nature" should always remember two very important points. The first was that all the latent and overt harmony of the world, and its perfection, wholeness, and regularity of form, was the result of the creative power and wisdom of the divinity. He loved to return to theological proof of the existence of God and reproduced it in various versions in most of his works, now in the spirit of Wolff's rationalist theology, and now in the physical theology of the early Kant. In fact, Shcherbatov considered belief in God to be no more than a rational persuasion of the existence of a Creator from knowledge of his creations.

The second point was that philosophy based exclusively on experimental knowledge was capable of discovering only the regular connections of the natural world. It was powerless to understand the essence and origin of the spiritual, and the character of its relation to the corporeal. "How is it possible," he asked rhetorically, "to achieve knowledge of immaterial things through a science that has only bodies as its subject?"[12] He stressed his skeptical attitude toward attempts to raise mechanico-materialist ideas and principles to the rank of general laws of the Universe, in particular when they touched on the essence and purpose of man and the relation of the physical and spiritual. Unlike the theorists of Masonry, he tackled this problem without any kind of mystification and without pseudodialectical tricks. Man was a dual creature who consisted of soul and body; these parts, like "heaven" and "earth," were not equivalent. He treated the body and bodily organs wholly in the spirit of the medieval Scholastics, as passive conductors of spiritual energy; the human soul that is "unsuitable for any division," i.e., something indivisible and without extension, is spirit. He considered spirit independent of the ontological and theoretical, cognitive plane of the system of bodily organs and, furthermore, the basis and factor uniting the latter into the living organism ("invigorating the body"). It followed from this that the human soul was immortal in its nature, which was the final goal of all his arguments.

Let us examine Shcherbatov's argument in more detail. In his *Conversation about the Immortality of the Soul* (*Razgovor o bessmertii dushi* [1788]) he adduced a quite developed system of proofs of the posthumous existence and activity of the human soul and rejected materialist theories of the soul. He called thinkers like Epicurus, Lucretius, Spinoza, and Hobbes "pseudo-sages," considering that they all proceeded from a false premise that the soul was an equal material part of the living, organic whole or, in other words, part of the body. In this case he opposed intuitive guesses that the interaction and combination of material bodies in the system of the whole could spontaneously give rise to the soul (spirit) in certain circumstances as a specific quality or characteristic. While rejecting that point of view, he rested his critique on the real difficulties and contradictions of the materialist theories of the soul that existed in the second half of the eighteenth century, difficulties and contradictions that thinkers like Locke and Toland, Lamettrie and Diderot had tried to resolve.

Man's soul, or consciousness, was potentially independent of the body in Shcherbatov's opinion but functionally displayed a relative dependence on it "in its acts." This was manifested to the highest degree in cognition. But intellectual activity could not be determined only by the physiological activity of the sense organs that carried objective information about the external world. The very possibility of obtaining it depended primarily on the activity of consciousness at its rational level. While knowing Rousseau's and Diderot's critique of the extremes of sensualism of a Helvetian type, Shcherbatov was inclined rather to epistemological rationalism, approaching in this question the position of Descartes, Spinoza, and Leibniz. He adduced many examples to prove the impossibility of drawing a hard-and-fast line between the rational (spiritual) and sensory (material) aspects of cognition. When we heard a loud sound, for example, it was not perceived solely in its concrete sensory form but immediately evoked in the mind, and included, a whole number of conjectures about its cause: the firing of a gun, thunder, and so on. He noted, moreover, that such "proper" faculties of the soul as memory and imagination were actively involved in perception. It is, furthermore, only their involvement that provided a possibility of "forming a judgment" about the object, while not simply remaining at the level of fixing sensations.

The "incorporeity" of the soul—its immateriality—was thus manifested, from the epistemological standpoint, as independence of "bodily," "material" sensations that, according to him, constituted yet another weighty proof of the immortality of the human soul.

Shcherbatov expounded his understanding of history not only in *Russian History* but also in his *Short Tale of Former Imposters in Russia* (*Kratkaya povest o byvshikh v Rossii samozvantsakh* [1774]) and certain essays. Rationalism was characteristic of his historical conception. While denying any social role of Providence, he made the development of society dependent on the spread of science and secular erudition. Czars, military leaders, and the "best men" from the aristocracy were the direct initiators of history. According to him, their activity rested mainly on selfish psychological motives: avarice, egoism, love of fame, and so on. When united with will, cunning, and intelligence, they were capable of stimulating the mass of the rank and file to action. While stressing the significance of the individual in history, Shcherbatov essentially belittled the role of the Church, noting its negative influence, particularly when it interfered in "worldly matters." He considered a cause of the enslavement of Rus by the Tatar-Mongols to have been the "spirit of intemperate piety" cultivated by the clergy, which gave rise to unforgivable "weakness" in the Russian princes.

He expressed his political ideal—a union of the grand princely (czar's) power and the boyardom—in his unfinished socio-utopian novel *A Journey to the Land of Ophir* (*Puteshestviye v zemlyu Ofirskuyu* [1783–1784]). In its pages the promised land was represented by a state in which the monarch's power was limited by a government of the upper aristocracy and by a council of the great magnates. Other estates, including the rank-and-file gentry, were completely alienated from power. Passage from one estate to another was, moreover, impossible (Shcherbatov contested Peter's "Table of Ranks"). In Ophir the privileges and rights of the nobility were sacred: only a nobleman could hold lands peopled by submissive slave-serfs. The involvement of the merchant estate was very limited, even in the drafting of commercial legislation. Shcherbatov dreamed of organizing military service by a type of military settlement. In the Land of Ophir religion and the Church were meant to defend the social order. The priesthood of the Ophirian Sun God were police officers. At the same time Shcherbatov upheld the need for dissemination of knowledge in all strata of society and stressed the importance of various educational institutions and schools. Education should aim to maintain stability of the estate-caste system; from their early years, it was proved to the inhabitants of Ophir that inequality among people was "natural" and the "difference" of the estates "logically" stemmed from it.

Both Shcherbatov and the Masons left marked traces in Russian culture. And although we do not find direct heirs to their ideas in the nineteenth century, there were no few successors who employed their ideas to various degrees. It is difficult to deny their contribution to the movement of philosophical thought in Russia, and to the creation of the intellectual state that determined the direction of the creative quests of the many Russian thinkers who succeeded and took the place of their half-forgotten predecessors. In that sense Shcherbatov's views are comparable, for example, with the positions of the early Slavophiles. The eighteenth-century Masons, who were at the beginning of secular, extraclerical idealism in Russia, to some extent anticipated the development of irrationalist trends in philosophy, religious-modernist ideas, and influenced the ethical quests of Leo Tolstoy.

NOTES

1. It is difficult to name any one metropolitan country. Scotland, Prussia, and France were influential at various times in the spread of Masonry in Russia. The first Russian lodge, known as the Apollo, was founded by Reichel in 1771 in St. Petersburg.

2. This in spite of Rosicrucians not being considered true Masons in the West, and Voltaire being one of the best-known Masons in Europe. The peculiar understanding of Masonry in Russia was manifested in this.

3. *Pokoyashchiisya trudolyubets* (Moscow, 1784), pt. 1, p. 4. This journal, published by N. I. Novikov, printed articles and essays by both Masons and enlighteners not associated with Masonry.

4. Ibid., p. 60.

5. I. P. Yelagin, *Ucheniye drevnego lyubomudriya i bogomudriya* (*The Doctrine of Ancient Philosophy and Theosophy*). Republished in *Russkii arkhiv*, No. 1 (Moscow, 1864), p. 106.

6. *Izobrazheniye vetkhogo . . . i dukhovnogo cheloveka* (*A Portrayal of Fallen . . . and Spiritual Man*) (St. Petersburg, 1798), p. 18.

7. I. V. Lopukhin, *Masonskiye trudy Lopukhina* (*Lopukhin's Masonic Works*) (Moscow, 1790–91), p. 29.

8. *Pokoyashchiisya trudolyubets*, pt. I, p. 56.

9. Alexander Pushkin, *Sobraniye sochinenii* (Collected works), 10 vols. (Moscow, 1978), vol. 6, p. 190.

10. A. I. Herzen, "Prince Shcherbatov and A. Radishchev," in *Sochineniya* (Works), 9 vols. (Moscow, 1958), vol. 7, p. 150.

11. M. M. Shcherbatov, *Sochineniya* (Works), 2 vols. (St. Petersburg, 1896), vol. I, p. 299.

12. Ibid., p. 317.

5

Alexander Radishchev
Pavel Shkurinov

THE PATHS OF HIS OUTLOOK

Alexander Radishchev (1749–1802) had an important place in the history of
Russian culture. His ode "Liberty" (*Volnost*), his book *A Journey from St.
Petersburg to Moscow,* and his treatise *On Man, His Mortality and Immortality*
(*O cheloveke, o yego smertnosti i bessmertii*) had a considerable influence
on the shaping of the sociophilosophical foundations of the Russian eman-
cipation movement.

He was the eldest child in his family, which was large even for his time
(seven sons and four daughters). His parents inculcated in him a feeling of
respect for simple peasant folk (serfs), permanent contact with whom introduced
the boy to the rich world of folk art and encouraged the molding of his
democratic convictions. First his nanny Praskovia Clementievna and later his
serf attendant Pyotr Mamontov taught him his letters. His main textbooks
were the *Psalter* and the *Book of Hours.* His parents' Rousseauian convictions
prompted them to bring their children up "naturally"; his childhood was spent
on his mother's estate in the village of Upper Ablyazovo on the Volga, in
the Saratov Province.

When Radishchev was seven he was sent to Moscow, to a relative who
was the head of the directory of the just-founded Moscow University. Radishchev was enrolled in the grammar school (gymnasium) of the university where
he may have met future figures of the Russian Enlightenment (Kozelsky,
Desnitsky, Novikov, Tretyakov, and Fonvizin), the first graduates of the school.
The youth of Moscow (the old capital) were feeling the influence of Russian
science and enlightenment. Apart from the great authority of Lomonosov

and his school in the university in the 1750s and 1760s, the works of Prokopovich, Kantemir, Pososhkov, and the ethnographic, historical, and economic works of Tatishchev enjoyed great respect.

In 1762 Radishchev moved to Petersburg where he was enrolled in the Corps of Pages. Four years later he was sent to Leipzig University with a group of young people to study jurisprudence. The Russian students (Radishchev among them) had the opportunity to become acquainted with new European doctrines in Germany (Saxony), and to clarify their notions about the character of the social changes in Europe and Russia. The works of Leibniz and Baumgarten, Lessing and Kant attracted them. Radishchev studied the works of Herder and subsequently cited them—as a sympathizer and a critic. He had great respect for Fritz Hommel and E. P. Plattner, professors who read lectures on philosophy and literature, and Christian Gellert, who took classes in ethics.

Judging by his autobiographical book *The Life of Fyodor Ushakov* (*Zhitiye Fyodora Ushakova*), Radishchev exhaustively read the works of European (especially French) enlighteners while in Leipzig. When characterizing Radishchev's attitude to the Western Enlightenment Pushkin wrote of him: "All the French philosophy of his age was reflected in Radishchev: Voltaire's skepticism, Rousseau's philanthropy, and the political cynicism of Diderot and Reynal."[1]

Recognition of the serious impact of the European culture on Radishchev does not, nevertheless, eliminate the question of the determinant role of Russian reality in the molding of his outlook. His student perception of the ideas of the European Enlightenment had been formed, in fact, in the preceding period, i.e., by his initial education in Russia. In Leipzig he received information about all the main events in the cultural and political, scientific and philosophical life of Russia. At the same time the forming of his outlook had been completed in the main in the seventies, i.e., in the period of his activity after his return to St. Petersburg.

As an official of the Senate, auditor of the staff of the St. Petersburg commander-in-chief, and finally as chief of the St. Petersburg Customs House, Radishchev was associated with dignitaries of the court; employees of the Imperial Chancellery; and writers, scholars, diplomats, and merchants, which facilitated his obtaining all sorts of information, enriched his intellectual interests, and fostered understanding of the new tasks facing his contemporaries. In the seventies and eighties he came closer to opposition-minded noblemen and *raznochintsy,* who were to some extent aware of the inadequate realization of Russia's objective development possibilities. Prominent among these people were the publishers N. Novikov and I. Schnor; the writers Fonvizin, Karzhavin, and Emin; the university professors Anichkov, Desnitsky, Kozelsky, Tretyakov, and Sokhatsky. The Russian Enlightenment contained a charge of ideas distinguished in their synthesis by an antifeudal, democratic, republican, humanist, and anticzarist trend.

The Pugachev rebellion, and the political events in America and France had a great influence on Radishchev. In that complex social situation he translated Mably's *Observations sur l'Histoire de la Grece* (1773), and wrote his *A Word on Lomonosov* (*Slovo o Lomonosove*) around 1780, then his *Letter to a Friend Living in Tobolsk on the Duty of His Rank* (*Pismo k drugu, zhitelstvuyushchemu v Tobolske, po dolgu zvaniya svoyego* [1782]), and his ode "Liberty" (1783). Analysis of these works shows that already the synthesis of rebellious, anticzarist, and republican views constituted the core of his sociopolitical convictions. Before the French Revolution he was already aware of the "spirit of Pugachev's war," and the meaning of the revolutionary movements in the Netherlands, England, and America. His most important conclusion was recognition of the historical, moral, and political rightness of the people who had risen in rebellion against czarism and serfdom. In his works of the second half of the 1780s there were, in *The Life of Fyodor Ushakov* and his essay "A Talk about What a Son of the Fatherland Is" (*Beseda o tom, chto yest syn otechestva*), attempts at a theoretical comprehension of the experience of the emancipation movement.

From then on Radishchev labored over *A Journey from Petersburg to Moscow,* in which he substantiated methods of fighting autocracy and serfdom and examined various philosophical, ethical, and scientific matters. In this work he expressed a spirit of asserting lofty ideals of benevolence, philanthropy, and civil spirit in concentrated form. Printed in May 1790 on his own press to evade censorship, *A Journey* evoked the admiration of some and the fury and indignation of "official thought." The Criminal Chamber and the Senate imposed a death sentence on him, but the empress commuted it to exile in Siberia.

The "dangerous state criminal" Radishchev was sent to the Siberian fortress of Ilimsk. His creative work did not cease there, however. In 1790–1795 he wrote his treatise *On Man, His Mortality and Immortality, The Letter on Chinese Trade* (*Pismo o Kitayskom torge*), *A Brief Narrative on the Acquisition of Siberia* (*Sokrashchennoye povestvovaniye o priobretenii Sibiri*), *Travel Notes in Siberia* (*Zapiski puteshestvujushchego v Sibir*), *Description of the Tobolsk Governorship* (*Opisaniye Tobolskogo namestnichestva*), and other works. He was interested in a broad range of matters relating to the interests of the population of the country and the rights of man. He analyzed several problems of the development of science and education. In remote exile he attempted, in his treatise, to formulate the main principles of a philosophy of man and the tasks of humanizing social reality.

Radishchev's activity in his last years was also fruitful. In 1796 he came back from Siberia in connection with the general amnesty on the death of Catherine the Great. At first he was permitted to live on his own estate in Nemtsovo in the Kaluga Province, and later in St. Petersburg. At that time he wrote several works and poems that witnessed to the broad range of his interests and his agonizing search for a theoretical expression of the complex problems of his time.[3] Not without passion, he called for a struggle for "the happiness of Russians" and the prosperity of Russia in the "new age." He hoped, for a brief time, to find an enlightened monarch like Peter the Great in the person of Alexander I, i.e., a ruler capable of progressive, reformist activity.

These illusions were dispelled, but not immediately. He therefore agreed to work in the commission to draft new civil legislation, considering it useful in the first months of the "dawn of the century," at the beginning of Alexander's reign. Radishchev's major legal drafts—"The Draft Civil Code" (*Proekt grazhdanskogo ulozheniya*) and "On Legislation" (*O zakonopolozhenii*)—were schemes for attaining people's government. In his *Historical Song* (*Pesn istoricheskaya*) he persuasively demonstrated the bankruptcy of autocracy as a political form of government, rejecting the idea of a limited monarchy and even of bourgeois democracy. These ideas were doomed not to find real embodiment even in the conditions of the nineteenth century. However, in the new century the philosophical, ethical, and esthetic views underlying them were destined to have a great life.

After a year of his work in the commission, Radishchev experienced an emotional breakdown and committed suicide.

THE ANTHROPOLOGICAL TREND
OF HIS PHILOSOPHICAL INTERESTS

Radishchev's philosophical conviction resulted from many years of meditation and creative searching. Its source was already to be found in his notes on Mably's *Observations sur l'Histoire de la Grece*; it got fuller expression in "Liberty," and the poems of the 1780s, in particular in "Epitaph"; in *The Life of Fyodor Ushakov*; and finally in *A Journey* and the treatise *On Man.*

The theoretical sources of his outlook were the works of both Russian and West European thinkers and political figures, anthropologists and ethnographers, scientists and publicists. Traditional "natural" theories of law and morals, history, and the state were given new treatment under the influence of ethnography and psychology, medicine, and anthropology. Together with English, French, and American figures of the Enlightenment, their Russian counterparts declared people's main needs and rights to be unalienable forms of human nature. They combined calls for a return to "natural rights" and a regeneration of "man's usurped essence" with analysis of the "state of social forces" and a call to fight for the emancipation of man, and his conversion into a "product of the free action of the forces of nature and society." The democratic social trend that stressed the role of the individual in society was enriched by ideas of dialectics and evolutionism and backed by anthropological and ethico-social arguments. There was also a noticeable striving not only in European but also in Russian social thought of the last third of the eighteenth century (Anichkov, Desnitsky, Novikov, Tretyakov, and Fonvizin) to deepen the anthropological problematic and to put forward concepts and ideas that emphasized the special role of social processes that supplemented, or essentially altered, the strength and character of the effect of the natural and cultural environment on human existence.

The humanizing tendency in philosophy, inclusion of the "human element" in it, went alongside its politicization. A specific feature of the all-European social philosophy in the seventeenth and eighteenth centuries was the growing role of the idea of the need to emancipate man from the yoke of feudal slavery. A utilitarian expression of this slogan was the wish to free man from the shackles of the traditional social and economic restrictions, and to transfer him to the "free" labor market. That kind of mood encouraged development of humanism and various more or less mature forms of philosophical anthropology in Russia.

In the late 1780s and early 1790s, Radishchev's ideas about man took an original turn. "I have found man a consoler in himself," is how he put it.[3] The main formulation of this orientation was expressed in some sort of "functional" approach that brought out the many-sided character of the essence of "human nature" and is to be found in many chapters of *A Journey*. Radishchev did not conceal his desire to alter the order of things existing in Russia—founded on the "inhuman right" to own one's kind—and called for expression of compassion for "one's suffering brothers." He emphasized his conclusion that the serf system deteriorated the physical nature of the peasant and prevented natural manifestation of his capacities and talents. The system liberated the landlords from the "natural functions" necessary to the human organism, viz., to work and create material values, which led to the "bodily and moral degeneration of the nobility." The anthropological inspiration of *A Journey* comes out in its calls to "save humanity from chains and captivity," to remove the bonds from the physical and mental "forces" inherent in the peasant as a person. All that presupposed recognition of the wealth, majesty, intellectual beauty, and implicit value of human nature's inner world, which was the supreme manifestation of the regular nature of being.[4]

From the 1770s onward Radishchev's work was concentrated more and more on the problem of man. He interpreted the phenomenon of man, moreover, as a peculiar measure of the possibilities of nature and history, a standard of the development of the real world. That perception was the cornerstone of his optimistic understanding of the world. It was no accident that, when he got away from the casemate of the Peter and Paul Fortress, he noted to himself, as it were, on the road to the Ilimsk Prison: "I am the same as I was and will be all my days—not a beast, not a tree, not a slave, but a man!"[5]

But the social philosophical problems he was deeply interested in are scrupulously revealed in his essay *On Man*. In it he put forward a set of problems relating to understanding of the subject matter, tasks, purposes, and social role of philosophy and posed those of the relation of matter and consciousness, of the nature of the ideal (psychic), of man and his place in the world, of mortality and immortality, and of the "means," "forces," and "capacities" of knowledge, and so on.

According to him, philosophy opened the eyes to earthly nature, cosmos, and man. It was called upon to demonstrate the essence, role, and place of man both in his connection with and in his difference from nature and society. He proclaimed man the main object of knowledge, which it was necessary to examine in the structure ("organization") of the world as a whole. The homeostasis of the Universe (which he characterized in detail in this essay) appeared not only as something dynamic, changeable, and mobile, but also as connected with its specific value, man.

Radishchev's main philosophical work *On Man* has great interest for the history of Russian philosophy. Acquaintance with his basic principles makes it possible to answer how his various "conjectural" and "affirmative" postulates with regard to the transcendent were combined with tendencies to materialist monism, and how the initial principles and main conclusions thereby corresponded to one another.

BEING AND ITS DYNAMICS

In Radishchev's opinion, "what is *common* to all impressions is *space,* and what is *common* to all conceptions is *time,* and what is *common* to space and time is *existence*,"[6] which united everything inherent in everything, and without which nothing could exist. The forms of the real world, and the "degrees" of its development, made it possible to see how being revealed its possibilities of ascending the "ladder of substances and essences." In his concepts, part, whole, and organization agreed with the categories of "materiality" (matter), motion, space, and time, and of consciousness, soul, sensitivity, etc. He put forward the idea of the complexity of the real process of the becoming and development of the diverse forms of being: from "primeval chaos" to the universal Cosmos, and from it to man and mankind.

The initial phase of being appeared in his works as a kind of "primeval chaos" of its diverse "elements." Radishchev spoke about that in the concluding chapter of *A Journey* as well as in his early work *The Creation of the World* (*Tvoreniye mira*).[7] It was important to him to understand the logic of and reasons for the "first shift" and "first turn." If such had happened, he argued, they must probably have been manifested in the "depths of space" as "something not adequately organized" yet capable (thanks to their property of altering the environment) of communicating to the material world a "constancy of fluctuations and motion" of the particles that "filled its completeness," generating the terrestrial "solid." Whole, but infinite being was the basis of the existent. In spite of its serving as a kind of "material" for "creative acts,"[8] it possessed "primordiality" as "materiality" (matter), even in relation to the "creative force."

At the same time the concepts of force and "self-actuating spring" gave rise to deistic contradictions in Radishchev's views. The "spring," being naturally self-actuating, presupposed and included acts of "first creation" and "first impulse" as well. Radishchev came to conclusions close to a materialistically understood Spinozism: he dissolved the concept "God" in the concept "nature." In his works of the 1780s and 1790s Radishchev showed that if the divine were taken as something absolute, all-embracing, and all-powerful, then God was the nature that was also absolute, all-embracing, and all-powerful.[9] Pantheism thus became a way of surmounting the contradictions of deism, and an expression of Radishchev's tendency to philosophical monism.

The analysis of the broad system of philosophical categories in *On Man* included statements about earthly nature and the Universe. Radishchev treated the earthly and the cosmic as a unity, and in this treatment he gave his own interpretation of the main ontological problems, atomistics, and the development of objective reality.

"SUBSTANCE" AND "ESSENCE"

Radishchev's interpretation of one of the most important philosophical definitions—matter—is of interest to the history of philosophy. He substantially supplemented and synthesized the notions of Böhme, Leibniz, Lomonosov, Helvetius, Anichkov, Holbach, Desnitsky, and Diderot. His term "materiality" (matter) itself was, to begin with, clearly borrowed from Lomonosov. He specified its meaning and compared it with other philosophical categories. The classical definition of the French Encyclopedists was also supplemented: "matter in general is everything that in some way or other affects our senses." It was clear to Radishchev that this formulation left open the question of the real (objective) existence of a world outside the subject, which did not, moreover, rule out an arbitrary interpretation of the interaction of object and subject.

The definition of "materiality" (matter) he put forward contained an essentially more precise wording. "The substance that is the object of our senses, understanding by that what is or could be the object of our senses, is called 'matter.' "[10] By "substance" should be understood "that which exists," something existent, i.e., some form of substance or other, something real, existing outside the subject. His division of the category of "matter" into the active and potential satisfied the tendency to a synthesis of sensualism and rationalism. His idea of the unity of the "four elements" (earth, air, fire, and water) with "matter" as the universe was intended to explain the logical transition from the general (matter) to the particular (element) and from the particular to the singular (atom, corpuscle, individual, etc.).

In the spirit of the ideas of the eighteenth century he gave space to a philosophical interpretation. In many places in *On Man* he affirmed the idea of the unity of space, time, and motion, demonstrating that the common foundation of these categories was a constantly altering matter, for which the original state was "to move and live." The idea of the all-embracing character of motion and its universal significance was constantly repeated in this essay.

Radishchev's reflections about material being were linked with an idea of the diversity of the action of the "force of motion" as a whole and in part, from which it followed that the "whole" was not reducible to the sum of the "parts." He saw, in the "complex," a qualitatively new, higher result compared to the sum of the parts: the elements could only be altered in "their summation" but were not quite like "their primevalness" in that connection.[11] The whole was not reducible to an enumeration of the properties that characterized the parts—their qualitative definiteness depended on "the way of summation," the "order of the parts," and the character of their inner mutability.

The idea of a dynamic interaction of parts and whole cleared the ground for evolutionism and dialectics. It was not fortuitous that Radishchev linked this problem closely with searches for answers to the cardinal questions of his time: the origin of life, the forms of organic evolution, the essence of epigenesis, the nature of the ideal, the peculiarities of the activity of the sense organs of animals and man, mortality and immortality, geogenesis, and cosmogenesis.

MAN AND MANKIND

Man, his essence, and the image of a single humanity were the most important aspects of Radishchev's philosophical-anthropological orientation. His examination of them was closely linked with the fundamentals of the "ladder of substances and living organisms," and the general theory of the "organization" of forms of matter, and with problems of anthropogenesis. He showed that "spiritual forces," which he interpreted attributively in the spirit of Spinozism, were typical of the material world as a whole. He united the principles of the unity of inorganic and organic nature with opinions about the possibility of self-generation of life and its evolution from the simplest organisms to complex ones right up to man, in whom he saw the measure of the highest organization, "the pinnacle of material formations," and the last page in natural and social history.

In his opinions about man Radishchev started from the latest scientific advances. He drew on the data not only of mechanics, physics, and chemistry, but also of biology, anthropology, and medicine, to reinforce his conclusions.

His appeal to science could not but lead him to a confrontation with the "abstract subjectivity of Christianity" and the Russian Masonic understanding of the world. At the same time he found it necessary to amend certain of the theories of Russian and European naturalists and philosophers. The theory of preformism, for example, became a topic of criticism.

In his striving to trace man's life from the embryo to death, he relied on the theory of epigenesis developed by Caspar Wolff, member of the St. Petersburg Academy. According to it an organism was not preformed in the sex cells (as preformists thought) but was formed during embryonic (fetal) development from new formations, that is to say, during a process in which one part appeared after another and they all successively developed, forming the mature organism.

Radishchev also examined the problem of the interconnection of man and the environment in connection with the theory of epigenesis. It was important for him to know how the psychic and mental "human powers" developed—in "prenatal existence" (embryonal) and in childhood, adolescence, and adulthood—how the sense organs functioned, how "the piece of bread one swallows is converted into an organ of one's thought," how the ideal was generated, and so on.[12] In his quest for "sound reasons," he turned to the materials of the celebrated anatomical-ethnographic collection assembled by Peter the Great, the exhibits of the St. Petersburg Kunstkammer.

Although Radishchev did not manage to frame his constructs without a large dollop of naturalistic notions characteristic of the philosophical anthropology of the eighteenth century, he was one of the first in science and philosophy to begin to investigate all the main components of man's genetic nature simultaneously. Real science, he considered, did not doubt that only in man were the following properties inherent: an erect gait, "the true distinguishing feature of the human brain," "miraculous speech," perfecting of external conditions and of himself, and also (thanks to the development of the hand) a capacity for labor.[13]

Radishchev assigned a special role in social life to reason, spirituality, and the active processes of the human soul. His appeal to the subjective principle in history helped surmount the contemplative character of traditional materialist conceptions of social development. The conception of psychic automatism of Leibniz and Christian Wolff also could not satisfy Radishchev. That is why a thesis of the mortality of the soul (disappearance of the ideal without trace), understood as a mark or a pattern on the material, was introduced in the first two books of *On Man*. All the spiritual in man died with the death of his mortal body (he thought), though he did not rule out the opposite opinion. His conjectural supposition of the material nature of the "spiritual force," the "imaginability" of the ideal, boiled down to a conclusion about the unity of the parts and the whole, the indestructibility of the material basis of nature in accordance with the law of conservation of matter.

Radishchev's argumentation about the immortality of the "spiritual sub-stance" had a pantheistic character since it employed Spinoza's idea of the eternity of the link of the spiritual and the material, and also Giordano Bruno's idea of the individual as sharing the fate of the whole. He understood that counterposing of the spirit (ideal, "imaginable") to the material could lead in the end to a need to recognize the spirit as a "miracle," or to agree with its "substantiality" (Leibniz), or finally to admit the idea of the equivalence and autonomy of the material and spiritual, remaining a dualist like Descartes. In all cases, however, the problem of *the nature of the ideal* was removed, and the question of how "substantiality" acquired the form of a living body, and began to think, was obscured. Radishchev's choice quite clearly indicated a connection of matter and consciousness in a single being—man. Radishchev's ideas of the immortality of the forms of the spiritual "organization," forces, and elements of universal matter were opposed to the mystic-religious doctrine of the eighteenth century. He also introduced serious amendments into the theory of natural right and the social contract. He did not agree with conceptions of Lamettrie (the man-machine), Montesquieu (the man-plant), and Rousseau (the man-animal). His interpretation of phenomena of social life required a comparison of man and the genus *Homo,* the social whole. His orientation to materialistically understood principles of philosophical anthropology prompted him to rely on the latest scientific data.

MAN'S TOOLS AND POWERS IN COGNITION

The inspiration for *On Man* was an endeavor to say what man was as a knowing being, by what means he was linked with the external world, and what study of the various problems of cognition could yield man. Radishchev's general declaration about the possibilities and powerful forces of human knowl-edge was supplemented by the materialist reflections and conclusions we find in all four books of his main philosophical essay, and in all his works of the 1780s and 1790s. "Man has the power," he wrote, "of being cognizant of things. Therefore he has a *power of cognition* which can persist even when man is not actually cognizing. Therefore the existence of things is independent of our power of knowing them."[14] He understood things, and the phenomena of nature, in a space-time continuum, but necessarily in an "experimental way."

Radishchev noted that man's cognitive capacities were realized through the sense organs, whose structure, functions, and activity had to be studied seriously in order to resolve the "difficulties of knowledge" and the search for truth by man, whose "zeal for science was insatiable." He called the sense organs the tools and forces of cognition, stressing that man was distinguished not so much by the highest form of his development as by his "proportionate structure" and by his ability to employ "skillfully constructed" instruments.

The eagle "was renowned" for unsurpassed vision, the bat for hearing, forest predators for sense of smell. A proportional development of the sense organs and their use, when necessary, in "combined unity" with such instruments as the microscope and telescope, were characteristic of man, Radishchev suggested, and he expressed an idea that the two forms of experimental knowledge (sensory and rational) could be mediated by "adaptive means."

According to him, sense experience provided knowledge of a fact, of the single, which was the lowest degree of knowledge. While the "lowest organization served the highest," the latter completed the pyramid of knowledge by means of rational experience. Truth required a uniting of sensory and rational experience, of the "lowest" and the "highest" knowledge.

Radishchev considered the brain—the peculiar generator of mental and psychic processes in man—to be the most important tool of cognition, in addition to the sense organs. The brain was the "receptacle of the soul" and the home of the "spiritual principle." Among its diverse "forces" he distinguished intellect, memory, reasoning, and imagination. Scientific knowledge was not sufficient to determine the essence of psychic processes and to make competent judgments about the nature of the "thinking substance." The physiology and psychology of the brain and nervous activity were then extremely undeveloped, and neurobiology had not yet taken shape. When entering the "realm of the unexperienced" and trying to find arguments in the works of eminent philosophers and scientists of that time, Radishchev pointed out the speculative and hypothetical character of their statements about the essence of cerebral processes.

He saw the "openness of the human soul" in the brain's capacity to reflect the external world and develop concepts. The brain was the regulator of people's deeds and actions. Everything that man had been up to then, and everything he would be, depended on the activity of the brain, which "made man human."[15]

Radishchev gave in several of his works a detailed description of cognition as a process of "imitation" and "participation." Man cognized the external world, himself, and the association of the like to himself by "imitating" the things and phenomena of nature and "participating" in his own nature. At the same time, when overcoming the "power of physicality," man was moved and controlled by the force of curiosity. And science, functioning as the concentrated expression of reason, became the "guide to knowledge."

The functions of the "rational force" in his idea went beyond the sphere of the sensory, reaching the limits of logical reasoning. Purposefulness and "premeditation" were inherent in rationality for Radishchev. And for him, as for Kant, reason was capable of performing not only epistemological function but others as well. He distinguished theoretical, operative, and social reason.

For Kant reason could appear in "pure form," but for Radishchev that was unnatural. Sensory and rational experience are the two parameters of a single function; feeling and reason, operating together, created a notion.

"Pure thought" and "pure reason" in the Kantian sense, as forms of the expression of maximum abstraction (which went as far as apriorism), were impossible in Radishchev's opinion.[16] In his epistemological categories, related to the description of rational experience, there were traces of the influence of Cartesianism, although his anthropological interpretation of the concepts "reason," "thought," "mind," etc., was undoubtedly quite original.

Radishchev tackled problems of both knowledge and self-knowledge in the spirit of anthropologism. The task of the latter was the individual's understanding of himself through his own powers of reason and will. Some of his theses about it had something in common with Descartes's philosophical reflections about intuition. Ideas of the causes of errors and of means of avoiding them or reducing them to a minimum supplemented a comprehensive analysis of the "logical forces" of knowledge, the sign structure of language and mathematics, and artistic images. Radishchev suggested that errors stemmed mainly from the subject's wrong perception of the form or an aspect of things during abstract argument, or because of a deviation of the organs of sense and thinking from the normal. Interestingly, he firmly believed that self-esteem could also "obscure the truth."[17]

The results of cognitive activity were certainly involved in people's relations with one another, according to him. Truth was thus "humanized" as it were, becoming a component of people's being and fate. Truth was an expression of the human striving for knowledge, a reflection of man's capacity to organize his creative powers for a search for new truths and for extending people's cognitive possibilities. Cognition aroused man's spiritual experiences and emotions.[18]

There were many guesses in Radishchev's epistemological conclusions that anticipated the ideas of certain humanist thinkers of the nineteenth century. His epistemology rested on the recognition of man's active role in cognition and also on its anthropological context.

HIS SOCIAL AND MORAL IDEAS

Radishchev's legacy witnesses to his bent for social and moral problems. The concepts "people," "society," "race," "mankind," "nature of man," freedom ("liberty"), necessity ("inevitability"), the "future of mankind," etc., were given a new sense in his works. He considered "social living together," the common and collective, the primary principle of history.

Considering himself an advocate of the conception of the "common good," Radishchev strove to show that improvement of public affairs was linked with emancipation of the popular masses (peasantry), "deliverance of mankind from the chains of slavery," and that only the emancipation of man led to a flowering of society and the individual. The mass character of the Pugachev movement, and the continuous peasant revolts in the last third of the eighteenth century, influenced the formation of these conclusions. The "inhuman existence" of the people was obvious. In Radishchev's social views the particular and singular were converted into the universal; man's individual features received generic significance. In that context the human essence was analyzed so as to clarify the general features of social being.

His sociophilosophical attitudes were clearly expressed in his endeavor to synthesize the different aspects of the theory of "natural right," early utilitarianism, and naturalistic and rationalistic views of man. In "Liberty," *The Life of Fyodor Ushakov,* and especially in *A Journey,* not only were ideas of republicanism propagandized but new ideas were also formulated relating to the description of society as a whole, the properties of "human nature," people's habitat, living conditions and circumstances, and the forms of morality and ideals.

A question that could not be resolved by anthropological philosophy alone was that of "society and man." Radishchev stressed that natural law functioned as something general and generic. The life of the population was higher than the interests of separate individuals. He declared the "socialized principle" to be the condition for humanizing social relations. He called interest, the "mercenary spirit," and profit "prompters of actions," valuable insofar as they encouraged the interaction of the individual and society. The "rule" of people's relations, he showed, was that "social benefit precedes private profit."[19] Only the collective, the "commune," could fully provide for the happiness of each member of society, since not every individual good led to prosperity of the people.

His treatment of economic, political, and legal problems (*The Letter on Chinese Trade, A Brief Narrative on the Acquisition of Siberia, Description of My Property* [*Opisaniye moyego vladeniya*]) often led Radishchev beyond an anthropological orientation. In those cases his system of views demonstrated a unity of anthropologism and humanism. The tasks associated with tackling social problems had as their objective reference point the "inhuman" position of the peasantry. That imparted both concreteness and broad democracy to his views. In contrast to the anthropocentric or plural-atomistic orientation of adherents of "natural right" and "social contract," Radishchev's conceptions of the 1790s contained an anthropo-humanist core that fostered the molding of notions of the estate division of society, social inequality, and the existence of conflicts between oppressed and oppressors.

The generic principle became a kind of measure in Radishchev's opinions of the fullness of the civil processes taking place. Like Desnitsky, he saw the criterion of the development of "community life" in strengthening the role of the "human principle," in a progressing humanization of public affairs, and in realization of the ideals of equality and brotherhood. History itself, moreover, was understood as a process of the actualization of the human essence, and conversion of the "truly universal" features into a real alternative to the existing social system. "Man's normal nature" was put forward as the principle of natural law, and sometimes even political forms of justice, "benefit," and activity.

Ideas of asceticism and puritanism were foreign to Radishchev. Limitation of human needs was only justified to the extent that it corresponded to the "natural measure" and the "general good." Yet he did not consider human needs themselves as stable; they developed and became complicated during man's achieving of freedom and the equality of people and nations. His concept of freedom of relations in the collective included a right to "selection of the best." It also contained a requirement of instilling a conscious preference for social interests in the members of society that rejected utilitarian individualism. "I call the habit of actions useful for the social good virtuous."[20]

It followed from this that a person taken separately was recognized as a more or less adequate embodiment of socio-ethical norms and generic moral forces. Radishchev's humanist notions called for recognition that not only each person, but also society had its own moral parameters. From his concept of the significance of "social forces" there stemmed a conclusion that it was these forces that were capable of realizing—and did realize in practice—a person's moral union with nature and the people around him. The source of morality was rooted in the people, imparting moral strength to the individual, and "support" and a criterion to the ethical. An early populist element was quite clearly manifested in that.

HIS POLITICAL PHILOSOPHY

Radishchev saw defects in the prevailing economic system of Russia that, he suggested, would certainly lead to the collapse of serfdom and the institutions of feudal society. "We must confess," he wrote, "that we ourselves, armed with the mace of courage and the law of nature for the crushing of the hundred-headed monster (serfdom) that gulps down the food prepared for the people's general sustenance—we ourselves, perhaps, would attempt at the autocracy's acts."[21]

He treated the possible peasant revolution, moreover, as justified retribution for oppression and the outraging of human dignity.

Radishchev's considerations of the questions of the future of serfdom and autocratic rule, and of the necessity of establishing a republican system in Russia in a radical way, were linked with awareness of the general historical trends of social development. "Man," Radishchev remarked, "does not achieve perfection in a single generation but over many."[22] If people had passed from hunting and fishing to pastoralism and agriculture, he argued, and had later built towns, and temples and palaces in them, that had been because of the action of three main "motive forces": (1) through "need," which increased as society developed; (2) in connection with the growth of "economic accumulation"; and (3) due to "inventiveness" and the advance of reason and science.

His understanding of historical development included the idea of the natural equality of people, and the principle of just civil relations. The laws of natural right and social contract were indisputable, according to Radishchev, and existed prior to every act of concrete social relations. By virtue of that they performed the role of "first rulers" in relation to whom the sovereign was "the first citizen of popular society." But since this principle was not observed in the conditions of serfdom and absolutism, "autocracy was a state most contrary to human nature."[23]

Radishchev's legacy was an important stage in the movement of political and philosophical thought in Russia at the end of the eighteenth century. It reflected many specific features of the European and Russian Enlightenment: the sharpening of social contradictions; the elevation of the value status of science; the secularization of consciousness; problems of public affairs, science, and culture. At the same time, Radishchev's enlightened and radical ideas, which grew in the soil of the reality of serfdom, reflected an orientation to popular forces (basically the peasantry).

NOTES

1. Alexander Pushkin, "Alexander Radishchev," in *Polnoye sobraniye sochinenii* (Complete works) (Moscow, 1947), vol. 5, p. 276.

2. *Proekt grazhdanskogo ulozheniya, O zakonopolozhenii, Pesn istoricheskaya, Zhuravli, Bova, Povest' bogatyrskaya stikhami, Oda k drugu moyemu, Soficheskiye strofy, Pesni petye na sostyazaniyakh v chest drevnim slavyanskim bozhestvam, Osmnadtsatoye stoletiye.*

3. A. N. Radishchev, *Polnoye sobraniye sochinenii* (Complete works) (Moscow-Leningrad, 1938), vol. 1, p. 227.

4. Ibid., p. 123.

5. Ibid.

6. Ibid., vol. 2, p. 77. Cited from J. M. Edie et al., eds., *Russian Philosophy*, 3 vols. (Chicago: Quadrangle Books, 1965), vol. 1, p. 85.

7. See *Polnoye sobraniye sochinenii*, vol. 1, pp. 18–21.

8. Ibid., pp. 391–92.

9. Ibid., vol. 2, p. 58. See also Edie et al., *Russian Philosophy*, vol. 1, pp. 78–79.

10. Radishchev, *Polnoye sobraniye sochinenii*, vol. 2, p. 74.

11. Ibid., pp. 100, 103–107, 112–14. See also Edie et al., *Russian Philosophy*, vol. 1, pp. 85–87.

12. Radishchev, *Polnoye sobraniye sochinenii*, vol. 2, pp. 40–43.

13. Ibid., pp. 48–51, 130.

14. Ibid., p. 59. Cited from Edie et al., *Russian Philosophy*, vol. 1, p. 79.

15. Radishchev, *Polnoye sobraniye sochinenii,* vol. 2, pp. 87, 95.
16. Ibid., pp. 117, 129, 133, 139.
17. Ibid., vol. 3, p. 312.
18. Ibid., vol. 2, pp. 125–26.
19. Ibid., vol. 3, p. 206.
20. Ibid., vol. 1, p. 191.
21. Ibid., p. 320.
22. Ibid., vol. 2, p. 66.
23. Ibid., p. 282.

6

The Decembrists

Vitaly Bogatov

PIONEERS OF THE RUSSIAN EMANCIPATION MOVEMENT

Decembrism was a political action of a large group of members of the Russian nobility aimed against serfdom and autocracy. The Decembrists' aim was to establish a republic in the country and to carry out radical political and economic reforms.

Their uprising seemed unbelievable in its successful beginning and rise, but its defeat was just as stunning. Around six hundred persons were investigated and tried by czarism. Five of them (K. F. Ryleev, P. I. Pestel, S. I. Muraviev-Apostol, P. G. Kakhovsky, and M. P. Bestuzhev-Ryumin) were executed; several hundred were sentenced to hard labor, exile, or were reduced to the ranks (most of the Decembrists had been officers of the Russian army).

Their movement had arisen amid conditions of mounting crisis in serfdom and was a natural product of it. The best people among the democratic-oriented nobility rose in arms against the feudal system. But at the same time it must be noted that Decembrism as a social phenomenon was still too narrow, and its members were far removed from the popular life. The significance of Decembrism was nevertheless great, since it exerted immense influence on the subsequent development of the political and radical thought of Russia.

The Decembrists' views had been shaped by the general historical needs of the country. In the aftermath of Napoleon's invasion of Russia in 1812 it had become clear that Russia's social and economic backwardness could only be overcome by abolishing serfdom and czarism's bureaucratic machine.

103

The patriotic upsurge of national consciousness as a result of the victory over Napoleon and the stationing of Russian troops in Western Europe inevitably challenged the minds of society with tasks of improving the spiritual and material well-being of the victor nation.

Serfs had enlisted in the Russian militia expecting emancipation at war's end, but these hopes of the peasants were not realized. Furthermore, czarism began an offensive against any opposition in the social and cultural spheres. Decembrism began to take shape in that atmosphere. The spontaneous unrest of the peasants and soldiers in Russia, and their oppositionist moods, had a direct influence on its proponents. In the words of Nikolai Bestuzhev, "The war still continued when the fighting men, returning home, for the first time spread a murmur of discontent among the popular masses. We have shed blood, they said, but we are being forced again to sweat for the landowners. We delivered the homeland from the tyrant, but the lords again tyrannize us."[1]

The sources of the ideas of Decembrism were primarily the Russian radical and antifeudal traditions and the heritage of Lomonosov, and especially of Radishchev. At the same time, the leaders of the movement were acquainted with the enlightened French and English thought of the eighteenth century: the works of Hume, Robertson, Rousseau, Mably, Holbach, Helvetius, Locke, Diderot, and Condillac. All that was evidence of a striving by the Decembrists theoretically to substantiate a program for creating new sociopolitical realities in Russia.

THEIR POLITICAL PHILOSOPHY

Decembrism was a multilayered, contradictory phenomenon. It did not have a single intellectual center, although its participants strove for one. The Decembrists drew up several written programs, but over time Pestel's *Russian Truth (Russkaya pravda)* more and more became a consolidating program; members of the Southern Society had been involved in creating it. But on several basic problems the Decembrists were still seriously divided. Among them, there were advocates of an enlightened monarchy, and republicans; there were also figures who considered it possible to draw the population into the revolution, and revolutionaries who wanted to make a radical change without involving the peasants and citizens.

The most balanced expression of the political philosophy of the Decembrists was given by Nikita Muraviev, a representative of the moderate wing of the movement, and by Pavel Pestel, who reflected the mood of the radical flank.

Muraviev proposed three versions of a constitution. Their content differences resulted from the impact criticism from the left had on him. He considered it necessary to proclaim political freedom for all social strata and supported abolition of personal dependence and autocracy. He recognized people's sovereignty as the supreme political principle. Private property in things rather than people was proclaimed the foundation of the future society. He proposed, at first, that the land should be retained (for money) by the landowners and clergy. Two dessiatines [approx. 5.4 acres] were to be allotted to the peasants, but would nevertheless he considered the landowners' possessions. In the second version of the constitution this matter was put differently: the land together with everything needed for working it was to be transferred to ownership of the peasantry.

Pestel's solution of the problem in *Russian Truth* was more radical. He considered the revolution's main task to be liquidating the old regime and suppressing the overthrown landowners. There should be a decisive restoration of justice in the new society "as fast as possible." The peasant was to become an equal citizen of Russia, and all citizens were to be ensured the means of livelihood. But each one should gain his own well-being himself. Pestel was an advocate of private property.

Pestel put forward an idea that "the land was common property of the whole human race, and not of private individuals, and could therefore not be divided among a few people only, to the exclusion of others."[2] After the revolution some of the land of the big landlords would have to be confiscated and the whole area of land for "free landholders" broken up into common and private land. The peasants would be allotted land for a comfortable existence from the common fund, and this land would not be subject to purchase and sale. But private land could be sold and purchased as a commodity. Furthermore, Pestel envisaged retention of part of the land for the nobility, although he also considered that it should be subject to the general laws of the state.

DEVELOPMENT OF SOCIETY

The Decembrists' political views were based on their more general philosophical and historical notions. Their philosophy of history developed on the whole in the framework of the radical tradition of European social thought of the eighteenth and nineteenth centuries.

The Decembrists saw the motive forces of the development of society in society itself. They started from the fact of the opposition of two forces, viz., the oppressors and the oppressed, whose economic inequality was fixed in political inequality. This social inequality gave rise to a struggle of estates because the dominant social group and its state took care of the "good of its members" irrespective of the interests of the "mass of the people." At the same time the Decembrists considered the existence of social strata eternal, since there would always be rich and poor. But serfdom was inordinate, artificial, a historically outlived inequality, and therefore needed to be abolished. For them feudal forms of inequality were unnatural, but inequality as such was natural. Equality extended to the sphere of politics and law but not to the economy. In that connection they stressed the great role of ideas, especially political ones, in social life.

Although supporters of ideas of constitutionalism and the legal state, they nevertheless criticized the formal democracy and extremes of economic inequality in Western Europe.

Most of the Decembrists (with the exception of certain members of the Society of United Slavs) were against involving the people in the revolution. Although the revolutionaries from the nobility saw the main social contradiction between "the masses of the people and the aristocracy of every kind," they tried not to permit acute social conflict.

Fear of popular actions predetermined the Decembrists' search for a specific tactic of revolution. On the one hand they were against a palace coup d'etat, on the other hand they did not want to draw the people into the revolution. So a tactic of a military, top-brass revolution took shape. Mikhail Bestuzhev-Ryumin admitted under interrogation: "We did not want to provoke the people to indignation. . . . We wanted the revolution to be brief and not bloody."[3] The Decembrists' attempt to seize power in the interests of the people, but without the people, ended in failure. They rejected the reformist path, even though they understood that revolution not only led to achievements and victories but also called for the greatest self-sacrifices.

THEIR IDEAS ABOUT THE STATE

To substantiate the new form of statehood and community the Decembrists relied on the theory of natural right and social contract widely held in Europe and Russia in the eighteenth century. Russian enlighteners drew broadly on this naturalistic, idealistic theory, while Radishchev was the first to render it in a revolutionary sense. The Decembrists, direct heirs of Radishchev's revolutionary ideas, developed them, and applied them in new historical conditions to substantiate the people's right to power and prosperity.

Starting from the requirements of "human nature," the Decembrists reflected on the good of the individual, the intrinsic character of the individual's inalienable rights, and the priority of these rights over juridical laws wherever the latter contradicted "man's nature." Nikita Muravlev, for example, stressed that freedom consisted not in doing what was forbidden by law but in "having laws corresponding to man's inalienable right to develop his natural capital, i.e., the aggregate of his physical and moral powers."[4]

Pestel, in his *Russian Truth,* set out not only a program of sociopolitical and economic reforms, but also a theoretical substantiation of it. In his opinion, separating the land from the landowners was necessary to ensure every-one's natural right to till a plot of land so as to meet his natural needs. He also pointed to man's natural "fundamental principles and foundations," which contradicted serfdom and monarchism.

Many Decembrists, when tackling the form of the state system, developed Radishchev's republican ideas. Like him they denied the possibility of a contract between the people and monarchs from the standpoint of natural right, because the latter always endeavored to break "the holiest ties of nature."

In his theory of the state Pestel formulated four basic requirements: state regulations should pursue the aim of social well-being; they should accord with natural laws; the private good could not be higher than the social good, because the social good presupposed prosperity of the "aggregate people" as well as that of the individual person; no one had the right to achieve good at the expense of another. Realization of these fundamental principles would lead to the achievement of freedom in society as an innate feeling of human nature. This freedom should be granted equally to all social strata of society of the future.

The main concepts of the Decembrists' philosophy of history were the state and the people. Pestel and his associates were convinced that the republican system of government best met the interests of the people. The main attributes of a republic were (1) the existence of a territory with convenient boundaries; (2) a single government ensured by a centralized state; (3) a single-mindedness of the members of society and a single morality, and unity of nation and language; and (4) the existence of a competent government apparatus. Fulfillment of these requirements would enable the state to perform its main obligation, viz., to provide prosperity for each and every member of society, and to ensure supremacy of the people through the electivity of the leading bodies (a People's Veche [National Assembly] and a State Duma), and the introduction of universal, equal franchise.

As we have said, the Decembrists, following the French philosophers of the eighteenth century, emphasized the role of ideas in the history of human society. But already problems like the following deeply interested them: What was the "spirit of the time"? what circumstances generated new ideas? By posing the problem that new ideas went before reforms, the Decembrists drew attention to the social and political education of revolutionaries and the creation of such an atmosphere in society that "the general idea would precede the revolution" (Pestel). It became more and more clear to them that new ideas were a reflection of the new social and economic needs of society as a whole. The quests of thought led them to study the economic factor in social development, and they displayed great interest in political economy.

THE ROLE OF THE PEOPLE AND THE INDIVIDUAL IN HISTORY

Decembrists recognized the problem of the role of the people and the individual in history as an important one. For them it was truly tragic: a strong conviction of the necessity of revolution in the interests of all society, including the peasants, on the one hand, and fear of the people's involvement in conflict, on the other; awareness of the historical place of the population, but also a deliberate exclusion of them from the revolution.

Meanwhile, there were various points of view among them on the people's role in revolution. The views of the leaders of the Southern Society and its associated secret organizations were distinguished by the greatest democratic spirit and profundity. There were also people in the Northern Society who interpreted this problem in a bold way. They all agreed, on the whole, that the history of the people was the history of its labor and saw in the people a fundamental, elemental, suffering mass, which would be rendered assistance from outside. One can say here that many Decembrists, in assigning the army a special position above the state and society, saw it as the main force and guarantee of success of the revolution.

Decembrists spoke quite rationally about the role of the individual in history. They highly valued the activity of Peter the Great, A. V., Suvorov, and the hero-commanders of the war of 1812. In their view historic personalities were above all "champions of any estate whatsoever" (Mikhail Lunin). Among these champions they numbered leaders of popular uprisings: Ivan Bolotnikov, Stepan Razin, and Emelyan Pugachev. An individual was great when he was the bearer of "indispensable historic laws" and capable of subordinating the circumstances of life to his aims, and eliminating what prevented realization of ideas advanced by the times.

But, while giving its due to, say, the personality of Peter the Great, some Decembrists justly condemned the antidemocratic methods by which the emperor implemented his reforms and recalled that the reforms of the early eighteenth century were carried out "on the shoulders of the people."

The Decembrists' movement demonstrated that a revolution was impotent without the support of the people. But their experience was useful because the best people among the nobility helped rouse the people.

TRADITIONAL PHILOSOPHICAL PROBLEMS

There was no unity among the Decembrists on the traditional problems of philosophy. Some of them can be considered materialists, others deists, and still others idealists. The proneness to materialism, it must be emphasized, was combined with political radicalism. The most consistent materialists were A. P. Baryatinsky, I. D. Yakushkin, P. I. Borisov, and N. A. Kryukov.

The materialistic Decembrists were the representatives of mechanistic materialism in Russia. Elements of dialectics are encountered, of course, in their works, but they did not determine the essence of their philosophical views.

The problem of man, of his specific features, and of his place in nature and society was the center of the Decembrists' philosophical searchings. That also determined their great interest in rationalism, problems of the theory of knowledge, and the materialist interpretation of the idea of being, which stamped their understandings of philosophy itself. Kryukov, for instance, saw its task as the "search for truth." Philosophy developed a person's mental capacities, and intellect was the "sole luminary" for understanding life. With its aid man could be liberated from "harmful prejudices." At the same time philosophy was an instrument and means for developing moral qualities in man, especially those needed by a revolutionary, viz., humanism and love of the motherland.

The Decembrist M. A. Fonvizin stressed the epistemological aspect of philosophy. To philosophize, he wrote, meant "to reflect nationally on the highest objects of human knowledge." For N. A. Bestuzhev, on the contrary, the social line of philosophy had priority, i.e., philosophy was the most necessary "thing for social well-being." Decembrists paid attention, in short, not only to the cognitive role of philosophy but also to its practical significance.

The materialist Decembrists paid much attention to the relation of the two kinds of reality—matter and consciousness. Having recognized nature or matter as primary and consciousness and the spirit as secondary, and having rejected the idea of God the Creator, they wrote enthusiastically about the eternally existing and developing material world. While holding an atomistic conception of the structure of matter, they considered everything that existed to be based on moving matter, which existed of itself and possessed magnitude, form, impenetrability, and divisibility. The different properties of matter were only the result of definite combinations of its elements, while human reason and consciousness were the product of complex organized matter.

In N. A. Bestuzhev's view space and time were forms of the existence of matter because "all material images were contained in a certain space, and all phenomena happened in a certain time."[5] The external world was governed by objective laws. "Everything in nature is in continuous movement. . . . Life in its manifestations, from fungus to man, has its degrees of development, and just as light is manifested at a high degree of heat, so thought is manifested at the highest development of life."[6]

Yakushkin sought the cause of motion in nature itself, in matter, and in the force inherent in matter. He rejected indeterminism, demonstrating that every phenomenon had its causes. Pestel, too, stressed the great cognitive significance of discovery of the objective causes of phenomena, pointing out that the investigator's attention should always be "turned to the general link, which naturally has also to be sought in the essence of an object."[7] The Decembrists surmised the role of contradictions as the source of motion.

The cosmological ideas expressed by Borisov in his *On the Origin of Planets* (*O vozniknovenii planet*) are of interest. In this small but meaty work he publicized the Laplace-Kant hypothesis of the formation of the solar system from a dust cloud. Atheistic positions were characteristic of the materialist Decembrists and were usually substantiated by the data of science, with the advances of which they were well acquainted. The link between materialist philosophy and natural science was clearly manifested in the works of Yakushkin (*What Is Life?* [*Chto takoye zhizn*]) and Kryukov (*Philosophical Notes* [*Filosofskiye zapiski*]).

Materialistically thinking Decembrists were advocates of a sensualist point of view in epistemology. The process of cognition consisted of two states in their opinion, the sensory and the rationalist. When speaking about thought as a function of the brain they did not vulgarize the connection of the ideal and the material. In *What Is Life* Yakushin wrote: "Thinking, being in direct dependence on this apparatus,* manifests itself as a consequence of the development of life; but the manifestations of thought themselves are as different from those of life as the manifestations of light differ from those of heat, although heat and light can manifest themselves in one and the same object."[8]

Thought was a product of history because it arose at a comparatively high level in the development of life. "The word 'life' itself signifies only a special mode and order of units, as a consequence of which form plants or animals."[9] At the same time these Decembrist theorists saw a link between the rational and emotional in man, and the pyschic and physiological in him. "To reflect or think always means to feel," said Kryukov. All spiritual faculties consisted precisely in that, in his opinion.[10]

Knowledge was a lengthy process of man's mastering the external world and a result of the brain's analytical function: "The property of analysis consists in passing from the known to the unknown by means of reasoning, i.e., by means of certain judgments, that follow one from the other."[11] Rational knowledge yielded truth, and reason was the supreme judge and criterion of it. Kryukov, like his comrades-in-arms, endeavored to overcome extreme rationalism. He widely employed the term "practice," which had many meanings for him.

The materialist Decembrists considered knowledge of the patterns and laws of nature and society, and of the conditions in which man lived, to be the main function of man's thinking. They criticized absolute idealism and mysticism and were among the first in Russia to call into question the solvency of the extreme Hegelian-Schellingian forms of rationalism. They had a profound respect for the work of Descartes, Locke, Helvetius, Diderot, and other West European thinkers.

One must count Lunin, Küchelbecker, D. I. Zavalishin, E. P. Obolen-

---

*The brain—*Ed.*

sky, P. S. Bobrishchev-Pushkin, and the Polyaev brothers among the members of the idealist trend in Decembrism. Some of them were deeply religious people; others, advocates of Schelling's natural philosophy. Some were attracted by mysticism.

Küchelbecker and Obolensky were admirers of Schelling's ideas. Küchelbecker belonged to the "wisdom lovers" circle and opposed both materialism and subjective idealism, seeing the "wise" principle of the Universe in faith alone. Obolensky explained in one of his letters his attraction to the system of transcendental idealism by its helping systematize man's world outlook: the "separate links" wandered in "my head without plan and without aim. Schelling's system united these isolated ideas into one, and to some extent met my requirements."[12] Obolensky demanded respect for different opinions from his friends, considering a democratic attitude to people's convictions a necessary condition of political unity and cooperation.

N. S. Bobrishchev-Pushkin and A. P. Belyaev were resolute advocates of theology. A tinge of religiosity was also apparent in the works of Nikita Muraviev, Mikhail Bestuzhev-Ryumin, Sergei Muraviev-Apostol (author of the notable "Orthodox Catechism"), and others. Most of them regarded religion ethically, seeing in it a real means of improving "national morality."

One of the most outstanding representatives of the radical wing of the Decembrists, Mikhail Lunin (a participant in the war against Napoleon who became closely acquainted with Enlightenment literature in France in 1814, was at the same time imbued with a deep sympathy for Catholicism, and was later a convert), did not leave any special philosophical works. But he obviously preferred religious faith and revelation to philosophy. Theology was profound knowledge that said that the divinity as the final principle of all that existed was known through revelation. In his words "the philosophy of all times serves only to designate the limits from which and to which the human mind can go of itself. The shrewd quickly see these limits and turn to study of the limitless Scripture."[13]

He saw the laws of logic as the basis of the world. He sharply criticized the Orthodox Church and considered it, with some truth, to be an ideological protector of the autocracy and not a defender of the peasantry. According to him, the true religion, i.e., Catholicism, unlike Orthodoxy, was not a servant of the sovereign; it admitted different forms of government, and that indicated that religion should not depend on secular authorities. He held the idea of an alliance of faith and reason: the religious truth of faith clarified by reason should be directed to the conscious service to God.

We must note here that not only Lunin but also certain other Decembrists were disappointed in their quest for answers to the spiritual needs of the time in the social and ideological practice of Russian Orthodoxy and turned to Catholicism.

While noting the existence of spokesmen of both materialism and idealism among other Decembrists, we must stress that there was no confrontation between them during the preparations for and carrying out of the mutiny on Senate Square in St. Petersburg. Sociopolitical problems and their sociophilosophical and legal substantiation were constantly at the center of their general interests.

NOTES

1. *Iz pisem i pokazanii debakristov (From the Letters and Testimony of the Decembrists)* (St. Petersburg, 1906), pp. 35–36.

2. *Izbrannye sotsialno-politicheskiye i filosofskiye proizvedeniya dekabristov (Selected Sociopolitical and Philosophical Works of the Decembrists)*, 3 vols. (Moscow, 1951), vol. 2, p. 134.

3. *Vosstaniye dekabristov (The Decembrists' Uprising)* (Moscow, 1950), vol. 9, p. 57.

4. *Izbrannye sots.-polit. i filos. proizv. dekabrisotv*, vol. 1, p. 339.

5. Ibid., p. 483.

6. Ibid., p. 166.

7. P. I. Pestel, *Russkaya pravda (Russian Truth)* (St. Petersburg, 1906), p. 167.

8. *Izbrannye sots.-polit. i filos. proizv. dekabristov*, vol. 1, pp. 168–69.

9. Ibid., p. 169.

10. Ibid., vol. 2, pp. 556, 410.

11. Ibid., p. 418.

12. Ibid, vol. 1, p. 426.

13. Ibid., vol. 3, pp. 189–90.

7

Alexander Nikolaevich Radishchev (1749–1802)

Among Russian intellectuals Radishchev is regarded as the first radical so-cial thinker and an outstanding philosopher of the period following the reign of Peter the Great (1682–1725). His major works are A Journey from St. Petersburg to Moscow *(1790) and* On Man, His Mortality and Immortal-ity *(1792–1796). The latter has been discussed in Russia in recent decades because of its obvious (and possibly deliberate) contradictory nature. First Radishchev exposes the materialist arguments in favor of man's mortality, then he argues for the immortality of the human being. There are a number of interpretations of this controversial treatise. The overwhelming majority of Soviet historians consider Radishchev to be one of the first (if not the first) Russian proponents of materialistic-oriented philosophical anthropology. The opposite interpretation can be found in V. V. Zenkovsky's* A History of Russian Philosophy *(trans. George L. Kline, 2 vols. [London and New York, 1953], pp. 83–90).*

Whatever the outcome of this debate, the fact remains that Radishchev expressed himself in an extremely passionate and sincere manner. He defended both mortality of body and immortality of personality within one treatise, which permits us to assume that he consciously left all possibilities open. Radishchev's position somewhat echoes Kant's dualism and his arguments for the impossibility of solving basic metaphysical questions with pure reason. *Later such Russian thinkers as Dostoyevsky and Shestov philosophized about human destiny in much the same way.*

ON MAN, HIS MORTALITY AND IMMORTALITY*

> Le temps présent est gros de l'avenir.
> —Leibniz

Book One

Begun January 15, 1792. Ilimsk.
To my friends.

. . . Let us turn our gaze on man; let us examine ourselves; let us penetrate with curious eye into our inmost being, and strive, on the basis of what we are, to determine or at least divine what we shall or may become. And if we find that our existence, or rather our individuality, the palpable *I*, extends beyond the limit of our days even for a single instant, then let us exclaim with heartfelt rejoicing: We shall be together once more. We shall know felicity, we shall!—But shall we? Let us defer our conclusion, dear friends! The rapturous heart has more than once thrown reason into error. . . .

This more than anything else is man's distinguishing quality: he can perfect himself; and he can also become depraved. The limit in either direction is still unknown. But what animal can accomplish so much, for good or for evil, as man? [Consider] man's language and all its consequences, man's boundless bestiality in murdering his fellow man in cold blood in obedience to a political authority which he himself has created. And what beast devours his fellow out of voluptuous desire if not he? On the other hand, what magnanimity, what self-abnegation—but this is not yet the place to speak of such things. . . .

Men are born for society. Their tardy maturity prohibits them from dispersing like the beasts. O, Rousseau! Where has your unbounded sentimentality led you?[1]

It is characteristic of man . . . and perhaps of animals in general, to have an inner sense of right and wrong. Do not do unto others what you would not have done unto you, is a rule if not proceeding from man's sensitive constitution then perhaps inscribed in us by the finger of the External. All man's depravities, lies, injustices, malice, and murder cannot overthrow this feeling. Passion comes and stifles the voice of sensitivity, but surely sensitivity does not cease to exist just because it lies trampled.

It is given to man alone of all the earthly creatures to know that there

---

*From *Russian Philosophy,* Volume 1, edited by James M. Edie, James P. Scanlan, and Mary-Barbara Zeldin, with the collaboration of George L. Kline. Copyright © 1976. Translated by Frank Y. Gladney and George L. Kline, from the essay, "O cheloveke, o yevo smertnosti i besmertii" ("On Man, His Mortality and Immortality"), as printed in A. N. Radishchev, *Izbrannyye filosofskiye sochineniya,* ed. I. Ya. Shchipanov, Moscow, 1949. Reprinted by permission of the University of Tennessee Press.

exists an All-Father, the origin of everything, the source of all energies. I shall not say that he arrives at this knowledge on the strength of his reason, moving from events to their causes and finally to the highest of all causes. I shall not say that the knowledge of God issued from terror or from joy and gratitude. Man has a conception of the Supreme Being; whether man formed this conception by himself, or received it from without is not the subject of our considerations. But it is true that when reason and especially the heart are unclouded by passion, man's flesh and his very bones feel a power over them which transcends them. Call it what you will, but Hobbes felt it and so did Spinoza; and if you are not a monster, O man, then you must sense your Father, for He is everywhere. He lives in you, and your very sensibility is a gift from the All-Loving. . . .

Man has the power of being cognizant of things. Therefore he has a *power of cognition* which persists even when man is not [actively] knowing. Therefore the existence of things is independent of our power of knowing them. . . .

We are cognizant of things in two ways: first, we know the changes which things produce in our power of cognition; second, we know the connection between things and the laws of our power of cognition, as well as the laws of things themselves. The first we call *experience,* the second *reasoning.* Experience is of two kinds: first, insofar as our perceptive power comes to know things through feeling, we call it sensitivity, and the change which takes place in this sensitivity is sense experience; secondly, knowledge of the relations among things we call reason, and knowledge of the changes in our reason is rational experience. . . .

We sometimes know the being of things without experiencing any changes in our perceptive power. We have called this reasoning. With respect to this faculty we call the power of cognition intellect or understanding. Thus reasoning is the use of the intellect or understanding.

Reason is only a supplementation of experience; only through experience can we be certain of the existence of things. . . .

When you consider the operations of the reasoning powers and determine the rules which they follow, there would seem to be nothing easier than the avoidance of error; but scarcely have you cleared a path for your understanding when prejudices enter, passions arise and, rushing headlong against the wavering helm of man's reason, sweep him more strongly than the mightiest of storms into the abysses of error. . . .

Animals, bent close to the earth, follow their inclinations in surfeiting themselves and in perpetuating their species. . . . But man, erect in posture and weak in constitution, having numerous defects, compelled to devise means for preserving himself, is free in his conduct. His inclinations and impulses are subject to his understanding. And although he has urges which would limit him, he is always able to weigh them and choose among them. Thus he is the only being on earth who knows good and evil, who is able to choose and is capable of virtue and vice, of misery and felicity. His free action bound him by an indissoluble bond to a wife, and through familial life he passed over to life in society, subjecting himself to law, to political authority, for he is capable of receiving reward and punishment. And entering upon the path of enlightenment through society, linking events to their causes beyond the limits of the visible as well as the invisible world, man came to know by the strength of his reasoning what before he could only sense: that God exists. . . .

Life extinguished is not annihilation. Death is destruction, transformation, rebirth. Rejoice, dear friends. The disease has disappeared, the agony has passed; there is no more room for misfortune and persecution, burdensome old age has faded, the bodily form is dissolved but renewed. . . .

Blessed are you, O man, if your death was merely your natural end, if only your physical and mental powers slackened, and you were able to die of mere old age. Your life was philosophical and your death an easy sleep. But such a death is seldom man's lot. He is swept by his passions against life's pricks and stings; excess rends his body and deprives him of understanding. Already grown old in his prime, it is not the weight of his days that closes his eyes. Rather, diseases which have taken root in his body stop his breath before his time, crushing the repentant man on his deathbed to the point of despair. . . .

Book Two

Hitherto two kinds of possible substances have been recognized in nature. Those of the first kind are called bodies, and the general or abstract concept concerning them is called matter or *materia*. Matter in itself is unknown to man; but certain of its properties are accessible to his senses, and on his knowledge of them rests all of his philosophizing about matter. Substances of the other kind are not accessible to our senses, but certain phenomena in the world have caused them to be considered not the action of materiality but the action of another kind of substance, the properties of which seemed to contradict the properties of materiality. Such substances are called spirits. At the first step into the region of the intangible we find an arbitrary judgment; for if spirit is not accessible to our senses, and if our cognition is not introspective, then our conclusion about the existence of spirits can be only probable and not certain, to say nothing of clarity or obviousness. . . .

Can materiality have life, feel and think, or spiritual substance have space, form, divisibility, hardness, inertness? In both instances the effect would be the same. If it is possible to prove this, the division of substances into material and spiritual will disappear, but if the arguments are insufficient and arguments are found proving the opposite, then it will be necessary beyond any doubt to posit the existence of two heterogeneous substances, spirit and materiality. . . .

Extension is that property of materiality in consequence of which it occupies a position in space, and inasmuch as extension has a limit, *every limited extension is called a form.* . . . Thus impenetrability, extension, and form are the inseparable properties of every substance which is accessible to our senses. Form gives definiteness to materiality; extension gives it position, and impenetrability gives it separateness. . . .

For since we have an impression of things through sense and receive conceptions, i.e., knowledge of their relationships, with the mind, and since what is *common* to all impressions is *space,* and what is *common* to all conceptions is *time,* and what is *common* to space and time is *existence,* then no matter what you imagine, whatever substance you take, you will find that first of all it must *exist,* because without that not even the thought of it can exist. Secondly, it must be in *time* because all things in their relationship or connection are conceived as either simultaneous or successive. Thirdly, it must be in *space.* . . .

Since limited and finite substances do not in themselves have sufficient cause for their existence, there must exist an unlimited and infinite substance. Since the essence of existent substances consists in the fact that by acting on us they produce the notion of space, and, existing in space, are by that very fact limited and finite, an infinite being cannot be grasped by the senses and must differ from the substances which we know in space and time. And since knowledge of the first cause is based on reasoning abstracted from what has been experienced, and is supported by the principle of sufficient reason, the concept and knowledge of the necessity of God's existence can be had by God alone. For it is impossible and forbidden to finite creatures to have certainty about the unconditional necessity of a higher being, because the finite is separated from the infinite and is not the same. . . .

If a body occupies a position in space, it must occupy it in a definite manner; if it has a definite position in space, it has form, i.e., extension, for form is a determination of extension. . . .

Force is necessary for two parts to be together in mutual penetrability, or even close to each other. It makes no difference where this force may be located, whether in the matter itself or whether it acts from without; it does act, it holds things together and gives them form. Consequently, form cannot exist without it. When cohesion is destroyed matter disappears. Therefore this force is consubstantial with all matter; one cannot and should not be imagined without the other. Thus hardness is a consequence of some force; it follows that this force is the cause, and substance the effect produced by it. . . .

We shall not say—it would be absurd—that feeling and thought are the same as motion and attraction, or some other property of materiality described above. But if we show that they can be or that they are indeed the properties of matter which feels and thinks, shall we not have the right to say that thought and materiality are one?—That feeling and thought are properties of materiality insofar as the latter takes the form of organic bodies? . . . —That life, this product of unknown matter, is scattered everywhere and various? . . . —That where organization is better there is a beginning of sense, which, ascending and gradually perfecting itself, finally reaches the point of mind, reason, and understanding?—That all these forces and life, sense, and thought themselves are nothing other than aggregate materialities? —That mind always follows materiality and the changes noted in thought correspond to the changes in materiality? If all this can be shown to be true, we shall conclude that homogeneous matter endowed with differing properties lives in the visible world, and that there are always forces in it which have belonged to it from time immemorial. But how this union is effected we do not know, for our understanding can rise only to a knowledge of the first cause, and this is our limit. . . .

Whatever exists can be only by being somewhere; for although space is an abstract concept, it indeed exists, not as matter but as the absence of matter. And in order to be convinced of this, if indeed it is not already incontestable that the void is necessary—since without it how can there be motion?—the position or point where the void is, provides a conception of space, i.e., of the receptacle, of being. It follows that mental matter must also be located somewhere. And since each mental entity is particular, endowed with individual existence, two such entities cannot be in the same place at the same time. . . . I say that your mind is extended, that your thought has form. . . .

Rather than create new entities, we place everything on a single scale and make manifest the inexhaustible variety of materiality and the infinite power of the All-Father. . . . Having shown that the properties of materiality are the properties of mind, we shall show, to the extent of its likelihood, that mind too is a property of materiality. First of all we shall inquire what are the properties of thinking matter, not as we may imagine it to be, but as we know it in fact to be.

The properties of thinking matter or the phenomena related to its activity are: life, feeling, and thought. These properties are something more than just motion, attraction, and reflection, although these forces probably play a considerable part in their production. . . . And so it is possible that life, feeling, and thought are the activity of a single matter which is different in different structures, or that feeling and thought are the effect of a distinct type of matter, which, however, includes in its composition something on the order of an electrical force. Thus thought is found only where we find sense, and if sense is inseparable from life, are we not right in saying that these three manifestations of bodies are effects of a single matter? . . .

Book Three

Hitherto, my dear friends, I have gathered all possible usable arguments in support of the mortality of the soul and tried to give them the greatest possible clarity and present them in all their glittering splendor, so that their weak side, if they have one, might thus be all the more obvious and so that the faulty reasoning, if it has taken root anywhere, should appear all the more clearly. In surveying man's mental and corporeal nature, and even penetrating to the invisible principles of things, we have paid attention only to what would tend to prove the proposition before us [i.e., that man is mortal.] Now let us go back over the path we have traced and gather everything we find in support of the opposite opinion; let us try to reinstate man in that true radiance for which he seems to have been created. . . .

For in what pertains to life and death our feelings can be less deceptive than our reason. And the man who has never had a presentiment [of death], even though he is sometimes able to divine that which other men feel with their whole inward being, usually bases his conviction on what he has heard or learned by rote, and merely seeks arguments to convince others of that of which he is himself convinced, not through feeling or through the understanding but only, as it were, by hearsay. . . .

Let us again ask what death is.—Death is nothing but the natural change of the human condition. Not only people, but also animals, plants, and other material entities undergo such a change. Death comes to all natural entities on earth, both animate and inanimate. Its sign is destruction. Thus no matter where we turn our eyes, we find death everywhere. But its gloomy face gives way before the face of life; it shamefully hides in the shadow of life, and life is spread everywhere. . . .

Change in general is the passing from one opposing determination of a thing to the other. . . . And the future condition of a thing already begins to exist in the present; opposed states are unavoidable consequences, one of the other. . . . The smallest instant can be divided into parts each of which will share in the property of time; and there are no two instants between which it would be impossible to insert a third. And since time is the measure of action and process, there are no two conditions of a thing between which it would be impossible to imagine a third. Furthermore, there are no two states between which it would be possible to indicate a boundary, because one has scarcely ended when the other already exists. And process is so dense, so continuous, that our thought can only follow after it, and not at the same level. For imagine an instant and the state of a thing during that instant: the instant has already passed, and you are already thinking in another instant; the thing is no longer in the same state as when you started thinking about it, and the instant is already behind you.

Let us apply this notion of change to man's mortality. Life and death are opposite states, and dying is an intermediate one, or rather it is that state through which life passes away and death comes to be. We have seen that there is not and cannot be discreteness in time; we have seen that there is no real division in the states of a thing, and that motion, once it has begun, is continuous until it ends. And since change is a passing from one state to the opposite through a middle state, one developing out of the other, life and death, since they are opposite states, are consequences of one another. And we may say that when nature produces man she is already preparing his death. . . . Reflect. Death was prepared at birth and is inescapable. Waking prepares for sleep and sleep for waking; why should we not think that death which is prepared by life prepares life anew? How continuous everything in the world is! Celebrate my death, dear friends. It will be a surcease of sorrow and torment. Since you have cast off the yoke of prejudice, remember that the dead are beyond the reach of misery. . . .

Life and death and even the essence of destruction are not so separate as they seem to our sense; they represent merely the judgments of our senses concerning material changes, and not states in themselves. . . .

The soul, being in the closest union with the body, follows all the changes which occur in the body, and, sharing in its joys and sorrows, in its health and sickness, gradually comes to the moment when the body dies. But will the soul die with the body, and is there a possibility of this? If it is to die, then either all its energies and powers, all its actions and passions will suddenly cease and the soul will disappear in an instant, or, subject like the body to a thousand changes, it will experience various transformations, and in this sequence of changes there will be a time when the soul will have changed completely and will no longer be a soul and will divide into parts like the body and enter into other bodily forms. There does not seem to be a third possibility, for nature, as we have seen, annihilates nothing, and non-existence or annihilation is a vain word and an empty thought. . . .

But if the soul is to live forever, will it act and be acted upon? To act and be acted upon for a soul is to think, desire, and feel, for these are the actions and the passive states of thinking matter. But how can a soul separated from the body feel and think, for it will be deprived of the organs of feeling and thought? This seems to be the case. But because the soul cannot participate in annihilation, thought will remain characteristic of it, as will existence. For all material entities whatsoever act according to their powers and capacities. Surely the soul alone cannot be deprived of its powers, becoming as immobile and inactive as prime matter. . . .

Mental energy cannot be produced by parts which lack such energy; therefore the mental energy of a simple or a composite whole must come from parts endowed with similar energies, i.e., from mental energies. . . .

The formation of our individuality requires that there be in us a single mental energy and, moreover, that it be indivisible, unextended, and without parts. . . . And what prevents us from calling this substance which constitutes our individuality, this energy of our thought, this power which unifies our conceptions, inclinations, desires, and strivings, this simple, uncompounded, and unextended substance, this substance known to us only through life, feeling and thought; what prevents us from calling this substance "soul"? . . . Simple, unextended, indivisible, the center of all feelings and thoughts . . . the soul [is] a substance distinct from materiality, and although there is a similarity between the two (their mutual influence proves this), the known energies of the one are different from those of the other. And although someone might wish to call the soul material, this would be a vain word. The thing in itself and that which constitutes thought and the individuality of each one of us, our inner *I,* is neither magnetic force, nor electrical force, nor the force of gravitation, but something else. . . . Without thinking substance there would be no past, present, or future; . . . time would disappear, motion would cease, ancient chaos would be reborn, and eternity would begin again.

For the sincere seeker after truth, proofs of the immortality of the soul can be multiplied to the extent of his desire to know this mystery, for they are scattered everywhere and we may say that all of nature bears witness to man's immortality. Moreover, man not only bears within himself arguments and proofs that death is not his end; he is also convinced of this truth with a conviction so strong that, in view of the weakness of intellectual proofs, it alone becomes his certainty. And although he does not have a mathematical clarity concerning his immortality, the voice of his inner feeling, the vividness of his personality, the uniqueness of his *I,* which is separated from everything in him and gathers everything to itself, gives rise in him to something like certitude about this proposition, which is subject to such dispute.

Heretofore my arguments have been simply metaphysical, solely speculative, based on a general examination of material entities. And though they may be convincing to some of you, to others they will appear weak. I myself know and feel that to be convinced of the truth of man's immortality something more is needed than intellectual arguments. . . . To produce conviction about man's immortality, reasons based on feeling, on the heart, are needed. . . .

Our assurance that man in his present form is not the end-product of organization, that he is a being with two natures, this assurance, drawn from the progressive gradation of the forms of organization, drawn also from the progressive gradation in the composition of natural energies, receives strong support from the following considerations based on an assiduous observation of nature. First, no force in nature acts without an organ, without a tool peculiar to it. Second, no force in nature can perish or disappear, and if both points can give rise to a conviction, then it will be evident that, first, in man there is a force for which his body is only the tool; second, that this force is not annihilated even with the destruction of the body, that it can always exist and live apart from the body, that it is therefore immortal.

That force is not an organ and that, on the other hand, force is not the action of an organ, that no force is known to us without a tool peculiar to it, and that force exists even without an organ—all this is proved by experience. For example, magnetic force is distinct from the piece of steel through which its effects are evident to us. . . . And since we cannot imagine a force being annihilated, how much more absurd it is to imagine that the principle which acts in man, his thinking substance, his soul, can be annihilated, when it is a force, and force is distinct from the organ and cannot be its action. Then how shall we imagine its annihilation, the annihilation of the force which is the most splendid on earth, which knows and governs itself and in its deeds is like the energy of the Creator? Can it be annihilated when not even a speck of dust, a single atom, can be lost to creation? For what is annihilation?— A removal from the universe, a conversion into nothing. Both of these are vain words, and to refute them would be only a fruitless and irretrievable waste of time. No, not only will the force which feels and thinks in man not disappear, but, as a result of the continuous process which is evident in nature, it will pass over into another order of things. . . .

The soul in man not only has the power to create conceptions, as we have seen, but it is their true sovereign. . . . Nothing, in my opinion, so supports the fact that the soul is a force and a force in itself, as its power to fasten by its own volition onto a single idea. We call this "attention." And indeed, when the will arises in the soul and by its command an idea is summoned from potentiality into actuality, behold how the soul surveys it, analyzes it, and considers all its aspects, faces, relations, and consequences. All other thoughts are summoned only so that the one on which the attention is directed can become clearer, more vivid, more radiant. . . .

Sleep is the animal's daily state of renewal, properly known as yet, in which the action of exterior objects on all or some of his senses remains unknown to him. In this condition his mind is incapable of discovering new concepts because the external senses are at rest, but its creative force does not stagnate. Passing through the storehouse of its thoughts, the mind arbitrarily abstracts properties from the concepts stored there and joins them according to completely new rules to produce forms, the very possibility of which is a complete mystery to the waking person. Nothing is impossible for this creative force; abstracted from the senses, mental power renders seemingly contradictory properties compatible. In dreams it makes right out of wrong, beauty out of ugliness; that which, waking, it scarcely suspected to exist, in dreams it summons into actuality. It compresses the events of whole centuries into a single minute. It almost annihilates the limits of space with its swift fluidity. It measures the limitless with a single step and, blocking the flow of time, embraces eternity. . . .

If a dreaming person's thoughts seem disordered, perhaps just because they are exceptionally vivid, sleepwalkers must be viewed with amazement. All known instances of somnambulism demonstrate that sleepwalkers not only follow the proper ordering of thoughts, but that in this condition the power of mind over body does not disappear, for somnambulists have the use of their members as do waking people. What they will undertake in this state is truly astonishing. Strangers to fear, they climb to high places which they would view with horror when awake. . . . The somnambulist, whose external senses are inactive, is led by his soul, the source of feeling and thought.

In the sleeping state, when the soul is deprived of its senses, a mere idea is just as vivid, just as evident, as the most lively feeling. The same thing takes place in certain diseases. . . . When I was sick once with a high fever (to cite an instance which is near at hand), there were moments when, in conversation with the doctor who had undertaken to cure me of this disease, I spoke Latin so fluently and correctly that when, after my illness had passed, I was told about this I marveled no little! For although I understood the language of ancient Rome, I did so very indifferently, not to say poorly, and never expressed my thoughts in it; and it always cost me great labor to compose even a single period. Thus, because of its inner force, because of the brain if nothing else, the soul, in whatever state it may be, cannot be estranged from its activity in the creating of ideas; if it cannot create something correct, it creates a monster, but create it will. . . .

It seems to me that human speech provides one of the strongest arguments for the incorporeality of the soul. It is the best and perhaps the only organizer of our thought. Without it we would differ in no way from the other animals, and this is proven by those who chance to live apart from human beings in complete isolation. Who can say that speech is something corporeal? Only someone who considers a word to be the same thing as a sound. But these differ just as the soul differs from the body. The sound signals the word; the word stimulates an idea. Sound is the movement of air striking the eardrum, but a word is something alive which does not pertain to our body. The word enters the soul; the sound disappears in the ear. . . .

The objection will be raised against those who affirm the incorporeality of the soul and thus also its immortality, that the body acts all-powerfully upon the soul. But have you never noticed by how much greater is the soul's power over the body? We have seen that the soul commands thoughts, that it gives birth to them. But it can or does have equal authority over our desires, and not only over the desires, but it can hold sway over physical illness itself. And not only can it hold sway over illness: man can deliberately put off sense and live incorporeally in the body itself, as he does involuntarily in sleep. . . .

Tell me, how does your arm work? Tell me, what moves your legs? Is a thought born in the head and do the members obey it? What excitation of the muscles produces movement? Or does electricity flow through your members? Both, of course, or something like them, are true. But how is it that a thought, and usually an unclear one, moves a member? You will say, "I do not know," and I shall say the same. But you must agree that however artful a machine, with whatever material energies—except thought—it be endowed, it will never produce action similar to yours. It will need the source of motion, which lives in you; it cannot command itself. Push it, and it moves; otherwise it stands still. But your movement belongs to you; you are its sole source. And what gives everything actuality? Thought, thc unspoken word. You say: I want to, and it happens so. Just as Eternal Thought rose to action before the beginning of time and the Almighty said: Let there be light—and there was light, so you say to yourself: Walk—and you begin to move. O man, in your environment you are all-powerful. You are the son of thought, the son of God!

Just as man rules his thoughts, so he rules his desires and passions. Although we see that most people give in to the promptings of desire, there are and have been instances of people who completely suppressed their passions. And although this seems or can seem to be madness and often perhaps it is madness, it shows the power of the soul over the body, and this power is autocratic. Read the lives of the ancient hermits and say that their bodies were not subject to their souls. If you marvel at the self-control of Scipio, who was unwilling to look upon his beautiful captives, why do you not marvel at the self-control of the hermits? Absolute mortification of the passions is unnatural, for it contradicts man's natural end, but it provides a clear and compelling proof of the power of the soul over corporeality. If the soul were the effect of its corporeality, a product of bodily organization, there could not be instances of such madness. And so you see that even in the alienation of the understanding the soul acts according to special rules, and not physically.

But the passions themselves, our very desires, are effects or actions of the soul and not of corporeality. True, their root is material and their goal is often the same. But what is it that gives man's passion so much energy and strength? What gives him the strength to overcome obstacles? Everything the body does is sluggish and heavy. The soul gives life to action and everything becomes light. Look at the lover, the miser, behold the man who lusts after fame. Perhaps you think they are led by corporeality alone? . . . Let us take an example of the most physical of passions, love. Who does not know that Platonic love on earth is nonsense, that the source and end of love are bodily? But picture to yourself what a man will undertake for love; review the numerous instances where love, parting from its origin and losing sight of its end, gives the enamored soul (yes, the soul! it is the soul which is enamored) such excellent strength, such divine energy apart from the flesh, that love then becomes spiritual. And in order to be convinced that passion is an action of the soul alone, consider that as soon as the body becomes privy to a part of it, passion disappears.

From this we may judge that the less material the object of the passion, the more lively and lasting the passion; the less physical the satisfaction of it, the more lasting it is. O friendship! O delightful passion of the soul! If you are the heart's most constant joy on earth, what will you be when the soul, freed from the external senses and concentrated in itself, will raise its reality to its most exalted power? . . .

That the soul or mind rules over the diseases of the body can be shown in two ways. It can make the body ill and can cure it of its illness. I do not contend that all diseases have their origin in the mind; that would be absurd and contrary to experience. But if some among the innumerable multitude of them are the direct result of mind, then what I am affirming is already more than likely. Nor do I contend that for all diseases there exists a medicine in the mind or soul. But if we have clear instances that may have been cured by the simple action of the soul alone, it would seem that these spiritual medicines deserve an equal place in the pharmacopoeia next to quinine, mercury, and the rest of the apothecary's store. Should someone ask me, in what way does the soul make the body sick and how does it cure it, I should answer: It cures it without feeling the pulse or examining the tongue, and it makes it ill without using poison. I shall say no more because I know no more, but my argument will be based on what can be known to everyone. . . .

Let us pass for a moment to the most cheerful of subjects and consider the soul's beneficial effect upon the body. On this point we can ask anybody, for who has not had occasion to experience in himself, or witness in others, or hear from reliable witnesses, how substantial the soul's effects sometimes are upon the body? Who has not had occasion to be ill and receive, or at least seem to receive, a momentary easing from a visit by those dear to him? . . .

One must have great concentration to decide to take one's own life without ever having had cause to conceive a hatred for it. Could it be said that here too only corporeality is acting? How can a thickening of the juices or some other failure in the vital structure produce a decision to commit suicide? This I think no one can grasp. But when the soul declares to the body: "You are my fetters! You are my dungeon! You are my torment! I want to act, you hinder me! Let our union be destroyed! Goodbye forever!" then no matter how painful the sting of death, it is blunted by the thought that it will be sweeter and more pleasant than all earthly comforts. If it should appear to someone that to take his life requires less firmness of spirit than would seem, since this transition is momentary, a single instant—then for those who still doubt the power of the soul we shall cite the example of those who not only despised death and gazed on it with equanimity, but so separated themselves in thought from the body that every torment was easy for them and torture did not touch them. . . .

The example of martyrs and of savages who laugh in the midst of tortures, is known to you. And if the power of the soul is not apparent here, where can it be? And if this too is still not convincing, then who does not know that Rousseau wrote many of his immortal works during unremitting sickness? Mendelssohn, who suffered from an unspeakable weakness of the nerves for many years, was able by patience and concentration to rise again in his old age to the heights of his youth. . . . Believe me, I know from my own experience that an effort of the spiritual power can strengthen the weakened body and to a certain degree give it new life. I also know that when the soul is at rest the excited blood also assumes a quiet circulation, and the agitated vital juices are calmed. The disease itself, if it is not too severe, retreats before the enduring patience of the resisting soul. . . .

Book Four

Dear Friends, this is all that can be said in plausible defense of the immortality of the soul. Our arguments, as you have seen, were threefold. The first group were drawn from the nature of things and are solely metaphysical. Through an uninterrupted sequence of premises, one giving rise to the next, they showed us that our thinking nature is simple and not compound, hence indestructible, and consequently immortal, and that it cannot be the effect of our bodily makeup, no matter how artful the latter may be. The second group of arguments, on the basis of the manifest ascending scale of all known beings, showed man to be the crown of this scale or ladder of visible creation and the most perfect of earthly organizations or structures. In him we clearly saw every natural force concentrated into one, but we also saw in him a force which was distinct from every natural force. From this we draw the plausible conclusion that man cannot be annihilated with the destruction of his body, for if it is impossible and self-contradictory for a force in nature to disappear, then his mind, being more excellent and perfect than any natural force, also cannot disappear. Arguments of the third kind, based upon our senses and drawn from our own experience, showed us that our intellectual energy or power of thinking is distinct from the senses and, although it receives all its concepts from the senses, is able to create new, complex, and abstract concepts. The thinking power rules over our conceptions, making them actual or bringing them into unity. In its occasional separation from the body, as in certain diseases and in sleep, the mind does not lose its creative power. The concatenation of our ideas since childhood, our speech, and most of all our manifest awareness of ourselves are convincing proofs that our thought is neither a manifestation of our corporeality nor the effect of our physical makeup. Finally we showed, in order to refute the impressive although shaky argument for the body's omnipotence with respect to the soul, we showed, I say, that the power of the soul over the body greatly exceeds it. And for this we cited examples from everyday experiences, affirming incontestably that the cause and root of all bodily motions is mind or thought, the source of motion. Can we not therefore say that this is also the source of life?

We cited instances of how man's thought so dominates his desires and passions as to bring disease and health and, we might add, death itself to the body. The effort of the mind abstracts thought from corporeality and makes man capable of overcoming difficulties, diseases, and everything which without the help of the soul cause the body to fail. Having thus affirmed the indestructibility of the soul, let us make bold to lift the heavy curtain of the future at least a little. Let us try to foresee, or to fore-feel, what may be in store for us beyond the limits of life. . . .

There are three possible forms of human existence after death: either I shall be a substance the same as I am now, that is, my soul after its separation from the body will pass into and animate another body; or the state of my soul after its separation from the body will be worse, i.e., it will pass into and animate an inferior kind of being, e.g., an animal, bird, insect, or plant; or my soul separated from the body by death will pass over to a better, more perfect state. . . .

Let us briefly repeat what we have said. After his death man remains alive; his body is destroyed, but his soul cannot be destroyed, for it is not a composite entity. Perfection is his goal on earth and it remains his goal after death as well. From this it follows that, just as his [bodily] organization was the means of this perfecting of himself, so he will have another, more perfect, organization commensurate with his perfected state.

The reverse course is impossible for man; his state after death cannot be worse than his present state. And for this reason it is probable or plausible that he will retain his acquired thoughts and his inclinations to the extent that they can be separated from his incorporeality. In his new organization he will correct his errors and direct his inclinations toward truth. Since he will preserve his thoughts, which received their scope from his speech, he will be endowed with speech. For speech, as a series of arbitrary signs denoting the significations of things, can be intelligible to every sense, so that no matter what man's organization may be, if sensitivity is a part of it, it will be endowed with the power of speech.

Let us put an end to our conclusions, lest we seem to be in quest of dreams and strangers to the truth. Be that as it may, O man, whether you are a composite or a homogeneous substance, your mind is not destined for destruction with your body. Your goal is felicity and perfection. Endowed as you are with varied qualities, use them in a way commensurate with your goal, but beware of using them for ill. Every abuse contains its own punishment. Your felicity and your misfortune are within yourself. Travel the path traced out by nature and believe in this: if you live beyond the limit of your days, and if the destruction of your mind is not your lot, believe that your future state will be commensurate with your life. For He that created you gave your nature a law to follow which cannot be eliminated or violated. The evil you have done will be evil for you. You determine your future with the present. And believe, I repeat, believe: eternity is not a dream.

NOTE

1. See *Discours sur l'origine de l'inégalité parmi les hommes.*

Part Three

The Idealism of the First Half of the Nineteenth Century

8

Pyotr Chaadayev

Zakhar Kamensky

BIOGRAPHICAL BACKGROUND

Pyotr Chaadayev (1794–1856) was born into an aristocratic family in Moscow. His father was a major landowner in the Nizhni Novgorod Province and well known for his liberal convictions. His mother was a daughter of Prince Mikhail Shcherbatov.

Chaadayev was orphaned in childhood, and he and his elder brother Mikhail were brought up by their aunt, Princess A. M. Shcherbatova. After an education at home, he matriculated to Moscow University in 1808, where he was close to such future figures of Russian culture as the poet A. S. Griboedov and the Decembrists N. I. Turgenev, I. D. Yakushkin, and the Muraviev brothers.

From 1812, when the war with Napoleon began, Chaadayev was on active service and fought in various battles, including Borodino. On returning home after the victory over the French, he continued in military service and had a successful career. But when he was going to be appointed an adjutant to Emperor Alexander I he suddenly retired, to everyone's astonishment, which was most likely evidence of Chaadayev's disapproval of the sovereign's policy.

Chaadayev had already become acquainted with Alexander Pushkin in 1816 and soon became not only his senior comrade but also his friend. The freedom-loving young officer joined the Decembrists' secret society, the union of Russians against absolutism and serfdom, but he did not take part in the uprising of 1825 having been abroad since 1823.

When abroad, Chaadayev observed the contrast between Russian and European reality; he reflected on how his country could achieve prosperity and sharply criticized Russia's order and customs, especially serfdom. On his return home in 1826 he came under surveillance by the secret police as a former member of the Decembrist organization. Having retired from the military, he devoted himself to theoretical activity. When endeavoring to comprehend the causes of Russia's economic, sociopolitical, and cultural backwardness in comparison with the most advanced countries of Western Europe, and to understand the causes of the defeat of Decembrism, he looked for both historical and philosophical explanations. For that purpose he studied the contemporary humanitarian sciences, the works of great thinkers of the past, and religious literature.

His main theoretical work, the *Philosophical Letters* (*Filosoficheskiye pisma*), was the creative result of this intense effort. Chaadayev naturally tried to publish it, if only in parts, but the strict censorship that existed in Russia allowed no works to be published that criticized Russian reality or contradicted the official position. Only several years later, through a lapse in censorship did the first *Letter* appear. But Chaadayev's success turned out to be tragic for him. The authorities, and above all the czar, were angered by the publication. The czar ordered the author declared a madman; N. I. Nadezhdin, the publisher of the journal *Teleskop* (Telescope), who had published the letter in the fifteenth issue of 1836, was exiled from Moscow, and the journal was suppressed. Not only was it forbidden to publish Chaadayev, but journals were even forbidden to mention his name and works.

For some time he was isolated and subjected to humiliating medical examinations, which were ultimately stopped. Chaadayev appeared in society and visited the salons of aristocratic Moscow families. He took part in the formation of and later in the confrontation between the two trends of Russian social thought—the Westerners and the Slavophiles. Although he had no opportunities to publish anything, he nevertheless continued intensive creative work, carried on an extensive correspondence, and worked on his manuscripts.

DEFINITIVE PRINCIPLES OF THOUGHT

Two main themes stand out in Chaadayev's theoretical legacy: philosophy and Russia. They were not isolated from one another. Problems of Russia and a philosophical interpretation of her history played a leading role in motivating his work.

The Russia of those days lagged appreciably behind the most advanced countries of Western Europe economically and especially socially. Serfdom continued and the monarch's absolute power prevailed. The country had neither a constitution nor any kind of significant representative institutions; the system of public schools (secondary and higher) was extremely narrow; and censorship of printed matter was extremely powerful. High aristocratic society was alienated from the people by its forms of life, education, and ethical principles. It is hardly surprising that many Russians who suffered from what they saw around them and were familiar with the achievements of Western culture and the Western social system, turned their minds to finding methods of reforming Russian society on principles of justice, universal well-being, and economic and social prosperity. Progressive minds, even those concerned with comparatively abstract things (philosophy, history, esthetics), associated the abstractions very closely with public affairs, and with the tasks of emancipation and reform of Russia.

Chaadayev was an ardent patriot, and although philosophy interested him as such, and although he had turned to its most abstract aspects—the theory of knowledge and ontology—he combined it with analysis of general problems of the philosophy of history. Through these he passed to contemplation of the historical development of his homeland to clarify why Russia was so behind England and France, and what needed to be done to overcome her backwardness and make her a prosperous, advanced country.

For Chaadayev philosophy and Russia were essentially a single theme of reflection, and his knowledge in this field was extraordinarily great. In his philosophical-historical intuition he did not lag behind contemporaneous professional philosophers, and even surpassed most of them.

Three periods can be distinguished in his intellectual life. The first was the shaping of the views summed up in the *Philosophical Letters,* written in 1829–1831. The second period covered the time from the early 1830s to the mid-1840s, when his philosophical ideas remained more or less unchanged but his understanding of Russia's historical destiny was very substantially altered. In the mid-1840s there was a new break, this time not only in his views about Russia but also in the field of the philosophical problems.

HIS EARLY PERIOD OF WORK
AND THE *PHILOSOPHICAL LETTERS*

We do not know much about the concrete circumstances that shaped Chaadayev's philosophy. Information about the time when he joined the Decembrist societies—first the Union of Salvation, and then the Northern Society—is particularly meager. Nevertheless it can be concluded from his correspondence and his admissions that "deadening deism" prevailed among them, from the recollections of contemporaries about his efforts to get Pushkin to accept Locke's ideas, from the fact that he gave up a brilliant court career, and from other similar information, that until his departure abroad in 1823 he was a typical representative of Decembrism and its political and religious freethinking.

His travels abroad were especially significant in shaping Chaadayev's views. He was affected in various and contradictory ways. His observations of West

European life, which had already begun when he crossed Europe from Moscow to Paris with the Russian Army, now continued, revealing to him the differences between Russia and Europe. Allowing for his political and ideological pre-disposition to radicalism, these impressions should, it would seem, have shaped corresponding social (quasi-democratic) and philosophical views in him. But during his travels he also experienced a strong influence of religious thought, especially the views of the later Schelling; in 1825, when Chaadayev became acquainted with him, he had already abandoned the dialectical ideas of his own natural philosophy and had evolved to religion and conservatism. Cha-adayev turned his mind to theology as a form of spiritual assimilation of the world. Events in Russia it would seem—the Decembrists' uprising and its defeat—had largely accounted for this turn. Chaadayev associated the causes of this defeat with the radical ideology (freethought, deism, and even atheism) that was characteristic of many of the most active Decembrists. He saw the root of the political defeat of the Decembrists in these theoretical precepts and this predetermined his transition to positions of religious philosophy.

At the same time the theoretical views he had set out in the *Philosophical Letters* had been formed under the influence of science as well as of religion, and that had affected both his general philosophical standpoint and his attitude to the future of Russia.

Chaadayev's deep interest in science was rooted in belief in the unity of the world, and of the human race in the unity of nations and all people. This conviction was realized ontologically in his world outlook, as a conception of the close tie of the spiritual and physical worlds; and epistemologically as the idea of the identity of subject and object, which accounted for the possibility and practical expediency of cognizing the existent. It figured in his understanding of social development as the principle of the wholeness of mankind and of historical regularity common for all nations; in ethics as an anti-individualistic idea of the morally perfect individual who constituted an organic element of the nation and, through it, of humanity as well; in the social utopia as the ideal of a society founded on these philosophical and ethical principles, a society in which all nations and people were in a harmonious accord that ruled out any kind of national inequality.

A critical fire predominated in Chaadayev's interpretation of Russian history in this period. Following the Decembrist tradition he condemned the civil state of Russia, especially the serfdom, decline of morals, blind imitation in culture, absence of democratic freedoms, and absolutism. He looked for explanations for this in national history and linked them with a certain anomaly in the development of Russia, namely, with the absence of a connection between its different stages, and with its departure from the traditions of European civilization. In his opinion Russia had fallen out of the civilized world, as it were, as a result of being drawn into Orthodoxy rather than the Catholicism that united the peoples of Europe. While not making an absolute of the achievements of West European civilization, he saw a need for uniting with other national cultures and with the human race as a whole. Since he believed in the possibility of such a development of Russia he was not a pessimist.

In the field of the philosophy of history, in the context of which he interpreted Russia's destiny, Chaadayev was on a par with the contemporaneous achievements of philosophical and historical thought and took into consideration the conclusions of German philosophy (Kant, Fichte, Schelling), French historiography (Guizot), and utopian socialism (Saint Simon, Lamennais). He criticized the old descriptive historical science that limited itself to simple statements and did not aspire to a theoretical explanation of concrete ideas about the history of mankind and of separate nations. He advanced the task of creating a new science of history that would be based on a specially developed philosophy of history. According to him the history of mankind was a process guided by Providence through the suggestion of opinions and ideas that directed it. He treated historical necessity in its dialectical unity with man's freedom, did not agree with the fatalism that denied the role of the individual in history, and with the voluntarism that did not recognize any objective determination of history.

Normal development of nations, in keeping with law, only happened (he considered) when their leaders assimilated these ideas. When they—the whole people together with them—fell into a false understanding of the main ideas and aims of public affairs, society took a false path of historical development as had happened, for example, with Russia. Then nations were faced with the task of returning to the true ideas of history and realizing a proper understanding of it. A correct or false interpretation of its tasks was realized through awareness of the goal that Providence set a given nation. But an individual nation was only an element of humanity, of the whole, and the whole of the human race was moved ahead through nations attaining their goals.

Chaadayev built his own social utopia starting from these ideas. He imagined the future society as an embodiment of unity of people, and as a harmony of personal and public interests and freedom of the individual. The main fault of modernity, according to him, was breach of this unity, isolation of the subject from objectivity, and the tragic estrangement of people and nations. Overcoming of this fault would enable man to find true freedom.

"Then instead of his present separation from nature would he not be fused with it? In place of the feeling of his own will which now sets him apart from the general order and makes him into an isolated being, would not the feeling of the universal will be found within him or, to put it another way, the intimate sensation, the profound consciousness of his real rapport with all creation?"[1]

The perfection and harmony of nations would correspond to the perfection and unity of the separate individuals, and the former would be "divested of their blindness and their impassioned interest," and would develop a "genuine national self-awareness." "We would see, perhaps, nations that stretched out a hand to each other in proper consciousness of the common interest of mankind, which would then be no other than the truly understood interest of each individual nation."[2] Chaadayev did not relate this ideal to some remote future and considered it subject to the control and action of people: "It is up to us to rediscover that lost, beautiful existence without leaving this world."[3] He saw the means of passing to this "beautiful existence" in the upbringing of a morally perfect and educated individual. He rejected forcible, revolutionary means of reforming society, means that in his opinion (based on the experience of the Decembrists' uprising and the European revolutions) did not lead to the desired result.

On the philosophical plane, Chaadayev regarded man as a unity of the physical and the spiritual, as realization of the principle of the identity of being and thought. He interpreted this unity as a "parallelism" of two worlds. The physical world consisted of atoms and molecules, the aggregate of which formed all bodies that existed in space, understood as the objective form of the external world, and in time that, on the contrary, was subjective. Motion in the world of nature he interpreted as mechanical, i.e., as impelled from outside, which in turn served as an argument to substantiate the idea of a first mover—God. The mechanistic model of the physical world served Chaadayev as a mode of religious explanation of consciousness as not subordinated to the mechanical laws of nature but communicated by the divinity. At the same time, he claimed that the physical world was cognized experientially and "through reasoning." The logic of reasoning was determined by the logic of natural phenomena. The mind therefore attained "supreme reliability" in the natural sciences, which made it possible to satisfy man's material needs. But experimental knowledge was powerless in cognizing the spiritual world, the objects of which were infinite and possessed freedom. Revelation was the specific form of comprehending phenomena of the spiritual world.

Scientific, rational and providential, irrational orientations were interwoven in the *Philosophical Letters*. The providential, irrational played an essential role in Chaadayev's world outlook, but it was not built up in any one of the Christian confessional traditions, Catholic, Protestant, or Orthodox. But whatever character his religiosity took in this period of his intellectual development, the contradiction between the two ideological orientations (to science and irrationalism) determined the inconsistency of his views in the years when he was writing his main philosophical work.

THE EVOLUTION OF HIS VIEWS ON RUSSIAN HISTORY

In the second period of Chaadayev's creative life, his philosophical convictions did not experience any essential change, but his opinions on Russian history underwent a marked evolution.

Whereas stress had been laid in the *Philosophical Letters* on a critique of the history of Russia, and on the social situation existing there, at the end of the 1830s and in the early 1840s the accent shifted to revealing her definite advantages over Western countries and outlining the prospects for and specific features of national development. Gradually Chaadayev came to a conclusion that a submissiveness to supreme authority was characteristic of the Russian people, which determined the specific relationships with it by virtue of which Russia was capable of advancing according to the instructions and under the guidance of this authority. This feature, in combination with the purity of the popular consciousness, the absence of cultural traditions, the amorphousness of the Russian spirit, and Russia's nonparticipation in the world-historical process, now seemed to Chaadayev to be a great advantage. They enabled Russia rapidly to attain the level of civilization of the West, since she could assimilate its achievements as ready-made results without having to take the long road of working them out.

PHILOSOPHY AND RELIGION

In the mid-1840s, during the third and final period of Chaadayev's work, there was a new turn in his conception of Russian history. His philosophical views also evolved. The transformation of the latter can be described as a de-religionizing of his ideas. He now understood faith as a certain epistemological function and not by any means traditional religiosity. It was now, for him, only one of the possible varieties of faith in a broader, philosophical sense: "Faith is not anything else but a moment or period of human knowledge, and nothing more."[4] For Chaadayev, who had previously counted on religion as a means of educating a truly free person, a perfect individual, it had become obvious that religious feelings could no longer win the masses. Philosophy was becoming free from religion, turning to its own range of problems and traditions developed over the centuries. At the center of philosophical comprehension stood the problem of subject-object relations most fruitfully developed by the German philosophers of the late-eighteenth and early-nineteenth centuries (Kant, Fichte, Schelling, and Hegel). What were the natural foundations of philosophy, Chaadayev asked. He answered: "The Ego and the not-Ego, the inner world and the external world, the subject and the object."[5]

Having changed his hostile attitude to Hegel, formed in the early 1840s, mainly because he had seen in Hegel's doctrine the theoretical basis of the idea of "reconciliation with reality" that had taken hold of Russian youth, Chaadayev now recognized Hegel as the greatest representative of German idealism who had fully and productively examined the main problems of philosophical science. But he understood that Hegel's system was not the last word in philosophy and drew attention to its inherent abstractness, spoke of its creator's predilection for a scholastic manner of thinking and "narrow logomachy" (playing with words), and considered that Hegel "obviously had not understood his century, a century so absorbed with ideas of the practical."[6]

Chaadayev was also familiar with the development of German philosophy after Hegel, and in particular with certain ideas of so-called Left Hegelianism or Young Hegelianism. He had read the works of David Strauss, one of the founders of this trend, and had studied the works of other Young Hegelians. Their ideas evidently impressed him, since they coincided with his own changing views. In gradually abandoning religiosity and treating philosophy as relatively independent, he brought to the fore the problem of the merging of philosophy with reality.

The process of de-religionizing also embraced his philosophy of history. That was expressed in his perceiving the course of social events more and more from the standpoint of historical realities, viz., the geographical factor, social relations, material needs, and political tasks and their solutions. Providentialism was pushed into the background in the interpretation of history.

Chaadayev's sociophilosophical views were growing more democratic and his critical mood intensified. He reproached the czar for intending "to turn a whole generation of free people into slaves" and accused the top echelons of Russian society of supporting serfdom, which was an "abominable abuse of autocratic power in its most vicious manifestation, namely, corruption of public consciousness."[7] Soon after 1848 (when the European revolutions were over), Chaadayev wrote an appeal to the peasantry, which stood in striking contrast to his *Philosophical Letters* with their antirevolutionary thrust. While not directly calling for a revolution in his appeal, he pointed to the example of nations that were trying to end oppression by revolutionary means. He took a negative view of the socialist doctrine yet still believed that "socialism will win, though not because it is right but because its opponents are wrong."[8] His former idea of Russia's leadership in movement along the path of human progress now gave way to an understanding that a country that enslaved its people and strove to oppress other nations could not be such a leader. He now understood particularly clearly that Russian society's task was above all radical reform of its own structure.

We must speak specially of Chaadayev's patriotism. The progressive people of Russia combined love of their homeland with criticism of its shortcomings and defects, and that combination reflected a deep-seated striving for social perfection. The idea of "true patriotism" permeated Chaadayev's whole life, and he expressed it in fine, fiery words. "It is true that I have not learned," he said in his second most important work, *The Apologia of a Madman* (*Apologiya sumasshedshego* [1837]), "to love my fatherland with my eyes closed, forehead bowed, mouth closed. I find that one can be useful to one's country only on the condition that one sees things clearly; I believe that the times of blind loves are over. . . ."[9] He expressed his patriotic convictions in the same spirit later as well, contraposing his own patriotism to its official form that demanded that Russia only be glorified. "Obviously, there are several ways of loving one's fatherland and serving it. I would prefer to flog my homeland, prefer to distress it, prefer to humiliate it, rather than to deceive it."[10]

Chaadayev's ideas had immense intellectual and moral significance. The publication of the first *Philosophical Letter* and his subsequent promotion of sociophilosophical views that he carried on by all the means available to him roused the Russian public from the despondency that had set in after the autocracy's defeat of Decembrism. Chaadayev restored the broken thread of the development of freethought in Russia. He played an outstanding role in the molding of Russian national self-awareness and had a direct influence on his younger contemporaries—the great Russian poets Pushkin and Lermontov, the young Herzen, and on many other notable figures of Russian culture. Thus not only in his homeland but also far beyond it he merited deep respect as one of the bright, original representatives of the intellectual history of Russia.

NOTES

1. Raymond T. McNally, *The Major Works of Peter Chaadayev* (Notre Dame: University of Notre Dame Press, 1969), p. 81.

2. P. Ya. Chaadayev, *Statyi i pisma* (Articles and letters) (Moscow, 1987), p. 97.

3. McNally, *Works of Peter Chaadayev,* p. 82.

4. Chaadayev, *Statyi i pisma,* p. 178.

5. Ibid., p. 179.

6. Ibid., p. 196.

7. Ibid., p. 185.

8. Ibid., p. 195.

9. McNally, *Works of Peter Chaadayev,* p. 213.

10. Chaadayev, *Statyi i pisma,* p. 161.

9

Slavophilism
Vyacheslav Serbinenko

SOCIAL AND HISTORICAL CONTEXT

Slavophilism was an organic part of the development of nineteenth-century Russian culture. Vissarion Belinsky, its constant opponent, wrote: "The Slavophile phenomenon is a fact, remarkable to some extent as a protest against obvious imitativeness and as evidence of Russian society's need for independent development."[1]

As a sociopolitical and intellectual trend, Slavophilism and its constant counterpartner, Westernism (a school of social thought that owed its name to its spokesmen's orientation to West European models of cultural and social development), were an important stage in the shaping of Russian liberal consciousness and actively encouraged the preparation and carrying out of the peasant reform of 1861. At the same time the Slavophiles made no effort to create anything like a complete political program, and the meaning of their philosophical and social views was far from covered by concepts of either liberalism or conservatism. In their polemic with Westerners and in their disputes among themselves the leading Slavophiles sometimes defended conservative ideas close to Western conservatism (Toryism). But this was not as a rule a narrow political conservatism, and ideas of that kind (for example, monarchism, anticonstitutionalism) need to be evaluated concretely and historically. Monarchism, quite obviously, was by no means a foreign element in the ideology of Russian as well as of European liberalism of the middle of the nineteenth century. The anticonstitutionalism of the Slavophiles was primarily associated with their dream of a state system in the "Slavonic spirit" and was not at all equivalent to antidemocracy: the Russian "Tories" constantly defended freedom of speech, freedom of the press, and freedom of conscience; opposed censorship; and recognized the inevitability of a development of elected representative institutions in Russia.

The major Slavophiles—A. S. Khomyakov, I. V. Kireyevsky, the brothers K. S. and I. S. Aksakov, and Yu. F. Samarin—based themselves in their dispute with the Westerners, and in their critique of the contemporaneous West, on a profound knowledge of European cultural traditions. They felt themselves sufficiently independent in the "land of holy miracles" (as the acknowledged leader of Slavophilism, Khomyakov, called European civilization) not to experience either an imitative urge or an obscurantist-nihilist complex that would lead to a negation of any "foreign" values and achievements. Through the Slavophiles post-Petrine Russian culture was actively and passionately involved in the all-European dispute on the meaning of history, real and illusory progress, and the national and universally human in culture. While intently following any pros and cons in Western social thought, the Slavophiles quite purposefully employed and, when necessary, criticized the ideas of Hegel, Schelling, and European romanticism. Their original evaluations and conclusions were determined in the end by the Russian rather than Western background, i.e., the general situation in Russia, torn by very acute social contradictions, and the specific features of the Russian religious and intellectual tradition. Being religious thinkers, they assigned a special role to Orthodoxy. Theological experience and the study of the works of the Church Fathers had a substantial effect on the whole complex of ideas developed by them and their followers.

The leading spokesmen of Slavophilism were not creators of finished philosophical systems. They were primarily known as public figures and representatives of Russian literature, therefore Slavophilism had little in common with the academic philosophical schools in the West. Each of the Slavophiles had his own independent position on many philosophical and social matters and resolutely defended it.

On the whole Slavophilism was a response to the historical processes of the time, and above all to the crisis of serfdom, and the establishment of capitalist relations in Russia. At the same time, the Slavophiles' ideas were an essential element of the Russian cultural tradition of the nineteenth century and an important milestone in its preservation and development.

ALEXEI KHOMYAKOV

Alexei Khomyakov (1804–1860) came from an old aristocratic family. In 1822 he passed the Moscow University examination for candidate of mathematical sciences. From 1822 to 1829 he was in military service, took part (in 1828) in the war with the Turks, and was decorated for bravery. Then he resigned and engaged in running his estate. The range of his intellectual interests and activities was exceptionally broad. He was a philosopher and theologian, sociologist, historian, an economist who drafted projects for the emancipation of the peasants, the author of several technical inventions, a polyglot linguist, poet, dramatist, physician, and painter.

In the winter of 1838–39 Khomyakov familiarized his friends with his work "On the Old and the New" (*O starom i novom*). This essay-manifesto, together with Ivan Kireyevsky's subsequent reply, marked the origin and began the rise of Slavophilism as an original current of Russian thought. In it Khomyakov outlined what was a constant theme of Slavophile discussions from then on: "Which is better, the old Russia or the new? Have many foreign elements come into her present organization? Are these elements good enough for her? Has she lost much of her native beginnings, and are they such that we should be sorry about it and try to resurrect them?"[2] The sociopolitical and philosophical-historical views of the Slavophiles were set out for the first time in this article. Khomyakov stressed the "beautiful, holy meaning of the word the state," pointed out the need for a strong central authority, and wrote about the time when "Old Russia will be revived on an enlightened, orderly scale, in the original beauty of a society that unites the patriarchal way of life in the province and the profound meaning of the state which presents a moral and Christian visage."[3] When listing the achievements of old Russia, Khomyakov did not so much follow ideal notions of the past as name the reforms the country needed: "literacy and organization in the villages"; "trial by jury"; absence of serfdom; an assembly of "deputies of all estates to discuss the most important matters of state"; freedom of the Church. In essence he set out a program of liberal changes translated into the language of historical reminiscences.

Khomyakov's philosophical views were closely linked with the theological system he developed and, in the first place, with his ecclesiology (theory of the Church). By the Church he understood primarily the spiritual link that united the host of believers in a "conciliar" way, and united them in "love and truth." In his opinion, the true ideal of Church life had only been maintained by Orthodoxy, which harmoniously combined unity and freedom and so realized the central idea of the Church, that of conciliarism (*sobornost*). This principle had been historically violated in Catholicism and Protestantism, in the former in the name of unity, in the latter in the name of freedom. But, as Khomyakov argued, betrayal of the *sobornost* principle had led, in both Catholicism and Protestantism, only to the triumph of rationalism, hostile to the "spirit of the Church."

When criticizing rationalism Khomyakov developed his own religious epistemology and ontology. The latter was based on the idea of the "free will of reason" (God)* as the first principle of everything existent: "the world

---

*The reason which has its own will and, at the same time, realizes its own will in action.—*Ed.*

of phenomena arises from free will." His ontology was essentially an experiment in philosophical comprehension of the intellectual tradition of the Church Fathers. It is also important that the appeal to will as the ontological root did not bring Khomyakov's conception close to irrational voluntarism (Schopenhauer, Hartmann, Shestov) that divorced will and reason, since he insisted on the rational character of will.

In his epistemology (which was not completed and systematized), Khomyakov, while rejecting rationalism, substantiated a need for integral knowledge ("living knowledge"), the source of which was also *sobornost*: "an aggregate of ways of thinking united by love." The religious and moral principle thus played a determinant role in cognitive activity as well, being both the premises and the final aim of this process. All the stages and forms of cognition, he wrote, "the whole ladder got its evaluation from the highest rung, faith."[4]

Khomyakov's philosophy of history was quite fully presented in his *Notes on World History* (*Zapiski o vsemirnoi istorii*), or *Semiramis* (*Semiramida*), his never-completed work of many years. This book, published after his death, was an attempt at an integrated exposition and interpretation of world history and a definition of its meaning and direction.

In *Semiramis* an image of world history that lacked in principle a permanent and rigidly fixed cultural, geographical, or ethnic center became an alternative to the Hegelian model of historical development, and to the Europocentrist philosophico-historical scheme associated with it. The historical link was maintained by an intense struggle of two polar spiritual principles: the "Iranian" and the "Cushitic," which operated partly in real cultural and ethnic areas and partly in symbolic ones. Very different ethnoses became involved in world history, developing their culture under the sign either of "Iranianism" as a symbol of freedom of the spirit, or of "Cushitism," which symbolized the predominance of material necessity, i.e., not a negation of the spirit but negation of its freedom in manifestation. In fact, according to Khomyakov, these were the two main types of man's perception of the world—its universal archetypes, one might say—since the idea of an initial unity of the human race was the cornerstone of *Semiramis*.

Khomyakov's conception of history, it must be noted, had nothing in common with racist or nationalist interpretations. First, the superiority of the "Iranian" cultural type in *Semiramis* was the superiority of a religious, metaphysical ideal whose real embodiment was not determined by any ethnic features. (In Khomyakov's philosophy of history, Christianity was the highest type of "Iranian" consciousness and at the same time its transcendence.) Concrete "historical Iranianism" was often presented in the book as degrading; and the colossal cultural significance of the achievements of nations that represented the "Cushitic" type was admitted many times. Second, Khomyakov was far from absolutizing any specific national-religious forms of historical life: history no longer knew pure tribes, as it did not know pure religions.

In addition to a clearly expressed religious and metaphysical approach to world history, *Semiramis* contains many interesting scientific observations and generalizations (including those pertaining to the theory of culture), which indicate the author's striving to apply broadly the results and methods of special sciences (ethnography, comparative linguistics, oriental studies, etc.).

In an attempt to overcome the "abstract rationalism" of Western thought Khomyakov looked for a way out not so much in history itself as in mythology and religion, which were interpreted in terms of theory of culture as a result. For him religious faith was "the most perfect fruit of public education, the extreme and supreme limit of its development. False or true, it contains the whole world of human thoughts and feelings."[5] While limiting the claim of rationalist dialectics to exhaust the meaning of history, and acutely sensing the fatalistic tendency of Hegelian thought, Khomyakov found no other version than a direct denial of rationalism and appeal to Christian tradition, which recognized in history a unity of the "combined efforts of human freedom and the universal will." He drew on the theory of culture in constructing his most serious "rational" arguments in his dispute with Hegel, in which he analyzed non-European intellectual traditions and cultures and subjected to essentially justified criticism the Europocentrism of the German philosopher. On the whole his Slavophile philosophy of history, in spite of its recognition of a specific dialectic and struggle of "Iranianism" and "Cushitism," was imbued with a spirit of Christian providentialism, and his general approach to history was a kind of "Orthodox" attempt at a religious, metaphysical interpretation of the past and present of world culture.

By contraposing "freedom of the spirit" ("Iranianism") to the "material," fetishistic view ("Cushitism"), Khomyakov continued in *Semiramis* the Slavophiles' key dispute with rationalism that, in their opinion, deprived the modern Western Christian world of any inner spiritual or moral content and put an "outwardly juridical" formalism of public and religious life in its place.

However, while constantly and sharply criticizing the West, Khomyakov was not inclined to idealize the Russian life of his time and critically evaluated practically all its social-historical forms. He also did not postulate any "golden age" in the past of Russia. He singled out three epochs of relative "spiritual well-being" of Russia, viz., the reigns of Fyodor Ioannovich, Alexei Mikhailovich, and Elizabeth I. His choice was explained by the absence in these periods of "military glory, great efforts, great deeds, brilliance and clamor in the world."[6] It was thus a matter of normal conditions (in his understanding) for organic natural development of the people's "spirit of life," and by no means of "ages of bliss," and still less of a lost "earthly paradise." He treated the rulers of these "happy" epochs without special reverence. What did he see as a way out of the generally unsatisfactory state of contemporary public and spiritual life, not only in the Catholic and Protestant West but also in Orthodox Russia? What hopes did Slavophile ideology place in the future?

An answer was provided, in particular, by the conception of the "education of society" developed by Khomyakov and his associates.

Khomyakov outlined the aim, the realization of which the Slavophile movement intended to promote, in particular in his essay "Concerning Public Education in Russia" (*Ob obshchestvennom vospitanii v Rossii* [1850]): "The domestic task of the land of Russia is to manifest a Christian, Orthodox society held together at the summit by the law of living unity, and standing on firm foundations of the village community and land."[7]

The road of the "education of society" should lead to attainment of that ideal. Therefore Khomyakov looked upon all the public activity of the Slavophiles as educational. The task of a religious and moral reconstruction of Russia was to be accomplished through a series of gradual, painstaking reforms ("cautious actions"), and by no means through sudden, radical social transformations.

The idea of the "education of society" reflected the liberal-conservative political premises of the Slavophiles' social philosophy. Top priority was given to "organic," evolutionary forms of the development of public and cultural life. While speaking of the inevitable utopianism of Khomyakov's program of education, we must not overlook its fundamental difference from the many versions of the educationist utopias. His religious, idealistic approach was beyond doubt, but a rationalist interpretation of the formula of the Enlightenment, "ideas govern the world," was essentially alien to him. His understanding of education was equivalent in a certain sense to enlightenment, but only in the sense that it was precisely the "upper social strata" that needed to be educated and enlightened, strata that "had been torn away from the conditions of historical development" and had abandoned themselves to worship of absolute, indeterminate being." This idea was directly opposed to educationist utopianism, whose faith in progress was based on a notion of the spiritual mission of the educated classes, who brought the light of knowledge to the ignorant, benighted masses of the people. Khomyakov rejected the road of a gradual raising of the people to the level of "society" because he was of the mind that the mental fare prepared by the worthy educators did not meet their needs, and that "sophisticated knowledge" was foreign to the people, who lived their own peculiar and organic life.

At the same time, Khomyakov was fairly critical of the contemporary state of the "peculiar life" of the Russian people, stating that "intellectual activity had grown weak in the lower strata." The general troubles in the intellectual sphere led, in his opinion, to retarding Russia's development, although the people were by no means alien to science: they would accept it only if it corresponded to their perception of life. The people "believed in their natural reason" and would reject everything that did not gratify their "rational feeling." The utopianism of the Slavophile conception of education was primarily associated with a dream of the possibility of a "new science," radically different from that "taken from the West," which, according to Khomyakov, had a "colonial character." The national science of the future, Slavophiles hoped, would become a necessary element of true people's enlightenment, which would appear, so to speak, in "the garment of Russian life." They also pictured the image of future society corresponding to this ideal "science." That society would not develop "along logical paths," and in it "the laws of the moral world" and not external juridical relations would assume paramount importance because they were "as immutable as the laws of the physical world."[8]

All Khomyakov's philosophical work was imbued with antirationalism, which was manifest not only in his epistemological and ontological constructs but also in his philosophy of history, theory of culture, understanding of science and knowledge, and in his sociopolitical views. In that sense, in spite of the incompleteness and fragmentary character of many of his works, he was a thinker of exceptional consistency. It was not fortuitous that many of his contemporaries repeatedly stressed the integrity of his world outlook. In his striving to transcend the limits of idealist philosophy of the "Western model" in both its rationalist and irrationalist versions, Khomyakov turned to the national religious-moral tradition, appealing to the spiritual experience of Orthodox Christianity. The theological searchings of the lay thinker had no serious impact on either public or ecclesiastical life in Russia (the greater part of his works were published in the West and not in Russia). But his ideas anticipated (and in some cases directly determined) much in the quests of Russian religious philosophical thought in the last third of the nineteenth century and the early twentieth.

IVAN KIREYEVSKY

Ivan Kireyevsky (1806–1856) came from an aristocratic family. In 1822, he attended lectures in Moscow University, and from 1824 worked in the Archives of the Foreign Collegium and then joined the Wisdom Lovers literary and philosophical society (whose members included V. F. Odoevsky, D. V. Venevitinov, A. I. Koshelev, M. P. Pogodin, S. P. Shevyrev, and others). In 1830, Kireyevsky went abroad, attended classes in Berlin and Munich universities, and met Hegel and Schelling. On his return to Russia Kireyevsky published a journal *Evropeets* (*The European* [1832]) which was soon suppressed. Later, in 1845, he edited the journal *Moskvityanin* (*The Muscovite*) for a short time.

Kireyevsky's ideas in many ways intersected with the principles developed by Khomyakov, forming with them a kind of initial basis of Slavophile philosophy. His position in his later years was that of a religious thinker, wholly absorbed in the study of the religious-mystical experience of the Church

Fathers and dreaming of the birth of a "new" Orthodox philosophy. But in his youth he became a follower of, in turn, Locke, Spinoza, Kant, Schelling, and Hegel. He went so far in lack of faith that he denied the necessity of God's existence. He was both repulsed and attracted to the cultural achievements of the West. It was so in his early life and at the end of it. Thus, in his main, so to speak, programmatic work *On the Necessity and Possibility of New Principles in Philosophy* (*O neobkhodimosti i vozmozhnosti novykh nachal dlya filosofii*), he spoke of Schelling with sincere admiration and love and noted the immense general cultural and not just philosophical influence of the Hegelian system. In this work he quite definitely formulated the kernel of his attitude to the philosophical tradition: "In the general life of humanity recent philosophy is not as new as is generally assumed. It is new for modern history, but for human reason in general it is a familiar thing, and hence the future consequences of its supremacy over the minds of men have been already more or less indicated."[9]

Kireyevsky did not deny development and progress in the history of philosophy, considering that its essence consisted not in invented "special modes of thinking and points of view," but solely in systematizing of what "man's curiosity has managed to amass for him in the course of his two-thousand-year search. Reason now stands on the same level, not higher, and perceives the same truth, not a more distant one. Only the contours of the horizon around us are clearer."[10]

The development of European philosophical rationalism was, in his opinion, a closed circle. Clear reverberations of the philosophy of the Eleatics and Heraclitus were to be heard in the manner of "dialectical thinking which is ordinarily deemed the . . . particular discovery of Hegel. . . . Hegel traveled a different road, which stood outside Aristotle's system, but just the same came to a meeting point with him, both in his final deduction and in the basic relationship of the mind to truth."[11]

Kireyevsky (like Khomyakov) saw the possibility of a way out of this vicious circle in transcending the limitations of rationalism. On the cultural-historical plane this meant a return of "abstract philosophy" to its "natural root," to religion, and in the realm of philosophical anthropology and epistemology a change in the very character of thinking and cognition, i.e., the achieving of a unity of "mind and heart," and of "living and integral vision of the mind." While paying their due to attempts to solve problems of this kind in the past (Pascal) and in modern times (Schelling), Kireyevsky considered that their failure had been predetermined. Philosophy, for all its immense significance and influence in society, depended on the general character of intellectual life in this society and in the first place "on the character of the dominant faith. Philosophy may not derive directly from faith; it may even be in contradiction to faith, but it is still born of that peculiar orientation of the mind given to it by the peculiar character of faith."[12]

In the Catholic and Protestant West, therefore, the critique of rationalism led to obscurantism and "ignorance" or, as happened with Schelling, to a striving to create a new, "pure religion." "A lamentable task," Kireyevsky wrote, "creating a faith for oneself. Schelling's Christian philosophy was neither Christian nor philosophy. It differed from Christianity by its most important dogmas, and from philosophy by the very manner of cognition."[13]

Kireyevsky's delimitation from Schelling, and from philosophical romanticism and pantheism (for he cast doubt on the conceptions of both F. X. von Baader and K. C. F. Krause), is quite obvious. He was oriented to Orthodox theism, and saw the future "new philosophy" (the idea of which arose in the current of the common Slavophile dream of a "new, national" science) in the forms of Orthodoxy, "true" realization of the principle of the harmony of faith and reason, which differed radically from its Catholic, Thomist modification. At the same time he did not by any means consider the cultural and historical experience of the European philosophy of rationalism senseless and futile. "All false deductions of rational thought resulted only from its pretension to the highest and complete cognition of truth."[14] The "recent philosophy" (the Schellingian-Hegelian system), which rejected such a "pretension," he wrote, "not only would not unconditionally contradict the concept of reason which we find in the philosophical works of the Holy Fathers,"[15] but would also be an essential and necessary supplement to the patristic literature since the following concepts were either absent or weakly expressed in it: "public" and "historical interest," and comprehension of "man's external life and the laws of development of family, civic, public, and state relations."[16] When completing his last work, Kireyevsky concluded that "German philosophy . . . could serve us as the most convenient point of departure in thinking . . . to an independent philosophy corresponding to the basic principles of ancient Russian education and capable of subordinating the split education of the West to the integrated consciousness of believing reason."[17]

Kireyevsky did not create a "new philosophy," not only because of his sudden death, which left the philosophical work he had begun unfinished. Like Khomyakov in his doctrine of *sobornost,* Kireyevsky linked the possibility of the birth of "love of wisdom," not with the construction of philosophical systems but with a general turn in public consciousness, "education of society," and the molding of a "genuine national science and enlightenment." The philosophy whose "new principles" he dreamed about should come to the life of society as part of this process through common ("conciliar") intellectual efforts rather than individual ones.

He formulated these principles quite definitely. A predominant place was given to the integrated character of spiritual life, the necessity of an "inner consciousness" that is the common living core in the depth of the soul for all the separate forces of reason, hidden from the usual state of the human spirit, but accessible to the person who seeks it, and is alone worthy of attaining the highest truth. Such consciousness constantly elevates man's manner of thought and, while humbling his rational conceit, does not constrain the freedom of the natural laws of his reason.[18]

Two main epistemological defects of intellectual life no longer threatened the individual and society upon attainment of harmonious "integral thought": "ignorance," which kept "peoples from lively intellectual interchange" and led to "deviation of the mind and heart from true convictions";[19] and the "detached logical thinking" that splits the wholeness of the spirit and was capable of diverting man from everything in the world except his "physical person."[20] The second danger for modern man, if he did not attain "wholeness" of consciousness, was the more real because, according to Kireyevsky, the cult of corporeality and material production and industry was still only gathering strength. By receiving ideological justification in rationalist philosophy, it would inevitably lead to a spiritual enslavement of the individual. Only a change of "basic convictions" and "alteration of the spirit and direction of philosophy" could modify the situation.[21]

Kireyevsky's views on the philosophy of history readily fit, at first glance, into a scheme of gradual transition from the "Westernist" convictions of his youth, which found reflection in his early essay "The Nineteenth Century" (*Devyatnadtsatyi vek* [1832]), to a persistent contrasting of Old Rus with Western civilization. But that is a schematization that explains little.

First of all, though Kireyevsky admired much in the life, culture, and social system of Old Rus, he by no means contrived a "conservative utopia," and did not call for a return to the past. In 1838 he wrote, in his "Reply to Khomyakov" (*Otvet Khomyakovu*), that, "The form of this life declined together with the weakening of the spirit . . . now this dead form would have absolutely no point. To bring it back forcibly would be ludicrous if not harmful."[22] Later, rejecting the idea of Slavophilism as a retrospective ideology, he expressed himself even more definitely:

> If I should ever happen to see in a dream that any of the external features of our former life, long dead, suddenly revived among us and came into our present life in its old appearance, that vision would not please me. On the contrary, it would appall me. Because such a transference of the past into the new, of the outmoded into the living, would be the same as transferring a wheel from one machine to another of different construction and size: in that case either the wheel or the machine would be broken.[23]

What had primarily attracted him in the Russian past was the "wholeness of life" inherent in it, and he wanted to see it in new forms of public and intellectual life that would not "oust European enlightenment." But he did not find such wholeness either in the West or in Russia developing under the influence of the West. He saw the reason for that in the "deterioration" of faith, and in the "heresy" of the Western Church. At the same time we must note that his evaluation both of the West and of ancient Rus by no means remained invariable.

For Kireyevsky, Old Rus (up to Ivan the Terrible) had, for quite a long time, been not so much a historical reality as an ideal image of the medieval Orthodox state, the antithesis of the Catholic and Protestant West, and even of Orthodox Byzantium. But in his *On the Necessity and Possibility of New Principles in Philosophy,* which can be regarded as Kireyevsky's philosophical testament, his critical study of the contradictions of intellectual life in the history of the Christian West and East (Byzantium), and of its contemporary decline, no longer contained references to Old Rus as the historical embodiment of the harmony of Christian principles and the social and state forms of the people's life. In his historical and philosophical reflections he came to the conclusion that such harmony could be attained in the future. In his religious utopia he dreamed of a synthesis of the best features (as he understood them) of the intellectual life of West and East, rather than of a negation of the Western tradition by a new "young" Russo-Slavonic culture that was succeeding it.

Kireyevsky considered that there had been the possibility of such a synthesis in the past, but it had not been realized; therefore he projected (not without some doubt) the religious, utopian ideal inspiring him into the future:

> The East would have given the West the light and strength of intellectual culture, and the West would have shared with the East the development of public life. . . . Public life, developing harmoniously, would not have destroyed earlier acquisitions with every new success and would not have sought the ark of salvation in the mundane calculations of industry or the starry-eyed constructs of utopias. Universal learning does not rest on a dream or on opinion, but on truth itself, which affirms it harmoniously and steadfastly.[24]

These hopes for a new culture in the future were undoubtedly utopian and far from the reality of Russian public life, which could not help affecting Kireyevsky's attitude to the changes taking place in it. The least "politicized" of the Slavophiles, Kireyevsky was the only one among them who disapproved of the plans for peasant reform. Fear of a catastrophic "antagonism between estates" and of "strife and useless war," and an indefinite hope of a rapid intellectual transformation of Russia that would make the road of liberal, essentially Western-type reforms useless and superfluous, all together constituted a specific element of his conservatism.

KONSTANTIN AKSAKOV

Konstantin Sergeyevich Aksakov (1817–1860) was the son of the famous Russian writer S. T. Aksakov. At fifteen the young Aksakov entered the philological faculty of Moscow University, from which he graduated in 1835. He was a member of the literary and philosophical circle of the well-known public figure N. V. Stankevich; like its other members (in particular, Belinsky) he was strongly influenced by the ideas of the German idealism of the late-eighteenth and early-nineteenth centuries. Ten years later this influence was clearly to be seen in his master's thesis "Lomonosov in the History of Russian Literature and Language" (*Lomonosov v istorii russkoi literatury i russkogo yazyka* [1846]), in which he consistently examined the stages in the development of literature in the spirit of the Hegelian conception of the cultural and historical process. At the end of the 1830s he was close to Kireyevsky and Khomyakov and became one of the leading theorists of Slavophilism. His creative activity was many-sided: poetry, publicistic writing, literary criticism, history, philosophy, and philology.

The main fields of Aksakov's theoretical research were social and political philosophy and esthetics. He had formulated his political views quite definitely in an essay "Voice from Moscow" (*Golos iz Moskvy* [1848]), written under the impression of the revolutionary events shaking Western Europe. Throughout the whole essay there was a contraposing of the "hideous storm of European West" and the "beauty" and "quiet" of the European East.

While condemning the revolution and demonstrating its "complete foreignness to Russia," Aksakov saw in the "European storms" the consequence of the Western tradition of "worship of the government" and concentration of public interests predominantly in politics and power. Orthodox Russia, he alleged, had never worshipped the government, "never believed in its perfection and did not demand perfection from it," and even looked on it as a "secondary matter." According to him, political and state relations were of "secondary" importance for the Russian people because their real interests, by virtue of historical tradition and features of the national character, lay entirely in the spiritual and religious sphere. There was only one form of authority that could harmoniously correspond to the people's "non-statehood," and that was the Orthodox autocratic monarchy. Later, in his memorandum "On the Internal Condition of Russia" (*O vnutrennem sostoyanii Rossii*) addressed to Alexander II in 1855, he stated: "The people can alienate the state from themselves only through unlimited monarchical power and rid themselves of any involvement in government and political affairs, having chosen instead a public life imbued with morality and an aspiration for spiritual freedom."[25]

The apology for the monarchy was accompanied with a very negative evaluation of other forms of the state system: a constitutional system of government was a "realized lie and hypocrisy"; a republic was "the most harmful governmental form."

Aksakov tried to grasp the essence of Russian history through comprehension of its specific features. Therefore he studied national literary traditions and folklore and conducted ethnographic research, seeking to confirm his own hypothesis of the absence of a tribal system among ancient Slavs, and of the decisive role of family-communal relations in their life. He wrote about the mainly peaceful character in the forming of Russian statehood and criticized the Petrine reforms for interrupting the organic development of Russian society and disrupting the age-old tradition of the Russian relationship of "land" (people) and "authority" (state).

The Slavophiles actively employed the conception of "land" and "state" (which became an important element of their ideology) in their criticism of the West and of Western influence. They substantiated, by means of it, the idea of a special historical road of the Russian people, who preferred the "road of inner truth" (Christian moral organization of life within the framework of the peasant community) to the "external truth" (a political and legal organization of society of a Western type). But, while Aksakov's general view of the relationship of "land" and "power" was shared by all members of the Slavophile trend, that cannot be said of some of his extreme conclusions, and particularly of the idea of the "non-statehood" of the Russian people. It not only oversimplified the picture of real Russian history but also deprived the road of liberal reforms of any historical perspective, which the spokesmen of Slavophilism aspired to carry out.

Although Aksakov categorically rejected any kind of reforms of a Western type in Russia, he was at the same time an active advocate of the abolition of serfdom and shared the Slavophiles' liberal hopes of the possibility of social and political reforms in Russia, endeavoring to deduce their necessity from the general postulates of his sociological theory. For instance, he deduced from the conception of "non-statehood" the idea of inalienable, sovereign people's rights (freedom of speech, opinion, and the press), which he declared to be nonpolitical and accordingly not subject to the jurisdiction of the state: "For the state an unlimited right of action and law, for the land full right of opinion and speech."[26] In the ideal civil system of the future Russia, he dreamed, *Zemsky sobor* (assembly of the land), representing all the estates, should be the form of cooperation between the "state" and the "land" (in his theory the "land" or people was primarily the peasantry). In contemporary Russia, beginning with Peter the Great, there had been "a yoke of the state over the land," as he remarked in his memorandum "On the Internal Condition of Russia." "Inner discord, covered up by a shameless lie," and "internal ulcers" (i.e., serfdom, disunity and schism, and the bribery of officials) were characteristic of this condition.

During disputes about the future peasant reform Aksakov categorically criticized schemes that proposed emancipation of the peasants without con-ferring land. "Until the question of property and ownership is settled," he wrote, "the landowner can consider the land his own property. . . . But as soon as the decisive question is raised, 'Whose land is it?' the peasant will say mine, and he will be right, at least more so than the landowner."[27]

The idea of "non-statehood" thus led him to democracy and rejection of any forms of aristocratism or manifestations of class exclusiveness. The same democratic tendency gave rise to his belief in the "communal principle" and its concrete historical model, the Russian peasant commune. But the elements of anti-elitism did not strip Aksakov's social philosophy of profound dualism. He did not see any other possibility of removing the (for him) obvious contradiction between state and people than calling on society to employ the historical experience of Old Rus and to "advance along the ancient road."

Aksakov's esthetic views had already taken shape in the 1830s, mainly under the influence of the ideas of philosophical romanticism, and in the first place of Schelling's philosophy of art. While regarding the idea as the "inner meaning and inner life of an object," he saw expression of the hidden "idea" of a thing through art as the aim of artistic creation.[28] A work of art was thus the highest degree of knowledge of an object's "inner life," and the artistic image the integral reflection of reality (which was close to Schelling's conception of the wholeness of artistic perception). Employing the idea of "integral natural art" to substantiate the development of an original national artistic culture, the young Aksakov sharply criticized the French romantics (for example, Victor Hugo) for artificiality and imitation, and an inability to express the "soul of the people" in their works. He contraposed the works of Schiller (Aksakov was not only a poet, but also a translator into Russian of the works of Goethe, Schiller, Herder, and others) to French romanticism preoccupied with an "outer decoration of form," yet at the same time did not see sufficient harmony of form and content in Schiller's work either. In his opinion, "thought" and "an ardent feeling" predominated in Schiller to the detriment of "proportionate form."

In the 1840s and 1850s Aksakov gradually abandoned the canons of German philosophical esthetics and concentrated on the philosophical inter-pretation of contemporaneous Russian literature. The Slavophile esthetics denied both the conception of "pure art" (art for art's sake) and "naturalism" in literature (the so-called natural school) and recognized *narodnost* (national character) as the main criterion for evaluating artistic creation and a sine qua non of the value of a work of art. In art, he argued, the "folk element was part of the task itself," the word as the material of poetry "carried in itself the expression of time, place, and . . . must of all, of the people." Therefore it was not only a means but also a "part of . . . the creative work itself." The subject-matter of literature should not necessarily be "only national," but any literature "should be an expression of the people's life in writing and word." It should not be "literature of the public" or "governmental" literature, "created by the government and eulogizing it," a literature of the "officials of all fourteen ranks," an "abstract" literature (i.e., remote from the main problems and contradictions of contemporary life).

Young Aksakov dreamed that in accordance with the classical Hegelian negation of the negation and his triad (thesis—antithesis—synthesis), modern literature, which had truly succeeded folk art and folklore, would play a necessary cultural role and, in turn, would give way to a "new," "synthetic" folk art. He saw the prototype of this art in Gogol's celebrated *Dead Souls,* and insisted that an "epic content" equally permeated this work and Homer's classical poems. Subsequently Aksakov became increasingly disappointed in contemporary literature, which held out little hope, in his view, of engendering a truly popular "synthetic" art of the future. He began to show more and more interest in the religious interpretation of painting and literature. In 1848 he stated that modern art was "paganism in the true sense of the word," incompatible with Orthodox faith and life, and recognized its "auxiliary" nature at best, citing icon painting as an example. In his esthetics, as in his social philosophy, the principle of "following the ancient road" presupposed the right to sit in judgment on contemporaneity, including contemporary art, and to require of it fidelity to the values and ideals of the past rather than a search for new forms. The religious ideas that permeated the whole system of Aksakov's philosophical views in the last period of his work began to play the dominant role in his esthetic conception as well.

IVAN AKSAKOV

Ivan Aksakov (1823–1886), Konstantin's younger brother, graduated from the Law School in St. Petersburg in 1842, and was in government service until 1851. After retirement, to the end of his life, he devoted himself wholly to literature and political journalism and public activity. He was a leading contributor to and publisher of the Slavophile newspapers and journals *Parus* (*Sail*), *Russkaya beseda* (*Russian Conversation*), *Den* (*Day*), *Moskva* (*Moscow*), *Moskvich* (*The Muscovite*), and *Rus.* In the 1870s he was the leader of the Moscow Slavonic Committee and an organizer of public aid for the people of Montenegro, Serbia, and Bulgaria during the war with Turkey.

The younger Aksakov's public activity and world outlook reflected the role and place of Slavophile theory in the social and cultural milieu of postreform Russia in the 1860s through 1880s. He tried to comprehend the new trends in Russian public affairs in the light of the religious and philosophical ideas of his brother and the "old" Slavophiles Khomyakov and Kireyevsky. The Slavophiles hoped that the peasant reform would lead to a rapprochement of the estates and that the institution of *Zemstvo* (organ of local self-government) would encourage return to the harmony of social relations that, in their opinion, had been characteristic of pre-Petrine Russia. Aksakov saw in the peasant reform the beginning of realization of the Slavophiles' forecasts and therefore spoke of it as a "grandiose social revolution." At the beginning of 1862 he proposed a scheme of self-abolition of the nobility as an estate and the "abrogation of all artificial divisions between the estates."

The idea of "self-abolition" of the nobility was put forward as a counterpoise to the gentry's constitutionalism that was gathering strength at the time. But Aksakov soon lost hope of rapid achievement in Russia of a social idyll where there would be no estates, although he continued to be a critic of constitutionalism, supported in this to the end of his life by Yuri Samarin. He declared "freedom of speech and thought, in both the press and publicly" to be the solely possible and necessary "constitution," following the principles of the theory of "land" and "state." The constitution being demanded by the gentry was foreign to the popular spirit and would lead to a final breach of the "vital alliance" between the people and the autocracy. As with other Slavophiles, monarchism and anticonstitutionalism were combined in Aksakov's views with recognition of the need for liberal, essentially democratic political freedoms for the individual and for society (freedom of speech, of the press, and of conscience) and substantiation of the inevitable imperfection and even "secondariness" of state legal relations and even of the state itself: "The state is necessary, of course, but one must not believe in it as the sole aim and most adequate norm of humanity. The social and personal ideal of mankind is higher than any . . . state, just as conscience and the inner truth are higher than the law and external truth."[29]

Aksakov continued the Slavophile critique of the relationship between the state and Church in post-Petrine Russia, opposing the established tradition of strict state control over the activity of the Orthodox Church. In his numerous articles he sharply criticized not only the Russian state for interfering in the religious affairs of citizens but also the Church authorities for conformism and violating the principle of freedom of conscience:

> The Church is inconceivable without freedom of conscience because the cause of the being . . . of the Church itself lies in man's spiritual freedom. . . . Freedom of the human spirit thus constitutes not only the sphere of the Church but also the object itself, so to speak, of its activity. . . . Obviously . . . in this sphere of free spirit its activity and direction can only be spiritual.[30]

Feeling himself a successor to the "old" Slavophiles and acting in a situation in which practical realization of their religious and moral ideals seemed more and more doubtful, Aksakov, though he continued the dispute with rationalism as "logical knowledge cut off from the moral principle," had to defend the Slavophile belief in the effectiveness of Christian values and ideals itself against numerous critics who belonged to the radical democratic and populist trends.

He wrote,

> One cannot but be astonished at the narrow and limited understanding of the universal mission of Christianity by the advocates of "modern progress." Now they lay the responsibility onto it for failing to establish universal well-being on earth in the last two millennia, and now they accuse it of un-practicality of the Christian ideal standing outside mankind's real histori-cal life. . . . The point is, however, that the Christian ideal is eternal, irrespec-tive of the conditions of place and time . . . it is not confined to life, has always been above it, and does not reconcile itself with it; it is eternally calling and rousing human society and guiding it forward and onward.[31]

In the early 1860s he formulated a theory of "society" on the basis of his brother's idea of "land" and "state," which represented a transformation of Slavophile ideology in the new social conditions. He defined "society" as "people aware of themselves," as the medium in which the "conscious, intel-lectual activity . . . of the people took place." "Society" arose from the people; it was "nothing but the people themselves in their forward movement." "So-ciety" lay between "the people in their direct being" and the state, viz., "the outward determination of the people."

In pre-Petrine Russia, according to Aksakov, there had been no "society," and that had made necessary a practically unlimited strengthening of state power and had justified the "autocratic initiative" that ensured the development of public life. The autocracy had originally successfully carried the burden of power entrusted to it by the "land," or people. Even "the torturer Ioann,* tyrant and despot," he wrote, "was at the same time a wise builder." But Peter the Great's reforming activity, "before which the despotism and tyranny of Czar Ivan paled," proved hostile to the "popular principles." The result of the Petrine reforms had been a "reaction of the popular spirit," and an awakening of "activity of self-awareness" in the people. The development and strengthening of this "self-awareness" led to the emergence of a new social force, viz., "society," "the people aware of themselves," or an "educated class" (essentially a popular intelligentsia). "Society" included, he considered, people of all estates and conditions who constituted a social and not a political force. People required freedom of speech for normal development (understood as an exclusively moral right, and not a political one). That also applied to freedom of the press, to which Aksakov attached greater significance than he did to representative institutions.

---

*Ivan IV (the Terrible)—*Ed.*

But already in the mid-1860s he had repudiated the idea of "society," believing that it had proved "powerless" in Russia since it had not become a "popular intelligentsia in the highest sense," and recognized the Slavophiles themselves as the sole representatives of the Russian educated stratum true to the "popular principles."

In the 1870s and 1880s Aksakov's social and political views more and more lost the liberal features characteristic of classical Slavophilism, and he came closer in his publicist works to spokesmen of the conservative camp (M. N. Katkov and others).

YURI SAMARIN

Yuri Samarin (1819–1876) came from a rich noble family and graduated from the Philological Department of the Philosophy Faculty of Moscow University (1838). In 1844 he presented a master's thesis on Stefan Yavorsky and Feofan Prokopovich. In the 1850s and 1860s Samarin was directly involved in the preparations for and carrying out of the peasant reform (1861) and worked in *Zemstvo* institutions. He was undoubtedly the most active public and political figure among the Slavophiles, who energetically contributed to the drafting and implementing of bills to abolish serfdom and of a number of other reforms during the reign of Alexander II.

Samarin, who had been deeply influenced in his youth by Khomyakov's religious and philosophical ideas, strove to find a practical application for them in the changing social conditions of postreform Russia, which was inevitably taking a road of capitalist development. Being well conversant with the nuances of European political and intellectual affairs, he defended the originality of Slavophile social philosophy, seeing in it a reflection of the specific features of Russian social history:

> De Tocqueville, Montalembert, Riehl, and Stein are Western Slavophiles. They are all closer to us in their main convictions and their final requirements than to our Westerners. As with us, so too in France, England, and Germany, one question is in the foreground: is an autocratic sovereignty of reason legitimate in the system of the human soul, civil society, and the state? Has reason the right to smash and deform spiritual convictions, family and civil traditions—in short, to reform life in its own way? The tyranny of reason in the realm of philosophy, faith, and conscience corresponds in practice, in social life, to the tyranny of the central authorities. . . . Power relates to society as reason to the human soul. A legitimate feeling of tedium and satiety caused by the absolute power of reason and government underlies the aspirations of Montalembert, de Tocqueville, and *Russkaya beseda*.[32]

Samarin saw the difference between the "Western" and the "Russian" Slavophiles in their different social biases. The former were drawn to aristocracy and the latter to the common people.

By cutting off Russian Westerners ("Whigs") from the "folk roots," Samarin assigned to the Slavophiles, or Russian "Tories," the role of a social, cultural force struggling for an organic development of society and against the dead-end road of building an "abstract civilization." The traditional "Western" classification of social movements into liberals and conservatives, he admitted, was not suitable to Russian conditions. Samarin's approach was reasonably justified: in spite of its ideological kinship to Western "Toryism," Slavophilism struggled, as a social movement, primarily for liberal reforms in society. But the *narodnost* proclaimed by Samarin had aristocratic origin, and history showed that Russian "Tories" could not take "refuge in the peasant's hut" and in essence did not set themselves the task of radically altering the traditional social hierarchy established in society.

Samarin, who did much to abolish serfdom, was the leading Slavophile theorist on the peasant question. He advanced his own version of the origin of feudal serf relations in Russia. According to him, serfdom in Russia was a "terrible accident," a "secondary" result of administrative measures. He was convinced that its abolition would be in the national interest. "The people surrendered to the landowners' power out of hard necessity and under coercion, as Russia had once surrendered to the dominion of the Mongols in hope of future deliverance."[33] The peasant reform should correspondingly have a national character, which meant first and foremost (for him) retention and consolidation of the peasant commune. A sober, even pragmatic politician, Samarin was not inclined to absolutize the significance of the commune as a concrete form of social and economic life, considering that "this form cannot be everlasting, and should be changed through free development." In defending the commune he acted, first, in the spirit of the general organicism of the Slavophile philosophy of history (for the Slavophiles the commune was an organic outcome of Russian history), and he warned that if "we thoughtlessly shake it and willfully introduce the chaos of private property into it, we shall kill then the rural commune for good and all; because, once it is broken up into units, it will never be brought together again into a single whole."[34] Second, Samarin believed that the Christian idea of *sobornost* (the doctrine of which constituted an important element in the Slavophile philosophy of history) was embodied in the Russian peasant commune, though not in an absolute form.

When considering the religious significance of the Slavic commune, Samarin wrote that,

> The communal life of the Slavs is based on free and conscious repudiation of their sovereignty and not on absence of individuality. . . . Christianity

introduced consciousness and freedom into the everyday national life of the Slavs. . . . The Slavic commune, which had dissolved, as it were, assimilated the principle of spiritual communion and became the secular, historical side, as it were, of the Church. . . . The task of our domestic history is defined as enlightenment of the popular communal principle by a Church communal one.[35]

Samarin saw Orthodoxy as the decisive factor in the historical development of Russia and, although he did not entertain illusions about the level of "Christianization," not only of its highest but also of its lowest social strata (the peasantry), was nevertheless guided by the common Slavophile ideal of an "Orthodox, Christian" society. As a religious thinker he saw in the Russian commune not an absolute, but an essential step toward realization of this ideal; as a liberal reformer who feared revolutionary upheavals, and who upheld the liberal idea of uniting all the forces of society, he associated hopes of avoiding social antagonisms of a "Western" type with the commune. In 1849, shaken like all Slavophiles by the European revolutions, Samarin wrote to Khomyakov that "in the West, where the idea of personal property had been developed so exceptionally, there was no mean between endless dividing up of the land and the proletarianization. Doesn't the longed-for reconciliation consist in communal property?"[36]

In his reflections on the revolutionary events of 1848 Samarin clearly expressed the reformer essence and consistent antiradicalism of Slavophile thought. He demonstrated that the revolution had been not so much political as social, since the cause of the uprising had not been discontent with the form of government but the "too long unheeded demands" of the working people. While condemning the Parisian workers for "bloody disorders," Samarin noted at the same time the abnormality of their position, their sufferings and lack of rights. He thought the sole way that could help avoid revolutionary upheavals in the future was the road of reform, "sincere" recognition of the imperfection of social relations, and their resolute transformation by "legitimate procedure." He was guided by the same idea of class collaboration in the preparation of the peasant reform of 1861 when, in spite of his generally critical attitude to the sociopolitical role of the gentry, he took care to observe the interests of the landowners.

Samarin's political philosophy embraced the principles of monarchism and anticonstitutionalism, which was typical of Slavophile views. But he categorically rejected the idea of divine sanction extended to the institution of monarchy itself, or to any other forms of government: "The Savior and Apostles created the Church and gave mankind the teaching of man's relation to God. But they did not create state forms and did not write constitutions."[37]

While an advocate of absolute monarchy, Samarin was an active theorist and practical organizer of *Zemstvo* self-government. Like Ivan Aksakov, he considered that all the estates of Russia (gentry, clergy, merchants, lower middle classes, and peasants) should be united in the elective *Zemstvo* bodies and together get down to "socially useful activity." He threw doubt on the claims to "exclusiveness" of the landowning class, and showed the necessity of the *Zemstvos* as supraclass institutions representing the interests of the whole people. In his opinion equality of the estates in elections to the *Zemstvos* would lead to estate uniformity of postreform Russian society. While disputing with representatives of aristocratic constitutionalism, he argued that the "parliamentary game" could ultimately lead to the domination of an irresponsible aristocratic oligarchy, even more intense exploitation of the common people, and a strengthening of the existing centralization of power. There could not yet be a people's constitution in Russia, but a nonpopular constitution, which presupposed the domination of a minority acting without a mandate from the majority, was a lie and deception, he wrote, believing that Russia had had enough of "pseudo-progress and pseudo-enlightenment." He was cautious about aristocratic constitutionalism, but still more did he fear the claims of the other estates to political power: in the first place, those of the "uneducated peasantry," who did not possess elementary political culture and experience in civic activity and were alienated from the other strata of society by centuries of slavery.

Samarin's system of philosophical views, alongside his sociopolitical and philosophy-of-history conceptions, included ideas of philosophical anthropology he had developed under the direct influence of Khomyakov's philosophy of *sobornost* and Kireyevsky's theory of "integral knowledge." While continuing the Slavophile critique of rationalism, Samarin sharply politicized it and equated rationalism with the hateful (for him) revolution; the latter, he claimed, was "rationalism in action" turned into a "battering ram" against the freedom of real, everyday life. Only philosophy was able to defend "real, everyday life" as a counterweight to rationalism, for, according to him, only philosophy reminded man that "full and supreme truth was attainable not through a capacity for logical speculation alone but through mind, feeling, and will put together, i.e., through the spirit in its living wholeness."[38] Rationalism and individualism were inseparable and presupposed one another. Samarin sharply criticized the "impotence" and "bankruptcy" of individualism. Christian philosophy, he argued, led to the overcoming of individualism and to free renunciation of closed, egoistic essence. Genuine development of the personality presupposed religious experience and was simply impossible without it. Individualistic rationalism split up social life and deprived it of its "absolute" unity and hence of any sense: "Only an artificial association can be based . . . on the individual, who regards himself the absolute measure of everything . . . but the absolute norm or law obligatory for each and everyone cannot be deduced from the individual by logic, and history cannot do it either."[39]

Samarin defined achievement of the wholeness of the spirit that was absent in history and individual life as the most important goal, realization of which depended wholly on consistency and fidelity to religious and moral guidelines. Just like Kireyevsky, he stressed the exceptional traditionality of his views, even stating that their essence was "ultimately reducible to the Christian catechism."

Though an ardent admirer of Hegel in his youth, Samarin later made rationalist idealism responsible for the "renaissance of materialism in the second half of the nineteenth century," since "materialism, according to the general law of logical retribution, . . . without going beyond the system of concepts of Hegelian philosophy, found justification of the self-essence of matter in the same law of necessity, only of material rather than logical necessity."[40] As a consistent opponent of any form of materialism, he saw in it the result of "abstract" philosophical idealism and not at all of natural science.

The development of capitalism in Russia, which was gaining momentum after the abolition of serfdom in 1861, inevitably put an end to the discussion in which the radical democrats and the Slavophiles had been engaged for several decades. Other trends of social thought took the place of Slavophilism and Westernism, among them populism, Marxism, and liberalism of the constitutional democrats.

But the clash of the Slavophile and Westernist ideals was by no means a mechanical reflection of the processes of Russian history, and not for them an ideological makeweight that automatically sank into oblivion together with the social relations that had given rise to it. The Slavophile philosophy was an element of Russian intellectual life of the nineteenth century, and at the same time an important and necessary stage of its development, without knowledge of which it is impossible to comprehend the complex, contradictory course of the self-determination of the Russian national cultural tradition. The sociopolitical theory of the Slavophiles, their philosophy of history, theory of culture, and anthropological philosophical conception, all this—to use the words of Belinsky—reflected "Russian society's need for independent development," and, one might add, contributed to the molding of the inimitable image of nineteenth-century Russian culture.

NOTES

1. V. G. Belinsky, *Polnoye sobraniye sochineniy* (Complete works) (Moscow, 1956), vol. 10, p. 264.

2. A. S. Khomyakov, *Polnoye sobraniye sochineniy* (Complete works), 8 vols., 3rd ed. (Moscow, 1900), vol. 3, p. 15.

3. Ibid., p. 29.

4. Ibid., pp. 281–82.

5. Ibid., vol. 5, p. 8.

6. Ibid., vol. 1, p. 25.

7. Ibid., p. 354.

8. Ibid., vol. 8, p. 362.

9. I. V. Kireyevsky, *On the Necessity and Possibility of New Principles in Philosophy,* in *Russian Philosophy,* ed. James M. Edie et al. (Chicago: Quadrangle Books, 1965), p. 181.

10. Ibid., p. 182.

11. Ibid.

12. Ibid., p. 196.

13. Ibid., p. 212.

14. Ibid., p. 207.

15. Ibid., p. 206.

16. Ibid.

17. Ibid., p. 213.

18. Ibid., p. 199.

19. Ibid., pp. 189–95.

20. Ibid., p. 189.

21. Ibid.

22. I. V. Kireyevsky, *Izbrannye statyi* (Selected articles) (Moscow, 1984), p. 126.

23. Ibid., p. 238.

24. I. V. Kireyevsky, *Necessity and Possibility of New Principles,* pp. 191–92.

25. K. S. Aksakov, "On the Internal State of Russia," in *Ranniye slavyanofily A. S. Khomyakov, I. V. Kireyevsky, K. S. i I. S. Aksakov (The Early Slavophiles: A. S. Khomyakov, I. V. Kireyevsky, and K. S. and I. S. Aksakov)* (Moscow, 1910), p. 78.

26. K. S. Aksakov, *Polnoye sobraniye sochineniy* (Complete works), 3 vols. (Moscow, 1861), vol. 1, p. 296.

27. Ibid., p. 511.

28. Ibid., vol. 2, p. 4.

29. I. S. Aksakov, *Polnoye sobraniye sochineniy* (Complete works), 7 vols., 2d ed. (St. Petersburg, 1891), vol. 2, p. 19.

30. Ibid., vol. 4, p. 86.

31. Ibid., p. 153.

32. Yu. F. Samarin, *Sochineniya* (Works), 12 vols. (Moscow, 1877–1911), vol. 1, pp. 384–95.

33. Ibid., vol. 2, p. 28.

34. Ibid., p. 71.

35. Ibid., vol. 1, pp. 63–64.

36. Ibid., p. 431.

37. Ibid., vol. 6, p. 557.

38. Ibid., p. 561.

39. Ibid., vol. 1, p. 41.

40. Ibid., p. 273.

10

The Philosophy of "Official *Narodnost*" and "Russian Theism"

Vitaly Bogatov

The 1840s were a period of self-determination of the various social forces of Russian society. The radical-democratic trend arose in those years, nascent Russian liberalism formed its principles, and the conservative outlook was modernized. The latter was most clearly expressed in the spread of the so-called theory of official *narodnost* (national character), which found philosophical substantiation in the works of theists.

This doctrine, as a system of views supporting the policy of preserving monarchy, on the social plane was a reaction to the Decembrist uprising and to the political events in Western Europe and a reaction to the spread of radical philosophical and scientific notions in the country. "Official *narodnost*" was an attempt to isolate Russia from the intellectual life of the West, to hold back Russia's historical advance, and to justify social and intellectual conservatism.

SERGEI UVAROV

One of the adherents to the theory of "official *narodnost*," Count Sergei Uvarov (1786–1855) held the high posts of president of the Academy of Sciences and minister of public education. Having put forward a triad formula that public education should be carried on "in a combined spirit of Orthodoxy, autocracy, and *narodnost*," he endeavored to integrate the religious, political, and ethical components of Russian culture into a single whole, seeing in it a social-psychological, moral, and emotional state in which loyalty to the monarch and deep religiosity were inherent. These features that, in his opinion, were essentially characteristic of the consciousness of the Russian people, were the foundation of the monarchist state, and consequently gave it stability.

As a dignitary and proponent of monarchy, Uvarov fostered the spread and consolidation in society of conservative political ideas. He waged a constant battle against democratic and radical ideas in philosophy and literature.

He did not formulate any system or even advance a total of philosophical views; his role was political. But the formula Uvarov proclaimed as the basis of the theory of "official *narodnost*" was developed by Mikhail Pogodin and Archimandrite Gavriil.

MIKHAIL POGODIN

The historian and publicist Mikhail Pogodin (1800–1875) was a leading theorist and advocate of the official conservative ideology. The son of a serf peasant who had been set free, he graduated from grammar school and then from Moscow University. He joined the Wisdom Lovers Society and from 1831 was a member of the academy. He was influenced by Karamzin, Schlözer, and Schelling. He was actively involved in publishing the journal *Moskvityanin* (*The Muscovite*). From the early 1850s he was engaged in publicist activity. Pogodin made a certain contribution to historical science; he gathered together extensive documents on the early period of Russian history and published several chronicles. His writings were mainly directed to the defense of the autocratic feudal system. His main aim was to substantiate historically the doctrine of "official *narodnost*"; for that he considered it necessary, from the methodological standpoint, to employ the ideas of the idealist philosophy of modern times, in particular Schellingianism. He fought bitterly against materialism and Darwinism and criticized positivism "from the right."

A characteristic feature of Pogodin's historical and sociological methodology was formalism. While paying lip service to natural science, he frequently drew analogies between the facts of history and phenomena of nature, endeavoring to give his conclusions a scientific appearance. He called this ploy a mathematical method intended "to eliminate harmful misconceptions." He saw the task of science and philosophy as "discovering the eternal laws of wisdom." But history, according to his reasoning, was unknowable in the scientific sense, since it was basically irrational, "the ways of Providence and of history are inscrutable."

While the nature created by God was governed by the laws of mechanics, the events of public affairs were not so obvious and could only be explained from the position of religion. "Providence and the guiding hand" were the starting point of Pogodin's views on social and historical development. The aim of the historian and sociologist was to comprehend "laws," but to do that, it was necessary to "sense God." The scholar's supreme task, consequently, was not to understand the destiny of people but to see "God's design" in them.

Pogodin rejected progress as natural, historical movement, denied the principle of a qualitative renewal of society, and took a stand for the circularity of history. He wrote frankly that "dilapidated, ramshackle forms are revived and continually begin a new life in history."[1] He did not accept social struggle either, preferring the idea of universal unity, which he associated mainly with unity of the state and the people—the most important categories of his sociology.

The state consisted of the government and the people. Pogodin regarded the people as such as a faceless, passive, and conservative mass, the background on which and for whose sake rulers acted. He supplemented his reactionary, essentially statist, bureaucratic theses about the passivity of the masses with the idea about the active role of the monarchical state. The monarch's activity was nourished by his link with God and therefore coincided with the "general laws." The "laws" received by mankind and the monarch's will were essentially one, and their unity was most obviously and fundamentally embodied in religion. That was why Pogodin believed that all the causes of human activity went back to a single source—to the "moral world," a synonym of religion in terms of the ideology of "official *narodnost.*" The true revolutionary in Russia was allegedly the monarch (for example, Peter the Great), and the people were the personification of the conservative principle in history.

Pogodin affirmed the idea of the impossibility of establishing real causes and effects in public affairs since, following his logic, every event in human life was unique because of the uniqueness of creative "divine Providence." "Providence" was a universal necessity, divine predetermination in humanity. The "upper," "top" sociohistorical phenomena were linked with it. The activity of mortal people, endowed with free will, constituted the second, "lower" order. People's individual free actions were offset by the "general law," by universal necessity, and by God. While Pogodin did not provide a rational answer of any kind to the question of the dialectic of necessity and freedom, he declared this interaction a mystery of history. As a social philosopher he often reasoned in the spirit of irrationalism and subjectivism. In his *Historical Aphorisms* (*Istoricheskiye aforizmy*), for instance, he expressed a conviction that it was impossible to know the real causes of events and supposed that "history can only be felt." "Events are hieroglyphs for us whose secret meaning we cannot fathom, and only external patterns of them attract us."[2] His final conclusion was very typical: the events of human history were dead if the researcher did not breathe his soul into them: a personal, subjective interpretation of history was thus the only true version.

The starting point of Pogodin's social-philosophical conception with regard to Russia was a contraposing of West European and Russian history. When substantiating the theory of the special "principles" of Russian history, he singled out three sets of attributes that distinguished Russia from the West: the historical, physical, and moral.

The historical tradition attested that while states had been formed in the West through forcible conquest, the Varangians were invited to Russia, this being an "amicable deal." That circumstance had put on Russian history the stamp of a special agreement and mutual understanding between all strata of society and had determined the course of its development right down to the nineteenth century. This specific made it possible to escape the tragic "trilogy" of the Western European world: the development of capitalism, class struggle, and lack of clear perspectives in public affairs.

The second feature of Russia—the physical—consisted in her unique natural conditions, which diverted Slavs from social matters and ruled out "all sorts of clashes and dissensions."

The third difference, the moral one—which included the character of the people, religion, and education—had a fundamental significance, according to Pogodin, for the distinctive "principles" of Russian life.

In his description of its moral distinguishing features Pogodin passed from history to the sphere of religious ethics. The Slavs, he said, as a northern, calm, quiet, and patient people, accepted the Varangians readily and without a murmur. He declared these features of the national character to be inborn and invariable, almost metaphysical: "We are the same in the nineteenth century as in the ninth."[3] He put forward this speculative doctrine about the moral qualities of the Russian people being conditioned by the natural environment itself, quite unsupported by any scientific data, as proof of the nonrevolutionary nature of the Slavs, turning revolution from a social problem into an ethnic one.

Pogodin treated the Orthodox religion as the inner essence of Russian statehood, which lent moral strength to the monarchy through its mystic link with God. The czar, moreover, who possessed absolute power over the masses of the people, was a kind of mediator. Pogodin ascribed a special sense of religiosity to the Russian people, which had to be consolidated and developed by religious and moral education. He therefore advocated broad dissemination of books with a religious content among the people.

The "historical," "physical," and "moral" distinctive features of Russian history constituted the "tradition" that determined not only the past but also the present and future of Russia, in Pogodin's opinion, and was the source and content of her social being. Permeated with antihistoricism and conservatism, his calls to re-establish the truly Russian "principles" meant a striving to restore the past, and an attempt to slow down progressive development of the country and to preserve the privileges of the ruling class. The Western world, unlike Russia, was full of contradictions and class clashes. Pogodin sensed a formidable force in the working class of Western Europe and was seriously worried that the revolutionary "poison had already begun to overwhelm the countryside in the West." The struggle of the Parisian Communards evoked a particularly negative reaction on his part. Seeing salvation in the monarchy's "rule with a rod of iron," he welcomed Thiers's reprisals against the workers.

In spite of the utopianism and unscientific character of his general historical views, Pogodin, being a consistent conservative, expressed a number of sober ideas. In drawing attention to the "bloody character" of West European history, he argued that there were no real grounds in Russia for proletarian class struggle. But he understood that any revolution was caused by the history of the country where it happened. Revolutions were not exported and each one took place in its own locale from its own causes. Imitations always came to nought. In that connection he was compelled to recognize the revolutionary potential of the "boorish muzhik" and the existence of a revolutionary "seed" in Russian society. "Mirabeau did not terrify us," he wrote, "but Yemelka Pugachev did. Ledru-Rollin and all the communists would not find admirers among us, but any village would gape in astonishment at Nikita Pustosvyat."[4]

Fear of peasant uprising caused Pogodin's deep dislike of radical ideas in Russia, of their proponents and theorists—the revolutionary democrats of the 1840s to 1870s.

STEPAN SHEVYREV

Pogodin's closest ally was the professor of literature Stepan Shevyrev (1806–1864). A nobleman by birth, Shevyrev had joined the Wisdom Lovers Society in his youth and had been influenced by the German idealist romantics. He was head of the Department of Criticism of the journal *Moskvityanin* and struggled against the ideas of Belinsky and the "natural school" in Russian literature. He spent his last years abroad, living in Italy and France, and was buried in Paris.

As an idealist mystic and advocate of theism, Shevyrev set himself the task of reconciling philosophy and religion. He rejected Hegel's philosophical system because of its inadequate religiosity and the "squabble" between spirit and nature, declaring dialectics a "trick of human thought." He rejected the materialist tradition in the history of philosophy on the grounds that materialism, in contrast to religion, was an egoistic persuasion. He opposed ideas of historical progress.

Shevyrev declared knowledge spiritualized by the religion of Orthodoxy to be universal. Science was needed only as a manifestation of a nation's "rational consciousness." The science of sciences was religion, in the context of which the subordination of the sciences was established, and also universal social harmony, which in turn served as the highest criterion of a worthy life and correct knowledge. In the interests of religion, he disparaged science and natural forms of personal and social existence, criticized any realistic world outlook, and attacked the materialism of Belinsky and Herzen particularly sharply.

Shevyrev was a metaphysician who denied real development and qualitative changes, and who rejected the dialectic of contradictions. While drawing his argumentation mainly from Scripture, he asserted that the concept of polarity "was completely contrary to Christian philosophy." His philosophical ideas did not, on the whole, go beyond the theistic notions of the first half of the nineteenth century.

Shevyrev was not especially interested in analyzing sociophilosophical questions, but he wrote much about the past, present, and future of Russian society. His philosophy of Russian history differed little from Pogodin's views. He saw autocratic Russia's mission as first of all to maintain her monarchical originality, and to ensure the universal victory of Orthodoxy. In his view Russia was "the kernel of the future development of mankind," and it was necessary for this kernel to put out shoots, to "hold out against Europe," which was "dying" and becoming a "corpse." He saw the decline of Europe in the West's loss of religiosity, no small part of the blame for which he put on the Encyclopedists, "who had plunged into the exclusiveness of reason." Unlike Pogodin, however, he made concessions to the spirit of the times. At the end of the 1840s he passed from complete denial of the Western "principle" and the idea of Russia's absolute uniqueness to recognition even to the role of the former as the second element needed to develop the Russian "principles" of the new epoch. True, he took an interest primarily in the experience of the ruling upper classes of Western Europe in their struggle against the revolutionary strivings of the masses, i.e., in everything that could further maintain and consolidate the autocracy.

Shevyrev paid main attention in his works to questions of esthetics and literary criticism. Basing his understanding of the subject matter of art on the Platonic definition of the beautiful as including the divine element, he contraposed art to life and saw a force in religion that ensured harmony of man's inner life. He banished any vital content from the "fine" and narrowed the genre diversity of art. He was an opponent of the realist trend in Russian literature; his literary criticism diluted the social content of Fonvizin's comedies, Krylov's fables, and the works of Griboyedov and Gogol. "True" art, in his opinion, had no connection with real life.

The central point of Shevyrev's attacks on Belinsky's esthetic theory was the principle of *narodnost*, which he interpreted in the spirit of the official ideology as an aggregate of all the intellectual and "physical forces given by Providence to any nation so as to realize its human purpose on earth."[5] While mystifying the category of *narodnost*, he called on writers to turn to religious themes and, in the light of them, to the past. In trying to weaken the high sociocritical spirit of progressive Russian literature, he accused it of a "one-sided" illumination of reality incompatible with artistry and insisted that art should reflect the "dark and bright sides of life" and so confirm the idea of the harmony of good and evil. Shevyrev declared that politics and art had no inner, indivisible link of any kind, that political trends were harmful to art, while true freedom of creation excluded any bias or partiality. From these positions he rejected the work of Herzen, Turgenev, Nekrasov, Dostoyevsky, Hugo, Balzac, and others.

But Shevyrev's "indifference to politics" turned into open politicking as soon as he had formulated the "positive" role of literature; since society was "tainted" and "irritated" by political troubles, it needed "soothing, reassuring spectacles" rather than new irritants that could only strengthen opposition tendencies, and literature should provide such spectacles. The aim of realism to depict reality in an all-round and objective way was "false," he declared, because "it is not reality that constitutes the achievement of art but the profundity of the artist who embraces that reality."[6] In contraposing the artist's reality, Shevyrev gave preference to the religious, spiritual world of the creative individual. He interpreted the creative process like an intuitionist, as an unconscious "choosing of the subject" and its depiction, and considered creative fantasy to be the result of religious illumination.

Shevyrev formulated several theses in this struggle against realist art that were subsequently employed by opponents of the principles of radical-democratic esthetics. He saw the bankruptcy of "St. Petersburg literature" in its realism, humanism, and social character. While understanding the strong aspects of realism, he nevertheless declared it a sign of the decline of Russian literature. In the end, however, he was compelled to admit that his main disagreement with the representatives of critical realism lay in the ideological and political sphere.

Shevyrev's literary critical positions were aimed against radical-democratic esthetics. While distinguishing between, or rather divorcing, the historical and esthetic in a literary work, he argued that literature was interesting in both its external value, i.e., its link with the spirit of the times, and its inner value, i.e., its artistic qualities. The esthetic element in art had a self-sufficing significance for him; the value of artistic works was consequently not determined by their link with real life. It was therefore esthetic rather than historical criticism that was called upon to "bring true benefit to the education of its people and fatherland." Shevyrev the critic strove to suppress the "historical" and social works of art by the "esthetic." But on that path he arrived at a contraposition of form and content in art that did not, incidentally, prevent him from defending the unity of the historical and esthetic when the "historical" was interpreted in the spirit of Uvarov's triad of Orthodoxy, autocracy, and *narodnost.*

RUSSIAN THEISM OF THE 1830S AND 1840S

Mystical, religious philosophy had a leading place in the system of conservative philosophies. Spokesmen for this philosophy tried to unite religion and philosophical idealism in order to renew traditional Orthodox conceptions, and to subordinate philosophy and science to theology. Theistic philosophy was contraposed to rationalism and especially to materialism, tried to substantiate the unity of reason and faith, and spoke of the powerlessness of the human mind to cognize truth without the "illuminating light" of revelation. Theism's main internal task was to protect the vitality of Church dogma, which saw a danger to itself in natural science, materialism, and, to some extent, in German classical idealism.

The Russian theistic literature of the first half of the nineteenth century drew primarily on a legacy of the Eastern Church Fathers; the West European mysticism of Boehme, Jacobi, and Baader; and certain propositions of the idealist philosophy of Plato, Kant, Hegel, and Schelling, interpreted in an Orthodox-mystical spirit. The theists, in Chernyshevsky's apt phrase, were trying to be philosophers but were afraid of not being also faithful to Orthodox Christians.

FYODOR GOLUBINSKY

Fyodor Golubinsky (1797–1854), a professor of the Moscow Theological Academy and an eminent exponent of theism in Russia, set himself the tasks of giving a metaphysical proof of the role of revelation in knowledge, and of substantiating religion by sanctifying it by philosophical knowledge.

His philosophy was a systematic attempt to employ science and reason to prove the truthfulness of religion. He used the term "philosophy" in two senses: as a striving for knowledge and wisdom, and as "initiation," i.e., science and knowledge. According to him the possibility of philosophy was rooted in man's innate love of wisdom and striving to God; philosophy was therefore knowledge of God. He declared that thinking is a formal principle, empty and lacking in content without the idea of God. The unity of God and man was realized in man's reason. Reason so interpreted absorbed and contained all external nature, because the supreme manifestation of reason was faith in being of the infinite. Golubinsky developed an idea of "inner and external experience," giving preference to the inner one that, in his words, "directly expressed divine perfections in itself." At the same time, insofar as external nature was devoid of all these perfections, "external experience" was empty, lacking in content and point. Golubinsky did not conceal his religious, mystical aspirations, declaring that the "practical aim of metaphysics was to make spirit, heart, and will of man communicate with God."

Golubinsky singled out four systems in the history of philosophy: materialism, idealism, pantheism, and theism. He was profoundly critical of the first three and criticized materialism particularly sharply as the lowest form of philosophizing, which he said could not comprehend the sphere of the spiritual. In that way he strove to refute the atomism, atheism, and anthropologism of materialist philosophy, and the evolutionary theory of development, as false doctrines incompatible with the religious world outlook.

FYODOR SIDONSKY

Fyodor Sidonsky's substantiation of theistic philosophy was not so straightforward. Sidonsky (1805–1873) was initially a professor of the St. Petersburg Theological Academy. Subsequently, from 1864, he was the chair of philosophy, and, in his last years, the chair of theology, in St. Petersburg University.

In his *Introduction to the Science of Philosophy* (*Vvedeniye v nauku filosofii*) he not only formulated the principles of philosophical theism but also, though timidly, defended philosophy's right to truth not reducible to the truths of theology. The book caused a great stir in its day, and its author was even expelled from the Theological Academy.

Sidonsky demonstrated the necessity of philosophy alongside theology, posing the question of an adequately rational foundation for the truths of religion.

His argument was centered on the problem of man and reason. He was interested in whether truth was accessible to man. The history of philosophy, he said, made it possible to give a positive answer: knowledge was a process of endless approximation to the truth, which was the "fruit of the age-old efforts of all mankind." Our knowledge grew and was perfected like social life, and "true" philosophy was emerging on the basis of the "true" Orthodox religion.

Sidonsky did not deny the role of sensation and experience in cognition, but, like Golubinsky, he did not include them in the subject matter of the analysis of philosophy. By linking the sensory and empirical levels of knowledge with the new sciences of nature, he thereby denied natural science the right to penetrate to the essence of things, reducing scientific knowledge to knowledge of phenomena and empirical facts.

At the same time he considered knowledge of nature as knowledge of the "source of all being," i.e., God. His idea of knowledge of God through knowledge of the world as endless material diversity was evidence of his certain pantheistic tendencies, and of tendencies to dissolve God in nature, which did not correspond on the whole to orthodox notions of the transcendent. He claimed, moreover, that philosophy, as a science, was no freer in its striving for truth than physics, because it depended on nature itself, and experienced the "always-needed guidance of Mother Nature." While relying on the concepts of nature, life, reason, and trust, Sidonsky interpreted them, however, in the spirit of rationalized mysticism, rationally interpreted knowledge of God.

Philosophy should be characterized by doubt as a means of affirmation and not negation of truth; "philosophy cannot prosper otherwise than hand in hand with the advances of the natural sciences." According to Sidonsky, although philosophy and faith were compatible, "the field of human thoughts was by no means limited to faith," because it would lead otherwise to "mental slavery," while "the authority of religion was still subject to confirmation." Philosophy, and not religion, was universal knowledge.[7]

But the certain contradictoriness of Sidonsky's views, and his endeavor to separate philosophy from religion and reason from faith, were sublated when he agreed in the last analysis that philosophy and religion followed different paths but had one goal, i.e., attainment of divine truth. He classed faith in the field of the emotions, devoid of rationalistic foundations; faith "only helps reason but does not create it." In contrast to religion philosophy was a necessary and natural product of our rationality; it took nothing on trust but tested everything by reason. When opposing Kant, Sidonsky declared: "Nothing in thought is the result of the pure work of mind alone, but is at the same time the result partly of experience."[8]

Sidonsky was the first to put forward the idea that Russian theistic philosophy was called upon to be the concluding stage in the development of world philosophical thought. Archimandrite Gavriil developed this idea. He regarded philosophy as one of the ideological bastions of the monarchical feudal system, meant to prevent the revolution's coming from the West. "Restless minds do not belong to philosophy," he wrote. Philosophy could not "approve of convulsive revolutions to renew the state machine."[9] In spite of his conservative philosophical views, Sidonsky was a philosopher attracted to a rationalism of an idealist hue, who tried to defend the duality of truth and the right of philosophy to real knowledge. That was evidence of the fact that objective development of natural science and philosophy put a stamp of rationalism on the world outlook of thinkers who saw their calling in the struggle against science, materialism, and ideas of the unlimited possibilities of reason.

VASSILY KARPOV

Vassily Karpov (1798–1867), professor of philosophy in the St. Petersburg Theological Academy, developed a version of theistic philosophy that should rank above materialism and idealism. These ideas were set forth in his *Introduction to Philosophy* (*Vvedeniye v filosofiyu*) and *Systematic Exposition of Logic* (*Sistematicheskoye izlozheniye logiki*). He was actively involved in the philosophical struggle in the 1860s, opposing the philosophical materialism of Chernyshevsky, Sechenov, and other radical democrats and natural scientists. Between 1863 and 1879 six volumes of the works of Plato were published in Russian translation by Karpov.

The philosophical principles that Karpov defended were in the general stream of the theism of the 1830s to the 1850s. He was one of the major adherents of Plato's philosophy in Russia. At the same time Karpov's treatment of problems of knowledge and logic contained serious admixtures of Kantianism. He called his philosophy "transcendental synthesis" or "synthetism," and declared philosophy to be a sphere that embraced nature and science in man's consciousness, and through it ensured subordination of everything that exists to theology. His synthesis was meant to unite doctrines of nature, man, and God, and to bring them into "perfect harmony."

Karpov paid predominant attention to questions of man's mental ("spiritual") life. At the center of his research was "self-knowledge and investigation of everything as a whole," and the "subject-object" problem that he interpreted broadly as a question of the unity of nature and God as conceivable and supersensory.

In Karpov's opinion philosophical knowledge was extraexperiential and was the result of "direct contemplation of truth in keeping with the nature of the mind." Such knowledge was derived through the "systematic" method. The foundation of knowledge was the "subjective sphere" ascending to the transcendental, because the idea of God lay in the "very nature of man" and led him to truth and the good.

While affirming that consciousness was the origin of both knowledge and being, Karpov called this beginning "formally real." From a position of recognition of the "realist" element in knowledge, he accused Kant of formalizing human consciousness and of neglecting the real, which was associated, for Karpov, with proof of the decisive role of God (the suprareal) in knowledge. Hegel's philosophical system also did not wholly satisfy him, since no convincing synthesis of the formal and the real was provided in it. Karpov's "synthetic philosophy" was meant to provide this synthesis.

Karpov regarded theistic philosophy as the antithesis of the "personal" philosophy of materialists and idealists, which led to "dissolution of social bonds." "Philosophy is needed so that everybody thought by the common mind . . . aspired to common truth and achieved a common goal."[10] Philosophy was a universal normative sphere of intellectual activity intended to strengthen ties between heaven and earth.

Karpov stressed the need to evolve an Orthodox philosophical system that would accord with the "laws of faith and conditions of Russian life," i.e., a system that would follow the stream of a conservative ideology, and "by acting in man's consciousness and holding the middle between Religion and Politics would give a hand to both."[11]

ARCHIMANDRITE GAVRIIL

The tasks of creating a system of theism called for a review of the traditional schemes of the history of philosophy from its followers. The six-part *History of Philosophy* (*Istoriya filosofii* [1839-1840]) by Archimandrite Gavriil (V. N. Voskresensky, 1795-1868), a professor of the Kazan Theological Academy, derives most interest from a description of the religious, Orthodox interpetation of the history of philosophy.

This book was the first original, systematic work in Russia on the history of philosophy. World philosophical thought was examined in it from the standpoint of Orthodox theology. Gavriil reviewed the then-known conceptions of the history of philosophy of Tiedemann, Buhle, and Ritter and rejected them as unacceptable.

Gavriil divided the history of mankind into two periods: "The age of inspiration" (the dominion of instinct) and "the age of philosophy" (the dominion of reason). But both of these ages were inspired by religion, which governed science and philosophy. In treating theology as a special, supreme philosophy, Gavriil came to a conclusion of the collapse of all preceding philosophical thought. Furthermore, he considered that mankind had not yet created a "full philosophical system," a task that could only be solved from the standpoint of the Christian world outlook. He pointed out that there were four main currents in philosophy: sensualism (materialism), idealism, skepticism, and mysticism, which were based in a one-sided way on one of the faculties of man's soul, but did not embrace it as a whole. While censuring the struggle of philosophical ideas, Gavriil endeavored to reconcile all these currents through faith, although materialism and atomism were a special object of his criticism.

Gavriil employed certain propositions of idealist philosophy in order to substantiate his synthetic theism. In his opinion the philosophy of the future, i.e., theology as a philosophical "limitless cosmorama," could borrow "universal concepts" from idealism adapting them to the "biblical principles."

Gavriil was one of the first to pose the question of the need to write a history of Russian philosophy. But being a proponent of the dominant religious ideology, he could not give any other conception of the history of Russian philosophy than one with a Christian orientation. He deduced theistic philosophy directly from the mystical and, at the same time, national features of thought ascribed to the Russian people. He declared theism to be a synthetic philosophy closely linked with the practical life of Russian society. It "has long belonged to a great and strong people who, considering rationalism correlated with experience to be the cornerstone of philosophizing, completed this temple of wisdom by a radiant dome, as it were, by revelation and the substance of allies, viz., the concept of God."[12]

Gavriil's conception of the history of philosophy pursued the aim of laying seemingly unscientific foundations under the ideological principles of the theory and policy of "official *narodnost.*"

Theistic ideas were developed further in the works of Orest Novitsky, Silvestr Gogotsky, and Pamfil Yurkevich, and found their completion in the works of Vladimir Soloviev and his successors, spokesmen of the "new religious consciousness" or "God-seeking."

NOTES

1. M. P. Pogodin, "Reply to My Reviewers," *Moskvityanin,* no. 3 (1847): 88.

2. M. P. Pogodin, *Istoricheskiye aforizmy* (*Historical Aphorisms*) (Moscow, 1836), pp. 29, 63.

3. M. P. Pogodin, *Drevnyaya russkaya istoriya do mongolskogo iga* (*Russian Ancient History Before the Mongol Yoke*) (Moscow, 1872), p. 153.

4. M. P. Pogodin, *Istoriko-politicheskiye pisma* (*Historical and Political Letters*) (Moscow, 1874), p. 262.

5. S. P. Shevyrev, *Istoriya russkoi slovesnosti* (*History of Russian Literature*) (Moscow, 1859), pt. 1, p. 7.

6. *Moskvityanin,* no. 2 (1846): 183.

7. F. F. Sidonsky, *Vvedeniye v nauku filosofii* (*Introduction to the Science of Philosophy*) (St. Petersburg, 1883), pp. 150, 179, 180.

8. Ibid., p. 192.

9. Ibid., p. 319.

10. V. N. Karpov, *Vvedeniye v filosofiyu* (*Introduction to Philosophy*) (St. Petersburg, 1840), p. 109.

11. Ibid., pp. 110–11.

12. Gavriil, *Istoriya filosofii* (*History of Philosophy*) (St. Petersburg, 1839), pt. 6, p. 23.

11

Pyotr Yakovlevich Chaadayev
(1794–1856)

The 1830s and 1840s were the crossroads of Russian thought—the time when its major trends were born: liberal-conservative Slavophilism (Ivan Kireyevsky, Alexei Khomyakov, et al.), radical democracy (Vissarion Belinsky, Alexander Herzen, et al.), right-wing conservatism or so-called "official narodnost*" with its idea-slogan "Orthodoxy, Autocracy, Nationalism" (Sergei Uvarov, Mikhail Pogodin, et al.).*

Chaadayev's Philosophical Letters, *parts of which are reprinted below, could be seen as a starting point for this process of differentiation among Russian intellectuals. Implicitly the* Letters *initiated discussion of a set of acute and most controversial problems of Russian philosophy of the nineteenth century: the character of the Russian style of thinking; the historical, cultural, and political identity of Russia; her attitude toward the West; and her place within a world community.*

PHILOSOPHICAL LETTERS*

Letter I

Adveniat regnum tuum

A certain portion of man's life pertains not to his physical, but to his mental existence. You must not neglect it. There is a mode of behavior imposed

*From *Russian Philosophy,* Volume 1, edited by James M. Edie, James P. Scanlan, Mary-Barbara Zeldin, with the collaboration of George L. Kline. Copyright © 1976. Translated by Mary-Barbara Zeldin. Reprinted by permission of the University of Tennessee Press.

on the soul just as there is on the body: man must learn to submit to it. This is an old truth, I know; but it seems to me that in our country it still has the value of novelty. One of the worst features of our peculiar civilization is that we have not yet discovered truths that have elsewhere become truisms, even among nations that in many respects are far less advanced than we are. It is the result of our never having walked hand in hand with other nations; we belong to none of the great families of mankind; we are neither of the West nor of the East, and we possess the traditions of neither. Somehow divorced from time and space, the universal education of mankind has not touched upon us. . . .

Every nation has its period of stormy agitation, of passionate unease, of hasty activities. In such a period men become wanderers over the world, both in body and spirit. This is an epoch of strong emotions, great undertakings, great national passions. At such times nations toss about violently, without any apparent object, but not without benefit for future generations. All communities have gone through such a phase. Such a period provides them with their most vivid memories, their legends, their poetry, their greatest and most productive ideas; such a period represents the necessary basis of every society. Otherwise, they would have nothing valuable or cherished in memories; they would cherish only the dust of the earth they inhabit. This fascinating phase of the history of nations represents their adolescence, the age when their faculties develop most vigorously, and whose remembrance brings both joy and wisdom to their maturity. But we Russians, we are devoid of all this. At first brutal barbarism, then crude superstition, then cruel and humiliating foreign domination, the spirit of which was later inherited by our national rulers—such is the sad history of our youth. We had none of that period of exuberant activity, of the fervent turmoil of the moral forces of nations. Our period of social life which corresponds to this age was filled with a dull and gloomy existence, lacking in force and energy, with nothing to brighten it but crime, nothing to mitigate it but servitude. There are no charming remembrances, no graceful images in the people's memory; our national tradition is devoid of any powerful teaching. Cast a look upon the many centuries in our past, upon the expanse of soil we inhabit, and you will find no endearing reminiscence, no venerable memorial, to speak to you powerfully of the past and to reproduce it for you in a vivid and colorful manner. We live only in the narrowest of presents, without past and without future, in the midst of a flat calm. And if we happen to bestir ourselves from time to time, it is not in the hope, nor in the desire, of some common good, but in the childish frivolousness of the infant, who raises himself and stretches his hands toward the rattle which his nurse presents to him.

So long as life has not become more regulated, more easy, more gentle than in the midst of the uncertainties of its earlier age, the true development of mankind in society has not yet begun. So long as societies waver about without convictions and without rules even for daily life, so long as that life has no form, how can the seeds of good ripen in them? This is the state of chaotic fermentation of the things of the moral world, similar to the revolutions of the earth which preceded the present state of our planet. We are still at that stage.

Our first years, spent in immobile brutishness, have left no traces on our minds, we have nothing that is ours on which to base our thinking; moreover, isolated by a fate unknown to the universal development of humanity, we have absorbed none of mankind's ideas of traditional transmission. Yet it is on those ideas that the life of nations is founded; it is from those ideas that their future develops and that their moral growth derives. If we want to have an outlook similar to that of other civilized nations, we have somehow to repeat the whole education of mankind. In this we can be assisted by the history of other nations, and we have before us the products of the ages. No doubt this task is difficult, and possibly it is not given to one man to exhaust this vast subject; but, first of all, we must know what we are talking about, what is this education of mankind, and what is the place which we occupy in the general order of things.

Nations live but by the mighty impressions which past centuries have left in their minds and by contact with other peoples. In this way every man is conscious of his ties with the whole of mankind. What is the life of man, Cicero asked, if the memory of past events does not come to bind the present to the past? But we Russians, like illegitimate children, come to this world without patrimony, without any links with people who lived on the earth before us. We have in our hearts none of these lessons which have preceded our own existence. Each one of us must himself once again tie the broken thread in the family. What among other people is a matter of habit, instinct, we can only get into our heads by hammer strokes. Our memories go no further back than yesterday; we are, as it were, strangers to ourselves. We walk through time so singly that as we advance the past escapes us forever. This is a natural result of a culture based wholly on borrowing and imitation. There is among us no inward development, no natural progress; new ideas throw out the old ones because they do not arise from the latter, but come among us from heaven knows where. Since we accept only ready-made ideas, the ineradicable traces which a progressive movement of ideas engraves on the mind and which gives ideas their forcefulness makes no furrow on our intellect. We grow, but we do not mature; we advance, but obliquely, that is, in a direction which does not lead to the goal. We are like those children who have never been made to think for themselves; once they have come of age they have nothing of their own; all their knowledge is on the surface of their being, their whole soul is on the outside. This is exactly our situation.

Peoples are moral beings in the same way as individuals are. As years make the education of persons, so centuries make theirs. In a way, one can say that we are an exceptional people. We belong to that number of nations which does not seem to make up an integral part of the human race, but which exists only to teach the world some great lesson. The lesson which we are destined to give will, naturally, not be lost; but who knows when we shall find ourselves once again in the midst of humanity and what afflictions we shall experience before we accomplish our destiny?

The peoples of Europe have a common aspect, a family resemblance. In spite of the general division of these peoples into Latin and Teutonic branches, into southern and northern, there is a common link which unites them into a fasces, clear to anyone who has studied their general history. You know that even recently all Europe called itself Christendom, and that word had its place in public law. In addition to this general character, each of these peoples has a particular character, which, however, consists of no more than history and tradition. It is what makes up the intellectual patrimony of these peoples. Every individual has a right to it, each amasses during his lifetime, without fatigue or labor, those notions scattered in his society, and profits by them. You can draw the parallel yourself and see how much we, on our side, can pick up in this way through the simple commerce of elementary ideas, to make use of them, for good or evil, to direct our lives. And observe that this is not a matter of study or reading, of anything literary or scientific, but simply of the contact of minds, of those ideas which a child receives in the cradle, which surround him in the midst of his play, which his mother breathes on him in her caresses; these are ideas which, in the guise of divers feelings, enter into the marrow of his bones with the very air he breathes, and which have already formed his moral being before he is delivered out into the world and society. Do you wish to know what ideas these are? They are the ideas of duty, of justice, of right, of order. They were brought forth by the very events which originated communities; they are integral elements in the social life of these nations.

Such is the atmosphere of the West; this is more than history, more than psychology; it is the physiology of a European. What have we to substitute for this in our country? I don't know whether one can draw any universal conclusion from what I have just said, but one can certainly see how the strange situation of a people which cannot connect its thought with any succession of ideas that have been progressively developed in society and devolved slowly one from the other, which has taken no part in the general progress of the human spirit save by blind, superficial, and often very awkward imitation of other nations, must powerfully influence the mind of every individual within it.

You will find that, as a result, a certain poise, a certain method in our thoughts, a certain logic is lacking to us all. The Western syllogism is unknown to us. There is more than frivolity in our best minds. But our best ideas are no more than sterile visions and remain paralyzed in our brains owing to lack of either connection or succession. It is a trait of human nature that a man gets lost when he can find no means to bind himself with what has come before him and what will follow upon him. Then all consistency, all certainty escapes him. Lacking the guiding sense of continuous duration, he finds himself lost in the world. There are lost souls in every country; but in ours it is a general characteristic. I don't mean the lightness with which one used to reproach the French—actually but an easy manner of conceiving things which did not exclude either breadth or depth of mind, and which gave infinite grace and charm to their transactions—I mean the flightiness of a life totally lacking in experience and foresight, a flightiness which results simply from the ephemeral existence of an individual detached from the species. Such a life holds dear neither the honor nor the progress of any community of ideas or interests, not even a traditional family outlook or that mass of prescriptions and perspectives which compose, in a state of things founded on memory of the past and awareness of the future, both public and private life. There is absolutely nothing general in our heads; everything in them is individual, and everything is transitory and incomplete. Even in our very eyes I find something strangely vague, cold, uncertain, something which resembles to an extent the aspect of people at the lowest scale of the social ladder. When I was abroad, particularly in the south where faces are so animated and expressive, I often compared the faces of my compatriots with those of the natives, and I was struck by this expressionlessness in our faces.

Foreigners have praised in us a sort of careless rashness which one finds particularly in the lower classes, but, since they could observe only certain isolated effects of our national character, they could not judge the whole. They did not see that the same principle which makes us sometimes so daring makes us also ever incapable of depth and perseverance. They did not see that what renders us so indifferent to the hazards of life renders us indifferent also to all good, all evil, all truth, all deceit, and that it is this which deprives us of the powerful motives which lead men to perfect themselves. They did not see that it is precisely this lazy boldness which is responsible for the fact that in our country not even the upper classes, painful though it be to say this, are exempt from the vices which elsewhere exist only among the lowest. They did not see, finally, that, although we have some of the virtues of a young people not much advanced in civilization, we have none of the virtues of a mature, highly cultured people.

I do not mean, certainly, that we have only vices, while European peoples have only virtues; God forbid! But I do say that in order to judge peoples fairly we must study the general spirit that constitutes their life, for that spirit alone, and not any other specific trait of character, can lead them on the road to greater moral perfection and indefinite progress.

People are subject to certain forces which themselves exist in the top social group. They do not think for themselves; there are among them a certain number of thinkers who think for them, who give the direction and put in motion the collective intelligence of a nation. While the small number thinks, the rest feel and the general motion occurs. This is true of all races on earth, except for some brutish ones in which there remains of human nature but the physical form. The primitive peoples of Europe, the Celts, the Scandinavians, the Germans [*Germains*], had their druids, their scalds, their bards: these were, in their way, powerful thinkers. Look at those peoples of North America which the materialistic civilization of the United States is so busily destroying: there are among them men of remarkable profundity.

Well, I ask you, where are our wise men, where are our thinkers? Who has ever thought for us? Who thinks for us now? And yet, situated between the two great divisions of the world, between East and West, with one elbow leaning on China and the other on Germany, we should have combined in us the two great principles of rational nature, imagination and reason, and have united in our civilization the past of the entire world. But this is not the part which Providence has assigned to us. Far from it, she seems wholly to have neglected our destiny. Suspending, where we were concerned, her beneficial action on the human mind, she left us completely to ourselves, she wished to have nothing to do with us, she wished to teach us nothing. Historical experience does not exist for us; ce..turies and generations have passed without benefiting us. To behold us it would seem that the general law of mankind has been revoked in our case. Isolated in the world, we have given nothing to the world, we have taught nothing to the world; we have not added a single idea to the mass of human ideas; we have contributed nothing to the progress of the human spirit. And we have disfigured everything we touched of that progress. From the very first moment of our social existence, nothing has emanated from us for the common good of men; not a single useful thought has sprouted in the sterile soil of our country; not a single great truth has sprung from our midst; we did not bother to invent anything, while from the inventions of others we borrowed only the deceptive appearances and the useless luxuries.

Strange. Even in the world of science, which touches on all fields, our history makes no connection, explains nothing, proves nothing. If the barbarian hordes which threw the world into confusion had not crossed the land we inhabit before swooping down on the West, we would hardly have provided a chapter to world history. For people to notice us we have had to stretch from the Bering Straits to the Oder. Once a great man wanted to educate us; in order to make us eager for enlightenment, he threw up the mantle of civilization; we picked up the mantle, but did not touch civilization. Another time, another great prince, associating us to his glorious mission, led us victorious from one end of Europe to the other; returning home from this triumphal march across the most civilized countries in the world, we brought back ideas and aspirations which resulted in an immense calamity that set us back by half a century. We have something in our blood which drives off all true progress. In a word, we have lived and we live but to be a great lesson to such distant posterity as will be capable of it; today, whatever anyone says, we mark a void in the intellectual sphere. I cannot tire of marveling at this void and this strange solitude of our social existence. It is due, certainly, in part to some inconceivable destiny, but doubtless in part, too, to man, as is true in all moral events. . . .

Letter III

. . . There is no reason which is not obedient reason. But that is not all. Does man do anything his life long but seek to submit to something? First, he finds in himself a power which he recognizes as different from that which determines motion external to him: he feels himself alive. At the same time he recognizes that his power is limited: he feels his own nothingness. Next he perceives that the power external to him dominates him and that he must submit to it. This is his whole life. From the moment that he begins to reason, these two notions—one of an internal and imperfect power, the other of an external and perfect power—come on their own to fill his mind. And although these two notions do not come so clearly and precisely as do those suggested to us by our senses or those transmitted by means of communication with beings similar to us, yet all our ideas of good, of duty, of virtue, of law, as well as their opposites, come to us only from the need we feel to subordinate ourselves to that which arises, not from our ephemeral nature, not from the restless stirrings of our inconstant will, not from the urgings of our anxious desires: all our activity is but the effect of a force which drives us to place ourselves in the general order of things, in the order of dependence. Whether we consent to this force or whether we resist it is immaterial; we are always under its sway. We have, therefore, no recourse but to give the best possible account of its action on us and, once we have discovered something about it, to give ourselves up to it with faith and trust: for this force which acts on us unawares is the never-failing force which leads the universe to its destiny. And what is the great question of life? This: What must we do to discover the action of the sovereign power on our being?

This is how I conceive the principle of the mental world, and in this way, as you see, it corresponds perfectly with the principle of the physical world. But one of these principles appears to us as an irresistible force to which everything inevitably submits, while the other seems to us to be no more than a power which is combined with our own power and is, to some extent, capable of being modified by our own power. This is the logical aspect imposed on the world by our artificial reason. But this artificial reason, which we have voluntarily substituted for that portion of universal reason which was imparted to us in the beginning, this bad reason which so often upsets observable objects and shows them to us completely differently from the way they are in fact, this reason still does not conceal from us the absolute order of things to such a point that we cannot see in this order the fact that passivity precedes freedom and that the law which we make for ourselves is derived from the general law of the world. It in no way prevents us, when we accept freedom as a given fact, from recognizing that passivity is the true reality of the moral order, just as it is of the physical order. All powers of the mind, all its means of cognition can, in fact, come to the mind only from its docility. The mind is powerful only because it is submissive. All human reason needs to know is to what it must submit. No sooner does a man except himself from this supreme rule of intellectual and moral activity than he falls instantly into vice, either of reasoning or of will. The whole mission of a good philosophy is, thus, first to demonstrate this rule, and then to show us whence shines the light which must guide us in our lives.

Why is it, for example, that in none of its activities does the mind rise so high as in mathematical computation [*le calcul*]? What is mathematical computation? An intellectual manipulation, a mechanical working of reason in which reasoning will counts for nothing. Why the prodigious power of analysis in mathematics? Because it is an employment of reason wholly subordinate to a given rule. Why the great efficacy of observation in physics? Because it does violence to the natural bent of the human spirit, because it subjects it to a pace diametrically opposed to its habitual pace, because it places it face to face with nature, in the humble posture which is proper to it. How did natural philosophy reach its great certainty? By reducing reason to a wholly passive, wholly negative activity. And what does logic do —that fine logic which has given this [natural] philosophy such enormous power? It puts reason in chains, curbs it to the universal yoke of obedience, and rends it as blind and submissive as nature itself, the object of its study. The only road, says Bacon, open to man to reign over nature is the same as that which leads to the kingdom of heaven: it can be entered only in the humble person of a little child. And logical analysis, what is that if not a violence which the mind does to itself? If you let your reason do as it will, it will operate only synthetically. We can proceed analytically only by acting on ourselves with tremendous effort: we always fall back into the natural procedure, into synthesis. Indeed, the human mind began with synthesis; synthesis is what characterizes the science of the Ancients. But however natural and legitimate synthesis may be—and quite often it is more legitimate than analysis—it is certain that it is only to the method of submission, to analysis that the most effective powers of thought belong. On the other hand, if one looks carefully one finds that our greatest discoveries in the natural sciences are never anything but pure, wholly spontaneous intuitions, that is, that they arise only from a synthetic principle. But note this about Intuition: although it essentially belongs to human reason and is one of its most active tools, we cannot understand it as we do our other faculties. That is because we do not possess it purely and simply like the others, because there is something in it of a higher intelligence, because its destiny is but to reflect that other intelligence in ours. And that is exactly why we owe to it our most beautiful insights.

Thus it is clear that human reason is not led to its most positive knowledge by a really internal power, but that its motion must always be impressed on it from without. The true principle of our intellectual power is, therefore, at bottom only a kind of *logical abnegation* identical with moral abnegation and derived from the same law.

Nature offers itself up to us not merely as experience and knowledge, but also as a rule of reasoning. Every natural phenomenon is a syllogism which has its major and minor premises and its conclusion. Thus nature itself impresses on the human mind the method which the mind must follow in order to know it; moral reason merely submits itself to a law which is offered to it in the very motion of things. Thus when the Ancients, the Stoics, for example, who had such magnificent presentiments, spoke of imitating nature, of obeying it, of conforming to it, they did so because they lived closer to the origin of things than we and had not yet shattered the world as we have: they were merely proclaiming this primitive principle of intellectual nature, namely that no power, no rule, comes to us from ourselves.

As for the principle that makes us act and which is simply desire for our good, where would the human race be if the idea of that good were but an invention of our reason? Every century, every nation would have a private idea of it. How would mankind as a whole advance along its indefinite progress if the human heart did not have a universal notion of a bond, common to all times and to all places, and consequently not a creation of man? What is the source of the morality of our actions? Is it not that commanding feeling which orders us to submit to law, to respect truth? But law is law only because it does not come from us; truth is truth only because we have not dreamt it up. If it happens that we take as the rule of our conduct what we ought not to take as such, that is because we are not strong enough to free our judgment from the influence of our inclinations (our inclinations then dictate the law we follow); but it is also because we expect to find in this latter law the general law of the world. Granted, there are people who seem to conform quite naturally to all the precepts of morality; such are many outstanding persons whom we admire in history. This happens because, in these privileged souls, the feeling of duty was not developed by thought but by those hidden means which lead men unawares, by those great teachings which life teaches without need of demonstration, teachings stronger than our personal thought, which constitute the general thought of man: now an example which strongly affects the mind, now a fortunate coincidence which takes hold of a man and raises him above himself, now the favorable arrangement of a life which makes of him what he would not have been without it—living lessons of history dispensed only to certain individuals according to a law unknown to us. If a vulgar psychology makes little of all these mysterious stimuli of the motion of the intellect, a more profound psychology, which considers the heredity of human thought as the first element of human nature finds in it a solution to most of its problems. Thus it is that when the heroism of truth or the inspiration of genius are not the thoughts of an individual, they are the thoughts of past ages. Whether we have thought or not, someone has thought for us before we were born. At the bottom of every moral act, however spontaneous it may be, however isolated it may be, there necessarily lies a sense of duty, i.e., of submission.

What would happen if man could make himself so submissive that he wholly rid himself of freedom? Clearly, according to what we have said, this would be the highest degree of human perfection. Every movement of his soul would then be produced by the principle which produced all other movements of the world. Thus, instead of being separated from nature, as he now is, man would fuse with it. Instead of the feeling of his own will, which separates him from the general order of things, which makes him a being apart, he would find the feeling of universal will, or, what is the same thing, the intimate feeling, the profound awareness of his real relation to the whole of creation. Thus, instead of the individual and solitary idea which fills him now, instead of this personality which isolates him from all his surroundings and places a veil over all the objects before him, and which is nothing but the necessary condition of individuation and hence the effect of his violent separation from general nature—by abdicating his fatal actual *self,* man would recover the idea, the vast personality, all the power of his pure intelligence in his innate bond with the rest of things. Then he would no longer feel himself living that narrow, niggardly life which compels him to draw everything to himself, to see only through the prism of his artificial reason. No, he would feel himself living the life which God Himself made for him that day when He drew him out of Nothing. It is that primitive life which the total exercise of our faculties is destined to find once more. A great genius said long ago that man has a recollection of a better life: this great idea was not cast upon the earth in vain; but what he did not say, what he should have said—and this is the conclusion which neither that great genuis nor any other man of his age reached—is that it is up to us to find this lost life, this more beautiful life, and that we can do this without ever leaving this world.

Time and space—these are the limits of human life such as it is today. But what is there to keep me from escaping the stifling embrace of time? Whence comes my idea of time? From the memory of past events. But what is memory? No more than an act of will: this is proved by the fact that one never has more memories than one wants to have, otherwise the whole succession of events that followed one upon another in the course of my life would always be present in my memory, would always press in my head; on the contrary, in the very moments when I let my thoughts flow most freely, I gather only the memories which coincide with the actual state of my soul at that time, with the feelings which move me, with the ideas which are in my mind. We make images of the past just as we do of the future. Then why could I not drive back the ghost of the past which stands motionless behind me, just as I can eradicate, if I wish, the moving vision of the future which floats before me, and escape that intermediary moment which is called the present, such a short moment that at the very instant when I pronounce the word that denotes it, it is no more? We ourselves make time, that is certain: God did not make time. He allowed man to make it. But then, where would time be? That fatal thought, time, which obsesses me and oppresses me on all sides, would it not vanish completely from my mind? This imaginary reality, time, which dominates and crushes me so cruelly, would it not be wholly dispersed? Then there would no longer be a limit to my existence, no longer any obstacle to infinite life, my gaze would plunge into eternity: the terrestrial horizon would disappear, the bulk of the heavens would no longer join the earth at the end of the immense plain which stretches before my eyes. I would see myself in that unlimited duration, undivided into days, hours, and fleeting instants, forever one, where there is no longer motion or change, where all individualities are lost one in another, where, finally, eternal objects endure. Every time that our mind knows how to disengage itself from the chains it has forged for itself, it conceives this kind of time just as well as that in which it lives now. Why does our mind again and again leap away from the immediate succession of things measured by the monotonous beat of the pendulum? Why does it leap again and again into that other world where the fatal voice of the clock is no longer heard? Because the infinite is the natural atmosphere of thought; because there is the only true time; because the other time is only that which we create ourselves, I know not why.

As for space, thought does not reside in space, everyone knows that. Thought naturally accepts the conditions of the tangible world, but it does not inhabit this world. Hence, whatever reality space may be supposed to have, it is no more than a fact external to thought and has nothing to do with the being of the mind; an inevitable form if you will, but only a form, in which the external world appears to us. Thus, even less than time can space enclose the new life of which we are speaking here.

This is that higher life toward which man must strive—the life of perfection, of certainty, of clarity, of infinite knowledge, but most of all of perfect submission; a life which man possessed in the past, but which is still promised to him. And do you know what this life is? It is heaven—there is no other heaven but this. We are allowed to enter it right now, do not doubt this. It is nothing but the complete renewal of our nature within the given order of things, the last stage of the labors of intelligent being, the final destiny of spirit in the world. I do not know whether each one of us is called to fulfill this immense career, to reach the glorious goal which is its end, but what I do know is that the final goal, the maximum point of our progress, can be none other than a complete fusion of our nature with universal nature, for only in that way can our spirit rise to the perfection of things which expresses the *very words* of the Supreme Intellect.

But in the meantime, while we have not reached the end of our pilgrimage, before this great fusion of our being with universal being is realized, can we not fuse at least with the mental world? Have we not in us the power to identify ourselves to an indefinite extent with beings similar to ourselves? Have we not the faculty of taking over their needs, their interests, of appropriating their feelings, and this to the point of living only for them, of feeling only through them? Of course we have. Sympathy, love, charity, whatever name you give to this unique capacity of ours to fuse with what is going on around us, it is certain that the capacity is inherent in our nature. We can, if we wish, so well mingle with the moral world that nothing can happen—so long as we know about it—such that we do not feel it as something happening to ourselves. Indeed, it is not even necessary that worldly events should particularly concern us; the general, the profound idea of the concerns of men, the intimate awareness of our real link with humanity, alone suffice to make our hearts beat with the destinies of all the human race, to make our every thought, our every action, accord with the thoughts and actions of all men in harmonious concert. By cultivating this outstanding property of our nature, by developing it more and more in our souls, we shall reach heights from which the rest of the road we must cover will be wholly revealed to us. Fortunate are those mortals who, once there, can remain at that height without falling back into the low regions whence they started! Until the moment when that height was reached, our existence was but a perpetual oscillation between life and death, a prolonged agony. From that moment, true life began, from that moment it is left up to us to follow the path of the true and the good, for from that moment the law of the moral world is no longer an impenetrable mystery.

But do things happen this way in the world? Far from it. It is not a matter of imagining this law of intelligent nature which appears to us only so late in life and so obscurely—any more than the law of physical nature is to be imagined. All that we can do is to hold our souls open for this knowledge when it comes to offer itself to our minds. In the ordinary course of events, in the daily concerns of our mind, in the habitual sleep of our souls, the moral law is much less clearly manifested to us than the physical law. It reigns over us absolutely, that is true; it orders our every act, every movement of our reason, and leaving with us, by a marvelous arrangement, by a perpetual miracle, the awareness of our own activity, it imposes on us a fearful responsibility for each thing we do, for every beat of our heart, for even every one of those fugitive thoughts which no more than graze our minds in passing. But in spite of this, it escapes from our intelligence into deep shadows. And what happens? Lacking knowledge of the true principle of which he was the agent, man unwittingly makes his own law, and the law which he thus sets over himself on his own is what he calls *the moral law,* or wisdom, or sovereign good, or simply law. And to this fragile work of his own hands, which he can break as soon as the fancy strikes him and which he does break at every instant of the day, in his blindness he attributes all the positivity, the absoluteness, the immovability of the true law of his being, that hidden principle of which, by his reason alone, he can know nothing but its inevitable necessity, nothing more.

Besides, although the moral law, like physical law, exists outside of us independently of our knowledge, there is an essential difference between these two laws. Countless multitudes have lived and live with no idea of the material forces which move the world of nature; God willed it that human reason should discover all that for itself, little by little. But however degraded an intelligent being may be, however limited his faculties, he cannot be wholly deprived of some knowledge of the principle which makes him act. Deliberation, judgment necessarily presuppose the notion of good and evil. If you take this notion away from man, he will not deliberate, he will not judge, he will no longer be a rational being. Thus God could not let us live a single instant without it; He made us this way. And this imperfect idea, placed in our souls in a manner we cannot understand, made the whole of intellectual man. You have just seen what could be derived from this idea if it could be found in its pristine purity, as it was given to us in the beginning, but we must [now] see what we can learn by seeking the principle of all our knowledge in our own nature alone.

12

Alexis Stepanovich Khomyakov
(1804–1860)

Khomyakov's On Recent Developments in Philosophy *represents some sort of essence of the Slavophiles' metaphysics expressed in a mature and lapidary form. While most works written by Slavophiles are devoted to ethics, social philosophy, and philosophy of history, the following pieces from* On Recent Developments in Philosophy *deal with classical ontological and epistemological problems: matter (world), time, space, energy, knowledge, consciousness, will, freedom, necessity, etc.*

ON RECENT DEVELOPMENTS IN PHILOSOPHY*

Letter to Y. F. Samarin

Dear Yuri Fyodorovich,

. . . *The world appears to reason as matter in space and energy in time.* German thinkers have already recognized such a division of concepts, and Schelling spoke about it at length in his "Propaideutics," incidentally calling time "life." But here the great philosopher lacks strength and clarity of thought. Indeed, metaphorical expressions (that is, elements of mysticism) take the place of strictly rational [*soznatelny*] expressions, and the apparent (merely apparent) consistency of the dialectical critique is illegitimately mixed with vague

*From *Russian Philosophy,* Volume 1, edited by James M. Edie, James P. Scanlan, Mary-Barbara Zeldin, with the collaboration of George L. Kline. Copyright © 1976. Translated by Vladimir D. Pastuuhov Mary-Barbara Zeldin, from A. S. Khomyakov, *Polnoye sobraniye Sochineni,* Moscow, 1900. Reprinted by permission of the University of Tennessee Press.

observations and illusions of representation (*der Representation*). The difference between space and time finds no logical formula in Schelling, and the
hesitancy of his expressions reaches such a point that in one place the only
meaning he leaves to space is that of impotent disintegration [*raspadeniye*].
This is, of course, contrary to philosophical common sense. I have said that
the world appears to reason as matter in space, as energy in time; but here
we encounter the question: What is matter? Let us put aside the foolish and
childish view [of matter as] an independent atom, a conception which does
not even deserve refutation (because the unchangeable—the atom—can be
neither the cause nor the instrument of action, and becomes the simple concept of an abstract point). Furthermore, matter, in relation to form, is a product of energy, while, apart from form, thought can affirm nothing at all beyond
matter. But energy appears as a change [of form], or, more exactly, as the
beginning of a change of form. Consequently, both space and time are categories of energy.

Their general relation to a single datum and to the single category of
quantity has given rise to a very legitimate and widely used expression, "a
space of time. . . ." But the difference between spatial and temporal deter-
minations with respect to energy, is the following: *time is energy in its
developments; space [is energy] in its combinations.*

In the face of thought, matter itself wholly loses its independence, being
evidently a product or a manifestation of energy, but in no case a principle
of energy. This is why the materialist school in our days, having recognized
the impossibility of preserving the autonomy of matter, has switched to the
teaching of pseudo-realism, without understanding that this pseudo-realism
is just as groundless as the earlier materialism, and for the same reason, i.e.,
precisely because [such a view] ascribes to what is partial and quantitative
properties which can belong only to what is whole and single. Spinoza stood
far above this. It seems that the materialists of the nineteenth century are
not even capable of understanding this great thinker; their minds are seemingly incapable of the effort of pure thinking, the contemplation of abstract
concepts. There is a kind of obesity about their minds; they are like the wife
of a country priest, for whom a light steam over a nourishing meat pie is
the ultimate representation of the spiritual. As soon as the materialist has
removed or hidden from his own view the obvious contradictions in his coarse
belief in the independence of matter, he becomes completely calm and boldly
looks you in the eye, not even understanding what else is missing. Such is
the clever Feuerbach, not to mention the *dii minores* whose obtuseness often
reaches comic proportions.

But Kant was right when he gave time and space the significance only
of categories of our own minds, i.e., when he took from them their independent status and renamed Leibniz' *ordo rerum* as an *ordo visionum*. Such
was the critical philosophy required in his day. Kant was right in this re-

spect, although his own definition, like that of Leibniz, is sheer nonsense. Because, as I have already said, the words *coexistentes* and *consequentes*, which he introduced into the definition of time and space, already include the same idea which they were supposed to define. Right now I am speaking only about the change of the word *res* to the word *visiones*. Kant, by this change, returned time and space to [the realm of] phenomena of our inner world from which, like all the other [categories], they had been illegitimately removed and ascribed to the unproven external world. I have already written about this. But, then, why am I again, so to speak, giving these categories an external significance? I shall try to explain myself. The whole of German criticism, the whole philosophy of the Kantian school, still remains at the stage where Kant left it. It has not advanced beyond understanding [*Verstand*], i.e., beyond the analytical power of reason [*Vernunft*], a power which is conscious of and capable of sorting out data received by it from integral reason. Since it has to deal only with concepts, it can never find within itself a criterion for the definition of the internal and the external, for it has to do only with what has already apprehended and which, consequently, has already become internal. You will remember, dear Yuri Fyodorovich, the great step forward made by our [Russian] thinker, I. V. Kireyevsky—who unfortunately died too soon—namely, the reasonable recognition of the wholeness of reason. Trying in part to expound this and attempting to continue his intellectual exploit along the road he indicated, I gave the name *faith* to that faculty of reason which apprehends actual (real) data and makes them available for analysis and awareness by the understanding [*Verstand*]. Only in this area do the data still have the fullness of their character and the marks of their origin. In this area, which precedes logical consciousness and which is filled with a living consciousness that does not need demonstrations and arguments, man realizes what belongs to his intellectual world and what to the external world. Here, by the touchstone of his free will [*volya*], man perceives what in his (objective) world is produced by his creative (subjective) activity and what is independent of it. Time and space, or, more exactly, phenomena in these two categories, are here perceived independently of subjectivity or, at least, as depending on it to a very small extent. That is why I was justified in speaking of [time and space] as categories of energy, apart from human individuality, and to define them in this sense. But thinking cannot stop here.

The fullness of reason, or the human spirit, is conscious of all phenomena of the objective world as *its own*, but, as I have already said, as emanating either from itself or not from itself. In both cases reason still accepts them immediately (as the Germans say), that is, on faith. The blind student of optics of whom I spoke knows the laws of a light which is inaccessible to him, but he accepts them as phenomena on faith in other men's senses, just as the man who can see has faith in his own senses, and the artist in his own creation. In all possible circumstances the object (or phenomenon, or fact) is an object of belief [*veruyemoye*]; it is fully transformed into an object of consciousness [*soznavayemoye*] only by the action of consciousness. The degree of consciousness never exceeds the limits, or more exactly, does not change the character of the way in which the object was initially accepted (thus, the blind student of optics will always know light only as an episode in another's life, not in his own). . . .

But, on the other hand, we can think about the object of consciousness only within the laws or categories of consciousness itself; otherwise, we are still thinking about it as an object of belief and imagining that we are thinking about an object of consciousness, i.e., we are no longer thinking, because [at this moment] there is an inner contradiction in our thought. The thought is not simply incomplete, as it would be in the case of lack of data, but self-destroying, i.e., false. Such is, in general, the shortcoming of mystics, such is the shortcoming also of most philosophers, when they begin to talk about the real world. This shortcoming is very striking in that definition of time and space which was given to us by Germany (for instance, in the words "subsequent" and "coexisting"). In the definition at which I arrived and in which energy is recognized simply as the unknown cause of phenomena as objects of belief, i.e., in the proposition "time is energy in its developments; space is energy in its combinations," the previous defect has been removed.

But you feel that the words "development" and "combination" still do not fully free us from unconscious objectivity and do not entirely transfer the definition itself into the area of strictly logical consciousness; they are not yet subordinated to the categories [of consciousness]. In fact, they do belong to the intellectual world and to the realm of pure consciousness, but there is already included in them an unnoticed, prior application of logical categories to the external world. Look at them carefully, and the words "development" and "combination" are transformed into the categories of *causality* and *reciprocity*. Therefore, a conscious definition of time and space would be: time is energy in the category of causality, and space in the category of reciprocity, i.e., *time and space are categories of causality and of reciprocity in the world of* [those] *phenomena* [which are] *independent of the subjective individuality of man.*

We have now purified the concept to such an extent that, with the full clarity of analysis, we can definitely distinguish the object of consciousness [*soznannoye*] from the object of belief, and see that the idea of appearance and externality with respect to human subjectivity refers only to the latter. Time and space have therefore lost all independent meaning in relation to reason in general, retaining a meaning only in relation to the individual. Such is the logical conclusion. Of course, it solves the problem positively only in relation to man, remaining negative in relation to cosmic universality. In this last relation it determines what we cannot say, but it does not state the actual situation. It cannot do otherwise, for neither appearance nor externality has a positive definition; they remain in the area of belief and not of knowledge, of which the ultimate goal—to be equal to belief, to be a fully conscious belief—has not been reached and cannot be reached by human thought.

But even so, the progress of thought is not yet finished, not even in this particular question. The word "phenomenon" keeps us in the material world because, for a reasonable man, the world of phenomena is the world of matter. . . . We know that another's thought, as long as it is only an expression and not a thought accepted within our own thinking and as an object of our consciousness, remains for us in the world of phenomena, in the world of formal and consequently material forces. We cannot say more than that. But this gives us the right to refuse to recognize any independent reality behind the formal energy. Consequently, energy stands before us as something external, alien, as non-ego, as something not posited by the creation of our subjective individuality, inaccessible to our positive consciousness, but [still] accessible, although [only] in part, to its negative criticism. Indeed, consciousness is not conscious of the phenomenon: it can understand its laws, its relation to other phenomena, and what is more, its inner sense (as, for instance, we understand the spoken or written word), but it does not understand it as a phenomenon. That is why the blind man does not see, although he grasps the laws of light, and the deaf man does not hear, no matter how competent he may be in acoustics, whereas full understanding [*razumeniye*] is a reconstruction, i.e., a transformation of the understandable [*razumevaye-moye*] into a fact of our own life. The phenomenon as a phenomenon is inaccessible to consciousness. But its laws, its inner logic are not alien to us. We study it, we define the connection and interrelation to its forms, we are able to lay bare the falsehood and the contradictions in judgments about it. Finally, in judgments about [the phenomenon] we attain whatever is accessible to negative, but not to positive, knowledge.

Reason, therefore, having given the general name of energy to the principle of the mutability of cosmic phenomena, demands of itself an answer to the question: Exactly what concept is contained in the word "energy"? Taine tried to prove the meaninglessness of the word itself and to interpret it as a mere algebraic sign in a meaningless proposition. His arguments are not without cleverness or a certain critical subtlety; but (as is almost always the case with the arguments of French writers) they do not exhaust the subject and they show a lack of intellectual depth. He denies independent existence to energy, and in this he is right; but he is right only against those who assume it—and what reasonable man does assume it? What thinker who has gone through the school of German thought would entertain such an assumption? Energy, whether we take it, with Hegel, as the law of a self-creating concept which is both object and subject of consciousness, or, with Schelling, as the law of a concept acting on the ground of divine thought, or as the law of the phenomenon in general and of its change—energy never and nowhere claims independent existence, but always designates a property of something else which makes a greater logical claim to independent existence. Excluding some very narrow-minded pseudo-philosophers, who do not deserve serious refutation, energy is for all others only a kind of algebraic name for the laws of motion (or of resistance, which means the same thing), and the concept of energy stands or falls together with the total system of which it constitutes a part or, more exactly, an abbreviated expression—since in fact a total system is always condensed in it. Define energy according to some one or other philosophical doctrine, and you have defined the doctrine itself. Of course, such a property belongs also to every element in a strictly consistent system; but in none, it seems, is it more apparent than in the word "energy." This is what Taine should have noticed and what he did not notice. In all that has preceded, I have considered energy in the sense of the law of the change of phenomena, not merely as the formula of this change (according to Hegel's doctrine, which is penetratingly thought out but, as I have already said, unfounded, since for Hegel the formula of the phenomenon is at the same time its principle), but as the actual principle of the change of phenomena. The following question naturally arises: how is the vital law of the changes of a phenomenon, or their principle, i.e., energy, related to the phenomenon itself?

I return to the two categories with which I began. We have seen that apparent space or so-called matter is not simultaneous in its interaction and that its simultaneousness resides in abstract thought, or else in atomistic concentration, or finally in subjective vision. We have also seen that apparent time or the so-called energy in matter is not contiguous [*odnoprostranstvenno*] in the order of causality, since phenomena linked by the mind in an instant of time were not yet able to react on one another and consequently to be in the conditions of true space. But we have also seen that time and space are so intimately linked together that (as real) neither can be thought without the other. Indeed, when one thinks about the phenomenon or about energy in the development of cause and effect, i.e., when one thinks of them in terms of time, one already posits the idea of form, i.e., of limit, and consequently of reciprocity—as Hegel showed in his splendid article "*Gränze und Schranke.*"

Thus one already posits space. And when one speaks or thinks about space in terms of interaction, one already posits the category of causality, i.e., time. The former false circle has been eliminated and the pseudo-definition replaced by a logical definition, but the link between the two categories not only has not disappeared—it has appeared even more clearly.

Thus, by discarding everything in the categories of space and time which was brought into them by sensuous representation, and restoring them by the natural path of dialectical thought to a more strict conception, we necessarily reach the proposition that the predominance of the element of thought leaves [to space and time] only the significance of something external, which consciousness does not transform back into something internal, consequently depriving them of independent existence. Actually, are not space and time created by different relationships of the mind toward itself and toward other things? You think about an object, concentrating only on its laws, be it [the laws of] your house, the earth, or the solar system—and nothing spatial or temporal enters into your thoughts. However, your thoughts, if I may use this expression, come into contact with one another, interact; inferences fly from premise to conclusion, concentrating all of them into a single instant, a single point. . . . During such purely internal work, in which there is an effort not to alienate your concepts, you often feel that, according to the order of external time, the conclusion precedes the premise. . . . You are entirely in the world of consciousness. But you do not want to treat your thought in that way. Whether it is an effort brought to bear upon what you have received or upon what you have created makes no difference. You want to have it not merely as a law but also as a fact. You want, as it were, to make it something alien to yourself. And this house, this country, this solar system, this statue, even this wooden spoon have already been spatialized, totally spatialized. They have occupied a place, they have been outlined by limits. These limits in their turn have put behind them the infinity of space. And time has flowed past, in days and years, or at least in its successiveness and gradualness of change. In what way is this not space or time? True, this is not the space common to all, not that time common to all, about which we are accustomed to speak. But they are real in just the same way. The law and the category of the objective world which you have just created, as well as the objects of your thought, are its material elements. They differ for you from so-called real objects in only one way: they are subject to your free will and you know it, as I have already said in an article (explaining the question: why the German philosopher is not content with the beer he has conceived by himself but buys his beer in a shop). They are yours, internal [to you], although alienated by your will, and not really external or common. *They are not only yours; they also are your creations.* But remember the marvelous tale of the *Thousand and One Nights,* about the sultan who plunged his head into a basin, or Mohammed's journey in the skies, or even less intelligent tales about visions induced by [animal] magnetism [i.e., hypnotism], visions on which the mystics build so many preposterous interpretations, being incapable of drawing any sound conclusion [from them]. (Between us, they are as dull-witted as the materialists; in fact they are materialists, or, to put it another way, they are those same country priests' wives, only more nervous.) Remember all this. True, I am talking about fairy tales; but there is profound wisdom hidden in these tales; more than that, a correct awareness of inner truth. . . . There is an irresistible conviction that, if it were given to man to look into another man's thought (this thought having already been alienated by the will of that other thinker in the activity of imagination), he would feel himself in a new time and a new space, independent to him, yet present to him as data, and not at all different from common [time and space], although completely other than they.

A clearer expression of this thought would probably be the following: Man feels that the external and sensuous world is related to him as a word is. One word is common, let us assume, to a whole people, but any other word, provided it is based on rational laws, is possible (C. S. Aksakov, in his grammar, states the profound thought that a word is the recreation of the world). The world of subjective creation with its space and time, is as actual as the external world, but the external world alone is common to all, is God's world [*Bozhi mir*], as Russian people say—God's world, God's sun, God's bread, etc. I know perfectly well that this expression "God's" has with us primarily the meaning of blessing or beneficence, but I think that it is not without an admixture of the concept of "general" or "universal," as for instance: "in God's world."

It seems that the relation of energy to the phenomenon is now clearly expressed. But let us approach it in another, still more empirical way, with the greatest possible analytical rigor. Where is the principle of a phenomenon, that is, its energy? The word "phenomenon" includes the concept of the relation between the subject and the object of consciousness, or, more exactly, the object of belief. If the principle of the phenomenon lies in a subjective consciousness, then evidently it is not contained in the phenomenon; but when we speak about the class of phenomena which is independent of subjectivity, i.e., about phenomena of the world common to all, we can no longer seek its principle in the conscious subject. Then is it contained in the phenomenon itself? The phenomena of the external world are all such that they really have no independent existence; they appear to experience as well as to reason as the product of forces, principles, or causes which exist apart from each particular phenomenon and merely combine for its creation. You tie off the vein of an animal, you stop the circulation of its blood, and you kill it; or you stop the flow of air and make it suffocate; you stop the growth of a tree or you drain a lake; a comet in its bold course pushes an asteroid from its path or destroys it, or it finds itself in the field of planetary gravity and flings itself onto a new course in space; or an entire solar system perishes (it makes no difference whether they really do perish or not, the mind is conscious of the inner possibility of such a disaster)—the destruction or the preservation of a phenomenon does not depend on it. The cause of its existence is not in it, but outside of it, in forces and causes which do not belong to it. It is itself contingent for itself, although it is not contingently but rationally deduced from universal cosmic laws. In its inner self it lives or exists not according to laws or principles set up by itself, but according to principles received from outside as a consequence of the universal life of the world. Thus, its essence [*sushchnost*] does not belong to it; consequently, every phenomenon is only a certain refraction or a combination and conjunction of general causes. The force or the cause of the being of every phenomenon is contained in the "all."

But this "all" is not a sum of phenomena. You can say that a yard is a part of a mile or of the earth's radius, but you cannot say that a yard is a part of the diameter of the universe, a part which transforms this diameter into a sum of yards. Similarly, you cannot say that the phenomenon is a part of the "all," a part which transforms this "all" into a sum of phenomena. The particulars cannot be summed into the infinite "all," but the principle of every phenomenon is evidently contained just in that "all," i.e., an "all" that is thinkable but not capable of representation or phenomenal manifestation.

But, is the principle contained only in the "all," or rather in its combination with a particular phenomenon? (Please notice that having separated the external from the internal in subjective consciousness, I no longer have the right, as German philosophy does, to place the "all" and all phenomena in the movement of the self-conscious subject. I think that I have earned the right to repudiate this illusory simplicity which, by the course of logical necessity, brought about the suicide of Hegel's system. Having recognized what is external to human thinking, i.e., to individually human thinking, I consider the world as external and must question it about the principles of phenomena, recognizing the possibility of its independent existence.) We have seen the contingency of a phenomenon in relation to itself; but with all this contingency could not the mind recognize [the phenomenon] as a polar factor in relation to the whole, a factor which produces a new phenomenon and consequently explains in turn all that preceded it, and is the eternal root of its own existence? Let us scrutinize any phenomenon, let us suppose that it is a shot which killed a wild animal. Let us admit the final result as a phenomenon. What is there that preceded it in which the factor creating the future could be included? You, with your rifle, your sharp eye and steady hand (as you see I have not forgotten what you justly boasted of in the past; I wish you the same in the future); but when, in all that, did the universal laws cease to work? The buckshot flew from the gun; but which aspect of the shooting was the actual phenomenon? Various forces acted throughout the flight of the buckshot: the [explosive] force of the gunpowder; the mass [of the buckshot] pushed in a straight line; the earth's gravity changing this line; the resistance of the air; even the slight effect of the head wind, tail wind, or side wind; chemical laws keeping the buckshot in its [original] state or oxydizing it during its flight and thus changing its mass. There is no point, no form at which we could stop and say: here is the phenomenon. And it's the same with what came before: your gun, your gunpowder, you yourself— all this never was, all this is a series of changes, or, more exactly, a continuous change, with respect to which the mind has no right to stop, is not able to stop, even for a minute, and to recognize something as a phenomenon.

And it's the same with what came after this. And the planet? The solar system? Consider them and [you will see that] they are exactly like this instantaneous shot. This hand, this foot, this blooming grass, this dried straw, all this on all their surfaces and in all their interiors are continually decomposing and forming new combinations. The bone inside the body, the stone in the bowels of the earth, do not stay without change even for a single instant. There is not a single moment of time during which even the smallest particle might remain itself. Nothing exists, everything is *im Werden,* as the Germans have already said (in *coming to be* [*gryadeniye*], I would say, because *werden* is nothing else than *to come to be,* or *gradior* in Latin. This etymology is obvious to me). True, we speak about a phenomeon; but what do we call by this name? Something snatched from the universal, something having no limits and defined only by our weakness and our individuality, which itself, aside from subjectivity, has neither limits nor form. Add to my words Pascal's wonderful lines *sur l'infiniment grand et l'infiniment petit,* lines which are even more understandable to modern science than to the science of his day, and you will see how the phenomenon in its growth went into the "all" which is thinkable but not capable of representation or phenomenal manifestation, just as, in its desire to define itself, crumbling away, it disappeared into the "atom" or into the moment—which is thinkable but not capable of representation or phenomenal manifestation. Both factors escaped before your eyes from the world of phenomena and passed into the world of thought. Both have freed themselves from form or were deprived of it and consequently no longer recognize its power over them, and now stand before our mental vision as that which positively is, appearing as abstractions because they were obtained by abstraction, but [in fact] being that which is and is self-identical, broken into the illusory polarity of the "all" and the "atom" only by the weakness of our subjective contemplation.

But people will say: this result is not necessary, since I have arbitrarily selected the path. No, it was not selected arbitrarily. A man can refuse to take it, as he can refuse any thinking at all, on the grounds of the enviable right enjoyed by so many, especially in our country. But this result is unavoidable for thought: it exists in each man of its own right and effectively, no matter how much one might like to deny it, and it is inseparable from a man's existence. This is the path of rigorous analysis; and the achieved result is necessary. That which is stands before us entirely freed from the phenomenon, from pseudo-real form, and accessible only to thought. But that which is, the "all," includes the thought which alone remained after the analysis of particular phenomena. Thus the character and the meaning of the thought stayed with it, now no longer subject to any external constraint but in its full freedom. The phenomenon is the movement [of that which is] as the object of consciousness; consequently, it is its movement for the subject of consciousness. It is free, but rational, i.e., in accordance with the laws of reason.

Rationality is not the same thing as necessity, although they are [often] confused, especially because of Hegel's logical theory. Rationality is not necessity, it is only the condition of possibility. A triangle is a triangle because "non-triangular triangle" is a mere sound, and not a thought. But this law concerns only the thought of the triangle in general and in no way conditions the existence of any particular triangle. The movement of thought includes the possibility of this movement, i.e., it does not admit anything contradictory to itself; but possibility does not determine actual existence. Possibility or rationality should rightly be called thinkability [*myslimost*], and if this word had been used by the German school, this school would have avoided a great many mistakes which it made because it used the word *vernünftig,* the ambiguity of which has constantly brought an alien and hence false element into the idea of thinkability. The correct development of any falsehood is rational only because an incorrect development is inconceivable, since it is not a development. But the correct development of a falsehood does not transform it into a truth, it does not change the initial dictum, and of course it will expose it as false in its final conclusion and hence will destroy it. But up to that time [the development of] a falsehood is thinkable, is possible, and often appears in the limited subjectivity of man or of the human race only because the inner contradiction of the initial datum is not immediately apparent to limited thought. Indeed, the correct development of a falsehood amounts to its unmasking and is not a development, and thus is wholly rational. But until the process is finished it has the features of development, while it is actually the annihilation of the datum. Properly speaking, falsehood is unthinkable and impossible in the world, for the world is the truth of that which is. Therefore, the freedom of the "all," i.e., of thought, is not at all hampered by being rational, i.e., thinkable.

But freedom, like possibility, does not include, and cannot include, the principle or the cause of phenomena; both these concepts are negative, for both of them define only external relations (i.e., of possibility to falsehood, of freedom to coercion); both of them being, as it were, to the passive area of the understanding and not to the activity of complete reason. They are not present in the object of consciousness or, consequently, in the phenomenon. Consciousness obtains them by means of opposition. Coercion, as force, does not reside in the object upon which it acts, but in that which is external to it, which acts upon it, and it is only from the negation of this coercion that the concept of freedom arises. The positive quality in the word "freedom" is not freedom but coercion; existence [*sushchestvennost*], as I have already said, belongs only to the positive. Therefore, that motion which we call free we consider to be nonexistent or non-self-existent. Freedom, in its positive meaning, cannot be the principle of the phenomenon [of motion], although by way of negation we acquired it as a quality of this principle. The principle of motion in that which positively is must be positive. The phenomenon as reality, as a sum of phenomena, cannot—as we have already seen—be recognized as a factor in the motion of the "all." The phenomenon as law, however, is only a possibility, and therefore cannot be a factor for the positive world. Aside from thought, only the "all" and the element or "atom" remained independent—both belonging to the world of thought and not to the world of the phenomenon or of representation. They [the "all" and the "atom"] are identical; but even if we should grant them this polar identity (which, by the way, is introduced by us and is not inherent in them), even so, their combination would be only freedom or possibility and nothing more. There is still no content. A mathematician would express this logical principle by the formula $\infty \times 0$, which is the formula for mathematical freedom, i.e., the possibility of any quantity, and, therefore (aside from external definition), the negation of any defining quantity because of the equality of all of them.

Therefore, as I have already said, freedom cannot include the principle of the phenomenon, but this principle is, by negation, determined as free by the consciousness of the understanding [*Verstand*] (according to the law which I explained in my article published in *Russkaya Beseda*). The principle is contained not in the *freedom of thought* which has remained the only determination of the "all," but in the *free thought, i.e., in the free will of reason.*

Here, dear Yuri Fyodorovich, is the root of the moving and changing world of phenomena to which the rigor of analysis leads us, no matter from what point we may have started our logical journey, provided only that we follow it steadily, putting aside the illusions of the world of representations and demanding a clear answer from any level of the development of thought at which we may have been pleased illegitimately to stop. Free will is the last word for consciousness, just as it is the first (and, just because it is the first) for actuality—*the free will of reason,* and—I add—*of reason in its wholeness:* because the change of phenomena is a change in the object of consciousness (and not in consciousness, which, from its side, apprehends every object equally), and the object of consciousness as such presupposes, or, more exactly, includes the inherent existence of pre-objective consciousness, this first stage of the being of thought, which does not and cannot pass into the phenomenon, but always precedes it. . . . Thus, the very change of phenomena, taking place as it does in the object of consciousness, sets up the fullness of the being of thought, and that is why we find the principle of the phenomenon and of its changes, i.e., of energy, only in total reason.

The *free will:* I have already stated that its concept is not given to man from outside. Man has obtained this concept not from without but from within himself, as a concept of reason itself. The outside world has not taught him such a concept; the outside world gave him neither foundations nor data for it. Entire categories of thought depend on it and could not exist at all without its existence, yet its existence cannot be explained by anything. Everything moves according to the law of cause and effect; everything is equally subject to necessity. Freedom can be no more than relative, i.e., in relation to one given force, but in no case in relation to all. Whence, then, has arisen the recognition of free will? Strictly speaking, as I have already said, it defines the limits of human subjectivity in relation to objectification or internal representation. It indicates to man, what, *in* himself, comes *from* himself, distinguishes [it from] what does not come from himself. It does not itself become known through any experience, through any phenomenon, and it does not pass into any phenomenon. Man does not know and has not seen a free object, that is, an object the action of which would give evidence of free will.

The only objection which could be made to my position would be the following: Man, being a concentrated reflection of the external world, is for himself the nodal point of its energies, and these energies, acting upon him, as it were, from the periphery, are recognized by him as an external necessity. But, acting again from this central nodal point (although, of course, also by necessity), he appears to have acquired independence and spontaneity. The center acknowledges as his, as his own, what actually is only the reflection of peripheral activity (as, for instance, we speak of the attraction of the center of the earth, whereas it is actually the attraction of all its parts crisscrossing and forming, as it were, a nodal point in the center). The mind, deceived, calls this illusion of central spontaneity free will and separates it from the activity of the forces of external nature which are clearly involuntary for us.

This is the only objection that is at all intelligent, at least at the first glance; but even it does not withstand criticism. To be sure, the consciousness of internal activity, of free activity, is so strong and primordial in us that the unenlightened man transfers this same thought to nature itself, believing, in the infancy of his mind, that every part of nature is spontaneous, be it animal or vegetable or even wholly inorganic matter. However, the first thought, which created a whole new category, could not have arisen from illusion. The false application of a category is an illusion, and a very common one, but the creation of a whole category is impossible, because categories are the laws of reason itself. Man comes to know the limits of his body, let us say, not from the limits of his free will but from the limits of his double impression (for the external gives only a single impression); but man ascribes to his free will far less than what is operative within these limits. Man does not recognize cramps, spasms, blinking, and a multitude of other actions as freely willed. A physiologist will say: this is not a function of the brain. But what sensible physiologist who has studied a certain number of abnormal and pathological phenomena of human nature can deny that man repudiates many actions which the same physiologist ascribes precisely to functions of the brain? "I did this, but I did not do what I intended to do. I said this, but I said it against my will. I felt and knew that I was not doing and not saying what I intended. I wanted to act and speak differently, but I could not." You constantly hear this kind of explanation from people with nervous disorders. "Tie me up, I want to bite you," says the unfortunate victim of hydrophobia. Is not rational free will separated from the needs of the animal center? But let us suppose finally that the body itself includes several centers, more or less independent, which by stimulation sometimes come to prevail over the brain center which man is accustomed to consider and call "himself." This concession (which I consider fully legitimate) leads to the same conclusion. All these movements of the tongue, throat, and limbs, about which I spoke, are again received only from the brain. Let us grant that another organ is acting through the brain: even so, all its powers are borrowed and are nevertheless considered by it as its own power, as its free will. Obviously, here too it could not consider an external power [as coming] from itself, since that power would fall into the common class. An illusion of the mind, its taking the centrality of impressions and reflections as its own free will, is inconceivable.

I repeat what I said earlier: at the infantile stage man is often mistaken, ascribing free will to objects of the outside world. This objection has been turned more than once against the existence of free activity in man by this school of blockheads who are called materialists, or, perhaps more politely in our polite century, realists. But what does it prove? Notice that the same infantile man who ascribes free will to matter also ascribes consciousness to it. How can that be? Man ascribes consciousness to an object because he obviously has it himself and ascribes free will to it because he does not have it himself! Isn't this an obvious absurdity? Isn't just one thing obvious, that man cannot conceive consciousness without free will? This deduction, this law of thought is irrefutable. Man cannot think otherwise, and when he persuades himself and others of the contrary, he merely collects sound, not thoughts, in just the same way as when he insists that he doubts the existence of his consciousness or of himself. Kant's analysis can be applied to either case. Nobody doubts his own free will, because he could not have received a concept of it from the outside world, the world of necessity; because whole categories of concepts are based on the consciousness of will; because in it, as I have already said, lies the differentiation between the objects of the existing world and those of the imaginary world; . . . because, finally, reason simply *cannot doubt its creative activity, i.e., its free will, as it cannot doubt its reflective susceptibility, i.e., faith, or its definitive consciousness, i.e., understanding* [*Verstand*].

That a phenomenon should precede its cause or force is logically as absurd, as unthinkable, as that an object should precede the subject of consciousness when [in fact] it is an object only for consciousness (because otherwise it would not be an object; and then what would it be?). Hence, the free energy of the nonphenomenal, of the mind, in other words of the free will, is such a strong requirement of reason that reason absolutely cannot fail to believe in it. It is not possible to condemn the infantile mind which ascribes consciousness as well as free will to objects of the external world. The infantile mind is perfectly right. It is far more faithful to the laws of reason than those pseudo-thinkers who deny (or imagine that they deny) both the one and the other. The mistake of the infantile mind consists in only one thing, that by transferring its human subjectivity to particular phenomena it equates them with itself and gives to the particular manifestation what belongs to the mental whole. Its great truth consists in that, in being conscious of external phenomena as a necessity with respect to itself, it recognizes active freedom, free will, at their original source. Here, it reflects profound awareness of the truth that *necessity is only the free will of another,* and since every objectification is a freely willed self-alienation of thought, i.e., is non-ego, so *necessity is free will made manifest.*

Law, i.e., the condition of concepts and consequently of the relations between everything that is, has nothing in common with necessity. It is nothing else than thinkability of the possibility of existence. Therefore, it is extremely illogical to recognize unfreedom [*nevolya*] (and consequently necessity) in thought only because all phenomenal manifestations of thought are always in agreement with the concept. If you formulate this pseudo-necessity, you will find the following: the manifestations of a thought are always in agreement with it, i.e., they are thinkable. This is indubitable; but where in this is necessity? What man of common sense will see it here? Hegel felt, or more exactly, knew this. That is why he recognized self-negating necessity, freedom, as a principle (*die sich negirende Negation und die Notwendigkeit*); but he vaguely felt that these formulae obtained by negation could neither positively explain that which is nor be its principle. That is why he introduced into his logic the doctrine of contingency (*die Zufälligkeit*), a doctrine which is remarkably profound in the coherence of its arguments. However, since contingency itself is only a law, he passed by an illegitimate leap from it to chance (*Zufall*), to that which actually is. (He makes the same leap from *Schein* to *Erscheinung* and many others, and all are conditioned by the same hidden demand for actuality, felt but not recognized or not realized.) Hegel did not arrive at the idea of free will and could not arrive at it for a very simple reason. He followed the path of analytical consciousness (understanding) and put the pole of positivity into it. Consequently, what precedes consciousness in reality always appeared to him with a negative sign, and free will—an essentially positive principle which, however, precedes both consciousness and its objects—appeared to him as a double negation of freedom, i.e., disappeared from the positive world. I repeat again: he was unaware, as all the German thinkers are unaware, of the rule that the path of analysis is identical with the path of reality, but leads in the opposite direction. . . .

And thus, wherever we start, whether from our own individual subjectivity and consciousness, or from the analysis of phenomena in their cosmic universality, one thing emerges as a final conclusion—that free will in its identity with reason as its active force is inseparable both from the concept of reason itself and from the concept of subjectivity. Free will posits everything that is, separating it from the possible or, in other words, *separating what is thought from what by the freedom of its creativity can be thought.* Free will is essentially rational because everything that is thinkable is rational, and because the will is reason in its activity just as consciousness is reason in its reflectivity or passivity or, if you prefer, receptivity. . . .

It is difficult or, more exactly, impossible, dear Yuri Fyodorovich, for a man to penetrate with his mind or to express in words this abyss of being in which he himself appears as such an insignificant whiff, something less than a grain of dust. But the mind sets endless demands for itself, requires an answer of itself, criticizes and rejects these answers, seeks in them harmony and strict consistency, feels that it is unable to stipulate the primary data, but strives to create for itself a mental world in which it would not be in contradiction with them. I shall, therefore, go further, retaining, I hope, a correct sequence and connection of concepts; but I shall not be going without fear, for I know how easy it is, even with apparent logical accuracy, to fall into the kind of logical mysticism which takes the word for the thought, just as the more common sort of mysticism takes representations for thought.

We have seen that the world of phenomena comes from free energy, from the free will; but this world arises as a combination of two factors, of the "all" and of the element, or "atom," both thinkable but not phenomenally manifested, called two, however, only by our subjective weakness which is deceived by our path through the world of representations. Both have already stepped out of the world of phenomena, have freed themselves from any features imposed from the outside, and have merged into a full identity so far as strictly logical understanding is concerned. But even after that, the illegitimate belief in duality may still remain, even though we cannot formulate this duality; there remains the rational conviction that individual consciousness sees necessity in a world which it could not recognize if that world were a fact of its free will. Finally, there remains the tendency to justify that which is phenomenally manifested, that which, so far as the unity of the subject is concerned, would be merely the thinkable or even the consciously thinkable in the phenomenon.

Everything that is appears to reason as a free energy of the mind, as freely willing reason, presenting itself as having been thought (for its own consciousness, of which it is unnecessary to speak now). In the form of the "all," and the fullness of the "all," it keeps this fullness of being even at the level where it appears as something thought. . . .

Part Four

Philosophy and
Radical Publicistic Writing

13

Vissarion Belinsky

Viktor Firsov

IDEALIST ENLIGHTENER

Vissarion Belinsky (1811–1848) was the son of a doctor in Sveaborg (now a district of Helsinki). In 1828, having finished gymnasium, he matriculated in the Philology Department of Moscow University but was expelled in 1832. He soon began to visit the literary and philosophical circle of N. V. Stankevich and to work actively in the journals *Teleskop* (*Telescope*) and *Moskovsky nablyudatel* (*Moscow Observer*). Several years later he moved to St. Petersburg, where he became a leading critic of the journal *Otechestvennye zapiski* (*Fatherland Notes*), and in 1847 head of the criticism department of the journal *Sovremennik* (*The Contemporary*).

In the process of his intellectual maturing Belinsky intensely studied not only the best achievements of Russian culture but also all the results significant in any way of West European philosophical thought, striving to find the answers to the metaphysical, ethical, and social questions bothering him. Despite the diversity of the ideas he assimilated, he was always distinguished by an original view of the world.

The specific feature of Russian philosophical thinking, i.e., its inherent closeness to literary and public activity, was clearly discernible in Belinsky's work. This feature was particularly characteristic of the nineteenth century, when a tempestuously developing Russian literature became a world phenomenon. Insofar as fiction and belles lettres were a highly important sphere where ideas of enlightenment and sociophilosophical conceptions were expressed, the philosophical, esthetic, and even political interpretation of literary works had an immense influence on the readers and on the shaping of public opinion in Russia. A fine analyst, Belinsky had an opportunity not only to make a profound examination of a literary work but also to compare it with the best examples of world literature, to acquaint readers with the achievements of philosophy, and on that background to single out the basic problems and trends in the development of Russian culture and of society as a whole.

He thought broadly, freely, and internationally. He wished to comprehend the development of social relations in Russia through universal values, and world development through the Russian people's involvement in it. His general ideological views could be called a philosophy of critical national self-awareness. His clearest gift as a thinker was a unity of philosophy and social and esthetic criticism. He considered the main task of modern times to be philosophical awareness of reality through the prism of literature and belles lettres.

Belinsky's intellectual interests began to take shape during his time in the Chembar *uyezd* school and the Penza grammar school, where he became acquainted with the works of Lomonosov, Sumarokov, Kheraskov, Griboyedov, Pushkin, Ryleyev, Bestuzhev, Schiller, and Byron. Possibly he even became acquainted with the works of Radishchev in that period. It was also the time when his interest in philosophical problems first arose.

His years at the university were hard and sometimes dramatic. This extraordinarily gifted young man, with an adequate knowledge of life, was registered in the first course for three years, and was expelled by a notice that read: "abilities weak; lacks diligence." The real cause of his academic difficulties was his poor health, which caused him to spend months in hospital.

The main reason for Belinsky's expulsion from the university was his political "unreliability." Not satisfied by the system of teaching, he attended lectures of freethinking professors that were required by the syllabus, but ignored the obligatory ones on theology. He subsequently wrote that, "It is impossible for a young man to lay firm foundations for his future scientific occupations in any Russian university," and that, "The time spent in a university is lost and wasted for a person who is devoting his whole life to knowledge."

The thinking young man made up for the deficiencies of university education independently, in many student circles. One of them was known by the number of the room where Belinsky lodged, viz., Literary Society Number Eleven; its members primarily discussed belles lettres and articles on current affairs. As a rule not one of the discussions passed without disputes on political themes. Belinsky acquainted his fellow members of the circle with excerpts from his drama *Dmitri Kalinin,* which had an antiserfdom bias. Its basic concepts, however, were contradictory, as it combined enlightenment ideas with hopes for a liberal form of czarism. Belinsky formulated in the play an idea that was to run through most of his works, namely, a conviction that much could be altered in peoples' lives through moral perfection. Belief in that permeated all his work right up to the mid-1840s.

Three very important features characterized Belinsky's intellectual development in his university days. One was associated with enlightenment. He early came to a conclusion about the incompatibility of serfdom with the nature of human relations itself. He saw the cause of serfdom in the backwardness of the Russian people, which could only be overcome through educational activity. A second feature of his search was increasing loss of faith in "official Orthodoxy," which led subsequently to his abandoning religion. The third line of his search was quests for ways to actuate the progressive political development of Russia. The attempts the young Belinsky made to resolve disturbing questions compelled him to concern himself more and more seriously with sociophilosophical problems.

After his expulsion from the university Belinsky grew close to the writer I. I. Lazhechnikov and to Professor N. I. Nadezhdin, of Moscow University, the editor of *Teleskop*. Through them he joined N. V. Stankevich's circle that united people of different convictions (K. S. Aksakov, Mikhail Bakunin, V. I. Krasov, I. P. Klyushnikov, Ya. Neverov, and others) and had a marked influence on his mental development. In this circle he took part in discussing the works of Kant, Fichte, Schelling, and Hegel, and polished his literary and critical skills.

In 1834 the weekly *Molva* (*Rumor*) printed Belinsky's first major work *Literary Reveries* (*Literaturnye mechtaniya*), in which he developed his enlightenment, sociophilosophical, and ethical ideas. Enlightenment was the driving force of social progress. A drawing together of the people and the educated part of Russian society would promote their awareness of their own importance and their own dignity. Belinsky advocated change in the system of education that would make it accessible to the broad masses of the population. The basis of enlightenment, he thought, was the principle of moral self-perfection. He regarded man as the incarnation of the moral idea, which was constantly moving toward perfection. The specific paths of achieving this were the overcoming of the egoistic element, the fostering of a feeling of respect for and love of people, and the developing of esthetic feeling.

Belinsky's philosophical position was brought out in *Literary Reveries*. It was largely determined by the influence of Schelling. Starting from a thesis of the identity of a single mind with itself, Belinsky wrote:

> The whole infinite, beautiful, divine world is nothing but the breath of a single, eternal *idea* (the idea of a single, eternal God) manifesting itself in innumerable shapes as a great spectacle of absolute unity in infinite diversity. Only the ardent feeling of a mortal can, at its lucid moments comprehend how great is the *body* of this soul of the universe, whose heart is formed by immense suns, its veins by Milky Ways and its blood by the pure ether.[1]

It can easily be noted that his early philosophical reflections were based on his intuitive knowledge of a cosmomorphous God (idea) in which the material and the spiritual coexisted without visible contradictions. The absolute appeared before man in concrete material forms. Man could only understand the infinity of the universe and the diversity of its manifestations as a cosmic divine essence intuitively, in a kind of revelation.

In the realm of esthetics Belinsky developed an idea of "intellectual intuition" of the beautiful, of the priority of art over science. He declared that man got his main notion of the world through inspired esthetic feeling rather than through reason. Since his intellect was not capable of grasping the "Life of the Universe," the "aim of art was to reflect the phenomena of life." In his reliance on intuition, Belinsky proceeded from the notion of an "instinctive" and unconscious character of creative activity (one of the results of which was knowledge of the phenomena of life).

Belinsky treated artistic creation as an unfathomable act of "mysterious second sight," and perceived it, in the spirit of romanticism, as a "synthetic" comprehension of the world. But in *Literary Reveries* anti-Schellingian motives were already discernible and were particularly clearly displayed in his appraisal of the new, realist trend in art that he lauded for its depiction of real life.

Belinsky's departure from Schelling's philosophy in 1834-36 coincided with a new stage in his study of German philosophy. He was then studying the main philosophical tenets of Fichte's doctrine. The latter's ideas of man's freedom and of the possibility of building an ideal society on the principles of reason and justice, on a foundation of universal moral principles, impressed Belinsky most of all at that time.

The publication of Chaadayev's *Philosophical Letter* in *Teleskop* in 1836 had a serious impact on Belinsky's intellectual interests. It pushed him to a more profound study of the historical past and present Russia.

THE PHILOSOPHICAL MEANING OF "RECONCILIATION WITH REALITY"

The next period in the evolution of Belinsky's ideas was complex and contradictory. This stage in his life is usually called the time of "forced reconciliation with reality."

In the words of Georgi Plekhanov, it was "a new phase in his philosophical development" that represented "an enormous stride in comparison with the preceding one." In order to understand Plekhanov's words, we have to take into account all the positive ideas in the field of contemporary philosophy Belinsky had assimilated by that time.

Since the end of 1837 and up to the early 1840s Belinsky was very systematically studying Hegel's philosophy. In Stankevich's circle Hegel's *Esthetics, Encyclopedia of the Philosophical Sciences,* and *Phenomenology of Mind* were actively discussed. Belinsky himself noted in one of his letters of 1837 that it was natural to go from Schelling to Hegel: "In order to understand Hegel it is necessary to become familiar with Kant, Fichte, and even Schelling."[2] At the same time, he wrote that, "Philosophy is the science of a pure, abstract idea; history and natural science are the sciences of the idea in phenomena."[3] Following Schelling he ovecame the Fichtean treatment of intuition (as the self-contemplation of Ego), understanding it as the form of the self-contemplation of the absolute, and advanced further, to the assimilation of Hegel's rationalism. He came to believe that truth did not come from experience and was not attained through inner feeling but was "transmitted from the spirit to experience." Theory underlies cognitive activity; "the facts should be explained by the idea, rather than ideas deduced from facts."[4]

The philosophical constructs of the period of "reconciliation" were marked by a critical attitude to French sensationalism and materialism. Belinsky ruthlessly criticized (sometimes a bit too harshly) the French Encyclopedists in his review of Fyodor Glinka's *Essays on the Battle of Borodino* (*Ocherki Borodinskogo srazheniya*).

> The materialists of the eighteenth century wanted to explain the origin of the world by the mechanical cohesion of atoms, by mechanical processes of the interaction of gravity and the attractions stemming from its mathematical laws; but this *explanation* only *obscured* the essence of the matter because, while being externally clear, it was internally *murk[y]*. And how could there be light in it and not gloom when they saw only some pulleys, cords, nails, and glue in the Universe and not hot blood and nerves tingling with electricity—a dead skeleton and not a living organism as the expression of the spirit of life moving in it?[5]

He was then convinced that materialism was not worth serious attention and interpreted the materialist tradition as an intermediate stage in the movement of thought to the true (Hegelian) philosophy.

There is no doubting the influence of Hegel on the evolution of Belinsky's views, but this influence was a shove toward construction of his own philosophical conception. It is important that his attention was centered on reality itself, which insistently called for understanding and interpretation. He gave Hegel's idea of development as a struggle of opposites concrete application. In this same review he showed up the contradiction between the individual and the social milieu. Man was the particular, the individual, the general, the embodiment of the idea. In public life there was an immanent, constant struggle in a person between the particular and the general. By sacrificing his own subjectivity, the individual could become a necessary part of the general, which would make it possible for him "to reconcile himself with the world, the general, having recognized it alone as truth and reality." Since the general was characteristic not of man but of the environment, man must "take to it and merge" with it.[6]

"Rational experience" suggested to man the inevitability of reconciliation with reality, because he drew everything necessary for his existence from the environment. The combination of the finite and infinite being in human reason was the grounds, according to Belinsky, for the reason of man as a private person reconciling with reality as the universal entity. He admitted the social milieu to be the supreme reality; a person was consequently obliged to reconcile himself with society, surrendering his own personality.

For Belinsky Hegel's absolute spirit was not only the rational foundation of existent and potential being, but also absolute love and absolute good. The absolute spirit was rational and moral. By excluding the moment of negation from it (which was of special importance for Hegel's system), Belinsky saw the road to social perfection in moral self-improvement: "If each of the individuals who constitute Russia, attained perfection through love, then Russia would become the happiest country in the world without any politics."[7]

So the formula "the real is rational, and the rational is real" was perceived uncritically. It was interpreted in the spirit of rigid determinism. By the category "rational" Belinsky understood "necesssary": "History can be *written* only by a nation that *makes* history with its own life, i.e., builds up a mass of *rational,* not *haphazard* events, such as constitute the subject matter of history."[8] A person could only act in reality by relying on it and by understanding its obligatory laws. He was incapable, according to Belinsky, of changing anything in real existence through his subjective wish. Reality was the first principle, and man one of its numerous products. From that Belinsky drew the conclusion that there was nothing left for a person than to recognize the "rationality" of existing reality.

Belinsky's philosophical development prepared, as it were, his temporary "reconciliation with reality," while rejection of those theoretical fallacies meant his final formation as a philosopher, critic, and public figure. But at the same time it also led to justification of the social order existing in Russia. While considering that serfdom had not outlived itself, Belinsky hoped for governmental measures to improve the position of the peasants.

Being in a state of necessity meant being rational, according to Belinsky. Social reality, which had its inner causality, acquired the character of necessity and so the status of rationality. The social milieu was the guardian of the rational idea of the state, which passed from abstract being to the existent and empirical. Progress of the state did not depend on people's activity, which could not lead to replacement of certain principles by others. No change in society should affect the main state principles, and any changes could only come from the state and be implemented by it. Belinsky came to idealize the state mainstays and the Russian autocracy. The position of the social strata of Russia, he believed, depended entirely on the czar. He had only to help the peasantry for the gentry to cease to be a privileged class. Belinsky saw an exceptional feature of Russia in the close "unity" of the people and the autocracy in both the past and the present.

FROM CONTEMPLATION TO DIALECTICAL NEGATION

A new stage in the development of Belinsky's ideas coincided with his move to St. Petersburg (at the end of 1839); it was associated first and foremost with his rejection in the early 1840s of reconciliatory moods and his working out of the methodological foundations for a reinterpretation of reality and clarification of its social perspectives. He set out his new demands on the social sciences in the following works: his reviews of Friedrich Lorentz's *Guide to World History ("Rukovodstvo k vseobshchei istorii"*[1843]), Nikolai Markevich's *History of Little Russia ("Istoriya Malorossii"* [1843]), and S. N. Smaragdov's *Guide to the Study of Modern History for Secondary Schools ("Rukovodsto k poznaniyu novoi istorii dlya srednikh uchebnykh zavedeniy"*[1844]).

Belinsky returned again and again to philosophical problems, and significantly altered his attitude to the concept of reality. From an understanding of it as an "existent being" he passed to awareness of the inner laws and patterns of its becoming and change, from a contemplative attitude to reality to a more active one. "A knowledge of facts is valuable *only because* facts contain ideas; facts without ideas are mental dross."[9] Any investigation should have a philosophical substantiation and unite an aspiration for truth with an underlying fundamental idea. The task of philosophy was to find "an uninterrupted thread that passes through all events and connects them, giving them the character of something whole and integral. This thread is the idea of consciousness evolving dialectically in events, so that every sequence is a necessary outcome of the precedent and the precedent is the origin and cause of the sequent."[10]

It was necessary, for objective investigation, to have a capacity for critical analysis. Any serious thinker analyzing problems of social development was obliged, according to Belinsky, to have a philosophical education because "history is not only art but also complex, many-sided science."

Belinsky began reconsidering his "reconciliation" from these methodological positions. In a letter to Konstantin Aksakov in 1840 he expressed his attitude to Russian reality: "Russia is not a society. We have no political, or religious, or scientific, or literary life."[11] On coming up against bureaucratic despotism in the capital, Belinsky declared that St. Petersburg reality was "a terrible rock against which my high-mindedness painfully banged." Herzen described the beginning of the mature period in Belinsky's creative life as follows: "He then won supremacy in the office of *Otechestvennye zapiski* in St. Petersburg, and dominated the Russian press for six years."

This stage in Belinsky's intellectual life was marked by a closer, deeper attitude to Hegelian philosophy, in the dialectics of which he had already identified the moment of negation of the old by the new. Negation was now wholly included in the idea and was declared a necessary aspect of its existence. The rationality of development consisted in that "the succeeding generation had what to negate in the preceding one. But this negation would be an idle, dead, and barren act if it consisted only in annihilation of the old."[12]

Understanding of negation as a necessary element of development helped Belinsky to overcome reconciliation with reality and substantiated and theoretically determined his transition to revolutionary democratic positions. His democratic views soon emerged with the ideas of utopian socialism. His letters to V. P. Botkin are clear evidence of this: "And so, I am now at a new extreme, which is the idea of *socialism*, that has become for me the idea of ideas, the being of beings, the question of questions, the alpha and omega of belief and knowledge. It is the be-all and end-all. It is the question and its solution. It has (for me) engulfed history and religion and philosophy."[13] A new social structure could only be achieved through negation of the existing order. "My God is negation! In history my heroes are the destroyers of the old—Luther, Voltaire, the Encyclopedists, the Terrorists, Byron (*Cain*), and so on."[14] The old could not be annihilated of itself, without sacrifices, "without violent changes, without bloodshed."[15] In short, Belinsky had come to the idea of the necessity of revolutionary overthrow of the autocracy. But he did not pose the question of an immediate peasant revolution, considering it a matter of the future.

In breaking with reconciliatory moods Belinsky also reinterpreted the role of philosophy, considering its essential mission to be to help the masses in becoming aware of their predestination, in reflecting their interests: "To determine the people's outlook is the great task, a gigantic labor, worthy of the efforts of the greatest geniuses, spokesmen of modern philosophical knowledge."[16]

Belinsky's philosophical views of the early 1840s were contradictory. Idealist and materialist trends were closely mingled in them. Thus, while stressing that philosophical knowledge included "the great questions inherent in man's very nature, with which he was born and which he bears in his breast" and that philosophy was "the science of the development in thinking of pretemporal and incorporeal ideas,"[17] he maintained at the same time that investigation of real things and clarification of the patterns of their existence came also into the province of philosophy.

Materialism became noticeably predominant in Belinsky's philosophical ideas only in the mid-1840s. Before that he consistently and deeply assimilated dialectics, in which he saw "the means to reach knowledge of the truth."

Belinsky realized the principle of dialectics most fully in esthetics, in the context of which every phenomenon was perceived as a particular case of the universal law of development. His esthetic conception was based on the principle of the activity of the hero and a conviction that the source of the beautiful lay in the real world around man and not in abstract self-development of the "absolute idea." The main task of a literary work was reflection of reality in all its beauty, complexity, and contradictoriness. The artist's creative work should be based not only on his philosophical and moral principles, but also on his civic position and his devotion to the principle of *narodnost* (national character) in literature.

FROM HEGELIANISM TO MATERIALISM

The mid-1840s were a special stage in Belinsky's intellectual evolution. Then a consolidation of his materialism and anticlericalism occurred. There were very specific reasons for these changes taking place. The transition to positions of materialism was encouraged by radically interpreted dialectics that called for taking reality as it was in its development and many-sidedness. Revolutionary democratic ideas, organically united with ideas of utopian socialism, played a great role in this. Belinsky's personal acquaintance with Herzen encouraged a strengthening of the materialist tendency in Belinsky's views; he was, in addition, strongly influenced by Ludwig Feuerbach's *The Essence of Christianity*.

Belinsky set out his materialist notions most fully in his surveys of Russian literature in 1846 and 1847, in which he formulated the iples of materialism in their application to the realm of art. He also examined the problem of human consciousness, which he defined as a function of the brain: "Psychology which is not based on physiology is as unsubstantial as physiology that knows not the existence of anatomy. . . . Mind without body . . . mind which does not affect the blood and is not affected by its operation is a logical dream, a lifeless abstraction. Mind is man in the flesh, or rather, man through the flesh, in a word, *personality*."[18]

In 1847, Belinsky criticized Auguste Comte, calling his pretensions to rise above the "one-sidedness of materialism and idealism" unsubstantiated. At the same time he treated Comte's philosophical quest as an alternative "to theological interference in science"[19] and put it down to the credit of positivism, though Belinsky considered fruitless Comte's positivist attempts to formulate a new philosophy. In Belinsky's opinion Comte "puts up with the old, thinking to create something new."[20] Belinsky stood for unity of theoretical thought and empirical knowledge. He saw the weakness of the positivist approach in its belittling of the significance of general theoretical knowledge and the generalizing role of philosophy. In striving to exclude everything supernatural and mystical from the realm of knowledge, and in affirming that objective laws of development operated in the world, he noted that for Comte nature and social life were full of "transcendental absurdities" and reality itself was missing.[21]

Two of Belinsky's works, which appeared under the common title *A View on Russian Literature in 1847* (*Vzglyad na russkuyu literaturu 1847 goda*), are of great significance for analyzing his creative evolution. Interpreting in them the relation of conservatism to the progress of society, he set forth an idea of an inevitably political character of all social philosophy. Falsifying reality, reactionaries wanted to "assure themselves and others that stagnation is better than movement, that the old is always better than the new and that living in the past is real, genuine life."[22]

Belinsky's esthetics also changed. He saw the strength of the "natural" esthetic school in a close unity with reality and a truthful reflection of life, and that was linked with a firm belief in social progress. He defined the development of this trend as progress of art, showing that it was a reproduction of reality, a "repeated, a newly created world, as it were." From such positions he, the founder of materialist esthetics in Russia, analyzed the work of Pushkin, Gogol, and other great writers.

When one is examining Belinsky's philosophy, one must mention his acquaintance with works of Marx and Engels. In particular he studied the *Deutsch-Französische Jahrbücher* for 1844. Marx's appraisal of religion made a special impression on him and influenced the shaping of his atheistic views. He wrote about his impressions to Herzen: "I have found the truth—and in the words *God* and *religion* I see darkness, gloom, chains and whip, and now I like these two words—like the four following them."[23]

HIS SOCIAL RADICALISM

The theme of criticism of religion as a premise of social criticism sounded most sharply in Belinsky's open letter to Gogol. While blaming the latter for his departure from realism in his *Selected Passages from Correspondence with Friends* (*Vybrannye mesta iz perepiski s druzyami*), he saw the falseness of this book in Gogol's thirst for clericalism. "Can it be that you, the author of *Inspector General* and *Dead Souls,* have in all sincerity, from the bottom of your heart, sung hymn to the nefarious Russian clergy?"[24] Belinsky thought the Russian Church had always been a bastion of the "knout" and "cringed to despotism"; it was a flatterer of authority, a champion of inequality, and an oppressor of the masses. In this letter to Gogol he formulated a program-minimum of Russian democracy: struggle to abolish serfdom and corporal punishment; a demand to observe at least those laws that had been officially adopted in the country. These issues he called "the most vital national problems in Russia today."[25]

Belinsky paid much attention to the philosophical aspects of world history; yet, all the same, his historicophilosophical interest was centered on Russian history, in which he distinguished two main epochs: pre-Petrine and post-

Petrine. He mistakenly supposed that the Russian state had been framed only under Peter the Great, and that before Peter there had been neither struggle of classes in Russia nor different estates. He treated the Petrine reforms as the boundary between the old Russia and the new.

Belinsky believed the main problem of his time to be the relation between the serf peasants and the landowners, and pointed out the poverty and complete lack of rights of the peasants. He thought that the basis of the contradiction was the agrarian question and the "evil of forced rent." These problems could only be resolved by revolutionary means. A necessary stage of capitalist relations that would further develop industry would be followed by Russia's transition to socialism, because moral perfection of the people, and the establishing of real equality among them, was only possible if changes in society eliminated its division into rich and poor.

Belinsky's understanding of the essence and historical destiny of the peasant commune was an important component of his social philosophy, and he differed significantly from the Slavophiles and from both Chernyshevsky and Herzen in his explanation of it. He did not consider communal ownership of land a feature of Slavonic tribes. The existence of a commune, like its absence, did not provide defense of the masses' interests. Novgorod, for example, had not been a patriarchal commune, but the position of the peasants there had been no easier than in other regions of Russia. Communes had existed among all peoples in the patriarchal period, according to him, so that it was ludicrous to speak of "special features of the Slavonic communal principle" inherent in the Russian people.

Although Belinsky did not have a thoroughly worked-out sociophilosophical conception, the radical democratic ideas he held were a notable contribution to the development of Russian self-awareness. Objectively speaking, Belinsky was the spokesman of peasant protest against serfdom and the forerunner of the leftwing populists and social democrats in Russia.

NOTES

1. V. G. Belinsky, *Selected Philosophical Works* (Moscow: Foreign Languages Publishing House, 1948), pp. 13–14.

2. V. G. Belinsky, *Polnoye sobraniye sochineniy* (Complete works), 13 vols. (Moscow, 1953–59), vol. 11, p. 147.

3. Ibid., p. 146.

4. V. G. Belinsky, *Selected Philosophical Works* (Moscow: Foreign Languages Publishing House, 1956), p. 106.

5. V. G. Belinsky, *Polnoye sobraniye sochineniy*, vol. 3, p. 328.

6. Ibid., p. 340.

7. Ibid., vol. 11, p. 148.

8. Belinsky, *Selected Philosophical Works,* 1948, p. 303.
9. Ibid., p. 300.
10. Ibid., p. 306.
11. V. G. Belinsky, *Polnoye sobraniye sochineniy,* vol. 11, p. 546.
12. Ibid., vol. 6, p. 459.
13. Belinsky, *Selected Philosophical Works,* 1948, p. 159.
14. Ibid., p. 164.
15. Ibid., p. 166.
16. Belinsky, *Polnoye sobraniye sochineniy,* vol. 4, p. 418.
17. Ibid., vol. 6, p. 471.
18. Belinsky, *Selected Philosophical Works,* 1948, p. 369.
19. Ibid., p. 491.
20. Ibid., p. 492.
21. Ibid., p. 493.
22. Ibid., p. 397.
23. Belinsky, *Polnoye sobraniye sochineniy,* vol. 12, p. 250.
24. Belinsky, *Selected Philosophical Works,* 1948, p. 506.
25. Ibid., p. 504.

14

Alexander Herzen

Alexei Pavlov

MILESTONES IN HIS LIFE AND WORK

Alexander Herzen (1812–1870) was one of the most influential Russian materialist philosophers of the middle of the nineteenth century. Together with Belinsky he opened a new page in the development of materialism in Russia; he tried to unite materialism with dialectics and interpret history from materialist positions.

Herzen was the illegitimate son of Ivan Yakovlev, a rich Russian landowner, and Henriette-Luise Haag, a native of Stuttgart, whom Yakovlev had brought to Russia from Germany in 1811. Herzen's surname was derived from the German word *Herz* (heart). He was brought up like a typical Moscow gentleman, but his "false position" in the family (his parents were not officially married) left a deep track on the impressionable boy's soul. The Decembrist uprising of December 14, 1825, had an immense effect on the molding of his views. The execution of Pestel and his colleagues "awoke the boyish dream of my soul," Herzen later recalled.

Hatred of any arbitrary rule and despotism, and an aspiration to do everything he could to liberate the people from social enslavement, became Herzen's prime motivators throughout his whole life. While a student of the Physics and Mathematics Department of Moscow University (1829–1834), he was drawn to the socialist ideas of Saint-Simon, particularly his "new Christianity," i.e., the idea of a modernized Christian teaching that would, when freed from the hypocrisy of the official Church, be able to rally the masses around it to struggle for the building of a society on principles of justice and fraternity. Herzen then believed that socialist ideas needed a religious envelope and that the masses were not capable of assimilating social ideas in their secular political form. The new social system could only win with the support of the masses; the failure of the Decembrists' action convinced him of that. Together with Nikolai Ogarev he formed a circle of friends that focused on debates about the future of Russia, socialism, and revolution.

In 1834, Herzen and Ogarev were arrested in connection with a "case of persons singing lampoons in Moscow." They were accused of forming a secret organization to overthrow the government by disseminating "revolutionary ideas imbued with the malignant doctrines of Saint-Simon." Herzen was exiled under police surveillance to the Russian interior, where he remained until 1839. In 1840 he settled with his family in St. Petersburg, but was again arrested in 1841 for "spreading baseless rumors." A Senate order appointed him counselor to the administration in Novgorod Province, where he had been exiled. His distaste for civil service that made him an accomplice in autocratic feudal oppression led him to apply for retirement and permission to move to Moscow in 1842. After moving to Moscow, he quit Russia forever in 1847.

In Italy, and later in France, Herzen saw the revolutionary events of 1848 with his own eyes, believing then that it was a struggle for socialist reforms. The shooting of Parisian workers and a reaction to revolution aroused great skepticism in him.

After the defeat of the revolutions of 1848 and 1849, Herzen, disillusioned with the ability of the West European nations to carry out socialist principles, became convinced that the village commune preserved in Russia, with its common ownership of the land and self-government, could become the groundwork for reforming society along the lines of justice. In 1853 he set up the Free Russian Printing House in London, and from 1855 he began to publish an almanac, *Polyarnaya zvezda* (*North Star*), in which he censured serfdom and autocracy. His propaganda for the ideas of "Russian" socialism laid the basis of Populism as a broad ideological trend, whose goal was a noncapitalist development of Russia through strengthening the economic basis of the peasant commune. From 1857 to 1867 Herzen, together with Ogarev, who had moved to London, published *Kolokol* (*The Bell*), the first revolutionary newspaper in the history of Russia; it was the first organ of the free Russian press, a weapon of effective criticism of czarist despotism and of the system based on serfdom, and a disseminator of ideas of free thought and radical social and philosophical views.

Herzen and Ogarev organized their circle in Moscow University and propagandized the ideas of Saint-Simon and the French Revolution right to the end of the 1830s. He won particularly broad popularity when he began to publish his works in *Otechestvennye zapiski* (*Fatherland Notes*) and *Sovremennik* (*The Contemporary*). His novel *Who Is Guilty?* (*Kto vinovat?*), his stories *The Thieving Magpie* (*Soroka-vorovka*) and *Doctor Krupov* consolidated antifeudal feeling in Russia, while his philosophical works *Dilettantism in Science* (*Diletantizm v nauke*) and *Letters on the Study of Nature* (*Pisma ob izuchenii prirody*) molded a critical attitude to the dominant religious and idealist views, and fostered a scientific mode of thinking and secular world outlook. In spite of the official ban on his works and their withdrawal from libraries, everything he published before going abroad was carefully hand-copied and preserved by his many admirers, and widely read.

Herzen's influence on Russian social consciousness and the emancipation movement peaked in the second half of the 1850s and early 1860s, when the uncensored *Bell,* which was secretly distributed in Russia, became a threat to czarism and a center of attraction for all the revolutionary forces of Russia. (Another center of opposition was the editorial board of *Sovremennik,* headed by Chernyshevsky.) The *Bell*'s publication not only inspired the anti-feudal forces but also affected the policy and behavior of the authorities. Alexander II's accession to the throne in 1855, and his announcement of his intention to emancipate the peasants, gave rise to hopes of their impending real liberation. But that period of counting on radical changes coming "from above" rapidly passed. The abolition of serfdom in 1861 was neither complete nor economically just, and therefore *The Bell,* following Chernyshevsky and Dobrolyubov, sharply criticized the reform. "The czar has deceived the people"—such was the political conclusion Herzen drew from analyzing the czar's manifesto on emancipation of the peasants. For all his waverings between democracy and liberalism, Herzen the democrat had usually come out on top in the past; now he completely broke with the ideas of reformism and came out without reservations for solution of the land question by the peasants themselves.

PHILOSOPHY AS AN INSTRUMENT OF ACTION

Herzen's series of articles under the general title of *Dilettantism in Science* (1843) was evidence of his persistent search for an explanation of the relation of matter and spirit. In the articles, he set himself the task of comprehending the role of philosophy as a science among the other sciences and its place in the life of society. The need for a close alliance between philosophy and religion was being argued at that time by the Russian intellectuals, especially the Slavophiles. Herzen came out against that with a thesis of the necessity of an alliance of philosophy with natural science rather than religion.

In this work there was a marked striving to get away from the influence of Hegel, whose ideas had then become quite widespread in Russia. Herzen protested against attempts to fence science and philosophy off from everyday life, and to shut them up within a circle of specialists. He reinterpreted Hegelian philosophy in the radical spirit and claimed that logic, knowledge should not only provide man with truth but also help him leave the realm of pure theory for real life and introduce the advances of science into practice. "Modern science . . . struggles for freedom, desirous of contributing a decisive voice in the practical spheres of life."[1] To confine oneself to cognition alone, without "activizing" knowledge, i.e., without using its results to transform reality, meant to reconcile oneself to that reality. Herzen rejected such a reconciliation, which was characteristic of the Right Hegelians, and of Belinsky, in the period 1837–1840.

Herzen interpreted Hegel's idea of man's active thought in terms of materialism. "Man's vocation, however," he wrote, "is not logic alone, but also the socio-historical world of moral freedom and positive action. . . . Man cannot forbear from the human work around him. He must act in his place and his time and this is his universal vocation, his *conditio sine qua non*."[2]

Dilettantism in Science was an important stage in the development of Russian philosophy. Now philosophy was seen as a theoretical activity that not only had a cognitive value but was also called upon to be an instrument transforming the existing socio-economic and political structures and not just explaining them. At that time, however, Herzen still accepted many propositions of Hegelian idealism and panlogism. But his striving to apply ideas in life, and to put philosophy on a scientific basis, took him beyond a contemplative and abstractly philosophical attitude to reality and forced him seriously to engage in analysis and interpretation of the latest achievements in natural science. In a letter of December 2, 1843, i.e., after having already completed publication of *Dilettantism in Science,* he remarked: "I am thus beginning to quarrel with Hegel because he extends idealism to everything. . . . It enrages me when he says that 'the Spirit descends to the multifariousness of being,' that it 'leaves the alien milieu of Nature'—and that is as stupid as to say 'children with whooping cough like to cough strongly.' "[3]

AN ALLIANCE OF PHILOSOPHY AND THE SCIENCES OF NATURE

In order to substantiate the impossibility of an independent existence of the spiritual without the material it was necessary to understand the laws of their interconnection and interaction, the mechanisms of the generation of the ideal by the material, and the transition of the ideal into the material. That is why Herzen began seriously to enlarge his knowledge in the natural sciences, believing that only they could cleanse the mind of prejudices and help pose and answer the traditional questions of philosophy.

In 1845–46 he published a series of articles under the general title of *Letters on the Study of Nature.* In that major philosophical work the results of his materialist interpretation of Hegel's dialectics were already clearly visible.

While criticizing idealism for deriving nature from reason and stressing that, on the contrary, reason was nothing else than "nature's cognizance of itself,"[4] he at the same time criticized naturalists and materialists for isolating thinking from nature, and for contraposing thinking to nature as something external to it. The perception of intellect as only the subject in contrast to nature as the object prevented naturalists from comprehending the unity of man and nature and grasping the objective character of cognition, i.e., from seeing it in a process subordinated to the universal laws of nature and interwoven in the latter. Instead of the metaphysical identification of spirit and nature proclaimed by classical German philosophy, Herzen strove to comprehend the idea of identity from a materialist position and to bridge the gulf between the subjective and the objective characteristic of the French and German materialists of the eighteenth and nineteenth centuries.

> The materialists, indeed, could not understand the objectivity of the mind and therefore they, naturally, falsely defined not only the historical development of thought, but also the general relations between mind and object and, at the same time, the relation between man and nature. For them, being and thought are either dissociated or react upon each other in an external way.[5]

In the *Letters* Herzen was striving to show the necessity of a dialectical method that could be realized in science. He was convinced that science alone could bring man closer to true comprehension of the world and at the same time noted the incapacity of scientists to provide a full picture of the development of nature because of their "empiricism," formalism, and lack of a philosophical and historical view of things. The idea of development, so comprehensively formulated by German idealism from Kant to Hegel, had not been adequately appreciated by scientists, who regarded nature not in its development and universality, but as a mechanical aggregate of various natural objects and processes that did not have an inner unity. "Neither mankind nor nature can be understood," he stressed, "apart from their historical development."[6]

As a philosopher, Herzen was inclined to look for the roots of human consciousness in nature, which evolved from the physical and biological to the social. He treated man and his thinking as the result of the motion of the material world as a whole and in the final analysis as a property, a quality of matter. Following Hegel he defended the unity of the laws of thought and nature, but in opposition to the great idealist he claimed that the laws of thought (i.e., "logic" in the terminology of the day) did not precede nature but stemmed from its development. For him the key to the solution of the relation of thought to being was the very fact of the development of nature. Those who divorced thinking from nature, he declared, proceeded from the idea that nature was incapable of qualitatively developing. But if nature was examined in development, i.e., "as it is," it turned out that "consciousness is by no means external to nature, it is rather the highest stage of its development."[7]

Analysis of man's cognition of the nature around him brought Herzen to a conclusion on the limited character of metaphysical materialism, for which consciousness was only a passive recipient of external influences. Consciousness was not passive in the act of cognizing and did not leave an object as it was but impressed on it a stamp of the universal.

But Herzen did not give an adequate explanation for the source of the activeness of consciousness, perceiving it as an inherent property of the latter. When explaining the unity of consciousness and nature, he focused on their genetic connection and ignored the social factors, practice, and labor activity, all of which generated consciousness. The concept of practice did not have its due place in his philosophy, so that he, as Lenin put it, "came right up to dialectical materialism, and halted—before historical materialism."[8]

The criterion of truth for Herzen was not practice (as for Marx and Lenin) but thought and reason. Feeling the inadequacy of this criterion, he defined his position more precisely, noting that truth could only be found in thinking liberated from personal character, and, furthermore, that "truth must be proven not by thought alone but by thought and being."[9] These corrections, however, did not lead to overcoming a certain naturalism in his understanding of consciousness and truth.

SOCIETY AND HISTORY

After his departure abroad, Herzen did not write any special works on philosophy; his whole attention was absorbed by the revolutionary events of 1848–1849 in Western Europe and the struggle against serfdom in Russia. That did not mean, however, that his philosophical views were not enriched. In his autobiographical work *My Past and Thoughts* (*Byloye i dumy*), which he wrote between 1852 and 1868, and in such works as *Letters from France and Italy* (*Pisma iz Frantsii i Italii*), *From the Other Shore* (*S togo berega*), *On the Development of Revolutionary Ideas in Russia* (*O razvitii revolyutsionnykh idei v Rossii*), *The Russian People and Socialism* (*Russky narod i sotsializm*), and *To an Old Comrade* (*K staromu tovarishchu*), he constantly discussed philosophical problems.

The major ones were connected with a set of philosophical-historical and social issues. What exerted a decisive influence on the development of social events? How was one to analyze the patterns of historical development and what was their essence? What were the sources and causes of mass movements? There was still another question of major importance for the Russian radicals who reflected on the people and revolution. How was the consciousness of the masses molded? Spontaneously, through the impact of the facts of life, or through the effect on them of the will and ideas of leaders, confident in their knowledge of the historical patterns and the direction of social progress?

His first impressions of public life in Western Europe brought Herzen to a clear awareness that the ideals that had been evolved by the philosophers of the Enlightenment and that had been struggled for during the French Revolution had not been realized. That threw doubt on the whole philosophy of history based on the ideals of the Enlightenment, together with its central thesis that reason played a decisive role in social progress. In December 1847 Herzen wrote: "We saw all the hopes of the theoretical minds derided, heard the daemon of history laugh at the expense of their science, ideas, theories. . . . Having made a deeper study of revolutionary questions, we demand today what they demanded, but in a greater and wider degree, yet even their demands remain as unapplicable as before."[10]

Herzen did more than criticize the philosophers of the Enlightenment for their excessively optimistic view of history as a process of continuous realization of rational ideas. He also drew attention to the defects of Hegel's notion of progress as the logical development of goals originally inherent in the absolute spirit. "Needless to say, the laws of historical evolution do not contradict the precepts of logic but they do not coincide with the ways of thought, just as nothing in nature coincides with the abstract standards set up by pure reason."[11]

As a result of his spiritual crisis Herzen ceased to believe in the rationality of history and the incontestability of its laws. Yet it would be erroneous to conclude that he had come to think of the dominance of chance and rationalism in it, and the impossibility of foreseeing the trend of social development. Herzen by no means denied regularities of historical development. However, he treated their action not as a fatal inevitability of certain paths of development but rather as the subordination of history to laws whose manifestation depended on the activity of the masses and that were not realized without their will. "Obeying one and the same law of gravity, a feather flies and lead falls," he remarked. The same in history: "The future does not exist; it is made up of the sum total of a thousand conditions, both essential and fortuitous, plus the human will."[12]

What then underlies historical circumstances? And what stimulates man's motives? Herzen had no clear answer to these questions, but he was aware that people's actions stemmed from their needs and interests. Being convinced of the impracticability of utopian ideals and the nondependence of the development of society on the subjective desires of outstanding individuals, he came to the conclusion that the root of all social change had to be sought in the life of the people and not in the minds of prominent historical figures.

When reflecting on the motive forces of history Herzen stressed the important role the economic foundations of society played in the perception and realization (or nonrealization) by people of political ideas, including the socialist ones. Having arisen among European nations, the latter could "germinate" only in soil where they met understanding and appropriate social conditions: "The fact alone of communal ownership of the land and the re-allotting of fields in itself justifies the assumption that our uncultivated soil, or black earth, is *more suitable* for the cereal crops harvested from Western fields. Better suited because of the elements it consists of, and more suitable because there is less rubbish and ruins of every kind of it than on Western fields."[13]

Why, then, did the "Russian soil" suit socialism better than the Western? Herzen took material factors primarily into account. The economic life of West European nations, he remarked, was based on private property, so that the consciousness of the masses was imbued with a spirit of individualism, while the Russian people had been accustomed to communal ownership of the land from time immemorial, thus the idea of social ownership was close to them and understood by them. That opened more prospects for implementing socialist principles in Russia. These arguments contained a true idea that the consciousness of a people was determined by its being. At the same time he did not renounce the idea of an immanent ability of consciousness to generate spontaneously ideas and programs of social development.

At the end of the 1860s Herzen was leaning toward recognition of a certain dependence of consciousness on people's activity. In a letter to his son in which he discussed free will, he expressed an idea that consciousness itself was the result of a long series of previous acts that man himself had already forgotten, that it was the result of human intercourse and historical development rather than a function of the organism as such. "Social man escapes physiology," he wrote, "while sociology, on the contrary, takes possession of him as he leaves the state of simple animal life."[14]

In the final analysis, Herzen tended to link together his conclusions that consciousness and ideality have a natural basis with an admission that society and historical regulations play an important role in determination of mind and possibilities for people freely to express and realize their will and aspirations.

THE INDIVIDUAL AND FREEDOM

Problems of ethics and the molding of the personality, and of the conditions for its comprehensive development, had a significant place in Herzen's theoretical searches. He treated these issues from secular positions and criticized in this context feudal and bourgeois morality. The latter was based, in his view, on a formal proclamation of rights without any attempt to secure sufficient guarantees (social and moral) of their realization. At the same time, the main point was harmoniously to combine absolute freedom of the individual with respect for the rights of other persons.

"True ethical interest does not consist in proscription of egoism (which will never be assimilated by fraternity), but rather in a search for means of joining these two great elements of human life together in a harmony in which they can help each other, instead of tearing each other to pieces as in the Christian world."[15]

A combination of egoism and sociality was possible on condition that the former was reasonable and the latter did not suppress the freedom of the individual. The nature of human relations itself was dynamic and that opened prospects for a search and establishment of adequate forms of human intercourse:

> The harmony between the individual and society is not established once and for all: it *becomes* with every period, in every country, and is changed by circumstances as are all things in life. There can be no universal solution, no common standards. . . . Unfortunately, it is not within our power to change the historical relation between the individual and society. Nor is this within the power of society itself. But it is within our power to be abreast of the times, to be in accord with our development, in short, *to shape* our conduct according to the circumstances. A free man does indeed *shape* his morals. . . . There are no unshakable, eternal morals as there are no eternal rewards and punishments.[16]

The evolution of moral standards was conditioned by the development of social relations and is at the same time inseparable from the self-awareness of the people who constituted society. However powerful the social factor might be, in the sphere of ethics it could not relieve man of personal responsibility for his actions.

THE ROAD TO "RUSSIAN SOCIALISM"

A central subject of Herzen's political philosophy related to domestic affairs was emancipation of the peasants, with retention of communal ownership of the land. He saw in that the shortest road to socialism, whose essence, he believed, was social ownership of the means of production.

An irreconcilable opponent of serfdom and a consistent advocate of the economic interests of the peasants, Herzen worked out his tactics for the struggle against feudal dependence in accordance with the possibilities of a peaceful or a violent road to emancipation of the peasants. While preferring a peaceful road to reform, he never rejected the possibility of armed struggle as an extreme, though at the same time very effective, means of achieving freedom.

The defeat of the West European revolutions did not kill Herzen's belief in the possibility of revolutionary social reform and the expediency—under definite conditions—of a forcible social revolution. True, when explaining his preference for peaceful means of deciding the peasant question in Russia, he said that the blood of the defeated insurgents "had entered my brain and nerves, and since then I have cultivated in myself a repugnance to blood when it flows without absolute necessity."[17] But that argument dated from the second half of the 1850s, when hope had developed for emancipation of the peasants with the accession of Alexander II. In the early 1850s, however, Herzen stressed that only armed struggle could bring about liberation of the peasants: "Because the nobles wait and do nothing, the government takes measures which it fails to execute. . . . There remain only two resources for the oppressed—if he wishes to gain his freedom, the scythe and the axe."[18]

The ignorance of the people and their low level of political self-awareness brought Herzen to the conclusion that the place of a leader of the revolutionary movement should be taken by a person or group of persons of a different social origin. The nobility could, in his opinion, lead the popular uprising. Why? Because the radical ideological, intellectual forces of the emancipation movement were concentrated precisely in the milieu of the gentry. The masses were dissatisfied with the existing situation; they were ready to rise up and smash the old social structure. But building of the new, socialist society called for knowledge, which the educated gentry, familiar with Western social science, had at its disposal.[19] The gentry had to lead the people's movement both to help peasants to satisfy their desires and to protect culture from destruction. Meanwhile Herzen appealed to the privileged social groups of czarist Russia to compromise and be ready to yield the masses their demands for social justice and equality. "It seems wiser and *more prudent* to give way than to wait for the explosion,"[20] Herzen appealed to the nobility in 1858. Recalling the sad experience of the Decembrists' uprising, he proposed the uniting of the gentry's and the peasants' movements under the motivation of one aspiration, viz., abolition of serfdom and retention of communal landownership as the most important step toward Russian socialism.

Proceeding from the rational premise that the masses play the decisive role in history, and that success or failure of the socialist "re-creation" of society depended on their activity, Herzen believed at the same time that since the masses were interested in economic reforms and improving their life and did not display interest in political forms of revolution or the state system as such (he was close to the Slavophiles in this), any means could bring about these reforms; only the result was important, viz., emancipation of the peasants and assigning of the land to them. Moreover, he was well aware that, while demanding abolition of serfdom, the peasants, as a rule, did not entertain antimonarchist views. Herzen even thought that the political indifference of the people actually meant that they were ready to support any government so long as it was capable of radically altering the economic position of the peasantry and giving it freedom and land.

The unduly moderate character of the peasant reform of 1861 finally dispelled Herzen's hope of the possibility of a just solution of the peasant question by the autocracy; from that time on he resolutely maintained a radical democratic position.

Nevertheless for decades the most important aspects of the philosophical heritage of the theoretician of "Russian socialism" were neglected or treated one-dimensionally. That is especially true in terms of Herzen's purposeful struggle for freedom and dignity of personality, his defense of the human right to resist the threat of society and state. For ideological reasons historians in the now defunct USSR deliberately avoided analyzing the elements of irrationality in Herzen's social philosophy as well as the tragic motives in his contemplations of world history. He admitted that the history of humankind is based not only on the social and economic regularities, moral and religious norms, etc., but also that at any moment the irrational (unknown), unpredictable, and tragic can interfere with world community. That is why it would be inaccurate to define Herzen's philosophy of history as rationalistic and naively optimistic. The vision of both rational and irrational aspects of history forced Herzen to look for the more universal, rich, and dynamic relations between human beings and the outside world.

NOTES

1. Alexander Herzen, *Selected Philosophical Works* (Moscow: Foreign Languages Publishing House, 1956), p. 51.

2. Ibid., pp. 83–84.

3. A. I. Herzen, *Sobraniye sochineniy* (Collected works), 30 vols. (Moscow, 1954–65), vol. 22, p. 162.

4. Herzen, *Selected Philosophical Works*, p. 117.

5. Ibid., p. 291.

6. Ibid., p. 135.

7. Ibid., p. 133.

8. V. I. Lenin, "In Memory of Herzen," *Collected Works* (Moscow: Progress Publishers, 1983), vol. 38, p. 5.

9. Herzen, *Selected Philosophical Works*, p. 254.

10. Ibid., p. 358.

11. Ibid., p. 394.

12. Ibid., p. 360.

13. Herzen, *Sobraniye sochineniy*, vol. 15, p. 148.

14. Herzen, *Selected Philosophical Works*, pp. 571, 573.

15. Herzen, *Sobraniye sochineniy*, vol. 12, p. 234.

16. Herzen, *Selected Philosophical Works*, pp. 457–58.

17. Herzen, *Sobraniye sochineniy,* vol. 14, p. 243.

18. Ibid., vol. 12, p. 40.

19. Subsequently Lenin expressed similar ideas in his work *What Is to Be Done?* when substantiating his theory of the party of a new type.

20. Herzen, *Sobraniye sochineniy,* vol. 12, p. 83.

15

Nikolai Ogarev

Alexei Pavlov

MILESTONES IN HIS LIFE AND WORK

Nikolai Ogarev (1813–1877) was the closest friend, ally, and associate of Alexander Herzen. They jointly published the journal *Kolokol* (*The Bell*) free from czarist censorship and fought together for the emancipation of the Russian peasants from serfdom; they shared similar views on the main philosophical and social problems. As youths they had sworn to dedicate their lives to the struggle for freedom and democracy against autocracy.

Soon after graduation from Moscow University, Ogarev and Herzen were brought to trial for participation in a circle claimed to have revolutionary inclinations. Ogarev was exiled to Penza under police surveillance. In 1839 he was permitted to move to Moscow, and in 1841 to go abroad.

Ogarev's stay in Europe enabled him to acquaint himself firsthand with the latest ideas of Western philosophers—Hegel, Schelling, Feuerbach, and others. Those travels shaped his materialist views. In France, and especially in Germany, he was shocked by the poverty of the factory workers and their lack of rights. That picture of social inequality, even more terrible than in Russia—where the commune helped even the poorest peasants to survive and not to die of hunger—gave rise to his interest in the peasant commune. He saw in communal, collective landownership the salutary rational principle on which a society could be based. But when he returned to Russia in 1846, and made closer acquaintance with the real state of affairs in the Russian village, he began to have strong doubts about the capacity of the peasant commune for movement toward a socialism that would ensure the spiritual freedom and human dignity of each particular person. "Our commune is the

231

equality of slavery," he said. Still he continued to regard the principles of collective landownership and self-government as important features of the communal system. In the absence of outside landlord and bureaucratic influence on the commune, sociality, collective ownership could develop into a system of socialist society.

In 1856 Ogarev again left Russia. On arrival in London he immediately joined in the work of the Free Russian Printing House founded by Herzen. On his advice Herzen began publishing the newspaper *Kolokol,* along with an almanac *Polyarnaya zvezda* (*North Star*) as a newspaper supplement. Between 1857 and 1867, in *Kolokol* and other publications, Ogarev published around 170 articles directly appealing to the peasants, Old Believers, dissenters, and schismatics, and containing revolutionary calls for an overthrow of autocracy.

He played an outstanding role in founding a secret society to prepare for a peasant revolution. From 1857 he had already begun to draw up a political program whose central idea was emancipation of the peasants and the land. At an 1861 conference in London attended by himself, Herzen, the Serno-Solovievich brothers, Sleptsov, Obruchev, and Kurochkin, it was decided to form a secret political society, Land and Freedom, which operated from the middle of 1862 to the end of 1864 and was the prototype of Populist political parties in postreform Russia.

PROBLEMS OF PHILOSOPHY

Ogarev was not only one of the leading figures of the Russian liberation movement of the mid-nineteenth century, but he was also an original philosopher. Philosophical subjects occupied a substantial place in his correspondence and publicistic writing. He repeatedly stressed his interest in philosophy and its significance in bringing about the goals of human activity and the sense of everything that exists. "It is as necessary for man to produce a theory of the universe as it is to eat," he wrote.[1]

For him philosophy was not an end in itself. He saw it as a means of clarifying general epistemological and social problems, without solutions to which it was impossible to tackle the specific political and economic tasks facing Russian society. Abolition of feudal slavery was the central concern But what awaited Russia after slavery was abolished? Would it be the bourgeois order like the one that had succeeded feudalism in Western Europe? Or was another road possible? If everything in the world was predetermined by some supreme power—ideas, God, fatalistic necessity—and if there was no regular pattern of social development, then what were the possibilities for people who had the will and who wanted to fight for their ideals and convictions? Did free will exist? Or were all human actions governed by circumstances? Could the man in the street influence history? When occupying himself with these matters Ogarev turned to philosophical theory, because he was aware that the answers to particular questions depended on the answers to general ones. In general, Ogarev tended to present materialistic views of nature, history, and personality. At the same time his knowledge of dialectics as a style of thinking and conception of universal development, worked out in German philosophy mostly by Schelling and Hegel, helped him to transcend the limits and weaknesses of mechanical (vulgar) materialism, represented by Foht and Moleschott. It is no accident that Ogarev named his philosophical views "realism" rather than "materialism." Within its framework he analyzed the structural aspects of space and matter and its movement.

Ogarev pursued the idea that substance and space did not exist separately in nature, and that these concepts were differentiated only from the "anthropological standpoint," while "in fact substance is the same series of planes that do not have thickness, and the same series of noughts in all directions, as a void." Just as substance and space were inseparable, so motion was inherent in matter, without which it could not exist. "The world is the immobility of motion. What we call inertness is only relative equilibrium."[2]

He also reflected on the problem of the thing-in-itself. Criticizing Kant's separation of essence and phenomenon, he remarked:

> The boundary does not lie in the difference between the phenomenon and the essence of things themselves; if their essence were in the difference between phenomenon and essence, and were inaccessible to us, we could not trace even this difference. The point is that the essence of a phenomenon is in the phenomenon, and the anthropological boundaries of reason are by no means in the inaccessibility of essence. The boundaries are in the relation of the cognizing person to the phenomenon which is being cognized.[3]

Though he had become a materialist by the mid-1840s and was firmly convinced that nature was primary in relation to man and society, in that period he tried to explain the origin of consciousness as the development of chemical and biological processes on the surface of the Earth. Meanwhile he had underestimated the role of labor and of society in the formation of the human mind, regarding the nervous system and man's organism in general as the immediate basis of psychic activity; consciousness evolved as a result of the evolution of nature.

NATURE AND SOCIETY

In the 1860s Ogarev began to guess at the role of "social organization," as he put it, in the development of consciousness, but his naturalistic approach was still strong. This was clearly manifest in his attempts to explain not only human life but also social phenomena by resorting to the arguments of anthropology and physiology. "Until we understand anthropology," he wrote to Herzen in 1845, "we are blind in the social world."[4] He considered anthropology a science of concrete man without which "one could not make a single step in history." He believed that human society itself is the "latest and consummate work" of nature. He therefore did not see the fundamental difference between the sciences of society and the sciences of nature. "Science is only one, and is absolutely not dogmatic," he wrote, "i.e., it is history, the history of nature, and its branch, the history of humanity."[5]

During the 1850s and 1860s Ogarev gradually changed his views on the basis of historical laws and regularities. That was a quite complicated business, accompanied with repeated retreats to naturalism. Thus he was still writing, in 1867, that, in spite of the substantial difference between materialism and positivism, the development of the two coincided since they "seek the foundations of the very history of the human race in the physiological laws of the human organism and, perhaps, in the mechanical laws of nature themselves."[6] But already in 1869 he explicitly posed the question of the qualitative difference between the evolution of society and the evolution of nature: "I cannot agree with the comparison of zoological and historical development. That each is a *Naturprodukt,* I do not of course dispute; but each of the two *Naturprodukte* has its own techniques, its own features, its own methods. . . . The gulf between the social and zoology is enormous."[7]

He came to the conclusion, while analyzing history, that the main thing in it was the activity of people, who were not only material, but also spiritual beings. Circumstances were made by people, and not by the will of mysterious fate. People were guided by ideals in their activity and aspired to realize definite ends. "All history follows this road, mankind lives by utopias, and aspires to a fantastic social system, and achieves substantial transformations on the way."[8] Ideals, he argued further, always constituted the goal without which any movement was impossible. Need, requirements gave birth to ideals, and ideals in their turn accounted for history's advance, created it insofar as man sought to attain those ideals through his actions.

But the indisputable fact that history was the activity of people and depended on their consciousness, will, and acts still did not mean that it was created consciously, on the basis of ideals and theories developed by the people of the period. "The development of the history of Europe is rational, as everything in nature is rational, i.e., each step is the consequence of a certain combination of causes."[9] However great the role of science in the affairs of society, he concluded, "we are unable to reduce the course of historical development exclusively to scientific development."[10]

Ogarev's searches for the mechanism of combining objective factors of the social development on the one hand, and human freedom, purposefulness, science, and morality on the other, led him to consideration of the phenomena that obviously include both material and ideal: consciousness, spirit, conscience, and will. Two such spheres of human life, he pointed out, are practice and economics.

In this connection he began to recognize the decisive influence of economic processes on the whole course of historical development. This idea found its realization in his analysis of Russian history. One of the starting points in this analysis was the period of the Petrine reforms, the underlying reason for which he saw in Russia's acute need for modernization rather than in a blind desire to imitate Western Europe. He considered the "need for new industrial activity" to be the most important factor of further historical advance of Russia. It was not only Peter the Great's reforms that were caused by this need. The Decembrists' attempt at a coup d'etat was also linked, according to Ogarev, with the need to solve the pressing economic problems of Russian society. Moreover, he explained the whole public movement in Russia for the emancipation of the peasants, which commenced in the mid-nineteenth century, as motivated not just by ethical considerations and the shamefulness of maintaining slavery in the age of enlightenment and cultural progress, but primarily by the needs of developing industry. "I shall not speak of the filth of landowners' petty oppressions in which the serf lives stifled; reform is needed for the simplest economic conditions."[11]

The new in society, Ogarev claimed, could only win when the material force, the majority of the people, were all for change. Why couldn't Babeuf's conspiracy succeed? he asked and replied—because French society did not have the appropriate economic base for a socialist revolution. "If Babeuf and his comrades had not been idealists they would, before believing in the success of their cause, . . . have looked for grounds in French public life whose consequences could coincide with their socialism." In that period, "the force of capitalism had grown from a vital, historical root; the expiring feudal dominion was being resolved into capitalism; capitalism was the ideal for all the aspirations of the proletariat."[12] Socialism could not win in France, because it had no economic ground there. It was another matter in Russia. Ogarev was convinced that he was thinking quite materialistically and rationally when he argued that socialist ideas had a firmer economic ground in Russia than in Western Europe. That ground, in his reasoning, was the peasant commune that was based on communal ownership of the land and had absorbed deep traditions of self-government. It seemed to him that the Russian peasants, who did not know private landownership, were spontaneously drawn to socialism as the most just social system. It would be enough just to free them from serf dependence and to secure for them the land that they owned by right of communal property for the age-old habits of collectivism to lead to a socialist society.

The Russian communal peasantry, he argued, jointly held the land, and this collective landownership was the material foundation of socialist development of the countryside. As for the urban proletariat, it did not possess any property and so lacked the material basis for restructuring society on socialist principles.

Ogarev considered the combining of collective and personal interests one of the most complicated problems of socialist theory. He was clearly aware of the danger of the flouting of a person's freedom by the commune and looked for means to harmonize this freedom with collective interests. While in exile, he wrote, arguing about what was the gist in the social question: "To combine egoism and self-sacrifice, that's the point; that is what the social system should strive for." To maintain full freedom of the individual in the setting of the highest development of the social—"that is the task for the life of the human race."[13]

Later, in a work of 1869, again reflecting on this theme, Ogarev said that capitalism showed the impossibility of resolving the problem of freedom of the individual through private property, since those who had no property lacked the chance of enjoying freedom. The guaranteeing of personal freedom for all was thus practicable only on the basis of social ownership. Yet he also sensed the danger of suppression of the rights and freedoms of the individual when public interests were given priority over personal ones. Without free development of the individual, he stressed, mankind's progress was not realizable, and therefore the communal system should be governed by norms that guaranteed individual freedom against suppression. If "*freedom,* i.e., the individual, is destroyed in the commune, i.e., the *collective organization* (let us call it socialism)," he wrote, then society would again come to a "repetition of old systems," to despotism.[14]

In formulating the most characteristic features of Ogarev's social views, we can single out two as the main ones. The first is his conviction that it was the people who shaped the historical needs that led to change in the character of social activity, economic relations, etc. The educated strata of society and scholars only studied and interpreted this creativity of the people. The second is his conviction that no forward movement, and no historical progress, were possible without freedom of the individual. The main, chief role of science was to develop such social mechanisms under which the collective could not suppress the individual and deprive him of freedom of creative realization of his requirements.

Unlike Herzen, who gave the prerogative to science in defining the paths of historical development, Ogarev relied much more on the natural historical process that was the sum total of the actions of human beings.

NOTES

1. N. P. Ogarev, *Izbrannye sotsialno-politicheskiye i filosofskiye proizvedeniya* (*Selected Socio-political and Philosophical Works*), 2 vols. (Moscow, 1952–56), vol. 2, p. 86.

2. Ibid., pp. 41, 53.

3. Ibid., pp. 46–47.

4. Ibid., p. 362.

5. Ibid., vol. 1, p. 409.

6. Ibid., p. 761.

7. Ibid., vol. 2, p. 221.

8. Ibid., vol. 1, pp. 371–72.

9. Ibid., p. 329.

10. Ibid., vol. 2, p. 217.

11. Ibid., vol. 1, p. 109.

12. Ibid., p. 705.

13. Ibid., vol. 2, p. 228.

14. Ibid., p. 195.

16

Nikolai Chernyshevsky
Mikhail Maslin

FROM ORTHODOX THEOLOGY TO POLITICAL RADICALISM

Nikolai Chernyshevsky (1828–1889) is considered to be the most prominent thinker among Russian radical democrats. He was a materialist philosopher, a theoretician of socialism, and a proponent of peasant revolution. His treatment of philosophical problems, his consistent radical democratic position on all the matters agitating Russia of the 1860s, his talent as a publicist and polemicist, and his lofty personal and moral qualities enabled him to become the head of a left-wing trend in Russian social thought of that time.

He was the son of a Saratov priest, who guided his education at home. His father came from the serf peasants of the village of Chernyshev in the Penza Province. Chernyshevsky was educated in the Saratov Theological Seminary and later in the History and Philology Department of St. Petersburg University between 1846 and 1850. His extant seminary compositions* are evidence of the religious (Orthodox) character of his views. Subsequently he called those years "the Middle Ages of my personal history."

Chernyshevsky had become a materialist by the time he finished university, but his political views had been radicalized earlier. In his student diary for 1848 he recorded that he still held Christian views, though more by habit than conviction because they "got along badly" with his new ideas. At the same time, he declared his adherence to the revolutionary way of thinking:

---

*"On the Essence of the World," "Do Our Sense Organs Deceive Us?" "Death Is a Relative Concept"—*O sushchnosti mira, Obmanyvayut li nas chuvstvennye organy? Smert est ponyatie otnositelnoe.*

"I have become a resolute partisan of the socialists and communists and extreme republicans in my views concerning the final goal of mankind."[1]

Chernyshevsky's world outlook was molded under the influence of ancient materialism, the French and English materialism of the seventeenth and eighteenth centuries, the works of natural scientists (Newton, Laplace, and Lalande), the ideas of utopian socialists, English classical political economists, Feuerbach's anthropological materialism, and Hegel's dialectics. His acquaintance with Hegelian philosophy, however, at first in the interpretation of the Left Hegelian Karl Michelet, and later from original sources, was preceded by the study of "Russian expositions of Hegel's system," works of Belinsky and Herzen.

The lectures of professors A. V. Nikitenko and A. A. Fischer, advocates of anthropological idealism, which turned Chernyshevsky's attention to the problem of man, had a certain effect on the shaping of his philosophical interests when a student at the university. But he was still at a loss to picture the mechanism of consistent "application to reality" of the principle of anthropology.

Such an important quality of Chernyshevsky's world outlook as the need to comprehend political events took shape while he was a student and was stimulated by the course of the European revolution of 1848 and study of the works of Louis Blanc, Proudhon, Lamartine, Leroux, and Ledru-Rollin. Already at university he had characterized his political convictions as "red republican and socialist."

"If power were now in my hands, I would immediately proclaim the emancipation of the peasants, discharge half of the troops, if not now, then very soon, limit administrative and government power as much as possible . . . and introduce education, science, and schools as much as possible. And I would probably try to give political rights to women."[2]

Chernyshevsky's interest in problems of politics and the theory of socialism, and especially in the teaching of Charles Fourier, was also stimulated through acquaintance with A. V. Khanykov, a member of M. V. Petrashevsky's democratic circle. His thirst for history was satisfied in the main by reading works of Thierry, Guizot, Barante, Becker, and other West European authors. In addition, he attended the lectures of well-known specialists in world history, Slavonic philology, and Russian literature. The breadth of his academic interests was, on the whole, striking. One can say without exaggeration that Chernyshevsky, who by his own admission "became a bibliophagist and devourer of books very early," did not ignore any branch of knowledge that in any way had social interest, particularly in his student years.

LEADER OF THE RUSSIAN REVOLUTIONARY DEMOCRATS

After finishing university Chernyshevsky worked as a teacher in Saratov and St. Petersburg and then was drawn into literary, publicist activity, writing many articles on questions of politics, philosophy, economics, and history. In 1855 he defended and published his master's thesis "The Aesthetic Relation of Art to Reality" (*Esteticheskie otnosheniya iskusstva k deistvitelnosti*). His contribution to the journal *Sovremennik* (*Contemporary*) was particularly seminal, and he was in fact its leader in the latter half of the 1850s and up to 1862. In that period he became the most popular and influential advocate of a radical, democratic solution of the peasant question, the main social problem in Russia. On the eve of the 1861 reform, a special section "Organizing the Life of Landowners' Peasants" began in *Sovremennik,* to which he was the main contributor. A leader of Russian radical democracy, he also cooperated with other progressive publications. For example, he edited *Voyennyi sbornik* (*Military Anthology*). The ideas propounded by the journal influenced a considerable number of the junior officers who considered themselves Chernyshevsky's followers. He propagandized ideas of socialism in journals and sought to substantiate Russia's transition to socialism through the peasant commune.

In the 1860s Chernyshevsky reached the apogee of his influence on Russian intellectuals and students. At that time he became the leader of a Russian school of philosophical materialism whose members included N. A. Dobrolyubov, D. I. Pisarev, N. V. Shelgunov, M. A. Antonovich, and N. A. and A. A. Serno-Solovievich. After his arrest on a false charge and being imprisoned in the Peter and Paul Fortress in 1862, Chernyshevsky was sentenced (in 1864) to seven years' hard labor and life exile in Siberia. While in the Peter and Paul Fortress he wrote his famous novel *What Is to Be Done?* (*Chto delat?*), which had a revolutionary effect on several generations of Russian left-wing intelligentsia.

Only in 1883, after nineteen years spent in Siberian exile, was Chernyshevsky permitted to settle nearer to the center of the country, in Astrakhan, and later, just before his death, in Saratov. But his studies did not cease in Siberia, and later in Astrakhan. Of particular importance as regards theory was the exposition of his philosophical stand, not distorted by the censor, that he gave in his letters to his sons Alexander and Mikhail between 1876 and 1878.

A HEGELIAN AND A MATERIALIST

Chernyshevsky's "The Aesthetic Relation of Art to Reality," which brought him fame in Russia, was his first philosophical manifesto. This treatise was a polemical attack on the idealist esthetics of Hegel and his followers.

In opposition to idealism in esthetics, which claimed that the beautiful in the material world around us was imperfect because it was unstable in its beauty, isolated, and sometimes inseparable from the coarse and anti-esthetic, Chernyshevsky turned, when tackling the problem of esthetic perception and the criteria of appreciation of the beautiful, to man's real experiences and to the features of his psychology and taste. The beautiful was manifold and diverse and was not reducible to some elusive and normative idea of the beautiful allegedly surpassing all real objects. For him the beautiful was in essence objective and at the same time the result of a generalization of real living impressions.

"The sphere of art," he wrote, "is not limited only to beauty and its so-called elements, but embraces everything in reality (in nature and in life) that is of interest to man not as a scholar, but as an ordinary man; but which is of common interest—such is the content of art."[3]

His philosophy of the beautiful had the aim of showing that the artist did not simply reproduce life but also explained it, aspired to understand it better and express his attitude to its ugly and negative manifestations. In the context of the confrontation of different philosophical trends in Russia, the thesis of the superiority of reality over art acquired a sense of assertion of the primacy of the objective world in regard to the products of human consciousness.

Chernyshevsky's idea of the sociocultural determinableness of esthetic judgments was new and provocative for many Russian intellectuals. Basing himself on concrete life examples he stressed that aristocratic ideals of the beautiful differed very much from concepts of beauty in the folk milieu.

His thesis brought out a strong tendency to interpret the external world as it is objectively. It was fortified by an attentive attitude to the ideas of the outstanding thinkers of the past, both materialists and idealists. The study in Hegel, Kant, Edmund Burke, and Friedrich Fischer greatly influenced his esthetics and his world outlook.

Chernyshevsky was doubtful about the importance of idealism of the late-eighteenth to early-nineteenth centuries, but did not deny its inherent valu-able features, in particular the dialectical method, justifiably noting that it had many constructive ideas that needed to be purged of mystifications and brought closer to people's real life. His critical view of Hegelian philosophy was reflected in *Essays on the Gogol Period of Russian Literature* (*Ocherki gogolevskogo perioda russkoi literatury* [1855-1856]). In his appreciation of the Hegelian system, he remarked: "Hegel's principles were extremely power-ful and broad; his deductions were narrow and feeble."[4] Here he had in mind the "dubiety" of Hegel's philosophy, the conflict between its principles and some political conclusions, and its "spirit and content," implying by "princi-ples" and "spirit" Hegel's dialectics and methodology.

Chernyshevsky included himself in the trend of interpretation of Hegel's doctrine that had been started in Russia by Belinsky. He saw the prospects of Russian culture in its intensive interaction with the latest developments of West European philosophy and social thought.

According to him the most promising line of philosophical development had already been revealed in the generation of thinkers, both West European and Russian, who came after Hegel. Chernyshevsky, following Belinsky and Herzen, suggested that Hegelian dialectics not be taken in "ready-made form"; he interpreted it "realistically," purging it of mysticism, panlogism, and a claim to absolute relevance.

In his *Critique of Philosophical Prejudices against Communal Owner-ship* (*Kritika filosofskikh predubezhdenii protiv obshchinnogo vladeniya* [1858]) he started from the idea of dialectical development. As he put it, "the great, eternal, omnipresent" law of dialectical development of everything existent is "the law of eternal change of form." Its action was traceable in all spheres of being, and was illustrated by physical, moral, and social "facts."

Beginning with an analysis of the simplest phenomena of physical nature, Chernyshevsky showed that development in nature was characterized by a "lengthy gradualness." Development in society was much more complex and, therefore, people had incomparably more chances "to pass given the favorable circumstances, from the first or second stage of development directly to the fifth or sixth."[6] Such a transition could happen as well in natural processes, but the changes in them were realized organically as a rule, of themselves, stage by stage, so long as there were no special circumstances.

DIALECTICS AND SOCIALISM

For Chernyshevsky, the dialectic of the eternal change of form was nothing else, in the final count, than the philosophical substantiation of the ideal of communal socialism, just like his social philosophy as a whole, which was based on a similarity and synthesis of ideas of dialectical development, moral, political and economic values of socialism. He wrote:

> The eternal change of form, an eternal rejection of form, generated by a certain content or striving, as a result of a strengthening of that same striv-ing, and of the highest development of that content—whoever has under-stood this great, eternal, omnipresent law, whoever has grown accustomed to applying it to any phenomenon—oh, how calmly he invokes chances that embarrass others! . . . he does not pity anything that has outlived its time, and says: "Whatever will be, in the end our day will come."[7]

He dissociated himself from Slavophile idealizations that were based on "outdated philosophemes" and presumed retention of patriarchal communal principles in Russia. In order to persuade the readers to remove "philosophical prejudices against communal proprietorship," he introduced a number of "politico-economic truths" into the arguments for preserving—in radically reorganized form—the Russian commune. In his substantiation of the advan-tages of communal (collective) proprietorship compared with private ownership, Chernyshevsky did not limit himself just to arguments of dialectical theory of development or historical proofs for it as Herzen, for example, had done. Chernyshevsky did not think the "old communal proprietorship" interesting in itself or from the angle of its historic stability, but found it effective as an economic principle, because it was the "sole rational and full means of uniting the farmer's gain with land improvement and farming methods with conscientious performance of work."[8]

Chernyshevsky was the most consistent defender of his day of the "Europeanization" of Russia, and of introduction into social life of the political and technological advances of the most developed Western countries.

In such works as "Economic Activity and Legislation" (*Ekonomicheskaya deyatelnost i zakonodatelstvo* [1859]), "Capital and Labor" (*Kapital i trud* [1860]), he developed an economic "theory of the working people" closely linked with socialist ideas. These works were highly appreciated by Marx and Engels. In his afterword to the second German edition of *Capital* Marx wrote of Chernyshevsky as a "great Russian scholar and critic."[9]

Chernyshevsky's "Letters Without an Address" (*Pisma bez adresa* [1863]) made clear the capitalist character of the peasant reform. Along with this he proved it to be inconsistent, because of its privileges to landowners who became a real obstacle to Russia's movement to "private enterprise." These "Letters" served Marx as a source for studying the 1861 reform. Marx's acquaintance with Chernyshevsky's works stimulated his interest in Russian affairs, especially in the last decade of his life, and his examination of the Russian socioeconomic situation.

There were many realistic tendencies in Chernyshevsky's sociological views: understanding of the conflict of economic and political interests of the laboring people and the property owners; sociology of revolution; and the role of material, economic needs in sociohistorical affairs. His socialism, which merged with democratism, did not suppose to precede the social changes through embodiment of some detailed and strict projects for the future. He saw the reliable road for tackling the social problems in a people's revolution as a precondition of the future economic reforms, conceived as a limitation of private property, elimination of wage labor, and development of collective proprietorship in agriculture and industry.

In his works, Chernyshevsky tended to bring the examination of political and general social problems down to concrete matters of practice. It was Chernyshevsky who was the first among radical democrat Russians who introduced the idea of more or less direct determination of social concepts by political life. He wrote,

Political theories and all philosophical doctrines in general, have always been created under the powerful influence of the social situation to which they belonged, and every philosopher has always been a representative of one of the political parties which in his time contended for predominance in the society to which the philosopher belonged.[10]

Thus with Chernyshevsky it was not simply a matter of the influence of political notions and views of thinkers on the molding of his philosophical ideas; the principle of their socially and politically determined character had a methodological significance for him and was employed to interpret the sociocultural context of philosophy, social science, and the humanities.

MATERIALIST ANTHROPOLOGY

While counting himself a representative of "modern philosophy," Chernyshevsky defined it as the theory of the solution of the most general problems of science that are usually called metaphysics, for example, problems of the relation between spirit and matter, free will, immortality of the soul, etc.[11]

When answering the question of what is primary—matter or spirit—in favor of the first he defined matter as what exists in an infinite diversity of properties, forms, and motions.

The interaction of the parts of matter is called manifestation of the qualities of these different parts. But the very fact of the existence of these qualities we express by the words "matter has the power to act"—or rather "exert an influence." When we define the mode of action of qualities, we say that we find "laws of nature."[12]

Chernyshevsky referred to the materialist trend represented by Feuerbach, which Russian radical democrats considered the most modern and scientific: "The theory which I think is right is the latest link in a series of philosophical systems."[13] By that he had in mind the contemporary anthropological, rather than vulgar, materialism. And so that readers would not be left in doubt about his philosophical loyalties, he pointed out that "not Büchner, not Max Stirner, not Bruno Bauer, not Moleschott, not Vogt" had his sympathy.[14]*

In his central philosophical work "The Anthropological Principle in Philosophy" (*Antropologicheskiy printsyp v filosofii* [1860]), Chernyshevsky rejected dualism, and objective and subjective idealist monism by the philosophical arguments of anthropologism, and substantiated the point of view of scientific monism in solving the problem of soul and body and the unity of human nature. "The principle underlying the philosophical view of human life and all its phenomena is the idea, worked out by the natural sciences, of the unity of the human organism."[15]

In defining philosophy as "the theory of the solution of the most general

---

*The context of Chernyshevsky's works indicated that his anthropological philosophy was related to Feuerbach but the very name of this German philosopher was prohibited by the censors.

problems of science," Chernyshevsky specially stressed the scientific orientation of his philosophical position. Modern materialism had originated, he said, in the depths of antiquity: "The principles that have now been explained and proved by the natural sciences were found and accepted as true by the Greek philosophers, and even much before them by the Indian thinkers. In all probability, they were discovered by men with powerful logical minds in all ages, and among all peoples."[16]

He included himself in the "scientific trend," considering the Spinoza-Feuerbach line its most productive embodiment. When working out the thesis of the material unity of the world and the objective character of nature and its laws, in particular the law of causality, he broadly employed data of chemistry, biology, and other sciences. When explaining the ideal as the outcome of the material and discussing the material foundations of consciousness, he also relied on data of experimental psychology and physiology, for example, the studies of I. M. Sechenov.

Chernyshevsky's development, together with Dobrolyubov, of a new version of the theory of "rational egoism" as the free subordination of personal gain to the common cause, from the success of which the individual's personal interest gained as a result, brought him wide fame. In their interpretation it was a kind of expression of "anthropological socialism" and was proposed as the basis of a revolutionary morality whose main content consisted in devotion to the ideals of the "common people," struggle against feudal prejudices, and a critique of both religious asceticism and vulgar utilitarianism.

Chernyshevsky's application of the anthropological principle, among other things in ethics, by no means meant just an appeal to utilitarian aspects of human nature. He defended the idea of the historically changeable character of moral standards and notions, which, he claimed, while differing on the individual level, diverged even more among the members of various social estates and nations. In the final count, he stressed, "the interests of mankind as a whole stand higher than the interests of an individual nation; the common interests of a whole nation are higher than the interests of an individual class; the interests of a large class are higher than the interests of a small one."[17]

The scientific, historical, and philosophical arguments he adduced to substantiate the materialist outlook were often supplemented by logical proofs based on the methods of inductive logic. He proposed a system of proof of the truth of materialism, for instance, that started from the methodology of negative inferences. According to it, human knowledge, by progressing from one known truth to another, and finding confirmation of them in scientific and everyday practice, acquired the force of certainty and graphic cogency.

"We are in most cases," he argued, "as yet unable with certainty to determine from the part of an object we have investigated the character of the uninvestigated part, we are always able to determine with certainty the character it cannot have."[18]

Chernyshevsky's materialist anthropologism at the same time characterized the inclination toward naturalism. The naturalistic element of Chernyshevsky's anthropologism cannot be identified, however, with the naturalistic conceptions typical of the Enlightenment of the eighteenth century. It was not only the matter of the difference in social ideals, which with Rousseau, for example, were connected with the middle class and with Chernyshevsky were of more plebeian character, but rather of the substantial disagreements. Rousseau's naturalistic distinction between true and artificial ("moderate" and "immoderate") needs, and "naturalized" attitude to ideal culture, understood as the embodiment of human nature's true needs, and other ideas of Enlightenment naturalism were not characteristic of Chernyshevsky. On the contrary, all forms of social function were important to him: in all branches "only those directions achieve dazzling development that are vitally connected with society's needs."[19]

Although the sources of Chernyshevsky's views were close to the theoretical sources of Marxism—i.e., comprised classical German philosophy, including that of Hegel and Feuerbach—all the same, there was not, and could not be, a direct contact of ideas in it with Marxism. However, the philosophical and cognitive principles developed by Chernyshevsky were always of interest for Russian Marxists, especially for Plekhanov and Lenin.

Chernyshevsky's ideas had a considerable influence on the development of the democratic culture of the many nations inhabiting Imperial Russia. During his lifetime he became well known not only in Europe but also in a number of countries in Asia and the Americas.

NOTES

1. N. G. Chernyshevsky, *Polnoye sobraniye sochineniy* (Complete works) (Moscow, 1939), vol. 1, p. 122.

2. Ibid., p. 297.

3. N. G. Chernyshevsky, *Selected Philosophical Essays* (Moscow, 1953), pp. 369–70.

4. Ibid., pp. 460–61.

5. Ibid., p. 484.

6. N. G. Chernyshevsky, *Izbrannye filosofskie sochineniva (Selected Philosophical Works)* (Moscow, 1950), vol. 2, p. 487.

7. Ibid., p. 492.

8. Ibid., p. 476.

9. Karl Marx, Afterword to the Second German Edition of *Capital* (Moscow: Progress Publishers, 1977), vol. 1, p. 25.

10. Chernyshevsky, *Selected Philosophical Essays,* p. 50.

11. Ibid., p. 69.

12. Chernyshevsky, *Izbrannye filosofskie sochineniya,* vol. 3, p. 701.

13. Chernyshevsky, *Selected Philosophical Essays,* p. 162.

14. Ibid.
15. Ibid., p. 70.
16. Ibid., p. 80.
17. Ibid., p. 125.
18. Ibid., p. 83.
19. Chernyshevsky, *Izbrannye filosovskie sochineniya,* vol. 1, p. 783.

17

Nikolai Dobrolyubov
Vitaly Bogatov

THE MOLDING OF HIS PERSONALITY

The outstanding philosopher, literary critic, and publicist belonging to the radical-democratic wing of Russian intellectuals Nikolai Dobrolyubov (1836–1861) was born in Nizhni Novgorod, the son of a priest. As a youth he received a good education at home; studied for some time in a theological seminary; read a great deal; and was especially attracted to Russian and West European literature, belles lettres, and publicistic writing. Even in childhood he had already begun to note the "injustice of certain principles" of the affairs of society, the brutality and evil, and complete disregard of the rights of the common man. In 1853, Dobrolyubov left his hometown and enrolled in the St. Petersburg Main Pedagogical Institute, from which he graduated in 1857. From that year on he was a regular contributor to the journal *Sovremennik* (*Contemporary*).

Dobrolyubov was thoroughly acquainted with the philosophical and political conceptions current in Western Europe, in particular with the works of the Left Hegelians (Strauss and Bruno Bauer) and of Feuerbach. But the ideas of Belinsky and Herzen, which furthered his transition to a position of materialism, had a decisive influence on the shaping of his outlook. The works and personal support of Chernyshevsky, whose closest assistant and friend he became, played the main role in the evolution of his thinking.

His early death from tuberculosis at the age of twenty five prevented Dobrolyubov's talent from flourishing to its fullest. He wrote a great number of articles and surveys during his mere five years of literary activity. The most important among them are the following: "The Organic Development of Man in Connection with His Mental and Moral Activities," (*Organicheskoe razvitie cheloveka v svyazi s ego umstvennoi i nravstvennoi deyatelnostiu*), "Robert Owen and His Attempts at Social Reforms," (*Robert Owen i ego popytki obshchestvennykh reform*), "From Moscow to Leipzig" (*Ot Moskvy do Leipzyga*), "What Is Oblomovshchina?" (*Chto takoe oblomovshchina?*), "The Realm of Darkness" (*Temnoe tsarstvo*), "When Will the Day Come?" (*Kogda zhe pridet nastoyashchii den?*), and "A Ray of Light in the Realm of Darkness" (*Luch sveta v temnom tsarstve*).

Dobrolyubov's literary legacy is remarkably harmonious and purposive. His ardent wish was to reorganize the life of the laboring people according to the principles of social justice. This, as well as the ideals of democracy and socialism, can be seen in every article. Defining his action program, Dobrolyubov wrote: "We are touching on great matters, and our dear Russia's great future concerns us most of all; for that we want to work tirelessly, unselfishly, and ardently, . . . I am unusually strongly preoccupied with this great goal . . . I seem to be called by fate to the great cause of revolution."[1]

Dobrolyubov's ideas greatly influenced the generations of Russian left-radical theoreticians and revolutionaries that followed. Karl Marx said of Dobrolyubov: "I compare him as a writer to Lessing and Diderot."[2]

HIS POLITICAL PHILOSOPHY

Dobrolyubov did not experience dramatic periods of spiritual evolution. When studying at the pedagogical institute, he had already consolidated a position of philosophical materialism and revolutionary democratic spirit, overcoming the remnants of religious ideas.

"All that I saw and all that I heard," he wrote, "developed in me a feeling of grave discontent. Very early in life, my soul became troubled with the question: 'Why is everybody suffering like this? Is there no way of alleviating this suffering into which everybody seems to be plunged?' I hungrily sought an answer to these questions."[3] The young man soon formulated the aim of his work: "From the abstract law of justice I passed to the more real demand of the good of mankind."[4]

Dobrolyubov's criticism was focused on the autocracy and serfdom. He saw it as his civic duty to expose the antipeople, antihumane character of the political regime of czarism, so as to convince the people to fight it:

> We must not act in an allaying way but rather the opposite. We should assemble the facts of Russian life requiring correction and improvement. We should draw readers' attention to what surrounds them, throw every abomination into their teeth, and hound and torment them without rest until the reader becomes disgusted by all this plethora of filth and finally,

stung to the quick, jumps up in excitement and shouts: "Such life is drudgery. I can't stand it anymore."—That is what we should make our readers to think.[5]

When Dobrolyubov's political views are being characterized, it must be stressed that he propagandized the idea of people's revolution, with emotion and determination, saying that all the muddle and confusion of Russian life could only be solved by "independent action of the people" through a peasant uprising. In his censored articles he had to substitute something for the word "revolution." Sometimes he spoke of a "serious operation" on society, sometimes about "special" and "unusual" circumstances, and so on. The Russian reader undoubtedly understood him.

Dobrolyubov considered revolution as a result of natural processes in the womb of a society. If the feudal, serf system had outlived itself, if oppression of the masses was increasing, and Russia's economic progress was retarded, the revolution in that case would be imminent. Whether he was talking about Oblomov types (as a phenomenon of social and personal spinelessness and passivity)[6] or about the "realm of darkness" (the hint at the political order of Russian czarism), or about the venality of the officialdom, or about the clergy breaking religious and moral norms, he saw the root of all evils in social injustice and economic iniquity, and in the people's lack of political rights. Absence of rationality and justice in society was another source of revolution closely connected with low level of life.

He believed that the people's movement had to be prepared and organized, that it had to be led by the best members of the intelligentsia, by middle-class, nonaristocratic revolutionaries.

A conception of educating "people of action," capable of leading a people's revolutionary movement, had a major place in Dobrolyubov's political philosophy. It was developed in a sharp struggle against both the proponents of serfdom and moderate reformers and liberals. He suggested that liberals represented the main danger for the revolution. He criticized them along three lines: (1) for their inconsistently liberal opposition to czarism and the serf system; (2) for their reformism, which rested on fear of the people and its revolutionary potential; (3) for the gulf between word and deed, for indecision and incapacity for practical action. He counterposed to liberal gradualism a people's revolution, which had to be prepared and led by the antipodes of liberalism, i.e., by "people of action," or revolutionaries.

"PEOPLE OF ACTION" AND THEIR MORAL STATUS

The focus of Dobrolyubov's attention was the issue of service to society, of man's social and political activity. His aim was to prove that "people of action," and not useless people like Oblomov, worked out the idea of progress, and incarnated it in life.

"People of action" were the future of Russia, people capable of realizing the formula: "man and his happiness." They belonged to the type of intellectuals with a deep, broad theoretical training; with knowledge of the laws of social development and an understanding of the masses' main needs; with a critical approach to social reality—they were ready to join the revolution with the people. "People of action" should be genuine, true democrats; believe in and work for the revolution; and build a society in which the intellect and initiative of the people could be displayed to the full. The heart of "people of action" means to be energetic, true to one's word.

The basic issues of their worldview Dobrolyubov formulated as imperatives of revolutionary ethics that were for him not some abstract knowledge, but a norm of behavior for real people in concrete life situations. His attention was centered on the principle of ethical behavior, which he defined as a unity of the dictates of duty and the inclinations of the heart.

His views on ethics were based on the premise that a forced performance of duty only recognized as formal and obligatory was not a moral act. A view of life as a hard reality full of tragedy and distress, in whose conditions following of the moral imperative was transformed into a constant overcoming of natural human feelings and affections, led to ethical rigor. Therefore, those who did their duty only because it was prescribed were not worthy of the warmest eulogies. The deserving were "those who were concerned to merge the requirements of duty with the needs of their inner essence, who strove to take them into their flesh and blood by an inner process of self-awareness and self-development so that they are not only made instinctively necessary but also cause inner delight."[7] According to Dobrolyubov a true revolutionary was distinguished by active virtues and a heroic essence, because he was capable of immersing himself wholly in the great cause and would battle for it as his joy, life, and happiness.

His moral philosophy was based on the principle of "rational egoism," i.e., a combination of one's personal aspirations and the public good. Like Chernyshevsky, Dobrolyubov rendered this principle a political content oriented to realization of revolutionary changes in society in the interests of the people. So the theory of "rational egoism" and political philosophy merged together.

Patriotism, a powerful stimulus of human activity, was another important quality of "people of action," according to Dobrolyubov. There was an elemental, natural patriotism, which was in essence an instinctive striving to love what was close and familiar, to love the nature of one's homeland, one's own people, and one's native land. But there was also another kind of patriotism that was conscious—such love of one's nation was a concretization of love of the common good and the happiness of all mankind. Such patriotism excluded chauvinism of any sort, any feeling of national exclusiveness and recognition of the special advantages of some one nation.

"People of action" are not isolated individuals, they have a sense of collectivism and solidarity.

It was thus possible to achieve revolutionary goals ("man and his happiness"), given that a new social movement of revolutionaries of a new type was formed. But for Dobrolyubov, to be moral was not enough if the cause of the revolutionary were to succeed. It was also necessary to solve a number of problems of his inner development, in particular to understand what the people's real happiness was, why they had the right to happiness, and how it could be achieved. That is why it was important to define man's place in nature and society clearly, to comprehend him in his actual relations with the outside world. And for that an advanced philosophical outlook of the world was needed.

MAN AND PHILOSOPHY

Dobrolyubov was a spokesman of anthropological materialism in philosophy. This philosophical conception centered on each man as an active individual; it concerned not only the sphere of emotions and interpersonal relations (Feuerbach), but the social sphere as well, i.e., the right of the individual to a revolutionary overthrowing of the outmoded social order (Chernyshevsky). That gave materialist philosophical anthropology the character of a doctrine of man's social essence. For Chernyshevsky and Dobrolyubov the individual was the subject of historical action, governed not only by the laws of nature but also by those of human existence, i.e., social laws. They treated philosophy itself as an important part of social science, which in turn was a means of bringing about economic and political changes. For such a philosophy truth was not an end in itself but an instrument for affirming social justice. As the theoretical basis of the activity of "people of action," philosophy served as a theory of revolutionary behavior, the method to realize the ideals of democracy and socialism.

At the same time, according to Dobrolyubov's anthropological materialism, man as a social being developed on his biological basis; consequently, to understand human nature both humanities and natural sciences were essential. In the final count a person was an individual in a unity of economic, political, and moral relations.

In his interpretation of the external world, Dobrolyubov started from the principles of materialist monism. The doctrine of matter was the central point of his ontology. While criticizing idealism and mysticism, he repeatedly stressed that the modern theory of matter could only be formulated with regard for the latest data of the natural sciences. As to the link of philosophy

and science, he continued the tradition of Lomonosov, Herzen, and Chernyshevsky, who supported the idea of their interaction and dialogue.

According to Dobrolyubov, it was not pure thought but the whole
development of science that proved the truth of materialist philosophy.

"In nature," he wrote, "everything advances gradually from the simple
to the more complex, from the imperfect to the more perfect, but everywhere
there is the one and the same matter, only at different levels of development."[8]
It was impossible to imagine an idea existing independently of material
substance. The things around man were not a reflection of some higher ideal
essence existing outside nature, but real, material objects.

Dobrolyubov paid much attention to proving the impossibility of separating force, energy, motion, and matter in nature. He wrote:

> In the material world we do not know of a single object in which each,
> even the tiniest particle of matter did not possess a force peculiar to it.
> Similarly, we cannot conceive of force independent of matter. Force is a
> fundamental, inalienable quality of matter, and cannot exist separately. It
> cannot be communicated to matter, it can only be roused in it.[9]

That conclusion, he said, became possible owing to the advances of science:
"The natural sciences have made such enormous progress and have reconciled
philosophical reflections about the forces of nature with the results of experimental researches into the nature of matter."[10] The external world, according
to Dobrolyubov, was thus in itself an assemblage of different forms of matter
capable of development owing to the force inherent in it.

When answering the question of what a real man was and what was
his real, and not fantastic, relation to the external world, Dobrolyubov started
from the idea of the unity of the human organism.

"Modern science," he stressed, ". . . refuted the scholastic dualistic conception of man and began to study him as a complete, undivided whole,
corporal and spiritual."[11] The soul was not an independent substance but a
force peculiar only to man, which was as inseparable from man's material
nature as force was inseparable from matter. At the same time he resolutely
rejected vulgar materialism, stressing the groundlessness of the claims of crude,
ignorant materialism that reduced the spiritual to the material.

Having advanced a thesis that thought was impossible without matter,
he attached no little importance to the philosophical interpretation of psychic
and cerebral processes and study of the functions of the brain as the organ
of thought, a problem to which he devoted one of his best works *The Foundations of Experimental Psychology (Osnovaniya opytnoi psikhologii* [1858]).

The problem of man's real and not fantastic relation to the external world
also had an epistemological aspect. If thought was impossible without objective
reality, then it arose only as a result of the impact of material objects on

man. The material of thinking always and necessarily constituted the object of consciousness. A thought without its object was something inconceivable. Underlying materialist epistemology there was the principle that man drew the content of consciousness and ideas from the world, so that "it is necessary not to adapt the facts to a previously conceived law but to deduce the law itself from the facts, without forcing them arbitrarily."[12] Dobrolyubov counted himself an advocate of an objective epistemology and critic of the theory of "innate ideas," about which he wrote in detail in his "The Organic Development of Man in Connection with His Mental and Moral Activities" (*Organicheskoe razvitie cheloveka v svyazi s ego umstvennoi i nravstvennoi deyatelnostiu* [1858]).[13] Stressing the role of the brain as the material substratum of thought, he considered cognition the result of the activity of the whole human organism, because it was impossible to separate the vital activity of our whole being from the activity of the brain. And in a spirit of epistemological optimism he concluded that man naturally possessed everything needed for advancing knowledge of the world.

In order to get true knowledge of nature and man, it was first of all necessary to examine objects and phenomena concretely, in unity with the real connections in which they existed:

> Help me to understand the character of a phenomenon, its place among the rest, its meaning and importance in the general course of life, and I assure you that in this way you will help me to form a far more correct opinion about the matter in hand than you will with all the syllogisms you may choose to prove your case.[14]

The fact of knowledge was a certain living, many-sided whole, interwoven in surrounding reality. But one and the same phenomena and facts had a different meaning in different connections and conditions.

The principle of evolution, by which the content of an object itself depended on the development, on the different stages of the object's (or the processes') inner changes, was one of the main principles of Dobrolyubov's method. He demonstrated the necessity of a historical approach to notions, concepts, and values developed by human culture.

> What has outlived its time no longer has sense. . . . The gods of the Greeks might have been beautiful in ancient Greece, but they are ugly in French tragedies and in our odes of the last century. The chivalrous appeals of the Middle Ages could draw hundreds of thousands of people to battle against infidels so as to liberate the Holy Land, but the same appeals repeated in Europe of the nineteenth century would produce nothing but laughter.[15]

Like other Russian radical democrats, Dobrolyubov remained true to the principles of rationalism, characteristic of the Enlightenment. Strong materialist tendencies were also characteristic of him, which were due in no small measure to the requirements of applying the principles of anthropological materialism to the study of society.

Among the many problems of social philosophy, he singled out those of the regularities of social life and the role of the people and of the individual in history. He strove to prove the legitimacy of man's active intervention in the course of history on the basis of an objective knowledge of its laws, thereby throwing doubt on both fatalism and voluntarism. People of the present generation, he wrote, having in mind revolutionary democrats, do not set unrealizable hopes for themselves, do not think that they themselves can remake history, do not think themselves to be delivered from the influence of circumstances. And he stressed that, "Conviction of the impossibility of remaking history at their will does not entail anarchy and quietism, or a fatalistic submission to the course of historical events."

He wrote,

Progressive people consider themselves a cog of the machine, one of the circumstances governing the course of world events. Since all world circumstances are connected and are in some mutual dependence, they submit to necessity and the force of things; but that subordination apart, they do not worship any idols, but defend the independence and rightfulness of their actions against all haphazardly arising claims.[16]

In its paradigmatic status and sources the radical democratic and socialist-oriented philosophy of Russian thinkers from Belinsky to the Populists (*narodniki*) of the postreform period—Lavrov, Mihailovski, and Tkachev—was rationalistic, related to the spirit of the Enlightenment. Great attention was paid to reason, ideas, and theories as means of changing and organizing society. But in contrast, let us say, French philosophers such as Voltaire, Levetius, Holbach, and Russian followers of this intellectual tradition emphasized the crucial role not of ideas and theories per se, but of their individual and collective possessors. Only a conjunction of ideas and a corresponding social movement or certain groups of intelligentsia can secure the success of such doctrines. In turn, the genesis of a theory cannot be purely logical or speculative. An idea is reliable, and we can trust it if there is an adequate reflection of objective reality, which is primary for any theory. This way of reasoning was especially characteristic of Dobrolyubov.

He did not consider that the simple spread of very attractive ideas could change people's being. In his view, ideas had a real force only when they arose from "existing facts" and preceded changes in reality itself. Life creates a need in society; this need is recognized; following the general recognition of this need an actual change must take place in the direction of satisfying this generally recognized need. Thus, after a period of *recognition* of certain ideas and striving, a period must arise in society in which these ideas and striving are *carried out*.[17]

Groups and organizations of revolutionaries begin to appear, the time of "people of action," i.e., the subjects of social action, comes.

LABOR, DEMOCRACY, AND SOCIALISM

What, according to Dobrolyubov, was the most important aim for which a revolutionary should act? "Despotism and slavery, being abhorrent to human nature, can never become normal,"[18] he wrote. Normal development of the individual is possible only through satisfaction of human nature's natural needs, i.e., material needs achieved by means of labor. The main condition for happiness of all members of society is to ensure free development of people's labor. The ideal essence of history is free labor. The good is in labor and "the natural aspirations of mankind, reduced to the simplest denominator, could be expressed in two words: the good for all."[19]

The conditions of labor and social justice, according to Dobrolyubov, were not provided either in Russia or in the West. The reason was the split of society into two strata—workers and drones—between which there was an age-old struggle. Social confrontation had no underlying ideological or general cultural reason.

> Of course, the struggle between aristocracy and democracy forms the entire content of history; but we would have a very poor understanding of history if we took it into our heads to limit it merely to genealogic interests. Behind this struggle there was always concealed another circumstance, far more important. . . . In the eyes of the truly educated man there are no aristocrats and democrats, nor lords and villains, Brahmins and pariahs, there are only *working people* and *parasites*. To destroy the parasites and to raise labor to a higher status—such is the constant trend of history.[20]

Dobrolyubov valued the historical role of labor in the spirit of a democratic outlook: "It is by the degree to which labor is respected and appraised in accordance with its true value that we can tell the degree of a nation's civilization."[21]

In an article "From Moscow to Leipzig" (1859) he stressed that, "With the development of education in the exploiting classes the form of exploitation is only altered and grows more flexible and more sophisticated; but the essence remains the same for all that, while the possibility of exploitation remains as before."[22]

Dobrolyubov saw the way out of the social impasse in the necessity of eliminating the division of society into workers and drones, and in the establishing of socialism by revolution. Calling himself a "fervent socialist," he believed that socialism was the future of mankind: "That day will come at last! At all events, the eve is never far from the next day; only a matter of one night separates them."[23]

Dobrolyubov displayed his democratic spirit and radicalism in his understanding of the role of the people and of the individual in history. He examined this problem from a practical rather than a theoretical point of view, i.e., he was interested in the mechanism that unites the ideas and social consciousness for real, practical action. In the formula "idea—ideologist—people" the decisive role belonged to the people—the subject and initiator of revolutionary action. Its "involvement can be active or passive, positive or negative—but, in any case, it must not be forgotten by history."[24]

Dobrolyubov reasoned as follows: Surely, soldiers are necessary in order to win a war, and citizens in order to found a state. In other words, material was needed on which the great men "performed their exercises." That "material" was the laboring masses. But historians were interested in their fate least of all; what attracted their attention were outstanding persons. Scholars "do not want to understand that this 'material' is always made ready by the circumstances of a nation's historical development and that the historical circumstances are individuals who express the needs of society and their times."[25]

Great men are pushed to the fore by the objective course of the life of the people and their task in history is to realize the goals that the age poses, and that have become a necessity, have matured in the people and in society. For him Peter the Great was an example of such an individual—"the powerful motor" of the new, the fighter against outlived relics of the past, the direction of whose activity had been prepared by the course of history.

Dobrolyubov dreamed about Russian revolutionaries who would realize the ideas of democracy and socialism in practice. He believed that within society a special, active historical force would develop. That would be a "type of real people with strong nerves and sound imagination."[26]

Subsequent developments in Russia fulfilled most of his expectations. However, the irony of Russian history manifested itself in the fact that the political struggle of revolutionaries against czarism went according to such a tough pattern that as a result of that permanent conflict of the intellectuals and the government a new "type of people" was born, not only tough but cruel and often fanatical. But this would become obvious only after the first Russian revolution of 1905–1907. In Dobrolyubov's time the principles of democracy were not yet substituted by the idea of proletarian dictatorship.

NOTES

1. N. A. Dobrolyubov, *Sobranie sochineniy* (Collected works), 9 vols. (Moscow-Leningrad, 1961–64), vol. 8, p. 463.

2. Karl Marx, Letter to Nikolai Danielson, 9 November 1871, in Karl Marx and Frederick Engels, *Collected Works* (Moscow: Progress Publishers, 1989), vol. 44, p. 238.

3. N. A. Dobrolyubov, *Selected Philosophical Essays* (Moscow, 1956), p. 429.

4. Ibid., p. 431.

5. Dobrolyubov, *Sobranie sochineniy*, vol. 9, p. 408.

6. In 1859 a well-known Russian writer Ivan Goncharov published his novel *Oblomov* wherein he depicted the life of a Russian landowner. The title character was immediately recognized by the public and since then references to Oblomov-type people are common; the social phenomenon of spinelessness and passivity was named *oblomovshchina*.

7. N. A. Dobrolyubov, *Izbrannye filosofskie sochineniya* (*Selected Philosophical Works*), 2 vols. (Moscow, 1945), vol. 1, p. 146.

8. Dobrolyubov, *Selected Philosophical Essays*, p. xxiv.

9. Ibid., p. xiii.

10. Ibid., p. 61.

11. Ibid., p. xix.

12. Dobrolyubov, *Sobranie sochineniy*, vol. 4, p. 258.

13. See Dobrolyubov, *Selected Philosophical Essays*, pp. 69–101.

14. Ibid., p. 258.

15. Dobrolyubov, *Sobranie sochineniy*, vol. 1, p. 81.

16. Ibid., p. 278.

17. Dobrolyubov, *Selected Philosophical Essays*, pp. 396–97.

18. Ibid., p. 485.

19. Dobrolyubov, *Sobranie sochineniy*, vol. 6, p. 372.

20. Dobrolyubov, *Selected Philosophical Essays*, pp. 641–42.

21. Ibid., p. 642.

22. Dobrolyubov, *Sobranie sochineniy*, vol. 5, p. 460.

23. Dobrolyubov, *Selected Philosophical Essays*, p. 441.

24. Dobrolyubov, *Sobranie sochineniy*, vol. 3, p. 15.

25. Dobrolyubov, *Izbrannye filosofskie sochineniya*, vol. 1, p. 125.

26. Dobrolyubov, *Sobranie sochineniy*, vol. 4, p. 57.

18

Dmitry Pisarev

Lyubov Byelenkova

A SHORT BUT BRILLIANT LIFE

Dmitry Pisarev (1840–1868) was one of the leaders of the Russian democratic publicists in the middle of the nineteenth century. His many works on philosophy, history, literary criticism, esthetics, sociology, political economy, pedagogics, and natural science were an impressive contribution to the development of Russian culture. His life was a short, but powerful flight of the human spirit aspiring to profound knowledge, to the revolutionary and democratic ideals of justice and freedom of the people. The broad spectrum of his enlightened activity reflected the radicalism of his position as a political thinker. While continuing in the 1860s to critique the autocracy and the "ideological establishment" along the same lines as his teachers and associates—i.e., Belinsky, Herzen, Chernyshevsky, and Dobrolyubov—Pisarev actively espoused and developed the ideas of philosophical materialism, atheism, Darwinism, and revolutionary democracy.

During the ebbing of radicalism in Russia, when Herzen and Ogarev were out of the country; Chernyshevsky, Shelgunov, and many of their sympathizers were in Siberian exile; and Dobrolyubov was no longer alive, Pisarev in fact became the ideological leader of the revolutionary-minded youth. His works had a great influence on shaping the outlook of the next generations of revolutionaries up to and including Lenin and the Bolsheviks.

Pisarev came from a poor noble family in the village of Znamenskoye in the Orel Province. In 1856 he graduated from grammar school with a gold medal and entered the history and philology faculty of St. Petersburg University. From 1858, while still a student, he began to contribute to the journal *Rassvet* (*Dawn*), in which his first articles were published. After becoming personally acquainted with Chernyshevsky in 1859, he paid increasing attention to the sociopolitical affairs of Russia and began an open battle of ideas against the autocracy, serfdom, and the official Church burdened with protective functions.

In 1861, Pisarev transferred to the journal *Russkoye slovo* (*The Russian Word*), in which his main philosophical and sociological essays were published—"Plato's Idealism" (*Idealizm Platona*), "Nineteenth Century Scholasticism" (*Skholastika XIX veka*), "Moleschott's Physiological Sketches" (*Fiziologicheskiye eskizy Moleshotta*), and "The Process of Life" (*Protsess zhizni*) in 1861; "Heinrich Heine" (*Genrikh Geine*) and "Bees" (*Pchyoly*) in 1862; "The Historical Development of European Thought" (*Istoricheskoye razvitie evropeiskoi mysli*), "Progress in the Animal and Vegetable Kingdoms" (*Progress v mire zhivotnykh i rasteniy*) and "The Birth of Culture" (*Zarozhdeniye kultury*) in 1863; "The Realists" (*Realisty*) in 1864; "The Turning-Point in the Intellectual Life of Feudal Europe" (*Perelom v umstvennoi zhizni srednevekovoi Evropy*), "The Collapse of Esthetics" (*Razrusheniye estetiki*), "The School and Life" (*Shkola i zhizn*), "Auguste Comte's Historical Ideas" (*Istoricheskie idei Ogyusta Konta*), and "The Thinking Proletariat" (*Myslyashchiy proletariat*) in 1865; and "Popularizers of Negative Doctrines" (*Populyarizatory otritsatelnykh doktrin*) in 1866. For his revolutionary article-proclamation "The Russian Government Under the Patronage of Schedo-Ferroti" (*Russkoye pravitelstvo pod pokrovitelstvom Shedo-Ferroti*), written in 1862 and intended for illegal publication, Pisarev was arrested and held in solitary confinement in the Peter and Paul Fortress in St. Petersburg. In that article he had called for a people's revolution, overthrow of the Romanov dynasty, and change of the political and social system. The proclamation was essentially a political program the ideological substantiation of which most of his works had been devoted. Though imprisoned and subject to a triple censorship, he did not cease to work. In the articles of that period he turned to problems of history, studied the development of the social thought of the past, and made a philosophical analysis of the contemporary socioeconomic reality of Russia.

In 1866, after four-and-a-half years' imprisonment, he was released. His publicistic activity continued in the journals *Delo* (*The Cause*) and *Otechestvennye zapiski* (*Fatherland Notes*). The journals *Russkoye slovo* and *Sovremennik* (*The Contemporary*), to which he had contributed earlier, had been shut down for revolutionary agitation. As before, he defended the ideas of socialism, revolutionary democracy, and materialism in his struggle against liberalism and conservatism in politics and in science. In 1868, his life was suddenly cut short; he drowned while bathing off the seashore near Riga.

Herzen expressed the impact of this irreparable loss on Russia and her democratic culture, comparing Pisarev to a bright star that rose up in the sky but was prematurely extinguished.

THE MAIN PHILOSOPHICAL PROBLEMS

Pisarev's philosophical views gave concrete expression to and further developed the materialist tendencies of Russian revolutionary democracy, whose representatives did not divorce theory from practical issues of political life. He linked the purpose of philosophy with solution of the vitally important socioeconomic problems and advocated a philosophy of action that would "smash the rubbishy idols and shatter the obsolete forms of civil and public affairs."[1]

He saw it as an important task of his historical and philosophical studies to spread materialist ideas. His sympathies for materialism were manifest in his great appreciation of the philosophical and scientific views of Democritus, Epicurus, Lucretius, Aristotle, Leonardo da Vinci, Francis Bacon, Thomas Hobbes, and Pierre Bayle. In his essay "Popularizers of Negative Doctrines," he dwelt specially on an analysis of the contribution to the development of materialism made by the French philosophers of the eighteenth century (Diderot, Helvetius, Holbach, and Rousseau). It is noteworthy that in this work the term "negative doctrines" denoted materialist philosophy, a term forbidden by the censor. In addition, he meant by "negative doctrines" a system of views that rejected all idealism and theology, and the economic and political principles and foundations of feudalism historically connected with them.

A strong motif of negation in Pisarev's criticism allowed researchers to define his philosophical views as nihilism. When stressing the confrontation between the materialist and idealist trends in the history of world philosophy, Pisarev pointed out its objective character, ultimately conditioned by social and class interests. He considered materialism to be the expression of the progressive in people's spiritual life, since its link with natural science, and science as a whole, was obvious, while idealism was historically inseparable from religion. And since the Church in Russia was on the right of the political process, he associated idealism with conservative principles.

Pisarev was one of the first in Russia (together with Herzen) to acquaint readers with many unknown pages of the history of world social thought. His surveys of Arabic philosophy, the art and science of the eighth to thirteenth centuries, and his analysis of their influence on European feudal consciousness and on the Renaissance were an important reference point for the radical Russian intelligentsia and youth in their process of assimilating world culture.

A central social-philosophical subject occupying Pisarev was the problem of revolution. In particular, when speaking of the French Revolution, he noted that the French Enlightenment, which had undoubtedly had a positive significance, had not for all that been a decisive factor. In his analysis of the sum total of historical conditions that shape a revolutionary situation, he categorically brought socioeconomic causes to the front. In his "Historical Sketches" (*Istoricheskiye eskizy*) he repeatedly stressed that in the slow but steady maturing of the national explosion, as during the revolution itself, "the driving force always and everywhere lay and lies in the general and pre-dominantly the economic conditions" of the existence of the masses rather than in individuals, circles, and literary works.[2]

Pisarev paid great attention to popularizing the latest discoveries and ideas of natural science. While Darwin's theory was encountering great obstacles to its spread and recognition in his home country, many Russian thinkers enthusiastically acquainted the public in Russia with the theory of evolutionary selection. Darwinism was interpreted as the scientific foundation of the materialist outlook and was actively employed for criticism of idealism and religion.

The ideas of Darwinism became a major component of Pisarev's anthropological materialism. They were a type of link between his assertion of the social nature of man and his belief in the inseparable unity between man and Nature. "Man's nature," he wrote, "has always been capable of limitless development, as the nature around him has always been capable of a limitless diversity of modifications and combinations."[3]

Subsequently many outstanding Russian scientists took the road of materialism under the influence of Pisarev's popularization of the natural sciences (suffice it to recall the names of Ivan Sechenov and Kliment Timiryazev).

Pisarev was profoundly interested not only in the link between philosophy and science but also between science and life, anticipating in essence the trend of studies in Russia that subsequently came to be called the sociology of science. He saw the most important social role of natural science in accelerating the development of industry and agriculture. In the context of his analysis of the functions of scientific knowledge he drew attention to the impact of the natural sciences on the methodology and style of philosophical thought.

"The educative influence of all the natural sciences," he wrote, "consists exclusively in their inculcating in man the concept of eternal and unshakable laws that govern the whole universe and prevail with identical power over all phenomena accessible to our study, from the simplest to the most complex."[4]

Natural science not only underlies a sober, realistic world outlook but also helps establish rational social relations. Pisarev shared Comte's idea of the positive sciences as the most fruitful phase in the development of human knowledge. Yet, unlike the French sociologist, he resolutely opposed limiting the role of philosophy in the life of society, though he subjected to harsh criticism the systems of classical idealism and religious philosophy. His theoretical cognitive principle presupposed opposition to agnosticism. He stressed the power of the cognizing human intellect and the critical possibilities of the mind based on sense perception of the objective world. He correlated the problems of knowledge, especially of scientific knowledge, with the practical needs and interests of the individual and of society.

The philosophers and sociologists of Russian revolutionary democracy were in opposition to the Church and religious ideology because they saw in them the obstacle to social progress. Pisarev was no exception, though his attitude to religion was not completely negative. He studied the origins, causes, essence, and aims of religious consciousness (primarily Orthodoxy and Catholicism). In his work "Apollonius of Tyana" (*Apolloni Tiansky*) he expounded his views on the evolution of Christianity, which he saw as a form of social consciousness engendered by definite psychological as well as socioeconomic conditions.

In spite of the fact that Pisarev had not worked out his own theoretical system, he was well aware that philosophical and sociological thought in Russia in the seventeenth and eighteenth centuries had lagged too far behind the demands of its time, had been too remote from the life of the people, and had ignored questions relating to the specific social and intellectual development of society. Though he set great store by the work of Lomonosov and his followers, Pisarev believed that their scientific work was more evidence of the possibilities latent within the seventy-million-strong people of Russia than of actual realization of their rich inherent capacities. When analyzing the reforms of Peter the Great, Pisarev pointed out the disproportion between the emperor's efforts to transport the achievements of Western civilization to Russian soil and his harsh, sometimes brutal measures of extra-economic coercion in order to increase the country's rates of sociohistorical development. Russia's dash ahead not only made her "rear," but also placed numerous strata of the population on the verge of physical extinction.

PROBLEMS OF HISTORICAL PROGRESS

The works by Pisarev reflected views of revolutionary democracy on the essence and laws of history and social progress. He treated history as society's progressive movement toward increased production of material goods and development of man's spiritual needs. Society was an organism developing according to its own objective social laws that integrated all the factors—from natural and economic to intellectual and religious. Its transition from one state to another (from slavery to feudalism, and then to capitalism and future socialism) proceeded in a natural, regular way.

Progress or stagnation in social development depended, correspondingly, on the growth or reduction in the productivity of labor. The latter was predetermined in its turn by social relations. In calling on Russian society to raise the productivity of agricultural and industrial labor, Pisarev pointed out that the main condition for this was a change in social relations between the owners of the means of production and the workers. His tendency for an abstract economic materialism in interpreting social affairs was also manifest in his describing social relations as objective ones independent of the will and consciousness of individual persons. "These relations were formed without us and before our birth; history has hallowed them, and no individual will will abolish them."[5]

The theme of classes and the class struggle in Pisarev's works is evidence of how close his thoughts were to the political doctrine of Marx. Division of society into classes was axiomatic to him. The clash of class interests and struggle between social groups were natural and ineradicable so long as socio-economic inequality existed.

The basis of social distinctions between people was their different relations to work and their places in the process of production. If a given stratum of society lived through its own labor, then it comprised the category of "lower classes"; if, however, it lived at the expense of another class, then it belonged to the "exploiter upper classes."

In his articles "Essays on the History of Labor" (*Ocherki iz istorii truda*), "Heinrich Heine," "The Thinking Proletariat," and "Time Will Show!" (*Posmotrim!*), Pisarev showed that property inequality and class struggle continued in bourgeois society, which meant that all history evolved as the history of the struggle of social classes.

He was an advocate of revolutionary means to achieve democratic aims. That determined his conception of historical development as of an indirect, contradictory, meandering, but at the same time objective and inevitable, ascent of mankind to justice and equality.

> Whoever recognizes the theory of progress also knows that this progress does not happen according to the will of separate individuals, but according to the general, inevitable laws of nature. . . . Mankind moves forward—that is true; but it should not be thought that each step of mankind's is without fail a step forward, and each movement, one for the better. On the contrary, mankind does not advance in a straight line, but by zigzags.[6]

The complexity of history was due to the spontaneous, sometimes bitter struggle of the old and the new. The direction of development depended in each historical period on which of the contending sides was the stronger. But in the final count, he noted, victory went to the progressive, life-affirming social elements.

In surveying the historical road traversed by mankind, Pisarev clearly discerned its ascending movement from the slave system to feudalism, and from the latter to capitalism. But none of these social formations was or could be eternal. Explaining the reasons for the death of ancient civilizations he wrote:

> Civilizations everywhere and always perished because their fruits grew and ripened for the few. The few enjoyed life; the few meditated, the few set themselves social problems and solved them; the few discovered universal laws. . . . Meanwhile, though art and science were in their heyday, the masses were suffering and running out of strength . . . the masses were, in very

truth, getting poorer, slower of understanding and dying out; the glorious flower of ancient civilization was wilting because the root was decaying.[7]

For history to become the full-blooded, real history of the people, one had to care first and foremost for the welfare of the people. Pisarev saw a means of humanizing history in uniting scientific knowledge with the emancipation movement of the masses. In his "Essays on the History of Labor" he put forward a program for a rise of the productive forces of society. He stressed the necessity for a harmonious development of industrial and agricultural labor, for development of culture and, in particular, for dissemination of the natural scientific knowledge. But all that would only become possible given a radical reform of the political and economic system through a social revolution.

"The awakening of the masses, which is necessary for people to enter genuine civilization, is always the outcome of some sharp turn in the course of social and economic life."[8]

Revolution, Pisarev maintained, was the result of the historical need not only for a change of the political system but also for a radical restructuring or the whole socioeconomic organization of life, and the creation of new forms of the people's labor. Revolutionary transformation was a total negation of social orders that had outlived their time and an equally all-embracing creation of new economic and spiritual realities. In order to understand the real significance of revolution it was important to examine it in indissoluble connection with what had been before it and what results were achieved afterward.

> The thinking champion of the interests of the nation who has a respectful sympathy for any upheaval is guided therein not by love for noisy demonstrations or amusing brawls, but only by love for the poor people for whom the upheaval has made life a little easier. If this relief could have been achieved by peaceful changes the thinking champions of the interests of the nation would be the first to condemn the upheaval as an unnecessary waste of physical and moral forces.[9]

While preferring a bloodless, peaceful road of social changes, Pisarev considered a violent road of revolution a forced and "urgent necessity."

His social criticism was not limited to condemnation of feudalism but was extended as well to capitalism. In his analysis of bourgeois principles of business management he proceeded from the experience of capitalist development in the countries of Western Europe, in particular in France and England. On the whole he recognized the progressive character of the bourgeois revolutions in Europe, but he also saw the limits of these upheavals:

"A new plutocracy established itself on the ruins of the old feudalism, and the barons of the financial world, the bankers, businessmen, traders, manufacturers and all the various swindlers were not disposed to share the advantages of their situation."[10]

Under capitalism, Pisarev showed, tyrannical relations of capitalists with wage laborers were established; consequently the reason for the unjust position of things lay in the very principle of wage labor. He linked the essence of capitalist ideology with liberalism, which he condemned for its ambivalent, hypocritical attitude to the needs of the broad masses of the people. He repeatedly pointed out the transitory historical character of bourgeois society and was deeply convinced of its inevitable replacement by socialism a higher sociopolitical system. "Medieval theocracy has fallen, feudalism has fallen, absolutism has fallen; the time will come when the tyrannical domination of capital will fall, too."[11]

THE IDEAS OF SOCIALISM

Pisarev's revolutionary democratic ideas gradually led him to socialism. His evolution in that direction progressed under the influence of Chernyshevsky. As a man who unswervingly defended the interests of the people, Pisarev considered only one question worthy of attention in the conditions of capitalism, a question that "engulfed all the rest," viz., how to feed the starving and provide for all.

His socialist convictions were expressed very clearly in his article "The School and Life" in which he wrote about the unsatisfactory regulation of the relations between labor and capital under capitalism. The people's revolutionary gains were usurped and the prevailing ideology tended to be antidemocratic and apologetic, all of which led to the rise of socialist moods and ideas. The "labor question," which had taken on "immense and terrible dimensions" in the capitalist countries in the West, would also rise in time in Russia, he suggested; and the sole alternative solution was socialism.

While a champion of the social ideals of Herzen and Chernyshevsky, Pisarev nevertheless did not share the views of his teachers on the peasant revolution. But nowhere in his works did he criticize their theory of communal socialism; on the contrary, in conformity with his democratic convictions, he called for a broad revolutionary movement (involving the peasants, too) against exploitation and spiritual oppression.

He dreamed of the new people of Russia who would express the masses' self-awareness. This would require not only education of the upper and lower strata of society but also a powerful influx of individuals from among the popular masses who would enter the forefront of public affairs. In other words, this would call for an increase in the mass of the "thinking proletariat." At the same time, the transformation of public affairs should not be limited to a political upheaval, which would only open up an opportunity for radical change of the economic foundations of society, i.e., "the forms of the people's work."

> Work should become pleasing, its results plentiful, and these should go to the worker himself, while manual labor should go hand in hand with an all-round intellectual development. Until that is achieved, any civilization will be in the state of unstable equilibrium of an inverted pyramid. How is all that to be done? I do not know. Many ways have been prescribed, but till now no universal remedy has been used to heal the ills of life.[12]

Under socialism, in his opinion, people should be specially disposed to collective work, and to the creation of voluntary associations. A voluntary association and the harmoniously developed individual not only did not contradict one another but, on the contrary, also presupposed each other and could not exist without mutual support.

An important acquisition of Pisarev's political philosophy was the idea that "to solve the problem of the starving, two conditions must be observed. First, the problem must necessarily be solved by those who find their personal benefit in its solution, i.e., the workers themselves. Second, the solution of the problem consists not in cultivating personal virtues but in reorganizing public institutions."[13]

A necessary condition for a successful solution of the problems was a link between mental and physical labor, the bringing of the proletariat close to science. Thus labor power, practical aptitude, and industry should be supplemented with a clear understanding of interpersonal and social relations. The cause of socialism was the cause of the proletariat itself; the concept of revolution, democracy, and socialism was therefore in essence a single whole. But the proletariat was not yet ripe for realizing this whole. The undeveloped character of capitalist relations in Russia of the 1860s, the small number of the proletariat, and the illiteracy and submissive state of the peasantry pushed Pisarev to such a cautious conclusion. That explained his idea of the "thinking proletariat," his appeal to intellectuals or, to be more precise, to democratic *raznochintsy* intelligentsia, in whom he saw a social force capable of educating the working masses and preparing them for revolution.

NOTES

1. D. I. Pisarev, *Sobraniye sochineniy* (Collected works), 4 vols. (Moscow, 1955), vol. 1, p. 126.

2. D. I. Pisarev, *Polnoye sobraniye sochineniy* (Complete works) (St. Petersburg, 1912), vol. 3, p. 171.

3. Pisarev, *Sobraniye sochineniy,* vol. 2, p. 242.

4. Pisarev, *Polnoye sobraniye sochineniy* (St. Petersburg, 1914), vol. 4, p. 546.

5. Ibid., 1909, vol. 1, p. 475.

6. Ibid., 1911, vol. 5, p. 509.

7. Dmitry Pisarev, *Selected Philosophical, Social and Political Essays* (Moscow, 1958), p. 277.

8. Ibid., p 283.

9. Ibid., pp. 606–607.

10. Ibid., p. 592.

11. Ibid., p. 270.

12. Ibid., p. 296.

13. Cited in the "Introduction" to Pisarev, *Selected Philosophical, Social and Political Essays*, p. 22; taken from Pisarev, *Polnoye sobraniye sochineniy*, vol. 5, pp. 408–409.

19

Vissarion Grigoryevich Belinsky (1811–1848)

Vissarion Belinsky (dubbed "Vissarion the Furious") was one of the early Russian radical thinkers of the nineteenth century. His enthusiastic, original reviews of Russian classic literature—works of A. Pushkin, M. Lermontov, N. Gogol, I. Turgenev, and F. Dostoyevsky—brought him popularity and authority as a leading literary critic. Being influenced by the German philosophers Schelling, Hegel, and Feuerbach, and the French socialists, he revised and applied their ideas to the Russian historical and cultural realities. Finally, his—as well as Herzen's—essays on politics, philosophy, and esthetics gave birth to a new intellectual tide that lasted from the late 1830s until the end of the nineteenth century and included the so-called Chernyshevsky school and Russian populists such as M. Bakunin, P. Lavrov, P. Tkachev, and N. Mikhailovsky.

Letters to Vassily Botkin, his Western-oriented and less radical, liberal friend, refers to the period of Belinsky's transition from "reconciliation with reality" to left-wing political philosophy, which involved drastic changes of his attitude toward German philosophy, especially to Hegel.

LETTERS TO V. P. BOTKIN*

I

Saint Petersburg, March 1, 1841

. . . I have long suspected that Hegel's philosophy is no more than a moment, though a great one, that its absolute results are not worth a ———, that

*From *Russian Philosophy*, Volume 1, edited by James M. Edie, James P. Scanlan, Mary-Barbara Zeldin, with the collaboration of George L. Kline. Copyright © 1976. Originally translated by Philip Rahv. Reprinted by permission of the University of Tennessee Press.

it were better to die than to be reconciled to them. Fools lie when they say that Hegel turned life into dead schemes; but it is true that he turned its phenomena into spooks clasping bony hands and twirling in the air over a cemetery. For him the subject is not an end in itself but only a means for the momentary expression of the Universal, and in relation to the subject this Universal becomes a Moloch; when the subject's day is over it is cast off by this Moloch like an old pair of trousers. I have especially important reasons for being incensed with Hegel, for in remaining faithful to him I managed to reconcile myself to the Russian reality, and came to praise Zagoskin and similar abominations, and to hate Schiller. . . . All of Hegel's reasonings about morality are sheer nonsense, for in the objectified realm of thought there can be no moral values, just as there are none in objectified religion (in Hindu pantheism, for example, Brahma and Shiva are equal gods, that is to say, good and evil are equally autonomous).

I know you will laugh at me, you baldpate, but I will stick to my idea. The fate of the subject, the individual, the person is of more importance to me than the fate of the whole world and the well-being of the Chinese Emperor (namely, the Hegelian *Allgemeinheit*). I am told: develop the treasures of your spirit for the sake of its free self-delectation, cry to console yourself, grieve in order to rejoice anew, strive to attain perfection, climb to the top rung of the evolutionary ladder and if you stumble down you go—to the devil, the son of a bitch! I thank you humbly, Yegor Fyodorovich [Hegel], and I bow down to your philosophical nightcap; but I have the honor to inform you, with all due respect to your philosophical Philistinism, that even if I succeeded in climbing to the top of the ladder I would still demand of you an account of all the victims of the conditions of life and history, of chance, superstition, the Inquisition, Philip II, etc., etc. Otherwise there would be nothing left for me but to throw myself down headlong from the very top of the ladder. Even if I were to receive it gratis I do not want happiness, so long as I am not reassured as to the fate of my blood brothers, bone of my bone and flesh of my flesh. It is said that disharmony is the precondition of harmony; perhaps so; lovers of music may find the prospect agreeable and advantageous, but it is not a bit agreeable for those doomed to express the "idea" of disharmony. . . . The extract from Echtermeyer delighted me, because it administers an energetic rap on Hegel's philosophical cap, thus demonstrating that for Germans too it is possible to cease being Germans and become human beings. . . .

I belong to those men who see the devil's tail in everything—that, it appears, is my very latest world outlook, the one I will die with. Even though it makes me suffer, I am not ashamed of it. Man knows nothing about himself—everything depends on the spectacles provided by his disposition and the caprice of his nature. A year ago my thought was diametrically the opposite of what it is today, and, in truth, I don't know whether I am fortunate or unfortunate in being so constituted that for me to think and to feel, to understand and to suffer are one and the same things. And this is where fanaticism comes in. Do you know that my present self hates my past self, and that if I had the power it would surely go ill with those who are today what I was a year ago? In finding oneself alive in a coffin with hands tied behind one's back, how can one help seeing the devil's tail everywhere! What is it to me that some day reason will triumph, that the future will be good, when fate has consigned me to the witness of chance, unreason, and brute force? What is it to me that your children and mine will enjoy the good, when through no fault of my own I am so badly off now? Shall I simply retreat into myself? No, far better to die, to be a living corpse! The promise of recovery is nothing but words, mere words! You write me that you have outlived your love and have lost the capacity for loving. . . . I feel the same; Philistines, men meanly concerned with immediate reality alone, are laughing at us and celebrating their victory. Ah, woe, woe, woe! But all of that later. . . .

A fine Prussian government, in which we fancied to see the ideal of a rational state! What is there to say?—scoundrels, tyrants lording it over mankind! A member of the triple alliance of the executioners of liberty and reason. So that's your Hegel. . . . The most rational government is that of the North American states, and right below it I rank the governments of England and France. . . .

II

Saint Petersburg, June 28, 1841

. . . On your advice I have bought Destunis's *Plutarch* and read it. It has driven me wild. Good God, how much life is still stirring in me that will go to waste! Of all the heroes of antiquity three have won all my love, adoration, and enthusiasm—Timeleon and the Gracchuses. The life of Cato (of Utica and not the Elder brute) exhales the somber grandeur of tragedy: what a noble personality! Pericles and Alcibiades have exacted from me the full tribute of wonder and delight. What about Caesar?—you will ask. My friend, let me tell you that at present I am utterly absorbed and devoured by a single idea. You know that I am not destined to hit the truth at its core, uniformly surveying all that surrounds it—no, somehow I always run to extremes. So I am now caught up by the idea of civic virtue, of the pathos of truth and honor, apart from which I can hardly respond to greatness anywhere. Now you will understand why Timeleon, the Gracchuses, and Cato of Utica (not that red-headed brute the Elder) have quite eclipsed Caesar and the Macedonian in my eyes. There has developed in me a kind of wild, frenzied, fanatical love of freedom and the independent human personality, which are possible only in a society founded on truth and virtue. In taking

up Plutarch I imagined that the Greeks would overshadow the Romans—
it turned out quite the other way. I raved over Pericles and Alcibiades, but
the austere grandeur of Timeleon and Phocion (those Greco-Romans) shut
off from me the beautiful and graceful images of Athens' representatives. In
the Roman lives my soul floated as in an ocean. Through Plutarch I came
to understand much I had not grasped before. A new humanity grew upon
the soil of Greece and Rome. But for them the Middle Ages would have
achieved nothing. I also understood the French revolution with its Roman
pomp at which I once laughed. I grasped, too, Marat's sanguinary love of
liberty, his sanguinary hatred of everything wishing to separate itself from
the brotherhood of man even by so much as an armorial carriage. How
fascinating is the world of antiquity. It contains the germ of all that is great,
noble, and virtuous, for the basis of its life was the pride of personality, in-
violable personal dignity. Yes, the Greek and Latin languages must be the
cornerstone of all education, the foundation of schooling.

Strange that my life is in sheer apathy, sloth, a stagnant mire. But at
the bottom somewhere there is a fiery sea. I was always afraid that with the
passing of the years my feelings would gradually die away—the exact opposite
has happened. I am disenchanted with everything, believe in no one, love nothing
and nobody, still the interests of prosaic life absorb me less and less, and
I am becoming more and more a citizen of the universe. The mad craving
for love is devouring me inside, the yearning grows ever more persistent and
painful. That is myself, mine, and that alone. But I am also strongly concerned
with what is not mine. Human personality so obsesses me that I am afraid
I will go mad. I am beginning to love mankind à la Marat: to make the
least part of it happy I would be willing to decimate the rest of it with fire
and sword. What right has a man of my type to place himself above humanity,
to divorce himself from it by means of an iron crown and purple robe which,
as Schiller, the Tiberius Gracchus of our era, has said, are still stained with
the blood of the first manslayer? What right has he to fill me with that awe
which is but another form of degradation? Why must I bare my head before
him? I feel that if I were a king I would most certainly turn into a tyrant.
Only an omniscient and passionless God can be a Tsar. . . . Hegel dreamed
of a constitutional monarchy as the ideal state—what a paltry conception!
No, there should be no monarchs, for a monarch can never be a brother,
always he will keep aloof from men even if only through empty etiquette,
and men will always bow down to him if merely for form's sake. Men ought
to be brothers and ought not to humiliate one another even by a shade of
external and formal superiority. How gifted of the French to grasp without
the help of German philosophy what German philosophy has still failed to
understand! Damn it, I must study the Saint-Simonists! I look upon woman
through their eyes. Woman is a victim, the slave of modern society. It is in
the body rather than in the soul that public opinion lodges a woman's honor. . . .

III

Saint Petersburg, September 8, 1841

. . . You know my nature: always it runs to extremes. . . . It is with difficulty and pain that I part from an old idea, but once I do so I renounce it utterly, attaching myself to the new one with the fanaticism of a proselyte. And so, I am now at a new extreme—it is the idea of *socialism* which has become for me the idea of ideas, the essence of being, the question of questions, the alpha and omega of belief and knowledge. It is at once the question and the answer. It has swallowed up for me history and religion and philosophy. Hence I am using it now to explain my existence and yours, and indeed that of everyone I have encountered on life's path. . . . Our most cherished (and rational) dream was to bring our lives, and our mutual relations as well, into some kind of viable contact with reality. Well, the dream was but a dream and such it remains; we were phantoms and will die as phantoms, yet we were not at fault and have nothing to blame ourselves for.

The Universal isolated from the particular and individual exists in pure thought alone; in vital, concrete, visible reality the Universal is but a lifeless maturbatory dream. Man is a grand word, a grand cause, but not man in general, only man as Frenchman, German, Englishman, or Russian. Yet are we truly Russians? No, society looks upon us as diseased growths on a body, and we in turn regard society as a dung heap. Society is right, and we are even more in the right. . . . Without purpose no activity is possible, and without interests there is no purpose, and without activity no life; and it is the substance of social life which is the source of all three—interests, purpose, and activity. Is that correct, logical, clear? We are men without a country— no, worse by far, we are men whose country is a phantom, and no wonder we are phantoms ourselves, that our friendship, our loves, and our doings and strivings are phantoms too. Botkin, you loved and your love came to nothing. It is likewise the story of my love. Stankevich was of a higher caliber than either of us, and that was his story too. No, we were not made for love, to be husbands and fathers of families. . . . There are people whose lives, lacking content, cannot take on form; we, on the other hand, are men with ample life-content for which society provides no given, settled forms. Outside our circle I have met excellent men of greater actuality than ourselves; but nowhere have I come upon men with such an insatiable thirst for life, with such enormous demands on it, and with such capacities for self-sacrifice for the sake of an idea. That is the cause of our appeal and of the disturbance our presence effects. . . . Looking for a way out, we threw ourselves with fervor into the alluring sphere of German philosophical contemplation, fancying that we could create a charming inner world full of light and warmth closing us off from the external environment. We did not understand that this contemplative subjectivism and inwardness comprised the objective interest of the German national character, and that it is for the Germans what sociality is for the French. Reality roused us and opened our eyes, but for what? . . .

Social solidarity [*sotsialnost*] or death! That is my motto. What is it to me that the Universal exists when the personality is suffering? What care I if on earth the genius lives as in heaven when the mass is wallowing in dirt? What care I that *I* grasp the "Idea," that the world of ideas is open to me in art, religion, and history, when I cannot share it with all those who should be my brothers in humanity, my brothers in Christ, but who in their ignorance are actually strangers and enemies? What is the felicity of the elect to me when most men do not even suspect its possibility? Away with felicity if it is granted to me as one out of a thousand! I will not have it so long as I cannot have it in common with my lesser brethren!

My heart bleeds as I watch the life of the masses. Grief, poignant grief overpowers me at the sight of the barefooted little boys playing knucklebones in the street, of the poor in their rags and tatters, of the drunken cab driver, of the soldier returning from duty, of the functionary hurrying along with his briefcase under his arm, of the self-complacent officer and the proud magnate. As I give the soldier a penny I almost cry, and I run from the begger whom I have given a penny as though I had done him an injury and am ashamed to listen to the sound of my own footsteps. And that is life: to sit in the street in rags, an idiotic expression on one's face, collecting pennies all day long to be spent on booze in the evenings—men see it and care not a whit! I don't know what is happening to me, but there are times when I gaze with unutterable anguish at a whore in the street; her senseless smile acknowledging her depravity lacerates my soul, all the more so if she is good-looking. Next door to me there lives a well-to-do official who has become so Europeanized that he sends his wife to the baths in a carriage; recently I learned that he smashed in her teeth and lips, that he kicked her, dragging her over the floor by the hair because the cream she had prepared for his coffee was not good enough; and she had borne this man six children, and whenever I meet her I feel so bad at the sight of her pale worn face on which tyranny has left its mark. On hearing this story I gnashed my teeth—to burn this blackguard over a slow fire seemed to me too easy a punishment, and I cursed my impotence at not being able to go and kill him like a dog. And that is society, built on rational principles, a manifestation of reality! And how many such families, such husbands are there! After all that, what right has a man to lose himself in art, in knowledge?

I am bearing down harder and harder on all the substantial principles that bind the will of man to a creed! My God is negation! In history my heroes are the disrupters of the old—Luther, Voltaire, the Encyclopaedists, the terrorists, Byron (*Cain*), etc. Intelligence now stands higher with me than reason, and that is why I now prefer the blasphemies of Voltaire to the authority of religion, society, anything or anyone! I know that the Middle Ages were a great epoch; I understand the sacredness, the poetry, the grandeur of medieval religiosity; but I am more pleased with the eighteenth century, the age of religion's decline; in the Middle Ages heretics, freethinkers, and witches were burned at the stake; in the eighteenth century the guillotine chopped off the heads of aristocrats, priests, and other enemies of God, reason, and humanity. And there will come a time—I ardently believe it—when no one will be burnt, no one beheaded, when the criminal pleading for death as his mercy and salvation will not be granted death, for life will be his punishment as death is now; when there will be no senseless forms and rites, no contracts and conditions binding the feelings, no duties and obligations, when will yields to love alone and never to will; when there will be no husbands and wives but only lovers, and when the mistress comes to her lover to tell him that she loves another he will answer: "I cannot be happy without you, I will suffer all my life, but go to the man you love." If through magnanimity she should wish to stay with him, he will not accept her sacrifice but will say to her: "I want blessings, not sacrifices." Woman will not be the slave of society and of men but, like men, will freely follow her inclinations without losing her good name—that monstrosity of conventional notions. There will be no rich, no poor, neither kings nor subjects, but only men and brothers, and, at the word of the apostle Paul, Christ will give back his power to the Father, and Father-Reason will again hold sway, this time in a new heaven and over a new world. Don't think that I am being excessively rational: no, I do not repudiate the past, I do not repudiate history—I see in them an essential and rational development of the idea; I want the golden age, not the unconscious animal bliss of the past but one prepared by society, laws, marriage, in a word by everything that may have been necessary in its time but is now stupid and mean. . . . It is ridiculous to imagine that all this could happen of itself, merely with the passage of time, without violent upheavals, without bloodshed. Men are so witless that they must be forcibly led to happiness. What is the blood of thousands compared to the degradation and suffering of millions? Therefore: *fiat justitia, pereat mundus!*

20

Nikolai Gavrilovich Chernyshevsky (1828–1889)

Chernyshevsky's legacy mirrors the highest point in the history of prereform (1861) radical democratic thought in Russia. As a leader of the left-wing intelligentsia he was supplanted—mostly because of his two-year imprisonment and nineteen-year Siberian exile—in the 1870s by populist theoreticians and revolutionaries: P. Lavrov, P. Tkachev, et al. But as a man of outstanding courage, political prisoner, and persistent defender of human rights, Chernyshevsky was greatly respected among all groups of Russian democrats and leftist radicals until the October revolution of 1917.

In these excerpts from Chernyshevsky's The Anthropological Principle in Philosophy *he discusses some key philosophical and moral ideas of his worldview: interrelations between philosophy and science, science and morality, good and evil, the theory of "rational egoism," personality, and so on.*

THE ANTHROPOLOGICAL PRINCIPLE IN PHILOSOPHY*

That part of philosophy which deals with questions of man, just like the other part which deals with questions of external nature, is based on the natural ooionooo. The principle underlying the philosophical view of human life and all its phenomena is the idea, worked out by the natural sciences, of the

*From *Russian Philosophy,* Volume 2, edited by James M. Edie, James P. Scanlan, Mary-Barbara Zeldin, with the collaboration of George L. Kline. Copyright © 1976. Reprinted, in edited form, from N. G. Chernyshevsky, *Selected Philosophical Essays,* Moscow, 1953. Reprinted here by permission of the University of Tennessee Press.

unity of the human organism; the observations of physiologists, zoologists, and medical men have driven away all thought of dualism in man. Philosophy sees in him what medicine, physiology, and chemistry see. These sciences prove that no dualism is evident in man, and philosophy adds that if man possessed another nature, in addition to his real nature, this other nature would surely reveal itself in some way; but since it does not, since everything that takes place and manifests itself in man originates solely from his real nature, he cannot have another nature.

This proof is completely beyond doubt. It is as convincing as the grounds on which you, dear reader, are convinced, for example, that at the moment you are reading this book there is no lion in the room in which you are sitting. You think that this is so because you do not see a lion or hear one growl. But is this alone a sufficient guarantee that there is no lion in your room? No, you have a second guarantee—the fact that you are alive. Were there a lion in your room it would have sprung upon you and torn you to bits. The inevitable consequences of the presence of a lion are absent, and therefore you know that there is no lion. . . .

But while there is unity in man's nature, we see in him two different orders of phenomena of what is called a material order (a man eats, walks), and phenomena of what is called a moral order (a man thinks, feels, desires). In what relation do these two orders of phenomena stand to one another? Does not the difference between them contradict the unity of man's nature that is demonstrated by the natural sciences? The natural sciences answer that there are no grounds for such a hypothesis, for there is no object that possesses only one quality. On the contrary, every object displays an incalculable number of different phenomena which, for convenience, we place in different categories, calling each category a quality so that every object has numerous qualities of different kinds. For example, wood grows and it burns; we say that it possesses two qualities: vegetative power and combustibility. Is there any resemblance between these two qualities? They are entirely different; there is no concept that can cover both these qualities except the general concept of quality. There is no concept to cover both categories of phenomena corresponding to these qualities except the concept of phenomenon. Or, for example, ice is hard and shiny. What is there in common between hardness and shininess? The logical distance between these two qualities is immeasurable, or it would be more correct to say that there is no logical distance between them, great or small, because there is no logical relation between them. This shows that the combination of completely heterogeneous properties in one object is the general law of things.

But in this diversity the natural sciences also discover connection—not in the forms of manifestation, not in the phenomena, which are totally unlike each other, but in the way the diverse phenomena originate from the same element when the energy with which it acts is increased or diminished. For example, water has the property of having temperature—a property common to all bodies. No matter what the property we call heat may consist in, under different circumstances it reveals itself in extremely diverse degrees. Sometimes a given object is cold—that is to say, it displays very little heat. Sometimes it is very hot—that is to say, it displays a great deal of heat. When water, no matter under what circumstances, displays very little heat, it is a solid—ice. When it displays somewhat more heat, it is a liquid. And when there is a great deal of heat in it, it becomes steam. In these three states, the same quality reveals itself in three orders of totally different phenomena, so that one quality assumes the forms of three different qualities, branches out into three qualities simply according to the different quantities in which it is displayed: quantitative difference passes into qualitative difference. . . .

The union of the exact sciences, under the government of mathematics —that is, counting, weighing, and measuring—is year after year spreading to new spheres of knowledge, is growing by the inclusion of newcomers. Chemistry was gradually followed by all the sciences concerned with plant and animal organisms: physiology, comparative anatomy, various branches of botany and zoology. Now the moral sciences are joining them. What is happening to the moral sciences is what happens to proud but poverty-stricken people when a distant relative—not, like themselves, proud and boastful of their ancient lineage and incomparable virtues, but a plain, honest man— acquires wealth. For a long time they live off his charity, considering it beneath their dignity to turn, with his aid, to the honest work which made him a success. But gradually, eating better and dressing better, they become more reasonable, their empty boastfulness subsides, they become respectable, and at last they understand that not work but pride is shameful. Finally they adopt the habits that enabled their relative to succeed. Then, with his assistance, they quickly attain a good position and begin to enjoy the respect of rational people, not for the imaginary virtues they had boasted of in the past, but for their new and real qualities which are useful to society, for the work they do.

Not so long ago the moral sciences could not have had the content to justify the title of science they bore, and the English were quite right then in depriving them of a title they did not deserve. The situation today has changed considerably. The natural sciences have already developed to such an extent that they provide much material for the exact solution of moral problems, too. All the progressive thinkers among those who are studying the moral sciences have begun to work out these problems with the aid of precise methods similar to those by which the problems of the natural sciences are being worked out. When we spoke about the controverises among different people on every moral problem, we were referring only to the old and very widespread but now obsolete conceptions and methods of investigation, and not to the character the moral sciences are now acquiring among progressive thinkers. We were referring to the former routine character of these branches of science and not to their present form. In their present form, the moral sciences differ from the so-called natural sciences only in that they began to be worked out in a truly scientific way later, and therefore have not yet been developed to the same degree of perfection as the latter.

The difference here is only one of degree: chemistry is younger than astronomy and has not yet attained the same degree of perfection; physiology is still younger than chemistry and is still further removed from perfection; psychology, as an exact science, is still younger than physiology and has been worked out even less. But, while differing from each other in the amount of exact knowledge acquired, chemistry and astronomy do not differ either as regards the validity of what has been learned, or in the methods employed to arrive at exact knowledge in the particular subjects. The facts and laws discovered by chemistry are as authentic as the facts and laws discovered by astronomy. The same must be said about the results achieved by present-day exact research in the moral sciences. . . .

The first result of the entry of the moral sciences into the sphere of the exact sciences is that a strict distinction has been drawn between what we know and what we do not know. The astronomer knows that he knows the dimensions of Mars, and he knows just as positively that he does not know the geological composition of that planet, the character of the plant and animal life on it, or whether there *is* any plant or animal life on it. If someone took it into his head to claim that clay, granite, birds, or mollusks existed on Mars, the astronomer would reply: you are asserting something you do not know. If the fantast were to go even further in his assumptions and assert, for example, that the birds that inhabit Mars are not subject to disease and that the mollusks do not need food, the astronomer, assisted by the chemist and physiologist, would prove to him that this is impossible. Likewise, in the moral sciences a strict distinction has been drawn between what is known and what is not known, and on the basis of what is known the unsoundness of some of the previous assumptions concerning what still remains unknown has been proved.

It is definitely known, for example, that all the phenomena of the moral world originate from one another and from external circumstances in conformity with the law of causality, and on this basis all assumptions that there can be any phenomena that do not arise from preceding phenomena and from external circumstances are regarded as false. Hence, present-day psychology does not accept, for example, the assumptions that in one case a man performs a bad action because he wanted to perform a bad action, while in another case he performs a good action because he wanted to perform a good action. It says that the bad action, or the good action, was certainly prompted by some moral or material fact, or combination of facts, and that the "wanting" is only the subjective impression which accompanies, in our consciousness, the genesis of thoughts or actions from preceding thoughts, actions, or external facts.

The example most often given of an action based on nothing but our will is this: I get out of bed. Which foot do I put out first? Whichever one I want to. But this only appears to be so at a superficial glance. Actually, facts and impressions determine which foot a man puts out of bed first. If there are no special circumstances or thoughts he will put out the foot that is most convenient for the anatomical position of his body in the bed. If there are special motives that outweigh this physiological convenience, the result will change according to the circumstances. If, for example, the thought occurs to the man: "I shall put out my left foot rather than my right," he will do so. Here, however, one cause (physiological convenience) was simply displaced by another (the thought of displaying independence), or it would be more correct to say that the second cause, being the stronger, triumphed over the first. But how did the second cause arise? Whence came the thought of displaying independence of external conditions? It could not have arisen without a cause. It was created either by something said in conversation with someone, or by the recollection of a previous dispute, or something like that. Thus, the fact that a man can, if he wants to, put out the foot that is not convenient for the anatomical position of his body in the bed does not prove that he can put out this foot or that foot without any cause. It only proves that the manner of getting out of bed can be determined by causes that are stronger than the anatomical position of the body before getting out of bed.

The phenomenon that we call "will" is itself a link in a series of phenomena and facts joined together by causal connection. Very often, the immediate cause of the manifestation of our will to perform a certain action is thought. But the definite inclination of the will is also due solely to a definite thought: whatever the thought is, so is the will. If the thought were different the will would be different. But why did a particular thought arise and not a different one? Because it, too, arose from some thought, some fact—in short, from some cause. In this case, psychology says the same thing that physics and chemistry say in similar cases: if a certain phenomenon occurs, we must seek the cause of it and not be satisfied with the vapid statement: it occurred of its own accord without any special cause—"I did this because I wanted to." That's all very well, but why did you want to? If you answer: "Simply because I wanted to," it will be the same as saying: "The plate broke because it broke; the house was burned down because it was burned down." These are not answers at all; they are only a cloak to cover up laziness in seeking the real cause, lack of desire to know the truth. . . .

But if the moral sciences are still obliged to say "We do not know" in answer to very many questions, we shall be mistaken if we assume that among the problems they have not yet solved are those which, according to one of the prevailing opinions, are insoluble. No, the ignorance in these sciences is not of this kind. What, for example, does chemistry not know? It does not at present know what hydrogen will be when it passes from the gaseous to the solid state—a metal or a nonmetal. There are strong grounds for assuming that it will be a metal, but we do not yet know whether this assumption is correct. Chemistry also does not know whether phosphorus and sulphur are simply substances or whether they will in time be resolved into the simplest elements. These are cases of theoretical ignorance. Another category of problems that chemistry cannot solve at present consists of the numerous cases of inability to satisfy practical demands. Chemistry can make prussic acid and acetic acid, but it cannot yet make fibrin. As we can see, these and other problems it cannot at present solve are of a very special character, a character so special that they occur to the minds only of people who are fairly well acquainted with chemistry.

The problems the moral sciences have not yet solved are of exactly the same kind. Psychology, for example, discovers the following fact: a man of low mental development is unable to understand a life different from his own; the more his mind develops, the easier it is for him to picture another sort of life. How is this fact to be explained? In the present state of science, a strictly scientific answer to this question has not yet been found; all we have are various surmises. Now tell us, would this question arise in the mind of anyone not familiar with the present state of psychology? Scarcely anybody but a scientist has even noticed the fact to which this question applies. It is like the question as to whether hydrogen is or is not a metal; people unacquainted with chemistry are not only unaware of this question, they are unaware of the existence of hydrogen. For chemistry, however, this hydrogen, the existence of which would not have been noticed had it not been for chemistry, is extremely important. Similarly, the fact that a man of low mental development is unable to understand a life different from his own, whereas a mentally developed man is able to do so, is extremely important for psychology. Just as the discovery of hydrogen led to an improvement in the theory of chemistry, so the discovery of this psychological fact led to the formation of the theory of anthropomorphism, without which not a step can now be taken in metaphysics.

[. . .] The following baffling question is asked: Is man a good or an evil being? Lots of people rack their brains attempting to solve this problem. Nearly half of them decide that man is by nature good; others, also constituting nearly half of the brain-rackers, decide otherwise; they say man is by nature bad. Outside these two opposed dogmatic parties are several skeptics who jeer at both sides and say that the problem is insoluble.

But at the very first application of scientific analysis the whole thing turns out to be as clear as can be. A man likes what is pleasant and dislikes what is unpleasant—this, one would think, is beyond doubt, because the predicate simply repeats the subject: A is A, what is pleasant to a man is pleasant to a man; what is unpleasant to him is unpleasant to him. Good is he who does good to others, bad is he who is bad to others—this, too, is clear and simple, one would think. Let us now combine the simple truths; we will get the following deductions: a man is good when, in order to obtain pleasure for himself, he must give pleasure to others. A man is bad when, in order to obtain pleasure for himself, he is obliged to cause displeasure to others. Here human nature cannot be blamed for one thing or praised for the other; everything depends on circumstances, relationships (institutions). If certain relations are constant, the man whose character is molded by them is found to have acquired the habit of acting in conformity with them.

Therefore, we may think that John is good, while Peter is bad; but these opinions apply only to individual men, not to man in general, just as we attribute to individual men and not to man in general the habits involved in sawing planks and forging iron. John is a carpenter, but we cannot say that man in general is or is not a carpenter. Peter can forge iron, but we cannot say that man in general is or is not a blacksmith. The fact that John became a carpenter and Peter a blacksmith merely shows that under certain circumstances, which existed in John's life, a man becomes a carpenter; while under other circumstances, which existed in Peter's life, a man becomes a blacksmith. In exactly the same way, under certain circumstances a man becomes good, under others he becomes bad.

Thus from the theoretical side the problem of the good and bad qualities of human nature is solved so easily that it cannot even be called a problem: it contains its own complete solution.

It is quite another matter, however, when you take the practical side; when, for example, it seems to you that it is much better for a man himself, and for all those around him, to be good rather than bad; and when you want to make everybody good. From this aspect the matter presents many difficulties. As the reader will observe, however, these difficulties relate not to science but to the practical application of the means indicated by science. In this respect psychology and moral philosophy are in exactly the same position as the natural sciences. The climate in North Siberia is too cold. If you were to ask how it could be made warmer, the natural sciences would have no difficulty in finding an answer: Siberia is closed to the warm atmosphere of the South by mountains, and its northern slope is open to the cold atmosphere of the North. If there were mountains on the northern border and none on the southern, that part of the country would be much warmer than it is now. But we as yet lack the means with which to put this theoretical solution of the problem into practice.

Similarly, the moral sciences already have theoretical answers to nearly all the problems that are important for life, but in many cases man lacks the means to put into practice what is indicated by theory. Incidentally, in this respect the moral sciences have an advantage over the natural sciences.

In the natural sciences, all the means belong to the sphere of so-called external nature; in the moral sciences, only half the means belong to this category, while the other half are contained in man himself. Consequently, half the matter depends entirely upon man feeling strongly enough the need for a certain improvement. This feeling in itself provides him with a very considerable part of the conditions necessary for the improvement. We have seen, however, that the conditions that depend upon the state of man's own impressions are not enough; material means are also needed. In respect to this half of the conditions, in respect to material means, the practical problems of the moral sciences are in a much more favorable position than they are in respect to the conditions which lie with man himself. Formerly, when the natural sciences were still undeveloped, insurmountable difficulties could be met with in external nature that prevented the satisfaction of man's moral requirements. This is not the case now; the natural sciences already offer man such powerful means of command over external nature that no difficulties arise in this respect.

Let us return, as an example, to the practical question of how people could become good, so that bad people should become an extreme rarity in the world, and that bad qualities should lose all perceptible importance in life because of the extreme rarity of the cases in which they were displayed. Psychology tells us that the most abundant source of the display of bad qualities is inadequacy of means for satisfying requirements; that a man commits a bad action—that is, harms others—almost only when he is obliged to deprive them of things so as not to remain himself without the things he needs. For example, when crops are poor and there is not enough food for everybody, there is a great increase in crime and of all sorts of evil deeds; people rob and cheat one another for a crust of bread. . . .

The next subject to be dealt with in our essays is man as an individual. . . .

We shall put aside for a time the psychological and moral-philosophical problems concerning man and deal with the physiological, medical, or any other problem you please, but not with man as a moral being, and try first of all to say what we know about him as a being that possesses a stomach, a head, bones, veins, muscles, and nerves. We shall examine him only from the side that the natural sciences find in him; the other aspects of life we shall examine later, if time allows.

Physiology and medicine find that the human organism is an extremely complex combination of chemicals that undergoes an extremely complex chemical process we call life. This process is so complex and so important to us that the branch of chemistry engaged in research in it has been awarded the title of a special science and is called physiology. . . .

Physiology is only a variety of chemistry, and its subject is only a variety of the subjects dealt with in chemistry. Physiology itself has not kept all its departments in strict unity under a common name; some of the aspects of the subjects it investigates, i.e., the chemical processes that take place in the human organism, are of such special interest for man that investigations into them, which are part of physiology, have been awarded the name of separate sciences. Of these aspects we shall mention one: investigation of the phenomena that cause and accompany the various derivations of this chemical process from its normal form. This part of physiology bears the special name of medicine. Medicine, in its turn, branches out into numerous sciences with special names. . . .

When a subject under investigation is very complex, it is useful, for the sake of convenience, to divide it into parts. Hence, physiology divides the complex process that goes on in the living human organism into several parts, the most marked of which are: respiration, nutrition, circulation of the blood, motor phenomena, sensation. Like every other chemical process, this entire system of phenomena has its birth, growth, decline, and end. Therefore, physiology regards the processes of respiration, nutrition, blood circulation, motor activity, sensation, and so forth, and conception or fertilization, growth, senility, and death, as if they were special subjects. But here again it must be borne in mind that these different segments and aspects of the process are divided only in theory, to facilitate theoretical analysis; actually, they constitute one indivisible whole. . . .

Some parts of physiology have already been elaborated very well. Such, for example, are the researches into the processes of respiration, nutrition, blood circulation, conception, growth, and senility. Motor phenomena have not been explained in such detail, and the process of sensation still less. . . .

We have said that some parts of the process of life have not been explained in as great detail as others; but this does not mean that we have not already positively learned a great deal about those parts, the investigation of which is at present in a very imperfect state. First, even supposing that some special aspect of the vital process were still totally inaccessible to exact analysis on the lines of mathematics and the natural sciences, its character would be approximately known to us from the character of other parts that have already been fairly well investigated. This would be a case like that of determining the shape of the head of a mammal from the bones of its leg. We know that merely from an animal's shoulder blade or collarbone science can fairly precisely reproduce its entire figure, including its head so much so that when, later on, a whole skeleton is found, it confirms the scientific inference concerning the whole which was arrived at from one of its parts. We know, for example, what nutrition is. From this we already know approximately what sensation is: nutrition and sensation are so closely interconnected that the character of one determines the character of the other.

Above we said that such deductions concerning unknown parts drawn from known parts are particularly valid and particularly important when they are presented in a negative form: A is closely connected with X; A is B;

from this it follows that X cannot be either C, D, or E. For example, supposing the shoulder blade of some antediluvian animal is found; perhaps we shall not be able unerringly to determine to what particular category of mammals it belonged, or perhaps we shall mistakenly put it in the cat or the horse category. But from this shoulder blade alone we can determine without error that it was neither a bird, a fish, nor a testacean.

We have said that these negative deductions are important in all sciences, but they are particularly important in the moral sciences and in metaphysics, because the errors which they have removed did exceptional practical harm to these sciences. In the olden days, when the natural sciences were still undeveloped, the whale was mistakenly regarded as a fish and the bat was regarded as a bird; but in all probability not a single person suffered as a result. Owing to the same cause, however, i.e., inability to subject a thing to exact anlaysis, mistaken opinions arose in metaphysics and in the moral sciences which caused people much more harm than cholera, plague, and all infectious diseases.

Let us suppose, for example, that idleness is pleasant and that work is unpleasant. If this hypothesis becomes the prevailing opinion, every man will take every opportunity to ensure for himself a life of idleness and compel others to work for him. This will give rise to every kind of enslavement and thievery, from so-called slavery proper and ways of conquest to the present more refined forms of these phenomena. This supposition has actually been made by people; it actually became the prevailing opinion and has prevailed to this day, causing incalculable suffering.

Let us now try to apply to the concept of pleasure or enjoyment the deduction drawn from an exact analysis of the vital process. The phenomenon of pleasure or enjoyment belongs to that part of the vital process which is called sensation. Let us suppose for the moment that we have not yet had exact investigation of this part of the vital process, as a separate part. Let us see whether anything about it can be deduced from the exact information that science has acquired about nutrition, respiration, and blood circulation. We see that each of these phenomena constitutes the activity of certain parts of our organism. We know what parts operate in the phenomena of respiration, nutrition, and blood circulation, and we know how they operate. Perhaps we would err if from this information we drew any conclusion about what particular parts of the organism operate in the phenomenon of pleasant sensation, and about how they operate; but we have clearly seen that only the action of some part of the organism gives rise to what are called the phenomena of life. We see that when there is action there is a phenomenon, and that when there is no action there is no phenomenon. From this we see that in order to obtain a pleasant sensation there must be some kind of action on the part of the organism.

Let us now analyze the concept of action. Action calls for the existence of two things, something that acts and something that is acted upon, and it consists in the former exerting effort to alter the latter. For example, the chest and lungs move and decompose air in the process of respiration; the stomach digests food in the process of nutrition. Thus, a pleasant sensation must also consist in the alteration of some external object by the human organism. We do not yet know exactly what object is altered, or exactly how it is altered, but we already see that the source of pleasure must be some kind of action by the human organism upon external objects.

Let us now try to draw a negative deduction from this result. Idleness is the absence of action; obviously, it cannot produce the phenomenon that is called pleasant sensation. It now becomes perfectly clear to us why the well-to-do classes of society in all civilized countries complain of constant ennui, complain that life is unpleasant. This complaint is quite justified. For the rich, life is as unpleasant as it is for the poor, because owing to the custom introduced in society by a mistaken hypothesis, wealth is associated with idleness, that is, the thing that should have served as a source of pleasure is deprived by this hypothesis of that possibility of affording pleasure. Whoever is accustomed to abstract thinking will be convinced in advance that observation of every-day relationships will not contradict the results of scientific analysis. But even those who are unaccustomed to abstract thinking will be led to the same conclusion by pondering the meaning of the facts that constitute so-called high society life. In it there is no normal activity— i.e., activity, the objective side of which corresponds to its subjective role; there is no activity that deserves the name of serious activity. . . .

The reader sees that the method of analyzing moral concepts in the spirit of the natural sciences, divesting the object of all pomposity and transferring it to the sphere of very simple and natural phenomena, places moral concepts on an unshakable foundation. If by useful we mean that which serves as a source of numerous pleasures, and by good, simply that which is very useful, no doubt whatever remains concerning the aim that is ascribed to man— not by extraneous motives or promptings, not by problematical assumptions, or by mysterious relationship to something which is still very uncertain— but simply by reason, by common sense, by the need for pleasure. That aim is—the good. Only good actions are prudent; only he who is good is rational, and he is rational only to the degree that he is good. When a man is not good he is merely an imprudent wastrel who pays thousands of rubles for things that are worth kopeks, spends as much material and moral strength in acquiring little pleasure as could have enabled him to acquire ever so much more pleasure.

But in this same conception of good as very durable utility we find still another important feature, which helps us to discover precisely what phenomena and actions chiefly constitute the good. External objects, no matter how closely they may be bound to a man, nevertheless are only too often parted from him: sometimes he abandons them, sometimes they desert him.

Country, kinsmen, wealth—all these things can be abandoned by man, or they can abandon him. But there is one thing he cannot possibly part from as long as he lives; there is one thing that is inseparable from him—himself. If a man can be useful to people because of his wealth, he can also cease to be useful if he loses his wealth. If, however, he is useful to other people because of his own virtues—because of his own spiritual qualities, as it is usually expressed—all he can do is commit suicide; but as long as he refrains from doing that he cannot cease to be useful to other people; not to be so is beyond his strength, beyond his power. He may say to himself: I shall be wicked, I shall harm people; but he will not be able to do it, any more than a clever man could be a fool even if he wanted to.

Not only is the good done by the qualities of the man himself much more constant and lasting than the good done merely because he owns certain external objects, but the results are far greater. The good or bad use to which external objects are put is casual; all material means are as easily, and as often, used to people's detriments as to their benefit. The rich man who uses his wealth to benefit some people in some cases, harms others, or even the same people, in other cases. For example, a rich man can give his children a good upbringing, develop their health and their minds, and impart much knowledge to them. All this would be useful to the children. But whether these things will actually be accomplished is uncertain; often they are not. On the contrary, the children of the rich often receive an upbringing that makes them weak, sickly, feeble-minded, vacuous, and pitiful; in general they acquire habits and ideas that are harmful to them. If such is the influence of wealth upon those whom the rich man cherishes most, then, of course, still more notable is the harm it does to other people who are not so dear to the rich man's heart. Thus it must be supposed that the rich man's wealth does more harm than good to the people who have direct relations with him.

But while it is possible to harbor some doubt as to whether the harmful influence wealth exercises upon these individuals is equal to the benefit they derive from it or, as in all probability is the case, greatly exceeds it, it is a totally indisputable fact that the wealth of individuals does far more harm than good to society as a whole. This is revealed with mathematical precision by that section of the moral sciences which began earlier than the others to be elaborated in conformity with an exact scientific system, and some of the departments of which have already been fairly well elaborated by the science of social material welfare that is usually called political economy. What we find in relation to the great ascendancy that material wealth gives some people over others, applies in an even greater degree to the concentration in the hands of individuals of another means of influencing the fate of the people which is external to the human organism—namely, power or authority. It too, in all probability, does much more harm than good even to the people who come into direct contact with it, and the influence it exercises upon society as a whole is comparably more harmful than beneficial.

Thus, the only remaining real source of perfectly durable benefit for people from the actions of other people are the useful qualities that lie within the human organism itself. That is why it is these qualities which are designated as good, and that is why the term "good" properly applies only to man. His actions are based on feeling, on the heart, and they are directly prompted by that side of organic activity which is called "will." Therefore, when discussing good, a special study must be made of the laws that govern the action of the heart and will. But the will is given means of gratifying the feelings of the heart by the conceptions formed by the mind, and therefore it is also necessary to pay attention to that aspect of thinking that relates to means of influencing the fate of other people. . . .

But we had almost forgotten that the term "anthropological" in the title of our essay still remains unexplained. What is this "anthropological principle in the moral sciences"? The reader has seen what this principle is from the very character of these essays. It is that a man must be regarded as a single being having only one nature, that a human life must not be cut into two halves, each belonging to a different nature; that every aspect of a man's activity must be regarded as the activity of his whole organism, from head to foot inclusively, or if it is the special function of some particular organ of the human organism we are dealing with, that organ must be regarded in its natural connection with the entire organism. . . .

As for the word "anthropology," it comes from the word "anthropos," which means "man"—but the reader knows that without our telling him. Anthropology is a science which, no matter what part of the human vital process it may deal with, always remembers that the process as a whole, and every part of it, takes place in a human organism, that this organism is the material which produces the phenomena; under examination, that the quality of the phenonmena is conditioned by the properties of the material, and that the laws by which the phenomena arise are only special cases of the operation of the laws of nature.

Part Five

Philosophy and the Revolutionary Movement

21

Mikhail Bakunin

Valery A. Kuvakin

POPULISM AS A SOCIAL PHENOMENON

Revolutionary Populism (Narodism) was the culminating stage of the history of Russian revolutionary democracy and of its philosophical and social thought. This trend was most prevalent politically in the 1870s and 1880s, i.e., in the postreform period. The 1861 reform had opened the road to the development of capitalist relations in Russia, but at the same time it preserved significant remnants of the serf system. Under such conditions the position of the peasantry remained difficult, and agrarian problems were not a priority. The situation gave rise to peasant protest movements; it was the revolutionary populists who gave voice to the peasant cause. Coming forward in the period of nascent capitalism, they posed the question of how it would develop in the future; that was their historical merit. But they could not understand or comprehend it, having declared it a sign of decline and regression for Russia.

The social soil for populism in Russia was the predominant class of petty producers who suffered from the weak development of capitalism. Its most prominent spokesmen were Mikhail Bakunin who, like Pyotr Kropotkin later, represented its revolutionary-anarchistic trend; Pyotr Lavrov, the leader of its revolutionary propagandist wing; and Pyotr Tkachev, the theorist of the conspiratorial trend. In the 1870s, Nikolai Mikhailovsky became associated with the revolutionary underground. We shall dwell on the views of each of these men, beginning with Bakunin, who, as a thinker and public person, was a figure of European stature.

BIOGRAPHICAL BACKGROUND

Mikhail Bakunin (1814–1876) was born into a noble family in the Tver Province. After finishing the Petersburg Artillery School in 1833 he became an officer, but by 1835 he had resigned his commission. He then lived in Moscow where he became close to Belinsky in N. V. Stankevich's circle. In that group he was one of the main translators, interpreters, and proponents of Hegel. Like Belinsky, Bakunin experienced a short period of reconciliation with reality.

In 1840 Bakunin went to Germany, followed the lectures of Schelling in Berlin University, and became close to the Young Hegelians. From the end of the 1830s to the early 1840s, his outlook was a quite radical though strongly colored Hegelianism. His article "The Reaction in Germany" (*Reaktsiya v Germanii*), written under a pseudonym and published in Arnold Rüge's *Deutsche Jahrbücher* in 1842, made Bakunin known. In addition to a call to fight German conservatism and the official ideology, its epilogue contained a purely Bakunian slogan: "The passion for destruction is at the same time a creative passion!"[1] This article caused a great commotion in the ruling circles of Germany, and Bakunin was forced to go to Switzerland. There he met Wilhelm Weitling, the well-known leader of the German utopian socialists, under whose influence his revolutionary communist orientation was strengthened. The development of Bakunin's outlook was also linked with the names of Ludwig Feuerbach and Auguste Comte. He assimilated the whole modern European intellectual tradition of his time and was well acquainted with the works of the English economists, French philosophers and political thinkers, and with German classical philosophy.

Bakunin was never an orthodox Hegelian, a positivist, or a disciple of Feuerbach. Bakunin was personally acquainted with many of the outstanding people of his time. People whom he held in particular esteem included Hegel, Feuerbach, Comte, Marx, Engels, Proudhon, Max Stirner, Herzen, and Ogarev. In 1844 he became acquainted with Marx, Engels, and Proudhon. He threw himself headlong into the European revolutions of 1848–1849, taking a direct part in the armed events in Prague and Dresden. In 1849 he was arrested and in 1850 sentenced to death by a Saxon court, and in 1851 he was subjected to an Austrian court-martial; both sentences were commuted to life imprisonment. He was transferred, in shackles, from prison to prison and ultimately handed over by the Austrian authorities to Nicholas I, by whose order he was imprisoned in the Peter and Paul Fortress, and later for three years in the Schlüsselburg Fortress, from which he was exiled to Siberia for life in 1856. In 1861 he escaped from exile and found his way to England via Japan and the United States. In Western Europe he became close to Herzen and Ogarev. He led an active political life, founded a faction within the First International called the Alliance of Socialist Democracy on ideas of anarchism, and began his uncompromising struggle against Marx and Engels. He did not break ties with the Russian revolutionary emancipation movement, with which he further allied himself in the 1860s and 1870s. He died in Bern in 1876.

Bakunin's literary legacy is extensive. From his most significant theoretical works we must single out "Federalism, Socialism, and Antitheologism" (*Federalizm, sotsializm i antiteologizm* [1867–1868]), "Statism and Anarchy" (*Gosudarstvennost i anarkhiya* [1873]), "The German Coercive Empire and Social Revolution" (*Knuto-germanskaya imperiya i sotsialnaya revolyutsiya* [1871]), "On Philosophy" (*O filosofii* [1839–1840]), "Philosophical Discourse about the Divine Apparition, the Real World, and Man" (*Filosofskiye rassuzhdeniya o bozhestvennom prizrake, o deistvitelnom mire i o cheloveke* [1870–1871]), and "God and the State" (*Bog i gosudarstvo* [1870–1871; English trans., 1885]).

THE WORLD AS UNIVERSAL LIFE, INTERCONNECTION, AND CAUSALITY

Bakunin saw the world and surrounding reality as an integral whole in dynamic motion. He profoundly felt the boundlessness and continuous changeability of nature, its majesty, and its eternity.

> Whatever exists, all the beings which constitute the undefined totality of the Universe, all things existing in the world, whatever their particular nature may be in respect to quality or quantity—the most diverse and the most similar things, great or small, close together or far apart—necessarily and unconsciously exercise upon one another, whether directly or indirectly, perpetual action and reaction. All this boundless multitude of particular actions and reactions, combined in one general movement, produces and constitutes what we call Life, Solidarity, Universal Causality.[2]

In this proposition, colored by an original philosophical impressionism, one may perceive some of the ideas by which Bakunin's understanding of objective reality can be judged. He obviously interpreted nature as dialectically moving, structurally organized, single ("united"), eternal, and limitless matter. He saw the real unity of the world in the endless development of matter rather than in its abstract being.

Bakunin was not a dialectical materialist, but the main elements of that outlook were undoubtedly inherent in his views of nature. That is shown (1) in his recognition of the existence of the dialectic of developing reality, and (2) in his assertion of a unity in nature that linked inanimate matter in the closest way with animate and thinking matter. Matter, according to him, was total, dynamic, eternally mobile, active, and fruitful; it was governed by law. "The sum of all known and unknown laws which operate in the universe constitutes its only and supreme law," and "they are inherent to matter—that is, inherent in *the real and only universal being.*"[3]

The maturity of his philosophical views consisted in his understanding the essence and meaning of the basic question of philosophy not only as regards nature but also in respect to society. And while giving priority to Marxist philosophical theory when posing this problem, he noted that this theory took as its basis a principle that was

> in absolute contradiction to the principle recognized by the idealists of all schools. The idealists deduce all the facts of history—including the development of material interests and the various stages of economic organization of society—from the development of ideas. The German Communists, on the contrary, see in all human history, in the most ideal manifestations of collective as well as individual human life, in every intellectual, moral, religious, metaphysical, scientific, artistic, political, juridical, and social development taking place in the past and in the present, only the reflection of the inevitable result of the development of economic phenomena.
>
> While the idealists maintain that ideas produce and dominate facts, the Communists, in full agreement with scientific materialism, maintain on the contrary that facts beget ideas and that ideas are always only the ideal reflection of events; that out of the sum total of phenomena, the economic material phenomena constitute the essential basis, the main foundation.[4]

While noting Bakunin's close acquaintance with the philosophical ideas of Marxism, it would nevertheless be a mistake to suggest that the doctrine of dialectical and historical materialism played a determinant role in his system of views. At the same time his materialist orientation is beyond doubt. And among the main constants of his philosophical ideas were those of the primacy of matter, the development of a single material world from the lower to the higher, from the simple to the complex.

> One can clearly conceive the gradual development of the material world, as well as of organic life and of the historically progressive intelligence of man, individually and socially.
>
> It is an altogether natural movement, from the simple to the complex, from the lower to the higher, from the inferior to the superior.[5]

Bakunin penetrated quite deeply into the complex interconnection of the material and the ideal and was aware of the unity of the ontological and genetic, and the identity of the laws of nature and the laws of thought. He went further by substantiating a thesis about the necessity of relating the principles of the development of the objective world with the principles of knowledge of it. In other words, he started from the point that the general cognitive methodology and strategy should be similar to the purposefulness and laws of the evolution of nature. Since intellect and thought are essentially natural phenomena, they cannot have any laws of functioning different in principle from the laws of the objective world. In order to understand reality one must trace the movement of the inorganic in the organic, the vegetable in the animal and human, the chemical in the biological, and the biological in the thinking process. Moreover, while cautioning against reductionism, or reducing the higher to the lower, he warned that it was impossible to understand the specific nature of any of matter's concrete forms, as was shown by the development of all the sciences (from physics to psychology and philosophy), without analyzing the genesis and preconditions of the emergence of higher levels of the organization and motion of matter from lower ones.

A feature of Bakunin's materialism was its anthropological dimension. His thought therefore seldom lingered on analysis of purely ontological problems. On the contrary, it sought to discover, already in the early stages of the development of reality, the preconditions that could unite the world (from "crude matter" to the loftiest human ideals) in a single, indivisible whole. This "channel," the link between man and nature, he represented as animality, understood very broadly, i.e., as the vital potential spread over and present in all material forms.

A leaning toward a kind of vitalism, an exaggeration of the phenomenon of animality, and hence a danger of reductionist anthropologism is distinctly palpable here.

"What we call the human world," Bakunin argued,

> has no other immediate creator but man himself, who produces it by overcoming step by step the external world and his own bestiality, thus gaining for himself his liberty and human dignity. He conquers them, impelled by a force which is independent of him, an irresistible force inherent in all living beings. This force is the universal current of life, the same one which we call universal causality, Nature, which manifests itself in all living beings, plants or animals, in the urge of every individual to realize for himself the conditions necessary for the life of its species—that is to satisfy his needs.
>
> This urge, this essential and supreme manifestation of life, constitutes the basis of what we call *will*. Inevitable and irresistible in all the animals, the most civilized man included, instinctive (one might almost say mechanical) in the lower organisms, more intelligent in the higher species, it reaches full awareness only in man, who, owing to his intelligence (which raises him above instinctive drives and enables him to compare, criticize, and regulate his own needs), is the only one among all the animals on earth, possessing conscious self-determination—a *free will*.[6]

The anthropological tendencies in ontology, which spread their roots into ideas of vitalism and voluntarism, essentially depreciated the elements of dialectical materialism in Bakunin's views about objective reality.

MAN AS A PLURAL UNITY

Man, as a creature simultaneously belonging to nature, society, and himself, was an important object of Bakunin's philosophical reflections. This pluralism in his understanding of man was expressed in the well-known thesis: "Three elements, or if you like, three fundamental principles, constitute the essential conditions of all human development, collective or individual, in history: (1) *human animality,* (2) *thought,* and (3) *rebellion.* To the first properly corresponds social and *private economy*; to the second, *science*; and to the third, *liberty.*"[7] In accordance with that approach Bakunin examined the impact on the development of man of (1) life as a whole (natural, biological, and social), (2) science, and (3) freedom and lofty aspirations.

In the light of the first principle the question of the origin of man and his place in the world acquired special meaning: "Our first ancestors . . . were . . . omnivorous, intelligent, and ferocious beasts, endowed in a higher degree than the animals of any other species with two precious faculties: *the thinking faculty and the urge to rebel.*"[8]

Bakunin stressed man's belonging simultaneously to the animal kingdom and to the world of the highest intellectual and moral values even more sharply in his following conclusion: "Real humanity presents us the assemblage of all there is of the most sublime, the most beautiful, and all there is of the most vile and most monstrous in the world."[9]

While one is sometimes tempted to agree psychologically and emotionally, such statements do not however help to clarify in any way the genesis, essence, and specific nature of man. Bakunin came closer to the truth when he linked this problem to the role of social being in the shaping of a real human being:

> Man becomes and arrives at awareness as well as realization of his humanity only in society and only through the collective action of the whole society. He frees himself from the yoke of external Nature only by collective and social labor, which alone is capable of transforming the surface of the earth into an abode favorable to the development of humanity.[10]

Without material emancipation there could be no intellectual and moral emancipation.

This understanding of the link between the human and the social brings out very clearly the essential aspect of Bakunin's conception of man. One cannot but agree when he stresses that man becomes human only through society, when he recognizes the influence of collective activity on the realization of humanity. But at the same time we should not forget that he did not accept the labor theory of the origin of man and consciousness. He perceived labor, moreover, not as a constantly operating and determinant factor of man's development but as a means of "freeing oneself from the yoke of external nature," while he saw liberation "from the yoke of one's own nature" not in labor but in upbringing and education.

The dialectical unity of the opposition of the natural and the social escaped him so that, in spite of the statement—materialistic in the whole—that "natural and social life always precedes thought," he seldom succeeded in demonstrating their specific character. On the one hand he identified animality with life and the current of life experience and spoke of its primacy as a material element. On the other hand he just as persistently declared the necessity of overcoming the animality in people. Such an ambiguity begot a corresponding approach to the rational in man and of the significance of science itself, i.e., of what constituted, in his view, the second element or principle of human development.

"Reason," "intellect," "thought," "knowledge," and "science" were concepts of the same order for Bakunin. Ontologically they rested on the natural-human connection and were related to being as the ideal was to the material. The duality of his attitude to science stemmed from the fundamentally different perception of thought, of the ideal, which he simultaneously lauded as highest in man and sharply criticized as secondary in relation to life. He regarded the ideal as capable of being socialized and taking the form of science, whose role in society was far from unambiguous.

"What I preach then is, up to a certain point, *the revolt of life against science,* or rather against *government by science,* not against the destruction of science—for that would be a high crime against humanity—but the putting of science in its rightful place so that it would never forsake it again."[11]

Science, he explained, was always an important instrument; "the sole mission of science is to light the way"[12] and especially to enlighten the masses, since "it will have to show us the general conditions necessary to the real emancipation of the individuals living in society."[13]

In order to understand the sources of Bakunin's opposition to science, we must take into account that he had at least two more reasons for his criticism. The first was rooted in the political unacceptability of Marxism for him as a current of scientific socialism. The second was associated with his exaggeration of the negative consequences of the misuse of science as a social phenomenon of the world of capitalism.

Epistemologically his critique of thinking followed a line of denying its ability to grasp the individual and personal and, in that sense, the vital. "Individuals are too elusive to be grasped by thought, by reflection, or even by human speech, which is capable of expressing only abstractions."[14] The irrationalism that was beginning to sound in that statement was only an echo of the voluntarism and anarchism that came to full expression in his social philosophy. This irrationalism got involved in the delimitation of the theoretical, scientific, and the practical in man's life:

> The living, concretely rational step, is the step in science from the real fact to the thought, embracing, expressing, and so explaining it; but in the practical world it is the movement from social affairs to their possibly rational organization, in conformity with the instructions, conditions, demands, and more or less passionate requirements of that life itself.[15]

Science was thus deprived of its practical significance and was limited as it gave way to the immediate demands of life.

It would obviously be wrong to see only the negative side of Bakunin's critique of science, as only the positive aspect aimed against scientism, technocratism, and capitalism's use of scientists for selfish, antipopular ends. Truth was mixed with fallacies in this criticism, but there is no doubt that Bakunin did not reject science.[16] While noting a certain contradiction in his appreciation of science as objective knowledge and as social phenomenon and trying to resolve it, he proposed rather inflexibly: "Science, as a moral entity, existing outside of the universal social life and represented by a corporation of licensed savants, should be liquidated and widely diffused among the masses."[17]

Much more attention in Bakunin's works was paid to the third element in the development of man—revolt and the freedom stemming from it. Freedom was one of his central philosophical themes; it was present in his comprehension both of the nature of man and of the essence of history; it was at the foundation of his understanding of social revolution.

Bakunin devoted all his life to struggle against the political tyrannies of Europe and Russia. For him freedom was not only a political slogan, but also a moral imperative and a philosophical principle. There are clear grounds to call him the philosopher and passionate admirer of freedom. But that does not mean that he treated freedom exclusively in a voluntarist way, having recourse to the laws of nature, objective necessity, or social order of any kind. Bakunin was sufficiently circumspect to understand the impossibility of deducing his whole outlook, social philosophy, and political ideal exclusively from the idea of freedom: "I recognize that a certain kind of discipline, not automatic, but voluntary and thoughtful discipline, which harmonizes perfectly with the freedom of individuals, is, and ever will be, necessary."[18]

He expressed himself just as definitely on the relationship between man's freedom and the laws of nature. As he put it, in slavery of natural necessity "there is no humiliation, or rather it is not slavery at all. . . . And it is only through those laws that we live, breathe, act, think, and will. Without them we would be nothing, *we simply would not exist.*"[19]

But we also do not exist, he insisted, without freedom, which, together with animality and capacity to think, constitutes the basis of man's nature. Furthermore, our innate freedom, as an indestructible capacity, need, and passion, sends its roots down into what is associated with the idea of revolt.

Revolt in turn is organically and directly linked with animality, since it is a particular human manifestation of universal life or will.

A feature of Bakunin's conception of freedom is that its ontology and epistemology were only indicated in general outline, while the sociomoral and political aspects were brought to the fore. According to him, freedom was originally given to the individual not as something ready-made and complete, but dialectically, as a striving, as the prospect of its own growth and development, as an ideal and a truly humane moral principle that coincided in its sense with humaneness: "Freedom is the source and the absolute condition of all good . . . *the good being nothing other than freedom.*"[20]

Freedom was just as closely linked with love and many other moral qualities of people. Bakunin justly noted that, "True, real love, the expression of a mutual and equal need, can only exist between equals."[21] Freedom was associated with a person's dignity, happiness, and creative activity, but especially with social equality. Like most thinkers who had passed through Hegel's philosophical school, Bakunin was inclined to treat history as the progress of freedom. But since the idea of freedom occupied a dominant position in his outlook, and since he was mainly a social thinker, he regarded history and social relations, and the various structures and institutions of society, primarily in the light of freedom, fully dependent on its suppression or flowering.

His general philosophical-historical scheme was quite simple and to some extent resembled Comte's philosophy of history: "Man emerged from animal slavery, and passing through divine slavery, a transitory period between his animality and his humanity, he is now marching on to the conquest and realization of human liberty."[22]

The origin of society, like the origin of the individual, was a link or moment in the dialectical development of the Universe, or, more concretely, of cosmic life:

> The social world, the human world properly speaking, in a word humanity, is nothing else than the last and supreme development—for us at least and relatively for our planet,—the highest manifestation of animality. But as all development necessarily implies a negation, that of the base or of the starting point, humanity is at the same time and essentially the reflected and progressive negation of animality in men; and it is precisely this negation, . . . at once historical and logical, and fatal, as are the developments and realizations of all the natural laws in the world—which constitutes and creates the ideal, the world of intellectual and moral convictions and ideas.[23]

History, according to Bakunin, is the flux of human acts unfolding in time that gradually draws in ever-newer peoples, thus converting itself into world history, into the history of humanity. The driving force of social progress was science and technology and the development of industry. At the same time mankind also existed through the succession of generations. "What is permanent or relatively eternal in real men is the fact of the existence of humanity, which passes, while constantly developing and becomes always richer, from one generation to another."[24]

But if there was a cosmic dialectic there were also acute, irreconcilable contradictions in human history, whose solution signified the onset of the realm of freedom or, according to Bakunin, of anarchy. The concrete personification of this antagonism was, on the one hand, the power of property owners, exercised by the state in alliance with the Church, and on the other hand the people's ideal, which took the form, in conditions of economic and spiritual domination by exploiter classes, of a striving for freedom through revolt, or social revolution.

Bakunin's sociohistorical conception was distinguished by naturalism, abstractness, and a metaphysical character. These drawbacks stemmed in the first place from there being to some extent a lack of serious political and economic grounding in Bakunin's social philosophy. People's material standard of living and their struggle against exploitation and oppression were therefore not tied together closely enough; he put the stress on the subjective-psychological and political factors of revolution and not on its social and economic sources. To that were added the idea of man's innate striving to revolt (which completely replaced the objective historical factor for Bakunin) and the idea of an ideal of full, unconditional, stateless equality spontaneously maturing in the people. In other words, the instinct of freedom was converted into the main, leading impulse of historical progress and the activity of the individual. Freedom was ambivalent and internally contradictory; Bakunin distinguished two elements in it, a positive one, "the full development and the full enjoyment by everyone of all the faculties and human powers through the means of education, scientific upbringing, and material prosperity," and a negative one, "revolt on the part of the human individual against all divine and human authority, collective and individual."[25]

HIS ANARCHISTIC PHILOSOPHY OF REVOLUTION

The negative, destructive aspect of freedom was linked above all with revolution, in which it was most broadly and fully revealed as revolt, as a spontaneous manifestation of the impulse, passions, and feelings of the popular masses.

> A rebellion on the part of the people, which by nature is spontaneous, chaotic, and ruthless, always presupposes a vast destruction of property. The working masses are ever ready for such sacrifices: that is why they constitute the rude, savage force capable of heroic feats and of carrying

out aims seemingly impossible of realization, and that is so because, having very little or no property, they have not been corrupted by it.[26]

Bakunin's stressing of the spontaneous character of revolutions fully accorded with his general philosophical position and the idea of the link between animality and the innate capacity to revolt, the striving for freedom. This motif of a vitalist or even cosmic irrationalism was heard with full force when he lapsed into a genuine apotheosis of the destruction of the old, "a salutary and fruitful destruction, since by means of such destruction new worlds are born and come into existence."[27]

Nevertheless, just a passion for destruction and destruction itself was not sufficient for a social revolution: a national ideal was still necessary:

That can take place only when the people are stirred by a universal ideal evolving historically from the depths of the folk-instinct, and—developed, broadened, and clarified by a series of significant events, and distressing and bitter experiences—it can take place only when the people have a general idea of their rights and a deep, passionate, one might even say religious, faith in those rights. When this ideal and this popular faith meet poverty of the kind which drives man into despondency, then the Social Revolution is near and inevitable, and no power in the world will be able to stop it.[28]

Such are the general features of Bakunin's philosophy of social revolution that make it so unlike and so opposed to the Marxian conception. It is Bakunin's understanding of the driving forces of revolutionary change that separates them above all. The passion for destruction flowing from the instinct of revolt and the internally inherent striving for freedom, plus the national ideal that instinctively takes shape, comprise in the anarchist conception the important motivations that put the revolutionary masses into movement. And that converts revolution to a significant degree into a kind of concentration of irrational elements in which something impossible and unfathomable—and unforeseen by reason—is possible.

Although anarchy as a social condition is fed by destructive ideas of negation, absence of state power, and a resolute and uncompromising uprooting of all statehood, together with all its Church, political, military, civil, legal, and financial and economic institutions, Bakunin also linked it with people's positive, constructive activity. "The whole organization of the future should be nothing else but a free federation of workers—agricultural workers as well as factory workers and associations of craftsmen."[29]

His program of social revolution as a version of utopian socialism included spiritual and socioeconomic emancipation; abolition of the right to inherit property; equal rights for women; elimination of family rights and duties and of Church and civil marriage; and transfer of children to the care of society.

He saw in radical economic reforms, in the "rise of labor," and in the spread of knowledge and science important factors of the highest form of communal life, in which "every individual . . . should find . . . approximately equal means for the development of his various faculties and for their utilization in his work,"[30] and in which "strict justice" would not be based on right, law, or the state, but "upon positive science and upon the widest freedom."[31]

On the whole Bakunin's anarchistic social theory expressed the mood of a certain part of the petit bourgeoisie, the content of a consciousness constantly arising and disappearing with the migration of its concrete bearers— the class-stratified peasantry, being ruined and enriched. It also included the labor aristocracy and lumpen proletariat, the intelligentsia and gentry, or bourgeois, becoming bankrupt, i.e., the strata of the population characterized by social and psychological instability. His ideas reflected the real quests for emancipation from harsh exploitation and poverty of broad strata of the laboring people of Russia. In that sense anarchism as a current of revolutionary populism played a relatively positive historical role.

NOTES

1. Jules Elysary (Mikhail Bakunin), "Die Reaktion in Deutschland," *Deutsche Jahrbücher für Wissenschaft und Kunst* V, nos. 247–51 (1842): 985–1002.

2. *The Political Philosophy of Bakunin,* ed. and comp. G. P. Maximoff (New York: The Free Press, 1953), p. 53.

3. Ibid., p. 57.

4. Ibid., pp. 64–65.

5. Ibid., p. 175.

6. Ibid., pp. 94–95.

7. Ibid., p. 172.

8. Ibid., p. 84.

9. Michel Bakounine, *Oeuvres* (Paris: P.-V. Stock, 1902), vol. 3, p. 46.

10. *Political Philosophy of Bakunin,* p. 266.

11. Ibid., p. 77.

12. Ibid., p. 76.

13. Ibid.

14. Ibid.

15. Mikhail Bakunin, *Izbrannye sochineniya* (Selected works), 5 vols. (Moscow, 1919–21), vol. 1 (1919), p. 234.

16. He affirmed, in particular, the "authority" but not the truth of the scientific fact and came out for the "absolute authority of science" but against the "infallibility" of its representatives.

17. *Political Philosophy of Bakunin,* p. 80.

18. Ibid., p. 259.

19. Ibid., p. 239.

20. Bakounine, *Oeuvres,* vol. 1, p. 204.
21. Ibid., p. 317.
22. *Political Philosophy of Bakunin,* p. 174.
23. Bakounine, *Oeuvres,* vol. 3, p. 19.
24. Ibid., p. 87.
25. *Political Philosophy of Bakunin,* p. 268.
26. Ibid., p. 380.
27. Ibid., p. 381.
28. Ibid., p. 370.
29. Ibid., p. 410.
30. Ibid., p. 409.
31. Ibid., p. 297.

22

Pyotr Lavrov
Vitaly Bogatov

MILESTONES IN HIS LIFE AND WORK

The activity of Pyotr Lavrov (1823–1900), a major philosopher, sociologist, and leader of the propagandist trend in revolutionary populism, is inseparable from the history of Russian social thought and the emancipation movement of the latter half of the nineteenth century. He was born into a family of the Pskov gentry. In 1837 he was enrolled in the St. Michael Artillery School in St. Petersburg. In 1844 he became a teacher of mathematics in the school and was later invited to lecture in the Artillery Academy. This period marked not only the further enriching of his knowledge in the natural sciences but also his thorough and independent study of philosophy and sociology.

Lavrov was molded as a thinker and revolutionary in the spiritual atmosphere of Russia in the 1840s to early 1860s, in the period of exacerbating social contradictions. He assimilated the ideas of Belinsky, Herzen, Chernyshevsky, and other radical democrats. Their views were his main source of acquaintance with the ideas of materialism. At the same time, he made a deep study of German and French philosophers and politicians of the eighteenth and nineteenth centuries and soon began to publish his own philosophical works.

In 1866, Col. Lavrov, professor of the Artillery Academy, was arrested as a member of the democratic movement, court-martialed, and exiled to the Vologda Province. There he wrote his "Historical Letters" (*Istoricheskiye pisma*), which brought him fame in revolutionary circles. Early in 1870 he succeeded in escaping abroad.

Participation in the Paris Commune, appraisal of its lessons and results, personal acquaintance with Marx and Engels and other leaders of the European socialist movement—all this deepened his understanding of the unity of the historical destiny of Russia and Western Europe. Living in emigration, he labored intensively on a multivolume history of human thought and problems of sociology, especially of socialism. He also did much to rally the forces of revolution in Russia and abroad and edited the journal and newspaper *Vperyod!* (*Forward!*) published in Zurich and London. Toward the end of his life he won wide recognition in scientific circles in America as well as in Europe. After his death Lavrov was buried in Paris.

HIS ATTITUDE TOWARD PHILOSOPHY

For Lavrov philosophy was a sphere of *consolidating knowledge.* He viewed it as having two parts, one theoretical and the other practical. Theoretical philosophy was concerned with science, problems of scientific knowledge, and the external natural world, i.e., with ontology and epistemology, and presupposed an objective method of study. The center of attention of practical philosophy (the philosophy of history, sociology, esthetics) focused on problems of social life; the anthropological, individual, and subjective element was therefore inseparable from it even on the plane of methodology.

Philosophizing was mainly the "realm of monism," or unity, and any tendency of consciousness to monism was a "philosophical striving." History and its principle of solidarity found its adequate epistemological expression in philosophy, which introduced unity into all life. Lavrov considered a scientific character and universalism the main features of the philosophical approach. He called the system of his philosophical views "realism," since he subordinated it to the main idea that all analogies needed for philosophical constructs should be "taken from the world of the real."

"Realism" as a philosophical system consisted of three parts: (1) *materialism,* which studied the external world and nature; (2) *positivism* (including "the philosophy of development," i.e., evolutionism), which presupposed a very close approximation to scientific data and a singling out from the world outlook the creative principle needed to connect the whole; and (3) *anthropologism,* which studied man and his inner world, the world of his consciousness. Materialists and anthropologists had to base themselves on science, i.e., they had to be positivists and advocates of the idea of evolution, the idea of development. It was in this sense that "realism" was a truly "scientific philosophy" for Lavrov.

He looked for an answer to the question of the uniting philosophical principle precisely where materialism looked for and found it. In the final count he declared it to be the category of "substance" (matter) and discovered the unity of the world in its materiality. Substance "constitutes, according to the inevitable laws of our thought, the simplest starting point for our understanding of the world."[1] By matter he implied an "essential" principle that was opposed to "substantiality" as a concept outside experience without an analogue in the real world. "Essence" was the natural quintessence of things, cognizable through phenomena. Materialism had to be supplemented by anthropologism because only the latter was the tool for resolving epistemological and social problems.

In his interpretation *positivism* meant fidelity to science, an intention to derive theoretical conclusions from it and link it up with the metaphysical (philosophical) trend. It was philosophy from the standpoint of science. Only Aristotle, Francis Bacon, and Auguste Comte had held such a philosophy. But whereas Aristotle and Bacon had created systems of philosophy that were scientific for their time, positivism was only an attempt at formulating such a system. It broke up into two lines, the scientific and the Comtian. Scientific positivism was a broader current than Comtism. Lavrov never reduced the "positive" philosophy to the ideas of Comte, Spencer, and their sympathizers. It could only be based on scientific thought, by making it "the guiding element of its structure." When criticizing those philosophers' agnosticism, Lavrov said: "*Objective* truth constitutes the content of our *knowledge* of the objective world in general and of the science of nature as a whole; for this science there is nothing outside *objective* reality, and apart from the *objective* method of cognition there is no means of knowing the truth."[2]

Lavrov approached the process of cognition from a historical angle. Analysis of the genesis of human knowledge was one of the ways of explaining its essence. He recognized the decisive importance of fact as the initial moment in knowledge. Man goes from fact to skill, from skill to knowledge, and from knowledge to understanding, the best theoretical form of expression of which is science.

Knowledge is infinite because the external world is infinite, and our knowledge has a relative character. But this is objective knowledge, through which man comes close to "reality as a whole and in its details, . . . the process and realm of knowledge lies in the requirement of truth and only truth."[3] Only from the standpoint of idealistic metaphysics could the existence of the external world be doubted, and the objectivity of logical and mathematical truths be denied. But, by taking "the standpoint of science it is impossible to doubt it," because we would otherwise abandon the soil of real, scientific thinking.

When studying the history of science Lavrov concluded that the scientific method is the way of approaching phenomena and facts without preconceived ideas and subjectivism, the way of "assimilating and verifying the truth," "the instrument for confirming knowledge." Man did not get scientific method from nature, and it was not an a priori form of human consciousness. It developed as knowledge grew, and in the process of satisfying men's vital needs. Lavrov's final conclusion about the significance of method reads: "Methodical thought creates . . . techniques of analysis and synthesis that underlie scientific understanding for the particulars of thought and the scientific philosophical outlook for the whole combination of the spheres of thought."[4]

Evolutionism was such a method for him. He treated it as the principle of the movement of everything that objectively existed: nature, man, and society. This principle also included comparative-historical analysis. Nothing happened in history, and in nature, all of a sudden, but everything had its genesis, beginning, and cause. He recognized the ideas of development and historicism as fundamental features of a truly scientific method, whose universalism was conditioned by the unity of everything that exists, of all phenomena, even those that seem at first glance to be remote from one another. By recognizing evolutionism he tried to dissociate himself from idealism and mysticism, and from philosophical mechanism and metaphysics (as antidialectical).

Lavrov saw evolution as progressive development in the context of which the old was rejected and the new asserted through the struggle between them. Each new stage of evolution was unique and at the same time was a necessary link in the chain of a developing phenomenon.

Anthropologism—the third component element of philosophical "realism"—consisted in explaining the phenomena of social life by the properties and needs of an integral, progressively developing and cumulatively cognizing individual, who was part of nature and at the same time opposed to it by his consciousness. Man was both the primary essence for himself and an element of social process. Due to the unavoidable presence of the human factor in cognition the anthropological ("personal") principle became the basis for constructing a science of society. For Lavrov anthropologism was not only a theory of man but also a specific philosophy of knowledge that included the theory and history of human reason and people's actions.

In Lavrov's words, "Anthropological viewpoint *in philosophy* differs from other philosophical points of view because in the foundation of the system of reasoning it puts the *whole* human being or physico-psychological species as undoubtably given. Everything related only to one side of the human being should be considered as separated (abstracted) from the wholeness of personality and criticized."[5] Within this approach, Lavrov stressed "the principle of reality of consciousness," "the principle of real knowledge" (in contrast to the "phenomalistic" one, existing only in our mind without any ontological correlations), and the "principle of skepticism in metaphysics," according to which the reality of the metaphysical is questionable, but metaphysical searches are inevitable and play an important role in people's lives as a part of their beliefs.

Skepticism as a universal principle of human attitude to reality was specified in Lavrov's writings in a form of sociological doctrine. According to him, "the person with critical thinking" (literally, the "critically thinking personality") stays or should stay in a center of historical activity. This critical thinker—being "practitioner"—has to be oriented toward the newest achievements in science and the highest moral standards.

THE PHILOSOPHY OF MAN

Lavrov approached the problem of the individual from two standpoints, the genetic (historical) and the rational (logical). The first presupposed a study of man's history, including his prehistory, i.e., evolution from the inorganic to the organic world. On the whole he regarded man as an inalienable part of nature, and the natural principle in man was the starting point of human evolution. The genetic interpretation of man revealed a dynamic unity of the natural and the social. The rational approach, proceeding from the reality of man, aimed at explaining the inner connection between the phenomena of the individual, society, and nature. Lavrov regarded the logical approach as the internal initial point of anthropologism, when man acts as a cognizing and self-knowing individual, as a creative force in philosophy, science, and life. But the logical principles of anthropologism were possible because man had traversed a long road of historical development, in which the natural genetically preceded the rational.

The pluralism of Lavrov's conception of personality was shown by his underlining of the idea that any human being is a unity of the natural, the individual, and the social. The "internal" personalism of every single individual expresses itself in the form of an irresistible tendency both to differentiation and to integration for the sake of development of the private and collective human existence.

When discussing the problem of the dialectics of the genetic unity and interaction of the natural, the social, and the rational in man, Lavrov set forth a conception of human needs. He divided them into three groups: (1) the basic, i.e., zoological (striving for social intercourse, sexual instinct, parental affection) and sociological; (2) provisional (creation of various state forms, forms of ownership and property, religions, and the division of labor); (3) the needs of development, which are of special importance for the beginning of mankind's historical life.

HIS THEORY OF SOCIETY

Lavrov's anthropologism was of essential importance for his understanding of society and history. In recognizing the great importance of economic factors in the formation of society (a clear indication of the influence of Marx and Engels), he considered the human individual to be the focal point of all social relations. From that angle he examined the problems of the origin and essence of the state, culture, and civilization, and of social evolution and historical progress. He was convinced that, "In order to derive sociological laws it is necessary to employ the subjective method, i.e., to adopt the position of the suffering or enjoying members of society, and not that of a dispassionate outside observer of the social mechanism."[6]

The subjective method was thus not relativism and arbitrariness for him, but a principle of interested, socially differentiated, and a class-conscious perception of history. To be subjective in sociology meant rejecting contemplation of history, overcoming the fatal character of social laws, recognizing the active role of the individual, of a social stratum, or of a class.

Lavrov's subjective method presupposed due consideration for the interests of both the individual and society. "A true social theory," he wrote,

> requires not *subjugation* of the social element to the personal and not *subsumption* of the individual under the society, but a *merging* of social and private interests. . . . *Individualism* becomes at that stage the realization of the common good by means of personal aspirations, but the common good cannot be realized otherwise. *Public-mindedness* becomes the realization of personal aims in public affairs, but they cannot be realized in any other medium.[7]

For Lavrov, social philosophy (the cornerstone of which was sociology) was a science of the laws of functioning of society, of the dynamics of development of human solidarity; therefore it was not an abstract theory but a world outlook, which comprised moral activity, the realization in life of a hierarchy of aims, and the understanding of the laws of truth and justice given by science. Sociology studied social laws and ideals, and the practical ways of translating them into reality.

Lavrov widely employed the principle of anthropologism to develop problems of social philosophy. He divided human history into two epochs, the anthropological and the historical proper. The anthropological period embraced people's activity at the instinctive, socially unconscious, precritical stage. History proper began with rational, critical comprehension of the past and present, with the developing of an ideal of the future and the struggle to realize it. Historical progress consisted in the overcoming of old forms of life and the assertion of a new civilization as a higher social level of the realization of critical thought. Lavrov believed in progress, which, according to him, was realized in the course of the development of the individual physically, mentally, and morally, and of the embodiment of truth and justice in social forms. The objective base of this process was human needs, economic ones included.

At the same time he was aware that there had never been in history sufficient conditions for harmonizing the human personality. Only few could develop comprehensively, but that was achieved at the expense of miserable existence of millions. A counterweight to this should be criticism of social evil and struggle against the masses' inhuman living conditions. The most perfect socioeconomic and political form of historical progress, he maintained, was socialism.

In the concluding period of his creative life, influenced by the ideas of Marx and Engels, Lavrov came to the conclusion that, "Under the diverse and motley phenomena of history a struggle of classes for economic interests has always been and remains the general foundation."[8] His view of the role of the economic factor evolved from an abstract notion of the importance of material needs to agreement with certain fundamental theses of Marxism on this matter:

We should recognize, following Karl Marx, that the sum total of the relations of production constitutes the economic structure of society, the real basis on which the legal and political superstructure is erected, and to which definite forms of consciousness correspond. The mode of production of material life determines the social, political and spiritual process of life in general.[9]

His views on socialism also took on a more concrete form:

First of all we do not speak of socialism in general but about the sole socialism whose program we consider ours, about *worker's socialism,* which paves the way for victory of the *social revolution.* About the socialism that proclaims the solidarity of all working people, declares war on all social parasites, and strives energetically to destroy the modern kingdom of competition and exploitation in order for the laboring proletariat to win a human existence on the real soil of economic security and full possibility of the intellectual and moral development of all individuals.[10]

Lavrov supposed that there would have to be a transition period between capitalism and socialism. He set out and substantiated his idea of this period in *The State Element in the Future Society* (*Gosudarstvennyi element v budushchem obshchestve* [1876]).

History, according to him, was not advanced by separate individuals. Progress was ensured by collective work and knowledge, i.e., by the laboring masses and progressive intelligentsia, because individuals "are only *possible* figures of progress. They only become its *real* figures when they know how . . . to turn into a collective force from insignificant units."[11] That was possible "when the advanced intelligentsia, settling its unpaid debt to the people, will work for the social revolution, for the overthrow of the whole contemporary political and economic system through a revolution organized among its worker brothers and realized by their outburst against their enemies."[12]

He considered the uniting of all advocates of socialism in an independent workers' party that would lead the masses, on the basis of a scientific political theory, to realization of their cherished goal, to be a necessary condition of the victory of socialist revolution.

At the same time, Lavrov's assimilation of certain ideals of Marxism did not mean his rejection of the principles of anthropologism, evolutionism, and positivism. To the end of his days he remained an advocate of pluralism as a philosophical world outlook and a practical attitude to reality.

NOTES

1. P. L. Lavrov, *Opyt istorii mysli* (*An Essay in the History of Thought*) (St. Petersburg, 1875), p. 102.

2. Ibid., p. 16.

3. Ibid., p. 360.

4. P. L. Lavrov, *Vazhneishiye momenty v istorii mysli* (*The Most Important Factors in the History of Thought*) (Moscow, 1903), p. 375.

5. *Entsiklopedichesky slovar, sostavlennyi russkimi uchonymi i literatorami* (*Encyclopedic Dictionary Compiled by Russian Scholars and Men of Letters*) (St. Petersburg, 1862), vol 5.

6. P. L. Lavrov, *Izbrannye sochineniya na sotsialnopoliticheskiye temy* (*Selected Works on Sociopolitical Themes*), 8 vols. (Moscow, 1934), vol. 1, pp. 417–18.

7. P. L. Lavrov, *Filosofiya i sotsiologiya* (*Philosophy and Sociology*), 2 vols. (Moscow, 1965), vol. 2, p. 98.

8. Ibid., p. 444.

9. P. L. Lavrov, *Opyt istorii mysli novogo vremeni* (*An Essay in the History of the Thought of Modern Times*), 2 vols. (Geneva, 1894), vol. 1, pt. 2, pp. 591–92.

10. P. L. Lavrov, "Socialism and Historical Christianity," *Vperyod!*, no. 23 (1875): 708.

11. P. L. Lavrov, *Filosofiya i sotsiologiya*, vol. 2, pp. 130–31.

12. Ibid., p. 437.

23

Pyotr Tkachev

Valery A. Kuvakin

BIOGRAPHICAL BACKGROUND

Pyotr Tkachev (1844–1886)—a theorist and one of the leaders of the conspiratorial (Blanquist) current in revolutionary populism—had a short but brilliant, eventful life. He was born into a poor gentry family in the village of Sivtsevo in the Velikiye Luki uyezd of Pskov Province. The family moved to St. Petersburg in 1851. The youth's radical outlook began to take shape while he was still at grammar school. A rebellious mood and a thirst for struggle against state power were obvious in his first verses. In 1861, Tkachev matriculated at Petersburg University in the Law Department but did not spend more than a week there, as he was arrested for taking part in student actions. After two months' confinement, first in the Peter and Paul Fortress and then in the Kronstadt Citadel, and expulsion from the university, his revolutionary and publicistic activity began. He ardently believed that it was the sacrificial mission of his own generation to save Russia from the political tyranny of the autocracy.

In the early 1860s he established ties with the revolutionary underground and drew close to the secret populist organizations. From 1862 he was repeatedly arrested and brought to trial. He was finally sentenced to imprisonment in the case of the pseudorevolutionary and adventurist Sergei Nechayev and subsequently exiled to Velikiye Luki, whence he escaped abroad in 1873.

Chernyshevsky, Shelgunov, Pisarev, and Mikhailovsky—these were the names of Tkachev's first teachers. He concerned himself with scientific, philosophical, historical, and legal self-education no less energetically than with political activity. In 1868 he passed the examinations for the full course of university education and defended a dissertation on "Educational-Reformatory

Institutions for Juvenile Delinquents" (*O vospitatelno-ispravitelnykh zavedeniyakh dlya nesovershennoletnikh prestupnikov*).

In his writings Tkachev elaborated on philosophical, methodological, psychological, economic, historical, sociological, and political problems. He contributed extensively to the journals *Vremya* (*Time*), *Epokha* (*Epoch*), *Biblioteka dlya chteniya* (*Library of Readers*), *Russkoye slovo* (*The Russian Word*), and *Delo* (*The Cause*).

A new stage in his revolutionary and literary work began in emigration, where there was no czarist persecution or censorship. He studied the European socialist movement closely and became acquainted with the leading members of Russian revolutionary émigré circles. But because of ideological disagreements, his relations with them, and with Marx and Engels, leaders of the First International, became tense, and Tkachev soon found himself in a kind of isolation. In 1875, in Geneva, and from 1879 in London, he managed to publish a journal *Nabat* (*Alarm Bell*), of a "Jacobinic," left-radical orientation. At the end of the 1870s, in the conditions of the revival of the revolutionary movement in Russia, his sociopolitical ideas began to enjoy a certain popularity and, to a certain extent, formed the basis of the political program of the largest Populist organization, People's Will.

Tkachev's last years were marked by a deep inner crisis aggravated by serious illness (progressive cerebral palsy), which led to his early demise.

HIS GENERAL PHILOSOPHICAL VIEWS

Tkachev left a large literary legacy, which contained few philosophical, sociological, or scientific works in the proper sense of the word. It was publicistic writing in the main, much of which consisted of thorough critical reviews of works on philosophy, sociology, economics, and other branches of knowledge. Among his major works the following ones should be mentioned: *The Economic Method in the Science of Criminal Law: Introduction* (*Ekonomichesky metod v nauke ugolovnogo prava: Vvedeniye* [1865]); *Essays in the History of Rationalism* (*Ocherki po istorii ratsionalizma* [1866]); *Introduction and Notes to Becher's "Arbeitsfrage"* (*Predisloviye i primechaniya k knige Bekhera "Rabochiy vopros"* [1869]); *What the Party of Progress Is* (*Chto takoye partiya progressa* [1870]); *The Tasks of Revolutionary Propaganda in Russia* (*Zadachi revolyutsionnoi propagandy v Rossii* [1874]); *"Alarm Bell": The Journal's Program* (*"Nabat" [Programma zhurnala]* [1875]); *The Anarchy of Thought* (*Anarkhiya mysli* [1875]); *On the Usefulness of Philosophy* (*O polze filosofii* [1877]); and *Mines of Information of Russian Philosophers* (*Kladezi mudrosti rossiiskikh filosofov* [1878]).

He was an original and profound thinker, distinguished by the consistency and sobriety of judgment and scientific objectivity. By temperament he was a passionate fighter for justice and freedom; he united in his person the emotion of Bakunin's intellect and Lavrov's discipline for keeping strictly to verified methods of analysis. If we compare Bakunin, Lavrov, and Tkachev, we can say, oversimplifying it a bit, that the first emphasized political problems; the second, social-philosophical and ethical issues; and the third, political and economic concerns.

As for his general philosophical position, Tkachev held materialist views on nature and knowledge. He was clearly oriented to the natural sciences and Sechenov's school of "objective" psychology. In his hostility to idealism he sometimes went as far as denying philosophy as a relatively independent field of knowledge and mental activity.

That does not mean, of course, that Tkachev himself did not philosophize and did not attempt to expound his consciously deepened and constantly enriched outlook in a more or less systematic way. The motives of his dissatisfaction with philosophy (which he usually identified with idealism) were, in terms of methodology, its scorning of science and the objective laws of nature; and in terms of ethics and social relations, its parasitism and privileged position as an exclusive concern of members of the propertied classes who undeservedly profited by the labor of the people. In that connection he developed Lavrov's idea of the debt the intelligentsia owed to the people, the idea of its compensating for the high price of progress by sacrifice and revolutionary educational activity. He asserted that it was impossible to be indifferent to philosophy, since it was

paid for by the productive labor of society. The last pennies are taken from the unskilled laborer and the philosophers are maintained by them, who give the laborer *nothing* in return for those pennies except for printed sheets botched and soiled by stupid phrases of a sort lacking human sense. . . . Therefore, as long as there are people who occupy themselves with philosophy, who write and print philosophical treatises and arguments, other, more sensible people must not cease to show these parasites that their work is equivalent to spitting on the ceiling and that such exploitation of human stupidity is immoral and disgraceful.[1]

Tkachev himself, "as a more sensible man," first, relied on science and the general scientific methods of knowledge when tackling philosophical questions, and second, endeavored, when treating the mission of philosophy as relief of the condition of the workers, to substantiate "a rational analytico-critical method" as a special philosophical form of reflecting people's objective and, above all, economic affairs. "Conviction will be more independent and stronger the more deeply it is thought out, i.e., the more critically and cautiously we accept and check the data on which it is based."[2]

In formulating his understanding of philosophy Tkachev pointed out its dependence on economics: "People's outlook and the character of their activity are always determined by the conditions of their economic life. In respect of separate individuals, of course, this thesis admits of many exceptions, but as applied to a whole estate or class it is undoubtedly correct."[3] He counted himself a realist (the term "materialism" was not permitted by the censor) and a radical and wrote that rationalism "implies a sober, rational outlook free from any superstitions and prejudices—a sober, rational attitude to phenomena of the surrounding nature and to people's relations with one another."[4]

His understanding of philosophy was revealed even more graphically in his analysis of the world historicophilosophical process, which he interpreted as the history of the struggle of materialism and idealism. His own position was definitely that of scientific materialism. Whereas the idealist never takes facts in their real form but looks at them through the prism of an abstract "little ideal," instilled in him by the prevailing ideology, the realist "takes the facts of actual life as they are, without embellishing and daubing them with figments of his own fantasy."[5]

Characteristic of Tkachev's materialist method were the principles of objectivity, the primacy of the fact in relation to the idea of it, a critical approach, and the inseparability of knowledge from the history of science and its achievements. As he put it, "Human thought can only act proceeding from observations and comparison." While asserting the principle of epistemological monism and of the comprehensive reliability of empirical knowledge, he explained mistakes in cognition by psychological factors that upset the normal course of perception and thought. He considered the link with *practice,* and with people's interests (primarily material, economic interests) an important feature of scientific philosophical knowledge.

"The character of conclusions and moods depends on two main causes: on the property of the facts themselves and on personal interest. . . . Historical examples show that the theories and principles that dominate in science and morality always coincide with . . . the egoistic interests . . . of classes."[6]

"ENERGO-ECONOMIC MATERIALISM" AND THE PROBLEM OF THOUGHT

Tkachev paid much attention to developing a scientific style of thinking based, on the one hand, on the general scientific modes of cognition worked out by the natural sciences, and on the other hand, on the materialist conception of consciousness and thought, whose foundations had been formed by Sechenov and his school. He highly appreciated the achievements of the "objective" psychology that took as its main subject of research the so-called unconscious soul (that term meant for him the quite material activity of the brain and of somatic unconscious psychic processes, not completely cognizable but amenable to experimental analysis). He linked with these achievements advances in the theory of knowledge.

> The objective method, having made the unconscious soul the starting point for study of the conscious soul, has restored the wholeness and fullness of our inner world and introduced a mass of new facts and phenomena into the field of psychological research without knowledge of which it is impossible to form even an approximately correct idea of the laws and nature of our spiritual life.[7]

But when explaining the essence of thought and psychic processes Tkachev sometimes drew risky conclusions that bordered on vulgar materialism or resembled insufficiently formulated hypotheses. In his opinion, for example, psychological processes were essentially nothing else than "the force of movement manifesting itself only in different velocities and modes of the oscillation or vibration of the molecular particles and atoms of matter."[8]

While founding his conception of consciousness and psychic and intellectual activity on the advances of science, Tkachev nevertheless did not draw a strict qualitative distinction between the ideal and the material, between cerebral neurophysiological processes and thinking as a property of the human brain. That led to a blurring of the question of primacy of matter or consciousness. "Thought, or rather, cerebral activity, like the activity of the digestive organs, and the activity of the lungs, heart, etc., can neither precede human, and consequently social, life, nor constitute its result; it forms one of its necessary and inalienable components. . . . Thought constantly altered society though it was itself only a product of this society."[9]

That statement is characteristic of Tkachev's views, first and foremost for its combination of a scientific and a sociological approach to thinking and to man as a whole. The striving for such a combination deserves high appreciation, since consistent attempts to bring the natural and social sciences together only began in Russia with Herzen and Chernyshevsky. At the same time, Tkachev did not succeed in making a harmonious synthesis of scientific notions about thought with sociology of consciousness and knowledge, primarily because he lapsed into errors of vulgar materialism on the one hand and on the other did not consistently adhere to the principle of the interconnection of consciousness and the material (economic) basis of social life. In addition, he was not much interested in the genesis of consciousness as a product of social labor. That gives grounds for defining his views about cognition as *energo-economic materialism,* since concepts of force and of the economic factor were central in this case. When linking the essence of man and his intellectual and material activity with needs and their satisfaction, Tkachev remarked:

The possibility of satisfying his needs is determined by man's *strength.* By that I mean here not just the development of his muscular system, not just the strength of his muscles, but the development of his organism in general and the economic conditions for this organism's life under which the organism would have *a real opportunity* (power) to satisfy its capacities.[10]

Such an approach to the problem of man and his knowledge, eclectic on the whole, did not prevent Tkachev from formulating original epistemological ideas. He quite consistently defended the principle of the knowability of reality, and the adequacy of its reflection in our sensations and notions. He ascribed identical importance to both the movement of cognition from sensations to ideas and then to thought, and the reverse move of thought to the facts of objective reality. He sought to establish the dependence of theories (their balance of truth and falsity) on economic relations within the framework of which a given doctrine emerged and developed. At the same time he named several attributes of intra-knowledge character as criteria of truth, among them the obviousness and transsubjectivity of our knowledge. *Obviousness* was an objective criterion of truth, he said, in the

exact sense by which the obvious signifies something that each subject— whatever his personal views in general—considers unconditionally convincing for himself, i.e., true. The commonness of our physical, and consequently psychic organization makes the existence of these *somethings* possible. We have the right to consider these somethings true in themselves because they are true not for me alone or for you but for all people in general.[11]

This point of view on the criterion of truth can be defined as a naive-realistic *transsubjective naturalism.*

THE "HYPOTHESIS" OF THE
ECONOMIC EXPLANATION OF HISTORY

A "hypothesis" of the decisive role of the economic factor in men's lives not only permeated Tkachev's epistemological ideas but also, in particular, his conception of sociohistorical development. This hypothesis had already received developed expression in 1866. "Social life," the twenty-two-year-old Tkachev wrote,

is nothing else in all its manifestations, with its literature, science, religion, politics, and legal existence, than the product of certain economic principles that underlie all these social phenomena. These economic principles, in the course of their successive development, combine human relations in a certain way, generate industry and commerce, science and philosophy, the corresponding political forms and the established juridical mode, in other words, give rise to our whole civilization, and *make* all our progress. If these principles are unjust and irrational in themselves, then their consequences will not be distinguished by the best qualities.[12]

This meant for Tkachev that economic principles themselves could, though not necessarily, involve an ethical and rational element. But only their existence ensured social progress: "If the principles that generate the constant movement and metamorphoses in the social world are rational and just," so there is social progress; but "if they are not . . . then there can be no progress. There is movement, there is modification, and there is development, but there is no progress in the sense of improvement."[13]

The "economic principle" thus played a greater role in Tkachev's thought than in Marxism since, in essence, it gave direct rise to the superstructure and was the source of progress or of stagnation. This gives one certain grounds for speaking of Tkachev's economic materialism. He saw the methodological significance of the idea of the dependence of social life on economic relations in tracing a concrete manifestation of the "generating" effect of the economy in concrete spheres of the social organism. He wrote,

If the economic method can be usefully applied to study of a development of society that is manifested in some sphere or other of practical or theoretical activity, it will, in that case, be suitable as well for study of the laws of social development in general. If the economic hypothesis proves correct for investigating all the parts that constitute a single whole, it will of course hold water for this whole.[14]

It should be emphasized that Tkachev's use of the "economic hypothesis" as a method of social analysis was not only the result of his attention to Marxism but also a consequence of his own conclusions drawn on the basis of his acquaintance with English political economy, especially the works of Adam Smith. At the same time his subsequent opposition to Marxism led to a hypertrophy and vulgarization of the abstractly understood idea of the "economic principle."

The difference between his views and Marxism was especially evident in his reducing of economic interest to *personal* economic interest as primary in relation to *social* needs. Tkachev's general anthropological orientation showed in that. In his view the needs and interests of the individual were as primary as economic principles, so that the theory he developed began simultaneously (or should have begun) both with the individual and his needs and with the material (above all economic) conditions of life. "Personal benefit, personal good—that is the sole stimulus of any human activity," he claimed.[15] But the relation between personal interests and economic conditions did not take shape in history in favor of the individual.

"The opposition between man's individual striving for personal happiness, on the one hand, and the harsh, intolerable misfortunes and disasters surrounding him, on the other, are not due to the intervention of gods or lack of utilitarianism in people, but are simply due to the antisocial, anarchic principles that underlie our life."[16]

In his *Essays in the History of Rationalism* Tkachev painted a picture of how in the history of mankind—from primitive society to the onset of capitalism in Europe—economic needs and interests had put religion and science into their service and how changing economic relations had given rise to new civilizations and destroyed the old ones.

THE THEORY OF PROGRESS

The economy thus became, in Tkachev's eyes, the true creator of history. Yet this by no means meant that it automatically guaranteed historical progress, i.e., movement from worse to better, from evil to good, from the irrational to the rational. The scheme of historical progress was not a simple one. The circular conception of history, and the rosy optimistic model of it symbolized by a straight, smoothly ascending line, were both alien to Tkachev. Furthermore, he was even inclined to deny the existence of any sort of determinant measuring rod of progress, since the objectivity of historical movement was governed by economics, which was by no means necessarily associated with movement to the better, and was something extrahuman in principle, with nothing in common with anthropomorphic ideas of society and its development. Even one fact of an utter disharmony in the explanation of history was evidence, according to him, that "we have no right to seek an objective criterion of historical progress in historical movement, and that we cannot even think of this movement as progress, because . . . we do not know whether it is circular or rectilinear, rhythmic or continuous."[17]

This idea of Tkachev's smacks not so much of skepticism as of an endeavor to stress the independent character of historical movement, lying *outside human needs,* aims, and ideals. He was drawing attention to the natural flow of history. It followed from the view he adopted that mankind's history had some irrational residuum, i.e., was irrational to a certain extent. History as such had neither eyes nor head. Society did not know its past or present or future as an economic process. History was basically only continuous movement from the past and existent to the unprecedented and nonexistent; that alone made it a maximally creative flow of the social form of matter.

Tkachev did not fully share historical agnosticism, but he, first, did impose certain essential limitations on how far history, especially its future, was knowable, and second, banned anthropomorphization, i.e., transfer of certain qualities of the human individual (thought, purposiveness, aspiration to good and justice, etc.) to the processes of the material (economic) production of life. His singling out from the stream of world history of two lines of development, viz., knowledge and social forms, was a peculiar retreat from the "economic hypothesis." While progress was obvious in the case of knowledge, the question of the perfecting of social (economic) forms was far from so.

When analytically surveying the most typical (in his opinion) ideas of history, Tkachev dwelt on the following ones: (1) "historical movement" follows a line of embodiment in social forms of the idea of justice; (2) a broadening and extension of "citizens' political freedom" is observable in history; (3) history gives evidence of progress in the "development of economic prosperity and the establishment of a more or less even distribution of material goods"; (4) history demonstrates a polarizing and deepening of property inequality and "this progressing unevenness threatens to paralyze the development of economic prosperity in general"; (5) "there is one trend in history obvious for each and everyone and that is man's intellectual development . . . man's brain is perfected and the amount of accumulated information increases"; (6) the progress of knowledge is not a criterion of historical progress—it could become a component of this criterion if it were shown that "perfecting of social forms went parallel" with "man's intellectual development."[18]

None of these points of view satisfied Tkachev, since they all ignored the problem of man's needs. It was his needs, together with objective economic development, that constituted the main content and causes of historical dynamics. Their role was particularly great from the subjective, human angle. Tkachev defined the individual not as an aggregate of social relations but as an aggregate of needs that were a unity of men's entire reactive activity, in which their inner aspirations and interaction with surrounding reality were reflected.

Tkachev distinguished between essential, secondary, and harmful needs. He stressed that change in social conditions led to change in needs, while there always existed in society a greater or lesser gap between the "sum total" of needs and the means of realizing them. Here he came to what was for him the very important problem of the means of satisfying the individual's needs. The volume of these means, he noted, depended to a decisive degree on the productivity of social labor, while the needs themselves depended on the individual's development.

Tkachev linked the aim of society itself with satisfaction of the individual's needs. In short, a chain of basic categories was formed—needs, means of satisfying them, the goal of social development—with the help of which he also formulated his ideas of due progress (not existing in reality) and its criteria:

> Society can realize its goal by regulating the individual's development in such a way that his needs are constantly harmonized with the *given* means of their satisfaction, i.e., with the means determined quantitatively and

qualitatively by the corresponding level of development of labor productivity; . . . any progress of the individual should at the same time be progress
in the productivity of labor.[19]

The model of desirable historical movement found completion in the
following formula: "The establishment of fullest possible equality of individuals . . . and the bringing of each and all to full harmony with the means
of satisfying their needs—such is the final and only possible goal of human
society, such is the supreme criterion of historical social progress."[20]

That is how matters stood from the angle of the due and proper necessity.
But, Tkachev continued, since man's objective vital needs differed with different
individuals and groups because of the diversity of the conditions of their social
being, neither harmony nor unity of aims was conceivable—they were mutually
antagonistic and society fell into self-contradiction. There was no way out
of the antagonism created, it would seem; the individual, like society as a
whole, was doomed to the impossibility of meeting his needs and attaining
his life goals. The course of development of capitalism suggested a way out
of this contradiction to Tkachev; he saw in it not only negative processes
but also forces capable of creating new social forms. Under capitalism, "the
general conditions of work generate a community of life, concepts, habits,
and capabilities."[21] Portentous social steps were also associated with scientific
and technical progress:

> On the one hand the machine, on the other the introduction of more or
> less uniform techniques and methods of research into the various branches
> of human knowledge have altered, or at least started a change of, the direction
> of social movement. That fact has again confirmed that the process of
> historical movement . . . has no constant, uniform trend . . . taken by itself
> it should not be thought of as either progressive or regressive.[22]

As we see, Tkachev's idea runs into a contradiction: while affirming the
independence of the flow of history from knowledge and the tasks posed
by man, he nevertheless links social progress with the satisfaction of the needs
of people, "whose life aim consists in preserving and maintaining their
individuality."[23] His interpretation of social revolution is a kind of way out
of this theoretical impasse.

THE SITUATIONAL-VOLUNTARIST
CONCEPTION OF REVOLUTION

Ideas of economic materialism, voluntarism, and involuntary extrapolation of
the absolutized political situation established in Russian society to understand-

ing of every revolutionary process were fantastically interwoven in Tkachev's notion of revolution.

It would seem that he thought quite soberly, considering that a situation had taken shape in Russia in which, after the abolition of serfdom, feudalism was already dead, and capitalism had not yet developed. But that was too abstract a judgment to substantiate resolute actions aimed at immediate seizure of power from those whose overthrow he called for, ignoring the economic foundations of the autocracy and underestimating the power of the state. The logic of his argument was as follows:

> The enemy we have to fight is our government. . . . Between it and the people there is not yet any mediating force that could stop and hold back the popular movement for a long time once it began.
>
> Our landowner estate, taken by itself, is isolated, weak, and insignificant both in numbers and in its economic position. More than half of our *tiers état* are proletarians and the paupers, and only a minority of it are real bourgeois beginning to develop. . . .
>
> We should not expect too long an existence of these social conditions favorable for us; we are somehow moving, though quietly and sluggishly, along the road of economic development. And that development is governed by the same laws and proceeds in the same direction as the economic development of West European states.
>
> The commune is beginning to break up; . . . a class of *kulaks* is developing among the peasantry; . . . all the conditions exist among us at the present moment for forming, on the one hand, a very strong class of peasant landowners and farmers and on the other, a monied, commercial, industrial, capitalist bourgeoisie. And to the extent that these classes are formed and consolidated, the position of the people will deteriorate and the chances of success of a forcible overthrow will become more and more problematic.
>
> That is why we cannot wait. That is why we maintain that revolution in Russia is an urgent necessity . . . precisely at the present time; we shall not permit any postponements and delays. *Now,* or in a distant future, perhaps *never!* Circumstances are for us now; in ten, or twenty years they will be against us.[24]

This excerpt from Tkachev's *Tasks of Revolutionary Propaganda in Russia* contains the core and psychology and tactics of his revolutionary program. The "situativity" of revolutionary political thinking was fed by a conviction that history was a changing combination of the progressive and the regressive, and that it was consequently sufficient just to exploit favorable objective circumstances in order to intervene decisively in it and so alter its course. He regarded the state, moreover, as a neutral institution, only employable by one economic class or another for its own ends. The situational-conspiratorial conception of revolution was also expressed in the idea that revolution "differs from peaceful progress precisely in that it is made by a minority, while the latter is made by the majority."[25] Tkachev clearly underestimated the role of the masses in a revolution.

"A violent revolution," he wrote,

> can only take place when the minority does not want to wait for the majority to become aware of its needs, but when it has resolved to bring to an explosion the blind feeling of dissatisfaction with its position constantly inherent in the people. And then, when the explosion occurs—and it will occur not by virtue of any clear understanding and awareness, etc., but simply by virtue of the accumulated feeling of dissatisfaction, animosity, and of the intolerableness of oppression—when this explosion occurs then the minority will try simply to give it an intelligent, reasonable character, direct it to certain goals, and clothe its rough sensuous basis in ideal principles. The people of a real revolution is a tempestuous element which annihilates and destroys everything in its path, which always acts instinctively and unconsciously.[26]

It follows from such an essentially anarchic understanding of the role of the masses in a revolution that since the people lack "the *spirit* to get out of their rut," they need a push from outside, so that any unexpected clash will knock them out of it—"and they will rise up like a tempestuous hurricane and make a revolution."[27] As is known from history, the part of this external push was played by acts of terrorism.

The idea of revolution as a unique situation favorable for seizure of power by a minority was embraced by Lenin and to a certain degree realized by him. When Lenin was appreciating this Blanquist position of his predecessor, he wrote: "The attempt to seize power, which was prepared by the preaching of Tkachev and carried out by means of 'terrifying' terror that did really terrify, had grandeur."[28] At the same time, Lenin theoretically condemned the tactics of conspiracy and terror as incompatible with the revolutionary tasks of the laboring people.

Subsequently the ideas of the radical wing of the Russian Populists was transformed partly into more liberal and moderate forms in the works by Mikhailovsky, partly into the ideas of terrorism maintained by the Socialist-Revolutionaries, and partly into the Bolsheviks' tactics of struggle for political power.

NOTES

1. P. N. Tkachev, *Sochineniya* (Works), 2 vols. (Moscow, 1905), vol. 1, p. 110.
2. Ibid., p. 116.
3. Ibid., p. 294.

4. Ibid., p. 119.
5. Ibid., p. 160.
6. Ibid., p. 280.
7. Ibid., p. 209.
8. Ibid., p. 574.
9. Ibid., vol. 2, pp. 109–10.
10. Ibid., vol. 1, p. 106.
11. Ibid., p. 470.
12. Ibid., p. 96.
13. Ibid., p. 97.
14. Ibid., p. 98.
15. Ibid., p. 120.
16. Ibid., p. 121.
17. Ibid., p. 489.
18. Ibid., p. 490.
19. Ibid., pp. 506–507.
20. Ibid., p. 508.
21. Ibid., p. 492.
22. Ibid., p. 493.
23. Ibid.
24. Ibid., vol. 2, pp. 22–23.
25. Ibid., p. 17.
26. Ibid.
27. Ibid., p. 24.
28. V. I. Lenin, "What Is to Be Done?" *Collected Works* (Moscow: Progress Publishers, 1986), vol. 5, pp. 510–11.

24

Nikolai Mikhailovsky

Vladimir Alexeyev

STAGES OF HIS CREATIVE ACTIVITY

Nikolai Mikhailovsky (1842–1904), a publicist, literary critic, and eminent theorist of populism, was born into a gentry family of modest means in the town of Meshchovsk in Kaluga Province. After finishing grammar school he studied in the Petersburg Institute of Mining Engineers, from which he was expelled in 1863 for taking part in student agitation.

Mikhailovsky's outlook was molded by the complex sociopolitical conditions of postreform Russia. He was one of the many members of the radical Russian intelligentsia who fought against the survival of serfdom and for democracy and enlightenment of the masses. Over the four decades of his creative activity he wrote many works on philosophy, sociology, history, and social psychology. His philosophical, publicistic, and literary legacy was oriented to analyses of problems of the natural and social sciences and ethical and esthetic problems existing in his time. It attests to the depth of his understanding of the philosophical systems of Fichte, Schelling, Kant, Hegel, Comte, Spencer, and other major Western European thinkers and demonstrates his knowledge of Greek and medieval philosophy and the history of Russian thought. While actively collaborating with a number of leading popular journals, he became "commander of the minds" of the democratic youth in Russia during the years from 1870 to 1880.

Two periods are distinguished in the biography of Mikhailovsky the writer. The first, from the mid-1860s, was characterized by championing in the illegal press the slogans of democratic freedoms and the political platform of the Narodnaya Volya (People's Will) group (A. I. Zhelyabov, A. D. Mikhailov, G. A. Lopatin). In his *Renan's Utopia and Dühring's Theory of the Individual's*

Autonomy (*Utopiya Renana i teoriya avtonomii lichnosti Dyuringa*) and especially in two articles under the common title "Political Letters of a Socialist" (*Politicheskie pisma sotsialista*) in *Narodnaya Volya* (1880, nos. 1 and 2), he called its readers to resolute political struggle against czarism. The historical moment, he showed, called for the setting up of a "secret committee for public security" to overthrow the existing regime. At the same time he opposed tactics of individual terror, because members of People's Will were faced by a "whole system," and it was necessary to fight the system in an organized way. He was convinced of Russia's irrepressible striving for new social forms. His *What Is Progress?* (*Chto takoe progress?* [1869]) as well as Lavrov's *Historical Letters* (*Istoricheskie pisma*), had a powerful effect on the forming of the "going among the people" movement in the 1870s.

In his works of this period, and in some cases of the following one, Mikhailovsky continued the revolutionary tradition of social thought formed by Belinsky, Herzen, Chernyshevsky, and Dobrolyubov. His attitude to the Russian translation of volume 1 of *Capital* made by Lopatin and Danielson is indicative. In articles entitled "A propos the Russian Edition of Karl Marx's Book" and "Karl Marx before the Court of Mr. Zhukovsky" (*Po povodu russkogo izdaniya knigi K. Marksa; Karl Marks pered sudom g-na Zhukovskogo*), he praised Marx's philosophical historical conception as well as his explanation of the bourgeois mode of production. Mikhailhovsky also did not deny the importance of the dialectical method at that time, defending Marx against accusations of Hegelianism.

In the mid-1880s the second period in Mikhailovsky's activity began, when his sociopolitical views became more moderate, and ethical and sociological problems more and more came to predominate in his works. The development of a subjective method in sociology was brought to the fore. In the 1890s, when he was at the head of the journal *Russkoye Bogatstvo* (*Russian Wealth*), he began to criticize Marxism from positivist positions. The Marxian understanding of history was reduced to economic materialism. While clearly sympathizing with basic ideas of Comte, he gravitated to an understanding of them that subsequently came to be called "materialistically interpreted positivism." This period was marked by a turn to problems of social psychology. From an analysis of fiction, court reports, and data of medicine and ethnography he elaborated a number of points that enriched social psychology theory and have not lost their scientific value to this day.

Like other theorists of Populist socialism Mikhailovsky would not abandon the idea of a distinctive noncapitalist development of Russia. The idea that the laboring people's political struggle would eventually lead to the advent of capitalism in Russia as had happened in West European history was assumed as a basis for Populist explanation of the dynamics of Russian social relations. Such a sequence of events was declared undesirable, dramatically ruining the organics of social life.

Mikhailovsky perceived Marx's *Capital* as a theory that realistically reflected the situation in Western Europe. While welcoming the political and economic ideas of this work as a whole and recognizing Marx's creative contribution to analysis of the history of Western Europe's social and economic development, Mikhailovsky suggested that Russia could and should have its own, qualitatively different road to socialism because of its quite original economic and cultural traditions.

At the same time, the intensifying political and economic contradictions between czarism and capitalism, on the one hand, and capital and labor, on the other, left fewer and fewer opportunities for retaining the best historic traditions amid the evolutionary and gradual change of economic and social life in Russia by the beginning of the twentieth century.

HIS GENERAL PHILOSOPHICAL POSITION

Mikhailovsky devoted most of his writing to social philosophy, although, as a broadly educated thinker, he paid much attention to epistemological, ethical, and anthropological problems, being clearly aware that it was impossible to separate them from the theoretical, methodological initial principles of understanding of history, sociology, and other social sciences.

Mikhailovsky paid special attention to the problem of the relation of the material and the ideal. He was drawn to a positivist treatment of this problem, claiming that the disputes around the materialist and spiritualist (idealist) answers to the question of the priority of being or spirit were outmoded and scholastic. Modern philosophy, he said, basing itself on the data of natural science, should overcome the "one-sidedness" and metaphysical essence of these philosophical trends.

Invoking the founders of positivism, Mikhailovsky wrote: "While we are still divided into materialists and spiritualists, advanced Western thought in the person of Comte, Spencer, and others is denying both systems. While reproaches of atheism are being perpetually heard in our society against progressive people, positivism calls atheists 'the most illogical theologians.' "[1]

That statement shows that Mikhailovsky shared the positivists' idea of the vapidity and unconstructiveness of what Engels called the basic question of philosophy in his *Anti-Dühring*. Nevertheless, Mikhailovsky examined both ontological and epistemological aspects of the relation of matter and spirit in quite some detail, trying to get away from orthodox positivism, and drawing close in many respects to the materialist conception. In that he relied on the works of such outstanding scientists as Charles Darwin, Ernst Haeckel, Jean Baptiste Lamarck, Ilya Mechnikov, Ivan Sechenov, and others.

Contradiction and skepticism in his philosophical views are to be seen in his answers to epistemological questions. He agreed with the agnostics' basic thesis about the impossibility of knowing the essence of things: "We do not and cannot know noumena, things in themselves; we know only phenomena in their connections, succession, and coexistence."[2] Attempts to comprehend objects of an intellectual contemplation, he thought, only led to mysticism and metaphysics alienated from life. He answered the question of truth in accordance with that. Truth and its criteria were wholly dependent on the individual's cognitive capacities.

At the same time, he adhered to the idea of the experimental and not a priori origin (as Kant held) of man's cognitive faculties, considering that nature, objective reality, by acting on the sense organs, evoked the appearance of corresponding sensations and images of surrounding objects and phenomena. But he interpreted that quite materialist proposition in the spirit of the sensualism and empiricism of the seventeenth-century English materialists Hobbes and Locke, criticizing the rationalism that contradicted the phenomenalist epistemological principle set out above.

THE SUBJECTIVE METHOD IN SOCIOLOGY

Mikhailovsky paid considerable attention to problems of the methodology of science, primarily accentuating social knowledge and the theoretical and practical aspects of historical knowledge.

In the traditions of positivism and neo-Kantianism he counterposed the sciences of society to those of nature, suggesting that while a strict determinism prevailed in nature, and that it was necessary to employ an objective method in studying it, in society we were dealing not only with the necessary but also with the desirable, so that it was important in it to rely on the subjective method:

> The sociologist, perhaps, does not have a so to say logical right to eliminate the man as he is, with all his griefs and desires, from his works; the terrifying image of suffering humanity, combined with the logic of things, perhaps takes its revenge on anyone who forgets it, and who is not filled by its suffering; the objective point of view, obligatory for the natural scientist, is perhaps quite unsuitable for sociology, the object of which—man—is identical with the subject; as a consequence of this identity, perhaps, the thinking subject can only attain the truth when he was quite merged with the conceivable subject and not parted from him, for a minute, i.e., entered into his interests, felt his life keenly, pondered over and considered his thought, felt his feelings, suffered his sufferings, and shed his tears.[3]

The difference between the natural and social sciences stemmed, according to Mikhailovsky, from the differences in principle of the objects of study themselves. Nature was not animate, and there was no purposiveness in it, from which it followed that a sociologist should experience his object from within and understand the inner experience of those who perform actions and who constituted the foundation of social processes. The search for truth was thus attended in sociology, according to him, with the ability to understand the inner states of the subjects of social affairs. He formulated the gist of his method as follows: "The mode of satisfying cognitive needs, when the observer puts himself mentally in the position of the observed person, is called the subjective method. The sphere of action of the subjective method and the scale of the area of study legitimately subject to it are determined by that."[4] History and sociology, he claimed, needed the subjective method, or what was the same thing, the investigator's "preconceived attitude" to the historical and social phenomena being studied. But this "preconceived opinion" was by no means the investigator's arbitrary opinion, it was the "thinking subject's" ability to put himself in the place of the "thought-of object."

The preconception governed by the acquired experience and moral standard of the investigator of social processes figured as an irremovable and real component of the method and instrument of social science. This factor could and should be authentic when it was clearly realized and contained progressive scientific, ethical, and sociopolitical ideas. Objectively this was the movement of Populist sociology toward objective sociology and psychology of cognition, understanding of socially and even individually determined history, and integral character of human knowledge. In this sense the conceptions of Mikhailovsky and Mannheim are obviously in accord.

At the same time, Mikhailovsky undoubtedly shared the Marxian point of view that history is nothing else than the activity of man pursuing his goals. For him, however, as for Lavrov and other Populists, the individual creator of history proceeded first and foremost and predominantly from his own personal qualities and not from something objective (from the level of development of productive forces or, say, labor relations developing unconsciously).

Mikhailovsky's striving to substantiate the specifics of social knowledge led him to assert that social events are intellectually and emotionally determined by the individual: "The living individual, with all his thoughts and feelings, becomes a maker of history on his own responsibility. He, and not some mystical force, sets the aim and goals in history, and sets events in motion toward it through the set of obstacles put in his way by elemental forces of nature and historical conditions."[5]

For its part, "subjectivism" of social cognition becomes objectively inevitable insofar as social events are studied not by abstract or anonymous sociology or history but by some one sociologist or historian, i.e., a specific scholar, the individual who necessarily has certain notions about good and evil, the progressive and the regressive. It remains only for the student to rid himself of bad subjectivism (in the sense of arbitrariness in judgments), to select the positive in this subjective in an appropriate, critical way, and to reject everything negative and undesirable.

The positive, according to Mikhailovsky, included the ideals of social justice and good common to all mankind, and the negative, idols begotten by the dominance of theology and people's prejudices. Sociological "subjectivism" means not only the inclusion of the personal into cognition, but also the right of a learning man to act in accordance with his own evaluations and results of cognition of society and history. The sociologist, he wrote, must declare: "I want to know the relations that exist between society and its members, but in addition to knowledge I want as well to realize such-and-such of my ideals to which I justify as follows."6

PRAVDA-TRUTH AND *PRAVDA*-JUSTICE

Mikhailovsky's idea of "*pravda*-truth" and "*pravda*-justice" had a great philosophical and sociopolitical response. It has been interpreted by many students of his work not only as a justification or original exposition of the subjective method itself, but also as a description of the distinguishing features of Russian philosophizing and of the style of Russian thinking. He himself, incidentally, admitted that problems of free will and necessity, the limits of our knowledge, the application of Darwin's theory to social sciences; problems of public interests and public opinions; problems of the philosophy, history, ethics, esthetics, economics, and literature had occupied him exclusively from the standpoint of this "great dual *pravda.*"7

"*Pravda*-truth," according to him, was a law of the physical world independent of man that expressed the causal connections of natural processes and of the vegetable and animal kingdoms. Knowledge of the phenomena of nature was achieved through objective methods (among which he distinguished experimental, observational, speculative, and inductive and deductive methods).

Scholars analyzing social affairs, on the contrary, willy-nilly turned to the concept of "*pravda*-justice," which inevitably had a subjective, personal character. The sociologist evaluated social phenomena having to do with people's activity or its results, and not with objective laws of history, which (Mikhailovsky suggested) might not exist. If their existence was admitted, however, they were inevitably colored by the individual's ideals, wishes, and aims. It was quite inadequate to argue, in the context of sociology, just about the necessity of being governed by objective laws; it was necessary to add: "Make history, moving it in the direction of your ideal, because that is what obedience to the laws of history consists in."8

In the final count Mikhailovsky resolved the problem of free will and conscious activity, on the one hand, and historical necessity, on the other, in favor of the subjective factor. The main point for him was the individual's ideals and activity and not objective social relations.

Nevertheless the concepts "subjective" and "subjective factor" did not include any irrationalism or voluntarism. According to him, "The subjective and objective methods are counterposed only by character, but nothing prevents them from getting on quite peacefully together, even when applied to one and the same range of phenomena."[9]

In his posing of the problem of historical necessity and freedom of the individual Mikhailovsky touched on a central sociophilosophical theme, viz., the distinguishing features of social determinism and the mechanism of the operation of social laws, which he reduced to two groups—the objective and the subjective. He understood that society was a special sphere of activity; that the causal connections in society included the activity of people who possessed freedom and awareness; that objective relations of cause and effect in society are only realized through people's activities. The idea of the subjective factor included a view of the activity of people as subjects of the historical process and of their impact on the course of events.

A direct reason for Mikhailovsky's subjective method was the dissemination in the sociology of his time of the ideas of social Darwinism, which characteristically reduced the patterns of existence of human society to the laws of biological evolution, and the advancing of the principle of natural selection as the determinant factor of social being, to which Mikhailovsky categorically objected. Calling this theory "a very disgraceful slur" on the intellectual life of the nineteenth century, he saw in it a form of apologetic for social inequality under capitalism. To social Darwinism he opposed a conception of "social solidarity" and "struggle for individuality." When rationally used these theories increased the possibility of emancipating working men from political inequality and economic exploitation. That explains his calls to create social conditions for all-round, harmonious improvement of the individual and for satisfaction of the individual's basic material and intellectual needs.

HIS CONCEPTION OF HISTORICAL PROGRESS

Mikhailovsky considered attainment of a rational, just consolidation ("uniformity") of society to be the main criterion of progressive development. That could be realized, in his opinion, through elimination of the negative consequences of the social division of labor, and through removal of the social antagonisms ("heterogeneity") that opposed the individual to society. Everything that furthered the movement of history to harmonious and all-round development of the individual should be considered an act of humanity and justice. Everything that on the contrary brings social inequality and conflicts should be recognized as immoral and undesirable, regressive and reactionary.

The influence of Comtian ideas about the three phases of the social movement of humanity put its stamp on Mikhailovsky's views on the philosophy of history. A novelty of his approach, however, was that unlike Comte, he did not make a periodization of history dependent on the character of the development of human thought: religious, metaphysical, and positivist (scientific) stages in social life. The place of the individual in the system of social relations and the forms of cooperation among people are of special importance for Mikhailovsky. In accordance with this he distinguished the following phases of history: (1) an objectively anthropocentric stage, when there was no social differentiation, and simple cooperation with property equality prevailed; (2) an eccentric stage when man was isolated from other people, there was social differentiation and no harmonious development of individuals, and complex cooperation and division of labor prevailed; (3) a subjectively anthropocentric phase that was a repetition, as it were, of the first stage at the highest social level and in the conditions of which man again proved to be at the center of social, economic, political, and moral and ethical values. The last phase embodied the version of the socialist future that corresponded to Mikhailovsky's ideals. It was based not on the primitive egalitarianism of primeval communism or competition of capitalist society, but on a harmonious uniting of individuals who had attained a certain degree of intellectual, moral, and physical perfection.

"Man for man, everything for man" was the motto of the future society, the society of social justice, Mikhailovsky stressed. By employing Hegel's method of dialectical negation with reference to history, he tried to show that the history of society was change in the forms of cooperation and production-consumer relations. At the same time he simplified the Hegelian-Marxian scheme, maintaining that, in the conditions of the highest, socialist type of social system, simple cooperation (the model of which he considered the peasant commune) would predominate.

When criticizing capitalist exploitation, Mikhailovsky wrote that in this case

> the people do not own the means of production. An indispensable person offers them to the people and receives the lion's share of the product for doing so. The point, of course, is simply to concentrate the means of production in the hands of the representatives of labor. . . . True freedom, that is properly organized and useful industry, lack of fraud in financial combination, a necessary railway, and true self-management cannot contradict the interests of the people or, what is the same thing, of labor.[10]

Social progress went hand in hand with people's endeavor to attain a certain (common), political, economic, and moral ideal that they desire and prefer. But what besides the "subjective" concretely determined this ideal, the desirable? Mikhailovsky did not, in essence, answer that question, which leaves his social philosophy and philosophy of history incomplete. As his opponent Lenin remarked, he "came to a halt before man's social ideas and aims" and was "unable to reduce them to material social relations."[11]

Actually, Mikhailovsky was not going to do that. He was a spokesman of the factor theory of social development. His sympathy with this conception was due to the unsatisfactory character of the sociophilosophical doctrine of Comte and Spencer, Hegel's idealist philosophy of history, and the economic materialism of Marx. The calls of Mikhailovsky and several other Russian thinkers (N. Kareyev, B. Kistyakovsky) to study society as the interaction of a host of causes (economics, politics, natural conditions, and so on) furthered an integral and balanced survey of social and historic realities. But the theory of factors was not free from certain contradictions. On the one hand, its advocates claimed that the sociologist had no right to single out any separate factor (economics, politics, morality, etc.) as the driving and determinant force of social progress, and that he was obliged to pay equally close attention to the whole aggregate of factors so as to grasp the laws of social dynamics. But on the other hand, the sociologist had to recognize the priority of one factor or another. Mikhailovsky, too, did not avoid that; as a sociologist of the subjective school he usually came to a conclusion of the determinant role of the psychological factor, although he did not deny the significance of others. In order to understand the laws operating in social affairs, he said that it was necessary to establish certain general features of the psychology of people's movements, which were the foundation of sociology.

PROBLEMS OF SOCIAL PSYCHOLOGY

While relying on the works of the German psychologists Wilhelm Wundt, Moritz Lazarus, and Heymann Steinthal, Mikhailovsky set himself the task of studying the mechanism of interpersonal psychic communication, understanding the nature of human behavior in large and small social groups, and discovering the phenomena of people's effect on one another through suggestion, hypnosis, and imitation. His long essay *Heroes and Crowd* (*Geroi i tolpa*) devoted to this theme is one of the most popular.

By "hero" he meant a person "who attracted the masses by his example to a good or a bad, a very noble or a very villainous, a reasonable or a senseless cause."[12] The "crowd," in his view, lacked a rational and motive principle; there was no initiative in it, while the impulsive and unconscious predominated. The "hero" can exert a magnetic influence on the "crowd" to cause mass movements and "epidemics," and to attract others by his impulse. "An obvious villain, a fool, a nonentity, and a half-wit are therefore as important for us in the context of our task as a world genius or an angel in the flesh, if the crowd follows them, if it obeys them sincerely and not through extraneous motives, if it imitates them and prays to them."[13] According to Mikhailovsky, the relations between "hero" and "crowd" were governed by psychological factors of imitation, suggestion, and hypnosis.

Mikhailovsky went into the problem of imitation in particular detail, using for this purpose numerous facts from fiction, publicistic writings, criminal records, and ethnographic studies. He particularly defined the phenomenon of "automatic imitation," calling it "moral contagion."

Mikhailovsky's study of questions of social psychology was engendered not only by the absence of any serious publications on the subject, but also mainly by the necessity of reinterpreting psychological aspects of democratic and revolutionary movements, for which "the personal energy, tenacity, convincing strength of thought, and force of example, shown by the hero" was decisive.[14] But the successes of the "hero" depended on the "crowd." Mikhailovsky drew special attention to that point: "As a ray of light is refracted differently in different media, so rays of thought have different effects, depending on the general conditions they penetrate."[15] That was why it was necessary, when appraising the role of leaders, to clarify how far they understood the feelings and moods of the masses and what good they brought to the people.

What is more, Mikhailovsky opposed the cult of the "hero," and the cult of the personality. He criticized the views of Thomas Carlyle, who claimed that "the history of the world is but the biography of great men."[16] And he stressed that there were many examples in history when people proved to be on the surface of historical events who by no means represented the best forces of the milieu and by no means corresponded to what is sometimes called the demands of the time. But a crafty, slippery individual who seized on the mass of various aspirations and interests could succeed and "color a certain, more or less long period of time with his hue."[17]

Mikhailovsky saw psychology as a new, young science capable of explaining important aspects of social affairs, especially under conditions of forming mass societies and broad social movements. He considered the advances of the revolutionary movement in Russia to depend directly on changes in the content of the "mass psychology," and that a revolution in the people's consciousness could and should precede the social revolution.

In that connection he substantiated the need to study the public mood, because it was the factor the "hero," the leader of the masses, had to take into account. Whereas in the past allowing for the mood of the masses had been only the ability of individual military men, orators, preachers, and teachers, the task now was to study this phenomenon broadly and scientifically.

Sociophilosophical, political, and psychological ideas were closely interwoven with moral problems in Mikhailovsky's work. An ardent advocate of enlightenment of the masses, and of the emancipation of working people from social injustice, he saw a major component of society's progress in the moral health of its members. Mikhailovsky gave vital importance to the moral consciousness of large and small communities of people. He pointed out not only universal values, but also collective and class ones that in their sum are the basis or concrete essence of social consciousness and culture.

As a critic of capitalism Mikhailovsky noted that the bourgeois form of social life made the individual reject some moral norms in favor of principles of the economic system of private enterprise. The socialist individual, on the contrary, was active and creative; for him the worst form of moral decline was reconciliation with reality and "slavish circumstances." In formulating the socialist's moral creed, Mikhailovsky declared: "Man is the slave of circumstances; therefore the circumstances must be changed in his favor."[18]

NOTES

1. N. K. Mikhailovsky, *Sochineniya* (Works), vol. 1, p. 17.
2. Ibid., vol. 4, p. 97.
3. Ibid., p. 69.
4. Ibid., vol. 3, p. 402.
5. Ibid., p. 448.
6. Ibid., p. 406.
7. Ibid., vol. 1, p. 3.
8. Ibid., vol. 4, p. 69.
9. Ibid., vol. 3, pp. 401–402.
10. Ibid., vol. 1, p. 660.
11. V. I. Lenin, *Collected Works* (Moscow: Progress Publishers, 1986), vol. 1, p. 141.
12. N. K. Mikhailovsky, *Sochineniya*, vol. 2, p. 97.
13. Ibid., p. 99.
14. Ibid., p. 386.
15. Ibid., p. 389.
16. Thomas Carlyle, *The Hero as Divinity*, vol. 1 of *Heroes and Hero-Worship*.
17. N. K. Mikhailovsky, *Sochineniya*, vol. 6, p. 103.
18. Ibid., vol. 4, p. 62.

25

Mikhail Alexandrovich Bakunin
(1814–1876)

The name of Bakunin, one of the leaders of the anarchist wing of the European socialist movement, is widely known both in Russia and in the West. Bakunin was not only a politician and social thinker but also a man gifted with obvious philosophical talent. His reasonings on social and political problems usually include long passages about nature, cosmic vitality, and the metaphysical foundations of human beings. His militant materialism is inseparable from his sometimes even fanatical atheism (which did not impede his calling Jesus Christ the first real communist in the history of humankind).

Fragments from Bakunin's God and the State *represent the core of his political thought and its close interconnection with his general understanding of God, matter, philosophy, science, human freedom, and personality.*

GOD AND THE STATE*

[The idealists] wish God, and they wish humanity. They persist in connecting two terms which, once separated, can come together again only to destroy each other. They say in a single breath: "God and the liberty of man," "God and the dignity, justice, equality, fraternity, prosperity of men"—regardless of fatal logic by virtue of which, if God exists, all these things are condemned to non-existence. For, if God is, he is necessarily the eternal, supreme,

*From *Russian Philosophy,* Volume 1, edited by James M. Edie, James P. Scanlan, Mary-Barbara Zeldin, with the collaboration of George L. Kline. Copyright © 1976. Excerpted from *God and the State,* Mother Earth Publishing Company, New York. Reprinted here by permission of the University of Tennessee Press.

absolute master, and if such a master exists, man is a slave; now, if he is a slave, neither justice, nor equality, nor fraternity, nor prosperity are possible for him. In vain, flying in the face of good sense and all the teachings of history, do they represent their God as animated by the tenderest love of human liberty; a master, whoever he may be and however liberal he may desire to show himself, remains nonetheless always a master. His existence necessarily implies the slavery of all that is beneath him. Therefore, if God existed, only in one way could he serve human liberty—by ceasing to exist.

A jealous lover of human liberty, and deeming it the absolute condition of all that we admire and respect in humanity, I reverse the phrase of Voltaire, and say that, *If God existed, it would be necessary to abolish him.*

The severe logic that dictates these words is far too evident to require a development of this argument. And it seems to me impossible that the illustrious men, whose names so celebrated and so justly respected I have cited, should not have been struck by it themselves, and should not have perceived the contradiction in which they involve themselves in speaking of God and human liberty at once. To have disregarded it, they must have considered this inconsistency or logical license *practically* necessary to humanity's well-being. . . .

The liberty of man consists solely in this: that he obeys natural laws because he has *himself* recognized them as such, and not because they have been externally imposed upon him by any extrinsic will whatever, divine or human, collective or individual. . . .

To sum up. We recognize, then, the absolute authority of science, because the sole object of science is the mental reproduction, as well-considered and systematic as possible, of the natural laws inherent in the material, intellectual, and moral life of both the physical and the social worlds, these two worlds constituting, in fact, but one and the same natural world. Outside of this only legitimate authority, legitimate because rational and in harmony with human liberty, we declare all other authorities false, arbitrary, and fatal.

We recognize the absolute authority of science, but we reject the infallibility and universality of the *savant.* . . .

We accept all natural authorities and all influence of fact, but none of right; for every authority or every influence of right, officially imposed as such, becoming directly an oppression and a falsehood, would inevitably impose upon us, as I believe I have sufficiently shown, slavery and absurdity.

In a word, we reject all legislation, all authority, and all privileged, licensed, official, and legal influence, even though arising from universal suffrage, convinced that it can turn only to the advantage of a dominant minority of exploiters against the interests of the immense majority in subjection to them.

This is the sense in which we are really Anarchists. . . .

To proclaim as divine all that is grand, just, noble, and beautiful in humanity is to tacitly admit that humanity of itself would have been unable to produce it—that is, that, abandoned to itself, its own nature is miserable, iniquitous, base, and ugly. Thus we come back to the essence of all religion—in other words, to the disparagement of humanity for the greater glory of divinity. And from the moment that the natural inferiority of man and his fundamental incapacity to rise by his own effort, unaided by any divine inspiration, to the comprehension of just and true ideas, are admitted, it becomes necessary to admit also all the theological, political, and social consequences of the positive religions. From the moment that God, the perfect and supreme being, is posited face to face with humanity, divine mediators, the elect, the inspired of God spring from the earth to enlighten, direct, and govern in his name the human race. . . .

In a word, it is not at all difficult to prove, history in hand, that the Church, that all the churches, Christian and non-Christian, by the side of their spiritualistic propagandism, and probably to accelerate and consolidate the success thereof, have never neglected to organize themselves into great corporations for the economic exploitation of the masses under the protection and with the direct and special blessing of some divinity or other; that all the states which originally, as we know, with all their political and judicial institutions and their dominant and privileged classes, have been only temporal branches of these various churches, have likewise had principally in view this same exploitation for the benefit of lay minorities indirectly sanctioned by the Church; finally and in general, that the action of the good God and of all the divine idealities on earth has ended at last, always and everywhere, in founding the prosperous materialism of the few over the fanatical and constantly famishing idealism of the masses. . . .

History, in the system of the idealists, as I have said, can be nothing but a continuous fall. They begin by a terrible fall, from which they never recover—by the *salto mortale* from the sublime regions of pure and absolute idea into matter. And into what kind of matter! Not into the matter which is eternally active and mobile, full of properties and forces, of life and intelligence, as we see it in the real world; but into abstract matter, impoverished and reduced to absolute misery by the regular looting of these Prussians of thought, the theologians and metaphysicians, who have stripped it of everything to give everything to their emperor, to their God; into the matter which, deprived of all action and movement of its own, represents, in opposition to the divine idea, nothing but absolute stupidity, impenetrability, absolute inertia, and immobility. . . .

See in how profound an error our dear and illustrious idealists find themselves. In talking to us of God they purpose, they desire to elevate us, emancipate us, ennoble us, and, on the contrary, they crush and degrade us. With the name of God they imagine that they can establish fraternity among men, and, on the contrary, they create pride, contempt; they sow discord, hatred, war; they establish slavery. For with God come the different degrees of divine inspiration; humanity is divided into men highly inspired, less inspired, uninspired. All are equally insignificant before God, it is true; but, compared with each other, some are greater than others; not only in fact—which would be of no consequence, because inequality in fact is lost in the collectivity when it cannot cling to some legal fiction or institution—but by divine right of inspiration, which immediately establishes a fixed, constant, petrifying inequality. The highly inspired *must* be listened to and obeyed by the less inspired, and the less inspired by the uninspired. Thus we have the principle of authority well established, and with it the two fundamental institutions of slavery: Church and State. . . .

Science comprehends the thought of the reality, not reality itself; the thought of life, not life. That is its limit, its only really insuperable limit, because it is founded on the very nature of thought, which is the only organ of science.

Upon this nature are based the indisputable rights and grand mission of science, but also its vital impotence and even its mischievous action whenever, through its official licensed representatives, it arrogantly claims the right to govern life.

The government of science and men of science, even be they positivists, disciples of Auguste Comte, or, again, disciples of the doctrinaire school of German Communism, cannot fail to be impotent, ridiculous, inhuman, cruel, oppressive, exploiting, maleficent. We may say of men of science, *as such,* what I have said of theologians and metaphysicians: they have neither sense nor heart for individual and living beings. We cannot even blame them for this, for it is the natural consequence of their profession. . . .

Science cannot go outside of the sphere of abstractions. In this respect it is infinitely inferior to art, which in its turn is peculiarly concerned also with general types and general situations, but which incarnates them by an artifice of its own in forms which, if they are not living in the sense of real life, nonetheless excite in our imagination the memory and sentiment of life; art in a certain sense individualizes the types and situations which it conceives; by means of the individualities without flesh and bone, and consequently permanent and immortal, which it has the power to create, it recalls to our minds the living, real individualities which appear and disappear under our eyes. Art, then, is as it were the return of abstraction of life; science, on the contrary, is the perpetual immolation of life, fugitive, temporary, but real, on the altar of eternal abstractions.

Science is as inescapable of grasping the individuality of a man as that of a rabbit, being equally indifferent to both. Not that it is ignorant of the principle of individuality: it conceives it perfectly as a principle, but not as a fact. It knows very well that all the animal species, including the human species, have no real existence outside of an indefinite number of individuals born and dying to make room for new individuals equally fugitive. It knows that in rising from the animal species to the superior species the principle of individuality becomes more pronounced; the individuals appear freer and more complete. It knows that man, the last and most perfect animal of earth, presents the most complete and most remarkable individuality, because of his power to conceive, concretize, personify, as it were, in his social and private existence, the universal law. It knows, finally, when it is not vitiated by theological or metaphysical, political or judicial *doctrinairisme,* or even by a narrow scientific pride, when it is not deaf to the instincts and spontaneous aspirations of life—it knows (and this is its last word) that respect for man is the supreme law of Humanity, and that the great, the real object of history, its only legitimate object, is the humanization and emancipation, the real liberty, the prosperity and happiness of each individual living in society. For, if we would not fall back into the liberticidal fiction of the public welfare represented by the State, a fiction always founded on the systematic sacrifice of the people, we must clearly recognize that collective liberty and prosperity exist only so far as they represent the sum of individual liberties and prosperities.

Science knows all these things, but it does not and cannot go beyond them. . . .

Now, history is made, not by abstract individuals, but by acting, living, and passing individuals. Abstractions advance only when borne forward by real men. For these beings, made not in the idea only but in reality of flesh and blood, science has no heart: it considers them at most as *material for intellectual and social development.* What does it care for the particular conditions and chance fate of Peter or James? It would make itself ridiculous, it would abdicate, it would annihilate itself, if it wished to concern itself with them otherwise than as examples in support of its eternal theories. And it would be ridiculous to wish it to do so, for its mission lies not there. It cannot grasp the concrete; it can move only in abstractions. Its mission is to busy itself with the situation and the *general* conditions of the existence and development, either of the human species in general, or of such a race, such a people, such a class or category of individuals; the *general* causes of their prosperity, their decline, and the best *general* methods of securing their progress in all ways. Provided it accomplishes this task broadly and rationally, it will do its whole duty, and it would be really unjust to expect more of it.

But it would be equally ridiculous, it would be disastrous to entrust it with a mission which it is incapable of fulfilling. Since its own nature forces it to ignore the existence of Peter and James, it must never be permitted, nor must anybody be permitted in its name, to govern Peter and James. For it were capable of treating them almost as it treats rabbits. Or rather, it would continue to ignore them, but its licensed representatives, men not at all abstract, but on the contrary in very active life and having very substantial interests, yielding to the pernicious influence which privilege inevitably exercises upon men, would finally fleece other men in the name of science, just as they have been fleeced hitherto by priests, politicians of all shades, and lawyers, in the name of God, of the State, of judicial Right.

What I preach then is, to a certain extent, the *revolt of life against science,* or rather against the *government of science,* not to destroy science—that would be high treason to humanity—but to remand it to its place so that it can never leave it again. Until now all human history has been only a perpetual and bloody immolation of millions of poor human beings in honor of some pitiless abstraction—God, country, power of state, national honor, historical rights, judicial rights, political liberty, public welfare. . . .

Nevertheless, theology alone does not make a religion, any more than historical elements suffice to create history. By historical elements I mean the general conditions of any real development whatsoever—for example in this case the conquest of the world by the Romans and the meeting of the God of the Jews with the ideal of divinity of the Greeks. To impregnate the historical elements, to cause them to run through a series of new historical transformations, a living, spontaneous fact was needed, without which they might have remained many centuries longer in the states of unproductive elements. This fact was not lacking in Christianity; it was the propagandism, martyrdom, and death of Jesus Christ.

We know almost nothing of this great and saintly personage, all that the Gospels tell us being contradictory, and so fabulous that we can scarcely seize upon a few real and vital traits. But it is certain that he was the preacher of the poor, the friend and consoler of the wretched, of the ignorant, of the slaves, and of the women, and that by these last he was much loved. He promised eternal life to all who are oppressed, to all who suffer here below; and the number is immense. He was hanged, as a matter of course, by the representatives of the official morality and public order of that period. His disciples and the disciples of his disciples succeeded in spreading, thanks to the destruction of the national barriers by the Roman conquest, and propagating the Gospel in all the countries known to the ancients. Everywhere they were received with open arms by the slaves and the women, the two most oppressed, most suffering, and naturally also the most ignorant classes of the ancient world. For even such few proselytes as they made in the privileged and learned world they were indebted in great part to the influence of women. Their most extensive propagandism was directed almost exclusively among the people, unfortunate and degraded by slavery. This was the first awakening, the first intellectual revolt of the proletariat. . . .

The revolution of July resulted in lifting its tastes. We know that every bourgeois in France carries within him the imperishable type of the bourgeois gentleman, a type which never fails to appear immediately the parvenu acquires a little wealth and power. In 1830, the wealthy bourgeoisie had definitely replaced the old nobility in the seats of power. It naturally tended to establish a new aristocracy. An aristocracy of capital first of all, but also an aristocracy of intellect, of good manners and delicate sentiments. It began to feel religious.

This was not on its part simply an aping of aristocratic customs. It was also a necessity of its position. The proletariat had rendered it a final service in once more aiding it to overthrow the nobility. The bourgeoisie now had no further need of its cooperation, for it felt itself firmly seated in the shadow of the throne of July, and the alliance with the people, thenceforth useless, began to become inconvenient. It was necessary to remand it to its place, which naturally could not be done without provoking great indignation among the masses. It became necessary to restrain this indignation. In the name of what? In the name of the *bourgeois* interest bluntly confessed? That would have been much too cynical. The more unjust and inhuman an interest is, the greater need it has of sanction. Now, where find it if not in religion, that good protectress of all the well fed and the useful consoler of the hungry? And more than ever the triumphant bourgeoisie saw that religion was indispensable to the people. . . .

There is not, there cannot be, a State without religion. Take the freest states in the world—the United States of America or the Swiss Confederation, for instance—and see what an important part is played in all official discourse by divine Providence, that supreme sanction of all states.

But whenever a chief of State speaks of God, be he William I, the Knouto-Germanic emperor, or Grant, the president of the great republic, be sure that he is getting ready to shear once more his people-flock. . . .

In this respect Protestantism is much more advantageous. It is the bourgeois religion *par excellence*. It accords just as much liberty as is necessary to the bourgeois and finds a way of reconciling celestial aspiration with the respect which terrestrial conditions demand. Consequently, it is especially in Protestant countries that commerce and industry have been developed. But it was impossible for the French bourgeoisie to become Protestant. To pass from one religion to another—unless it be done deliberately, as sometimes in the case of the Jews of Russia and Poland, who get baptized three or four times in order to receive each time the remuneration allowed them—to seriously change one's religion, a little faith is necessary. Now, in the exclusive positive heart of the French bourgeois, there is room for faith. He professes the most profound indifference for all questions which touch neither his pocket first nor his social vanity afterwards. He is as indifferent to Protestantism as to Catholicism. On the other hand, the French bourgeois could not go over to Protestantism without putting himself in conflict with the Catholic routine of the majority of the French people, which would have been great imprudence on the part of a class pretending to govern the nation.

There was still one way left—to return to the humanitarian and revolutionary religion of the eighteenth century. But that would have led too far. So the bourgeoisie was obliged, in order to sanction its new State, to create a new religion which might be boldly proclaimed, without too much ridicule and scandal, by the whole bourgeois class.

Thus was born *doctrinaire* Deism. . . .

Its boldly avowed object was the reconciliation of Revolution with Reaction, to use the language of the school, of the principle of liberty with that of authority, and naturally to the advantage of the latter.

This reconciliation signified: in politics, the taking away of popular liberty for the benefit of bourgeois rule, represented by the monarchical and constitutional State; in philosophy, the deliberate submission of free reason to the eternal principles of faith.

26

Nikolai Konstantinovich Mikhailovsky (1842–1904)

If Bakunin's works exemplify the beginnings of the Populist intellectual stream in Russia, Mikhailovsky's could be considered the end of Russian populism's classic stage of development. While his more radical counterparts P. Lavrov and P. Tkachev lived in exile, Mikhailovsky remained in the motherland a legal spokesman of Populist social, philosophical, moral, and esthetic ideas. His philosophical interests were focused mainly on the problems of personality and society. Advocating a concept of "the struggle for individuality" and a theory of human progress he also pioneered the development of foundations of social psychology in Russia.

What Is Progress?, Mikhailovsky's most extensive and systematic treatise, was written in the form of "an examination of the ideas of Herbert Spencer." It allowed Mikhailovsky to express his own philosophy of history and propose answers to the questions of evolution of man and society.

WHAT IS PROGRESS?*

Spencer repeatedly cites Guizot's *History of Civilization*, drawing arguments from it to support his analogies and conclusions. But he seems to have overlooked a suggestion the book contains that is not devoid of interest— the suggestion, namely, that there are two types of progress—the progress of society and the personal development of man—and that these two types

---

*From *Russian Philosophy*, Volume 2, edited by James M. Edie, James P. Scanlan, Mary-Barbara Zeldin, with the collaboration of George L. Kline. Copyright © 1976. Translated by James P. Scanlan from *Chto takoye progress?* 1896. Reprinted by permission of the University of Tennessee Press.

of progress do not always perfectly coincide and sometimes form unequal parts of the sum total of civilization. The word "progress" is used here in the generally accepted sense of improvement in the direction of welfare— the sense Spencer repudiates as interfering with research.

Whatever Guizot's inferences and conclusions, his thesis of the dual character of progress has its share of truth. And however assiduously Spencer tries to avoid the teleological sense of the word "progress," his survey of the possible types of evolution must contain either an estimate of *both* personal evolution and the evolution of society, or else an indication that these two types of progress coincide. Now he has shown very well and in quite adequate detail that society—the ideal person—evolves like an organism: it proceeds from the homogeneous to the heterogeneous, from the simple to the complex, through gradual disintegration and differentiation. Very good. But what is happening all this time to the real person—the member of society? Does he himself experience the same process of evolution, on the model of organic progress? Spencer answers this question in passing, affirmatively. We shall try to answer it in more detail, negatively.

Primitive society is on the whole an almost completely homogeneous mass. All its members are occupied with the same tasks, possess the same knowledge, have the same customs and habits. But each of them taken separately is quite heterogeneous: he is a fisherman, a hunter, and a herdsman; he knows how to make boats and weapons, how to build himself a hut, and so on. In a word, each member of primitive, homogeneous society combines in himself all the powers and capacities which can develop, given the cultural level and the local physical conditions of the time.

But then the society first begins to divide into rulers and ruled. Certain individuals come from without or are singled out from the most homogeneous mass, and in the course of time they adopt a mode of life distinct from that of the remainder of the society; they leave the muscular labor to others, while they themselves gradually become specialists in activity of the nervous system. The society has taken a step from homogeneity toward heterogeneity, but the individuals who make it up have moved, on the contrary, from heterogeneity to homogeneity. With some, the muscular system has begun to develop at the expense of the nervous system, and with others, vice versa. Previously, each member of the society knew how to build a hut and how to catch animals, but now half of them have lost the habits connected with these occupations, while on the other hand they have learned how to rule, to heal, to tell fortunes, and so on. . . . Subsequent differentiations within the ruling class have the same dual character: they breed heterogeneity within the social order and, on the contrary, homogeneity and narrowness in the separate individuals.

We get the same result when we compare primitive society with the present condition of the lower classes. Take the labor of the savage on the one hand and of the contemporary factory worker on the other. The savage decides to build himself a hut. He himself chooses the right trees, fells them himself, hauls them into place himself, makes the framework and does the finishing himself. Suppose that the hut he has built is a very poor one—that is not the point. All the time he was working he was living a full life. While he was sweating and straining in the forest his labor was not merely physical: the choice of trees, of the route for transporting them, of the place to build—all this demands a certain intellectual effort. Furthermore, all the time he is working the savage is thinking of his future life in the hut he is struggling to build, thinking of the comforts that will grace his life and the life of his family; every corner and every chink suggests things to him. Similarly, he brings his pitiful conception of beauty into play in planning the hut and puts to work all of his meager knowledge of physics and mathematics. In short, in his work the savage is living with his whole being.

Quite the contrary picture is presented by the labor of the factory worker today in those areas in which the division of labor has proceeded furthest. For example, the manufacture of pocket watches, according to Babbage, consists of 102 separate operations, in accordance with the number of separate parts in the watch mechanism; each of a hundred men engaged in this work spends his entire life bent over the same wheels or screws or cogs, and only the master watchmaker who puts the separate parts of the mechanism together knows how to do anything besides his own specialty. Naturally such monotonous occupation excludes any kind of intellectual activity, or at least reduces it to the bare minimum. As Schiller says: by eternally occupying himself with some fragment of the whole, man himself becomes a fragment.

In the armaments works at Tula, the division of labor has been carried to such a point that the gunsmith not only spends all his life fashioning triggers or firing pins or boring the holes in barrels, but bequeaths his specialty to his children. Unvarying, monotonous activity can only result in simpler rather than more complex organization, and in the organism must lead to a more or less extensive homogeneity, which its posterity could acquire simply through the hereditary transmission of the organism's characteristics, were it not that in this case the natural factor of inheritance is further intensified by the social factor. It is understandable, then, that in the course of a few generations of Tula gunsmiths we encounter an ever-increasing transition from heterogeneity to homogeneity. Their ancestors made entire guns, and thus had to take into consideration facts which are completely unnecessary and useless to the descendants, who are only boring barrels or making firing pins. Thus the ancestors were more heterogeneous than the descendants, and at the same time the rise of these specialist descendants has promoted the heterogeneity of society, i.e., its evolution.

In constructing his outline of social evolution, Spencer refers to the works of economists in which there are detailed descriptions of the transition of industrial organization from homogeneity to heterogeneity through the division of labor. But Spencer seems to forget here that, if not the corporation economists, then their adversaries have examined in no less detail the double import of the division of labor, namely its property (retaining Spencer's terminology) of increasing the heterogeneity of society while at the same time diminishing the heterogeneity of the worker. . . .

If every development of the whole can take place only at the expense of the development of the parts, if in every particular act of evolution there exist two elements: one active, progressive, passing from homogeneity to heterogeneity, and the other passive, a victim of evolution, as it were, passing from heterogeneity to homogeneity—then how is the evolution of society reflected in the fate of its members? The answer is clear: if society makes a transition from homogeneity to heterogeneity, then the process of integration in the citizens which corresponds to this transition must proceed from heterogeneity to homogeneity. In short, individual progress and social evolution (on the model of organic evolution) are mutually exclusive, just as the evolution of organs and the evolution of the whole organism are mutually exclusive. . . .

What do the advocates of the so-called "woman question" (which in reality is just as much a man's question) want? They are demanding the extension of women's intellectual horizons and a certain role for women in social affairs, i.e., they are demanding individual heterogeneity, which must make society less heterogeneous, for to a certain degree it lessens the difference between men and women. What do their opponents want? To maintain the *status quo*, i.e., to keep women homogeneous and society heterogeneous. In what do the reforms of the present reign consist? In making society less heterogeneous and the individual more heterogeneous. What are the abolitionists striving to attain? The reduction of the differences between the white and colored populations, i.e., social homogeneity, and at the same time the extension of the rights of the colored people and a rise in their moral and intellectual level, i.e., individual heterogeneity. In a word, every social question takes both of these forms at once, because the differentation of society, as a whole, is always and everywhere accompanied by the integration of the citizens, as parts. . . .

To plumb Spencer's error to the bottom, let us examine the analogy he sets up between an organism and society. . . .

Though Spencer counsels us not to forget what is, according to his own opinion, the most important point of difference between society and an organism, he nevertheless forgets it himself. This is shown most clearly in the cleverest part of his analogy—the parallel between Parliament and the brain. If the individual's brain receives not the actual sensations immediately impressed upon the nerve-endings, but rather representations of these sensations, nevertheless the organism, possessing a corporate consciousness, experiences pain and pleasure as a whole. Consequently, to express it in the metaphorical language of Spencer's analogy, the interests of the brain are in solidarity with the interests of the whole organism, and in it there are no Tories and Whigs, no radicals and Chartists. But the English workers in no way benefit from the fact that their interests and sufferings are not immediately felt by the House of Commons but are "represented" in it. In an organsism it is the whole that experiences pain and pleasure, not the parts; in society it is the parts that experience pain and pleasure, not the whole. And no cleverness or erudition can abolish this fundamental difference, connected with the fundamental difference between the physiological and the social division of labor, which in its turn is connected with the equally fundamental difference between organic and social evolution.

This is in fact the third time Spencer has ignored human joys and sorrows, though all three times the wings of his thought have beat against them and he has bypassed them by the most diverse routes. Ordering art to depict past life only, he omits the concerns of the present through simple oversight, since the principle of contrast does not exclude from the tasks of art the communication of contemporary phenomena. Pursuing the parallel between organic and social progress, he consciously turns away from the happiness of mankind, since he frankly declares his disapproval of this point of view. Setting up an analogy between natural and social organisms, he ignores the pain and pleasure of men through a double oversight: he forgets not only the pain and pleasure but also his own reminder of them.

If in all these cases Spencer had actually reached the truth, we would say nothing and could say nothing against his objective method. In this event success would justify the means, whatever we had thought of them apart from their results. But we see that this is not so; . . . in all three of these cases he has fallen into gross errors. And since there can be no question of Spencer's intellectual prowess, the question arises: Is it legitimate to eliminate the teleological element from sociological investigations? Can the objective method give good results in sociology? Perhaps the sociologist has no logical right, so to speak, to eliminate man from his work—man as he is, with all his sorrows and desires. Perhaps the terrible image of suffering humanity, in league with the logic of things, revenges itself upon anyone who forgets it, upon anyone who is not imbued with a sense of its sufferings. Perhaps the objective point of view, obligatory for the natural scientist, is completely unsuitable for sociology, the object of which—man —is identical with the subject. Perhaps, as a consequence of this identity, the thinking subject can attain to truth only when he is fully merged with the thinking object and is not separated from him even for an instant— i.e., when he enters into his interests, lives his life, thinks his thoughts, shares his feelings, experiences his sufferings, weeps his tears. . . .

In the first half of the present century a new philosophical school arose in the West which sought to avoid . . . the interference of the subjective element. We speak of positivism. . . .

Every ethico-political doctrine has its motto, by which, as an end, its practical motives are summed up. But on the banner of positivism there is no such motto. Its principles are purely scientific, not philosophical. Positivism prides itself on the fact that in it philosophy and science blend into one whole—and it so prides itself with perfect justice. By this I do not mean to credit the principles of positivism with philosophical significance, but only to say that positivism does not embrace all aspects of life.

The principle of the conformity of phenomena to laws is as pure and irreproachable as a virgin. But like a virgin it may remain sterile, for it contains no fertilizing principle; as with a virgin, there is no guaranteeing into whose hands it will fall, and what it will give mankind. Comte himself felt this. "One must be very careful," he says, "that the scientific conviction that social phenomena are subject to immutable natural laws does not degenerate into a systematic tendency toward fatalism and optimism, which are equally immoral (*dégradants*) and dangerous; thus only those whose moral level is sufficiently high can profitably study sociology" (*Cours de phil. pos.*, vol. IV, p. 190). . . .

But why, from the point of view of positivism, are fatalism and optimism immoral and dangerous? "Without praising or condemning political facts," Comte says, ". . . positive sociology, like all other sciences, sees in them nothing but simple objects of observation and views each phenomenon from a dual point of view—from the point of view of both its harmony with co-existing facts and its connection with antecedent and subsequent states of human evolution" (*Cours,* IV, 293 . . .) . How can we connect this purely objective attitude toward political facts . . . with deprecatory remarks about fatalism and optimism? Fatalism and optimism are simply political facts, not subject to condemnation from the standpoint of positivism; they necessarily harmonize with co-existing facts and are connected with antecedent and subsequent facts. If it is said that the expressions "immoral" and "dangerous" themselves define the connection of fatalism and optimism with subsequent facts, this can only mean that the program of approaching political facts objectively is unrealizable; that in the realm of the phenomena of social life observation is inevitably linked with moral evaluation to such a degree that one can refrain from "praising or condemning political facts" only by failing to understand their significance. But moral evaluation is the result of a subjective process of thought, whereas positivism particularly prides itself on using an objective method in sociology.

Further, if the subjective method is fully adequate to sociological investigations, then why is a high moral level needed? Apparently the conviction that phenomena conform to law is, by itself, not enough. Very good. But how is one's presence on a higher moral level expressed in sociological investigations? Evidently from this height a man can see something which is not accessible to the objective investigation which alone is recognized as legitimate by positivism. Thus it turns out that there is something lacking in Comte's system, and something very important.

I am pleased to be able to refer here, in support of my own cursory observations, to an outstanding article by Mr. P. L. [Peter Lavrov], "Problems of Positivism and Their Solution" (*Contemporary Review,* May): "The objective element in ethics, politics, and sociology," says this esteemed author, "is limited to the actions of individuals, to social institutions, and to historical events. These are subject to objective description and classification. But to *understand* them, it is necessary to consider the *ends* for which the actions of individuals are only means, the *ends* which are embodied in the social institutions, the *ends* which generate the historical event. But what is an end? It is something desirable, agreeable, obligatory. All these categories are purely subjective and at the same time are accessible to all individuals. Consequently, when these phenomena are involved in an investigation they compel us to employ a subjective method and at the same time permit us to do so fully scientifically" (137). In another place Mr. P. L. quite rightly observes that by eliminating the subjective method in politics and ethics, positivism even prevents itself from justifying its own existence.

Teleology, in the sense of a doctrine of the ends which the individual sets himself, has no place in positivism, as a consequence of the absence of the subjective method and consequently of moral evaluation. Thus when Comte or one of his disciples . . . approves or disapproves of some social phenomenon, then however apt the evaluation, it is alien to the system, is not connected with it organically. Where there is no teleology there can be no moral rules, no praise or blame such as Comte himself pronounces, as we have seen. . . .

Similarly, when Comte says: "This new social philosophy (i.e., the positive), by its nature, is capable of realizing today all the legitimate desires which revolutionary politics can produce" and so on (*Cours,* IV, 148)—when Comte says this, the expression "legitimate desires" is left quite undefined. We know what desires are legitimate from the standpoint of the present political theories of the reactionaries, the conservatives, and the revolutionaries, from the standpoint of the individualists, the socialists, the clericalists, the eclectics, and so on. . . . From the standpoint of the objective method which is the characteristic feature of positive sociology, the expression "legitimate" desire can mean only "attainable" desire. But every ethico-political doctrine that has ever existed has regarded its desires as attainable. Let us suppose that positivism, linked so closely with science, can determine better than other philosophical systems and political theories which desires are attainable and which are not. But to do so it is first necessary to have a desire, and while of course every *positivist* has them, *positivism* poses no ideals, because an ideal is the result of a subjective attitude.

Mankind has harbored many unattainable and in that sense illegitimate desires, and many minds and lives have been destroyed by them. Perhaps the greatest service of positivism is to show man the limits beyond which he faces eternal and invincible darkness. To try to transcend these limits is to have unattainable and illegitimate desires. So teaches positivism. We shall go further. These illegitimate desires are a crime against that humanity to the service of which all man's powers should be dedicated. We are speaking here of purely theoretical questions, of the essence and the beginning of things, of ultimate principles, and so on.

But in the realm of practice the matter is complicated both by the complexity of the questions themselves and by the absolutely unavoidable interference . . . of the subjective element, i.e., personal feelings and desires. On a given practical question at any given moment several diametrically opposed desires may be attainable, and in this case what solution a positivist will adopt will depend upon his personal character. But this, of course, will always be the case, and not with positivists alone. The difference is that the follower of any other doctrine receives from it a more or less powerful immediate impulse in one direction or another. But the positivist receives no impulse from his doctrine. He can remain a positivist and move to the right or to the left, can, like Dumas, Nélaton, and other scientific luminaries of present-day France, prove to be the most humble servant of the Second Empire, or follow some completely different program. . . .

The exclusive use of the objective method in sociology—if that were possible—would be tantamount to measuring weight with a yardstick. From this it does not follow, however, that the objective method must be completely eliminated from this field of investigation, but only that the supreme control must be vested in the subjective method.

But then the question arises: if the objective method cannot satisfy all the demands of social science, cannot give it a supreme principle, which of these several subjective principles that can be suggested should be chosen as the best? This is the question we have been answering in this entire article. The fullest possible and most diversified division of labor among man's organs, and the least possible division of labor among men—such is the principle we propose, such is the goal we point to as the best.

It seems to us that this principle is free from every one of the defects inherent in all the principles of politics, ethics, and economics hitherto accepted. They are all either intended for one particular field, as a consequence of which no reconciliation can be effected between the different departments of social science; or else they are reached by a metaphysical route, are lacking in empiricism, and illegitimately ignore the science of nature, as a consequence of which no reconciliation can be effected between science and life. On the other hand, our principle embraces all realms of human activity, all aspects of life. We do not draw it from the depths of our personal spirit, and we do not recommend it as acquired via a supernatural route. It is firmly rooted in objective science, because it flows from exact investigation of the laws of organic evolution. It is true that Spencer, Draper, and many others, men of substance and authority, have taken their departure from these same laws and have arrived at diametrically opposed conclusions. But this circumstance in no way shakes our principle, since guided solely by it we have shown the complete groundlessness of Spencer's views and have even found it possible to suggest their historical causes.

Setting aside everything that is unfinished and incompletely expressed here, the reader is left with a clear and simple question: can the division of labor among individuals and the division of labor among the organs of a single individual be reduced to a common denominator, as Spencer and others suppose, or are they two phenomena which are mutually exclusive and which exist in eternal and inevitable antagonism, as we affirm? This question can be decided by the facts of objective science, and moreover by facts which are already established and are not open to doubt. If these facts actually support Spencer's answer to the question of the division of labor—which we consider the fundamental question of social science—all our considerations must fall by the wayside. If not, if truth is on our side, it remains only to apply the principle we have proposed, as a sociological axiom, to the solution of particular questions.

To the question we have posed—what is progress?—we answer: Progress is the gradual approach to the integral individual, to the fullest possible and the most diversified division of labor among man's organs and the least possible division of labor among men. Everything that impedes this advance is immoral, unjust, pernicious, and unreasonable. Everything that diminishes the heterogeneity of society and thereby increases the heterogeneity of its members is moral, just, reasonable, and beneficial.